# Structured ANS COBOL

**Mike Murach & Associates, Inc.**

2560 West Shaw Lane, Suite 101
Fresno, California 93711-2765
(209) 275-3335

# Structured ANS COBOL

Part 1: A course for novices using a subset of 1974 or 1985 ANS COBOL

Second edition

Mike Murach
Paul Noll

**Editorial team**

Mike Murach
Paul Noll
Judy Taylor
Pat Bridgemon

**Production team**

Steve Ehlers
Lori Davis
Carl Kisling

**Other products in our COBOL series**

*Instructor's Guide* for *Structured ANS COBOL, Part 1*
*Minireel* for *Structured ANS COBOL, Part 1*

*Structured ANS COBOL, Part 2* by Mike Murach and Paul Noll
*Instructor's Guide* for *Structured ANS COBOL, Part 2*
*Minireel* for *Structured ANS COBOL, Part 2*

*How to Design and Develop COBOL Programs*
by Paul Noll and Mike Murach
*The COBOL Programmer's Handbook* by Paul Noll and Mike Murach
*Instructor's Guide* for *How to Design and Develop COBOL Programs*
*Minireel* for *How to Design and Develop COBOL Programs*

*Report Writer* by Steve Eckols
*VS COBOL II: A Guide for Programmers and Managers (Second Edition)*
by Anne Prince
*VSAM for the COBOL Programmer (Second Edition)*
by Doug Lowe

*CICS for the COBOL Programmer, Part 1* by Doug Lowe
*CICS for the COBOL Programmer, Part 2* by Doug Lowe
*Instructor's Guide* for *CICS for the COBOL Programmer*
*Minireel* for *CICS for the COBOL Programmer*

*IMS for the COBOL Programmer, Part 1* by Steve Eckols
*IMS for the COBOL Programmer, Part 2* by Steve Eckols

*DB2 for the COBOL Programmer, Part 1: An Introductory Course,*
Steve Eckols
*DB2 for the COBOL Programmer, Part 2: An Advanced Course,*
Steve Eckols


Printed in the United States of America.

20 19 18 17 16 15 14 13 12 11 10 9 8 7 6

Library of Congress Catalog Card Number: 86-61654

ISBN: 0-911625-37-2

# Contents

# Preface

This book is a long overdue revision of our 1979 book: *Structured ANS COBOL, Part 1*. The first edition was used in dozens of colleges and junior colleges for classroom instruction, and in thousands of businesses for inhouse training. Nevertheless, it needed revision badly, due to changes in COBOL, changes in data processing procedures, and changes in training requirements.

## What this book does

The main objective of this book is to teach you how to use a subset of COBOL to develop structured programs that prepare reports. This subset consists of COBOL elements that conform to both the 1974 and the 1985 ANS standards (the standards published by the American National Standards Institute). Although most businesses use 1974 COBOL today, the trend is obviously toward the use of 1985 COBOL. That's why this book teaches you how to write programs for either version of COBOL.

Because we feel it's impossible to teach students how to code structured programs without teaching them how to design programs, this book gives extensive coverage to modern design techniques. Specifically, it shows you how to design a program from the top down using a structure chart, and it shows you how to plan the modules of a program using pseudocode. In addition, this book teaches you how to test a program from the top down. As a result, students who complete this course should not only be able to code COBOL, they should be able to develop programs using effective procedures for design, planning, and testing.

When compared with other introductory COBOL books, this book presents less COBOL than the average book does, but it teaches more about the structure and logic of programs that prepare reports. This makes sense because most students have more trouble with structure and logic than they do with COBOL. As a result, this book is a truer test of a student's programming aptitude. If a student can study this book and do the case studies in appendixes C and D with little outside help, we're confident that he or she has the aptitude required of a professional programmer in industry. On the other hand, if a student has considerable difficulty with the case studies, COBOL programming probably isn't the right vocation for him or her. In general, we feel that any student who successfully completes this course has the qualifications of an entry-level programmer in industry.

**Who this book is for**

This book is a first course for anyone who wants to learn how to use COBOL. Since it assumes that you have no data processing experience, the first two chapters present the background you need for COBOL programming. As a result, if you've had experience with computers or programming, you may be able to skip portions of these chapters.

Since this book presents standard COBOL as defined in the 1974 and 1985 standards, it teaches COBOL that can be used on any computer system that supports COBOL. Although standard COBOL has minor variations as you move from one computer system to another, examples are given throughout the book that apply to microcomputers, minicomputers, and IBM mainframes. In general, any program in this text will run on any system that supports COBOL with only a couple of minor changes, and these changes are clearly specified.

Since IBM mainframes are the most widely-used systems today, all of the program examples in this text have been run on an IBM mainframe. As a result, this book is particularly easy to use if you're going to develop your programs on an IBM mainframe. As I said, though, the variations required by other systems are also presented, and they are trivial.

**How to use this book**

If you're reading this book as part of a course, your instructor should guide you through it. On the other hand, if you're reading this book on your own, you should realize that the chapters don't have to be read in sequence from chapter 1 through chapter 13. Instead, the chapters are grouped into five sections as shown by the table in figure P-1. As you can see, you can read section 3 any time after you complete chapter 3 in section 2, and you can read section 4 any time after you complete chapter 4 in section 2.

This type of organization, which we call *modular organization*, gives you a number of options as you use this book. If, for example, you want to learn all of the COBOL elements in section 2 before you learn program development techniques and structured programming techniques, that's one option. Then, you just read the 13 chapters in sequence. On the other hand, if you want to start the case study in appendix C right after you complete chapter 3, you can study section 3 next to find out how to compile and test your case study program. Similarly, you can study section 4 right after you complete chapter 4 to find out how to design typical report preparation programs.

| Section | Chapters | Section title | Prerequisites |
|---|---|---|---|
| 1 | 1-2 | Required background | None |
| 2 | 3-7 | A professional subset of COBOL | Section 1 |
| 3 | 8-10 | Program development techniques | Chapter 3 |
| 4 | 11-12 | Structured programming techniques | Chapter 4 |
| 5 | 13 | Related subjects | Sections 1-4 |

**Figure P-1** The basic organization of this book

To help you learn from this book, each topic or chapter is followed by a terminology list and behavioral objectives. If you feel you understand the terms in each terminology list, it's a good indication that you've understood the content of the topic or chapter you've just read. In other words, we don't expect you to be able to define the terms in a list, but you should recognize and understand them. Similarly, if you feel that you can do what each objective requires, it's a good indication that you've learned what we wanted you to learn in each topic or chapter.

To give you a chance to apply your learning, appendix C presents a chapter-by-chapter case study. You can start working on this case study when you complete chapter 3. Then, as you complete each new chapter, the case study asks you to modify or enhance the program that you developed for the last chapter. If you can code and test all phases of this case study so they work correctly, we feel that this book has accomplished its primary objective.

To help you apply your COBOL knowledge to more demanding problems, appendix D presents four more case studies. You can start on these any time after you complete chapter 4. These case studies require you to develop four different types of report preparation programs, programs that require four different types of structure and logic. If you can develop all of these programs, we feel that you have the qualifications of an entry-level programmer in industry.

## Related books

This book is only one book in our COBOL training series. *Structured ANS COBOL, Part 2* is an advanced book that starts where this book ends. It teaches an entry-level programmer how to use advanced

COBOL elements to develop batch edit and update programs. Then, *Report Writer* teaches you how to use the Report Writer module of COBOL.

Perhaps the most important book we've ever done for COBOL programmers is called *How to Design and Develop COBOL Programs*. It shows experienced COBOL programmers how to design, code, and test programs that are easy to debug and maintain. And it shows them how to increase their productivity, often by 200 percent or more. As an accompanying reference, we offer the *The COBOL Programmer's Handbook*, which summarizes the procedures and techniques presented in the text. It also presents seven model programs that you can use as guides for developing your own programs. Because this text and handbook present techniques and examples that will help you at any stage of your COBOL training, we recommend that you get them and use them throughout your training and career.

Beyond this, we offer books that teach the COBOL programmer how to use CICS and IMS or DL/I on IBM mainframes. We have books on other subjects that the IBM COBOL programmer must know, like VSAM, TSO, ICCF, and JCL. And we are publishing new books each year. So please check our current catalog for titles that may be of interest to you.

### Instructor's materials

If you're an instructor in a school or business, you will probably be interested in the *Instructor's Guide* that is available with this book. It presents complete solutions for the case studies in appendixes C and D. It gives you ideas and summary information for administering a first course in COBOL. And it gives you masters for most of the figures in the text so you can make overhead transparencies from them.

A *minireel* is also available with this course. It is a 1600-bpi tape that contains files of test data, COPY members, and source programs. In short, it provides all of the complete program examples used in this book, as well as all of the files you'll need for running the case study solutions on your system.

Incidentally, we also offer instructor's guides and minireels for other courses in our COBOL series. These courses include *Structured ANS COBOL, Part 2* and *How to Design and Develop COBOL Programs*.

### Reference manuals

Although this book represents a complete first course in COBOL, we recommend that you have access to the basic COBOL reference manuals for your system. On an IBM mainframe, two manuals are usually enough for the version of COBOL that you're using: the COBOL reference manual and the programmer's guide for using COBOL. On other systems, one manual is usually enough.

In general, you shouldn't have to refer to these manuals as you do the case studies. Occasionally, though, a problem may come up that is specific to your system, not to standard COBOL. Then, you can research the problem yourself in your system's manuals. Also, as we point out in chapter 13, it's good to page through your system's COBOL manuals at some time during your training to find out what features your version of COBOL provides.

## About Paul Noll

Paul Noll originated the program development techniques we recommend in this book when he was working as a training manager for Pacific Telephone back in the mid-1970's. In 1978, he became an independent COBOL consultant. Since then, he has conducted seminars in hundreds of companies throughout the United States and Canada. His books have been used by thousands of programmers around the world, and, based on a COBOL survey we did in 1984, we believe that more than 3000 COBOL shops now use Paul's methods for program development. As far as we can tell, that means that Paul's methods are the most widely-used methods for structured program development. We've used Paul's methods in our own company since 1979, and we're convinced that they're the most effective methods currently available.

Paul is listed as a co-author of this book in the sense that he developed the basic methods that are taught in this book. He also reviewed the manuscript for this book as a double check on its technical accuracy. As a result, we feel that he has made an important contribution to the educational and technical quality of this book.

## Conclusion

Paul and I believe that this book will help you learn COBOL better than any competing book or course will. We're confident that you'll learn a usable subset of COBOL from this book and that you'll learn it with maximum efficiency. We're also confident that the case studies will let you discover on your own whether a career in COBOL is right for you.

If you have comments about this book, we welcome them. If you check the last few pages of this book, you'll find a postage-page comment form. You'll also find a postage-paid order form in case you want to order any of our products. We hope you find this book useful, and thanks for being our customer.

*Mike Murach*
Fresno, California
May 20, 1986

Section 1

# Required background

Before you can learn to develop programs in COBOL, you need some data processing background. The two chapters in this section present the minimum background that you need for this programming course. Chapter 1 introduces you to computers, computer applications, and computer programs. Chapter 2 presents a procedure you can use when you develop the COBOL programs required by this course.

Of course, if you already have computing experience or programming experience in another language, you may already know much of the material in this section. If so, you can review the objectives and terminology lists at the end of each chapter or topic to see whether you need to study it.

Chapter 1

# An introduction to computers, applications, and software

This chapter consists of three topics that introduce you to computers (*hardware*), computer applications, and computer programs (*software*). If you've had no experience at all with computers or programming, these topics provide the minimum background you need for COBOL programming. On the other hand, if you're already familiar with computers and programming, much of this chapter will be review for you. In that case, you can review the terminology list and objectives at the end of each topic to determine whether or not you need to read the topic.

# Topic 1 An introduction to computer hardware

Today, computer systems vary tremendously in size and price. On the low end, you can buy a home computer for less than $2,000. On the high end, a large IBM system may *rent* for over $1,000,000 per month. Nevertheless, the same basic concepts apply to both types of systems. In fact, you can run COBOL programs on both types of systems. This topic introduces you to the *hardware* concepts that apply to all business computers.

All business computer systems today consist of the four components shown in figure 1-1: processor, visual display terminal, disk device, and printer. A large system will have many more than four components, as I'll explain in a moment, but it will have at least one of each of the four components shown. In addition, a computer system may have one or more tape drives and one or more card readers, and it may have any number of special-purpose devices. In simplest terms, you can classify the components of a computer system into two groups: processors and input/output devices.

## Processors

The center of a computer system is the *processor*. All the other devices that make up the system are attached to it. Conversationally, it is the "brain" of the system.

In simple terms, a processor consists of two main parts: the central processing unit and main storage. The *central processing unit* (or *CPU*) is a collection of circuits that execute program instructions for calculation and data manipulation. *Main storage* (or *main memory*) is the high-speed, general-purpose electronic storage that contains both the data the CPU operates upon and the program instructions it executes.

The smallest unit of main storage is called a *byte*. In general, a byte of memory can store one character of data, such as the letter K, the digit 3, or the symbol for dollars ($). Later on, you'll learn that numeric data can be stored in more than one form within a byte, so two or more digits can be stored in a single byte. For now, though, just assume that one byte of memory holds one letter, digit, or special character.

To refer to the amount of main storage a system provides, the symbol *K* has traditionally been used. Because the word *kilo* refers to 1,000, one K (or *KB* for *kilobyte*) refers to approximately 1,000 bytes of storage. Thus, "a 128KB system" means a computer system with approximately 128,000 storage positions in its main storage. I say "approximately" because one K is actually 1,024 storage positions.

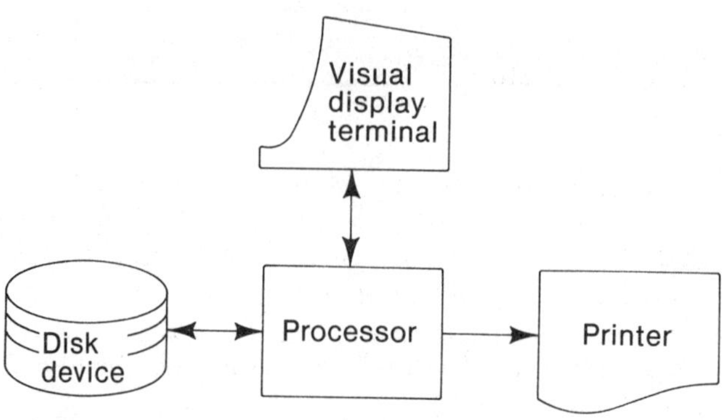


**Figure 1-1** The four components of any modern computer system

Today, however, large computers are sold with much larger memories than can be expressed conveniently in K's. For instance, a small computer may have one megabyte of storage (expressed as 1*MB*). The term *megabyte* refers to approximately 1,000,000 bytes of storage. More precisely, a megabyte is 1,024KB, or 1,024 times 1,024 bytes of storage.

Although a processor consists of millions of electronic components, you really don't need to know much more about one than what I've just told you. As far as you're concerned, a processor is a black box that stores programs and data and does what your programs tell it to do.

### Input/output devices

The second group of computer components is made up of *input/output devices*, or just *I/O devices*. Input devices send data to the processor, and output devices receive data from it. Some devices can perform both functions.

Because dozens of different devices are available for use within a computer system, many with a variety of special features, I'm not going to try to describe all of the possible I/O devices of a computer system. Instead, I'm going to concentrate on the three I/O devices shown in figure 1-1, because these are the ones you'll be using most frequently. In addition, I'll briefly mention tape drives and card readers: tape drives because you're likely to use one someday, and card readers because of their historical significance.

**Disk devices** *Disk devices* provide permanent storage for the programs and data of a system. They are both input and output devices because data and programs can be written on them or read from them. Because disk devices allow direct and rapid access to large quantities of data, they are a key component of all modern computer systems. In contrast to the permanent storage of a disk device, processor memory is only used to store programs *while they are being executed* or to store data *while it is being processed.*

The most common type of disk device is the *disk drive*, a unit that reads and writes data on a *disk pack*. A disk pack, illustrated conceptually in figure 1-2, is a stack of metal platters that are coated with a metal oxide. Data is recorded on one or both sides of each of the platters. A disk pack can be removable or it can be fixed in a permanent, sealed assembly inside the drive.

On each recording surface of a disk pack, data is stored in concentric circles called *tracks*. This is also illustrated conceptually in figure 1-2. Although the number of tracks per recording surface varies by device type, the surface illustrated in figure 1-2 has 200 tracks, numbered from 000 to 199.

The data stored on a track is read by the disk drive's *access mechanism*, which is an assembly that has one *read/write head* for each recording surface as shown in figure 1-2. As you can see, the access mechanism is positioned over the same track on all recording surfaces at the same time. As a result, all of these tracks can be operated upon, one after another, without the access mechanism having to move. Because the access mechanism can be positioned on any track of a device in a fraction of a second, any record on a disk drive can be accessed in an instant.

To specify the capacity of a disk drive, megabytes are normally used. For instance, a disk drive on a personal computer may have a capacity of 10MB, while a disk drive on a minicomputer may have a capacity of 75MB. On the largest computer systems, though, *gigabytes*, or *GB's*, are used to record disk capacities. One GB is equal to 1,000MB, so a GB is approximately one billion bytes of storage. On some systems, a single disk drive can store more than one GB of data.

For the most part, you can think of a disk device as a black box, just as you can a processor. In other words, you don't need to know how many disks it consists of, how many tracks are on each disk, and so on. All you need to know is that your program can write data on the disk device, and it can access and read any of the data on the disk device at a high rate of speed.

**Terminals** On a modern computer system, *visual display terminals*, or just *terminals*, are used to enter data into the system and to display data stored in the system. As a result, terminals are both input and output devices. Each terminal consists of two parts: a keyboard, which is similar to that of a typewriter, and a display screen, which is somewhat similar to the screen of a TV. Since you've probably used a terminal at one time or another, I won't dwell on one's operational characteristics. If you haven't used one before, you probably will as part of this course.

You should know, however, that terminals are also known by many other names. They can be called *VDT's*, using the acronymn for

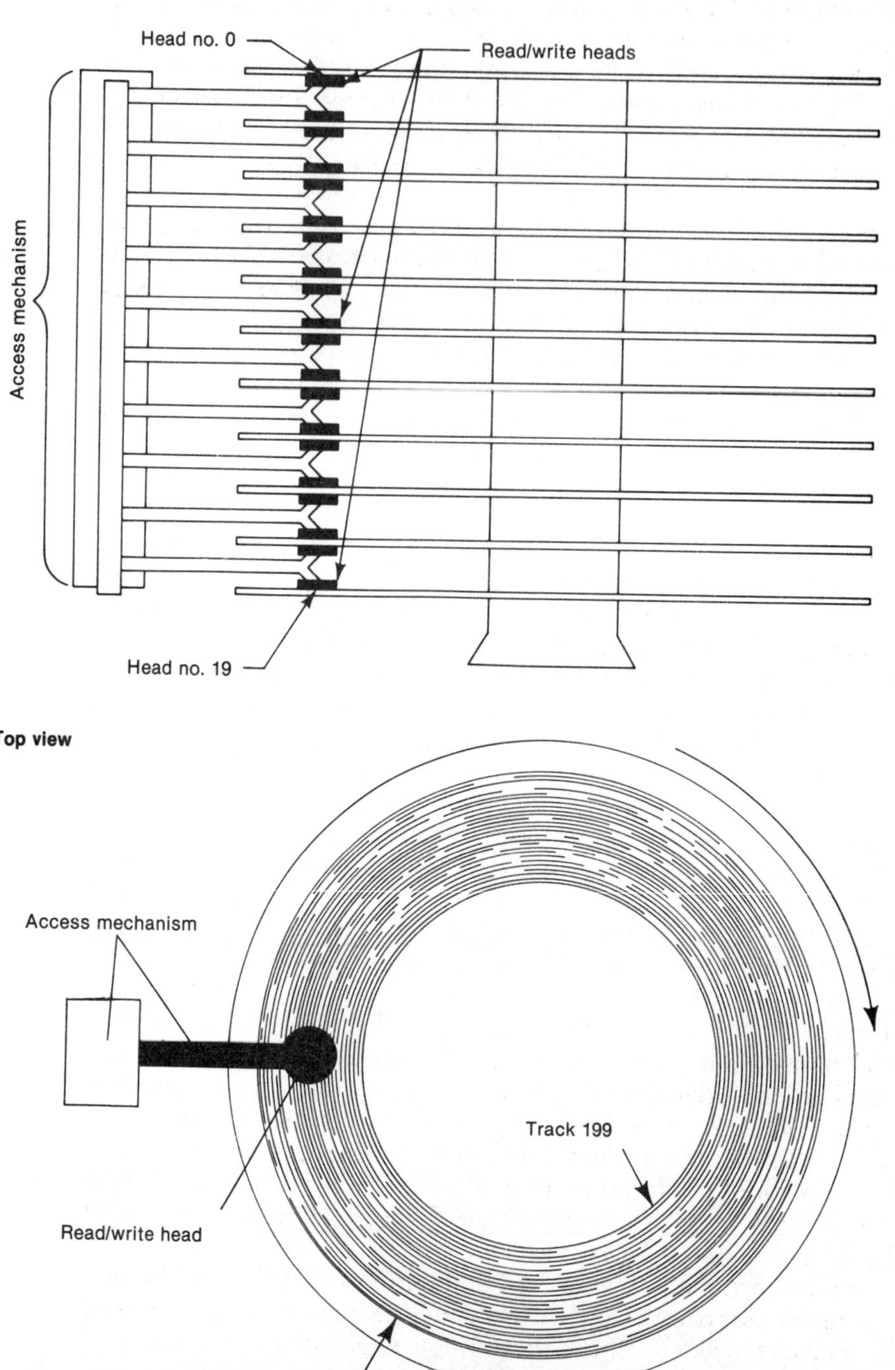


**Figure 1-2** Conceptual drawings of the access mechanism and disk pack of a disk drive

visual display terminal. Since they contain cathode ray tubes, they're sometimes called *CRT's* or "tubes." Since they're used as workstations by computer operators, they're often just called "workstations." "Terminal" is perhaps the least descriptive name for a VDT because it just means that the device is at the end point of a line leading from the processor (the "terminal" point). Nevertheless, "terminal" is a commonly used term, so it's the one we'll use in this course.

**Printers** *Printers* are used to print the output of a computer system. That includes documents like invoices, statements, payroll checks, and management reports. So they can print at high speeds, most computer printers print on *continuous forms*, forms that are connected in a continuous sequence. Since you've probably seen or used continuous forms in a computer printer, I won't dwell on the operational characteristics of printers. Although there are many varieties of printers, all you have to know is that they can be programmed to print data from the main storage of the processor.

**Tape drives** A *tape drive*, or a *magnetic tape unit*, reads and writes data on a *magnetic tape* that's a continuous strip of plastic coated on one side with a metallic oxide. How much data a reel of tape can store depends on how long the tape is and the density used to record the data on the tape. *Density* is a measurement of how many bytes are recorded in one inch of tape. For example, some common densities are 1,600 and 6,250 bytes per inch (bpi).

In contrast to disk data, tape data has one serious drawback: it must be processed sequentially. In other words, to read the 50,000th record on a tape, the computer must first read the preceding 49,999 records. On the other hand, tape provides an inexpensive way to store data. For instance, a typical tape may cost around $30, while a typical disk pack may cost $500 or more. Tape drives are found on most large computer systems just to provide this storage.

**Card readers** You won't find *card readers* on many systems today. They're worth mentioning, however, because they were the primary means of entering data into a system for many years. First, input data was punched into 80 column (80 character) cards by keypunch operators. Then, it was read by a card reader into the computer system so it could be stored on tape or disk. Today, of course, data is entered directly into the system by operators using terminals, so a card reader isn't a required I/O device.

Because card readers were so dominant in the 1960's and 70's, you can see many carryovers from the punched card era in the practices of today. For instance, the standard screen of a terminal is 80 characters wide. Similarly, the format of a COBOL statement is 80 characters long. It's even possible that your company or school may still use punched cards and card readers for one or more applications.

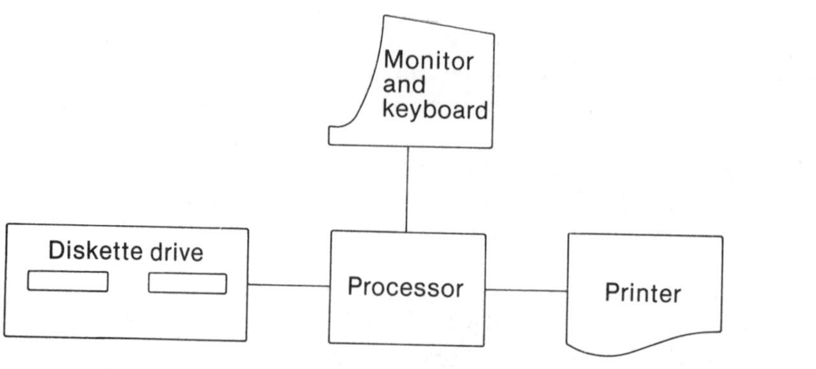


**Figure 1-3** A typical configuration for a microcomputer

### System configurations

Today, computer systems can be divided into three types: microcomputers, minicomputers, and mainframes. Because the terminology for the components of a system varies somewhat by system type, I'm now going to describe these system types in more detail. As I do, I'll present some typical system configurations. A *system configuration* is simply one combination of processors and I/O devices that makes up a complete computer system.

**Microcomputers** *Microcomputers* are the small, one-user systems that you're probably already familiar with. At the least, you're sure to have seen them on television. The Apple II and the IBM PC (Personal Computer) are two of the most common microcomputers in use today. You can buy most microcomputers for less than $5,000.

Figure 1-3 presents a typical microcomputer configuration. On a system like this, the screen of the terminal is often called a *monitor* and the *keyboard* is often detached from the monitor. Also, instead of a disk drive, a microcomputer is likely to have a single or dual *diskette drive* that can perform I/O operations on diskettes instead of disk packs. A *diskette* is a flexible disk (often called a *floppy disk*, or *soft disk*) with a relatively small storage capacity. For instance, the standard diskette on an IBM PC can store only 370K bytes of data.

Sometimes, one of the drives on a dual diskette drive is replaced by a *cartridge disk*. A cartridge disk, often referred to as a *hard disk*, has a much larger capacity than a diskette, and it can't be removed from the disk drive. The hard disk on a standard IBM PC XT today has a capacity of 10MB.

A few years back, 64K was a large capacity for the main memory of a microcomputer's processor. Today, however, it's common for a microcomputer to have 640K or more of main memory. The increased storage capacity just means that microcomputer programs today can

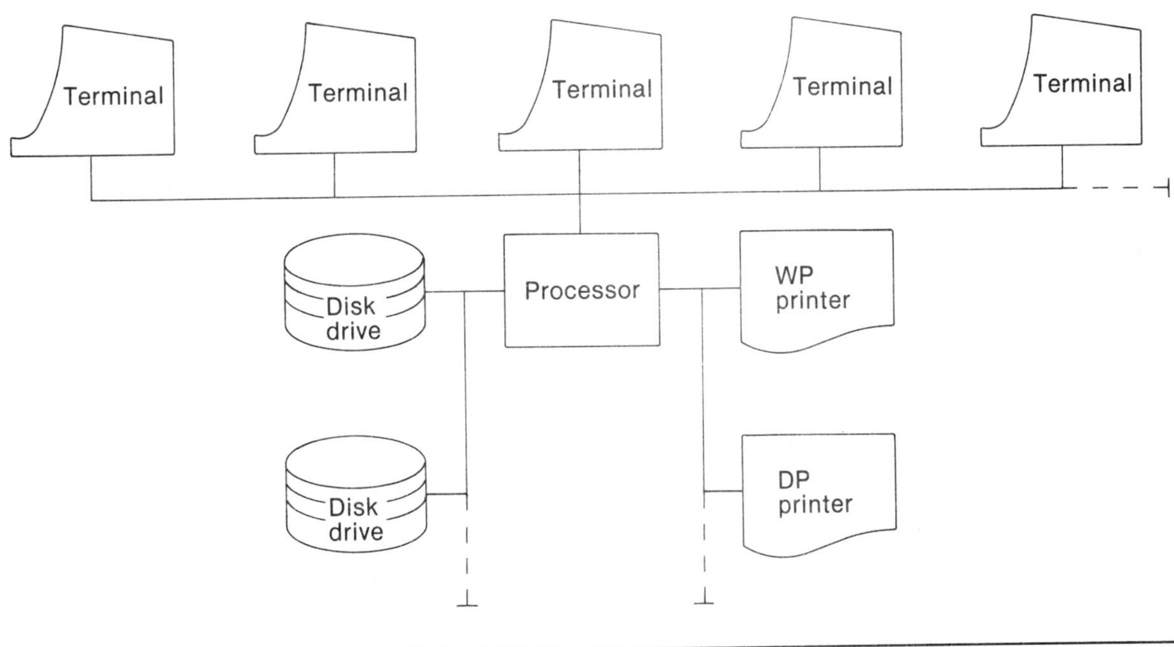


**Figure 1-4** A typical configuration for a minicomputer

be much larger, so they can do much more than the programs of just a few years ago.

I mention microcomputers because COBOL can be used on the larger ones. From a practical point of view, you need a system with a hard disk in order to develop COBOL programs effectively. However, the programs you develop can run on systems with only diskette drives. Although COBOL isn't used much for program development on microcomputers today, we expect it to be used more on these systems in the future.

**Minicomputers** A typical *minicomputer* configuration is shown in figure 1-4. In contrast to a microcomputer, most minicomputers provide for more than one terminal so more than one person can use the system at the same time. A system like this is referred to as a *multi-user system*.

Since many minicomputers provide both word processing and data processing capabilities, you'll often find more than one printer in a minicomputer configuration. One of the printers will be used for the high-speed printing of data processing (DP) applications; the other will be used for the lower-speed, typewriter-quality printing that is typical of word processing (WP) applications.

A typical minicomputer will have one or more disk drives connected to it with a total disk capacity of 20MB or more. Also, to provide for more than one user, a typical minicomputer will have

1MB or more of main memory. With capacities like this, COBOL can be used on most minicomputer systems, and much of the program development on minicomputers today is done with COBOL.

**Mainframes** Figure 1-5 presents a typical configuration for a *mainframe*. As you can see, it's the same basic idea as for microcomputers and minicomputers, but the mainframe has more I/O devices and larger storage capacities. On a mainframe, it's common for the system to include four or more tape drives so data can be written and stored on tapes. It's also common to refer to the disk devices as *direct access storage devices*, or *DASD's*. The term "DASD" is more inclusive than the term "disk device" because it can refer to direct access devices that aren't disk devices. From a practical point of view, though, you can assume that all the DASD's you will write programs for will be disk devices.

Oddly enough, most mainframes today don't provide word processing capabilities. As a result, you aren't likely to find a word processing printer attached to a mainframe system. On the other hand, it's common for a mainframe to include two or more high-speed, data processing printers.

A typical mainframe is likely to have dozens or even hundreds of terminals attached to it. Also, it is likely to have DASD capacities of several GB or more and a main memory capacity of a dozen MB or more. The large mainframes may even include more than one processor.

The vast majority of program development for mainframes is done using COBOL...perhaps 80 percent or more. It's not unusual for a large company to have a staff of 100 or more COBOL programmers who develop and maintain the programs for their mainframe. And COBOL programmers on mainframes probably make up more than half of all the programmers in industry today.

### Discussion

To develop COBOL programs, you don't need to know much more about the hardware for a computer system than the little I've just presented. Before you continue, though, you should find out what type of system you're going to be working on and what its configuration is. That way, you'll be able to recognize any references to your system as you go through this book.

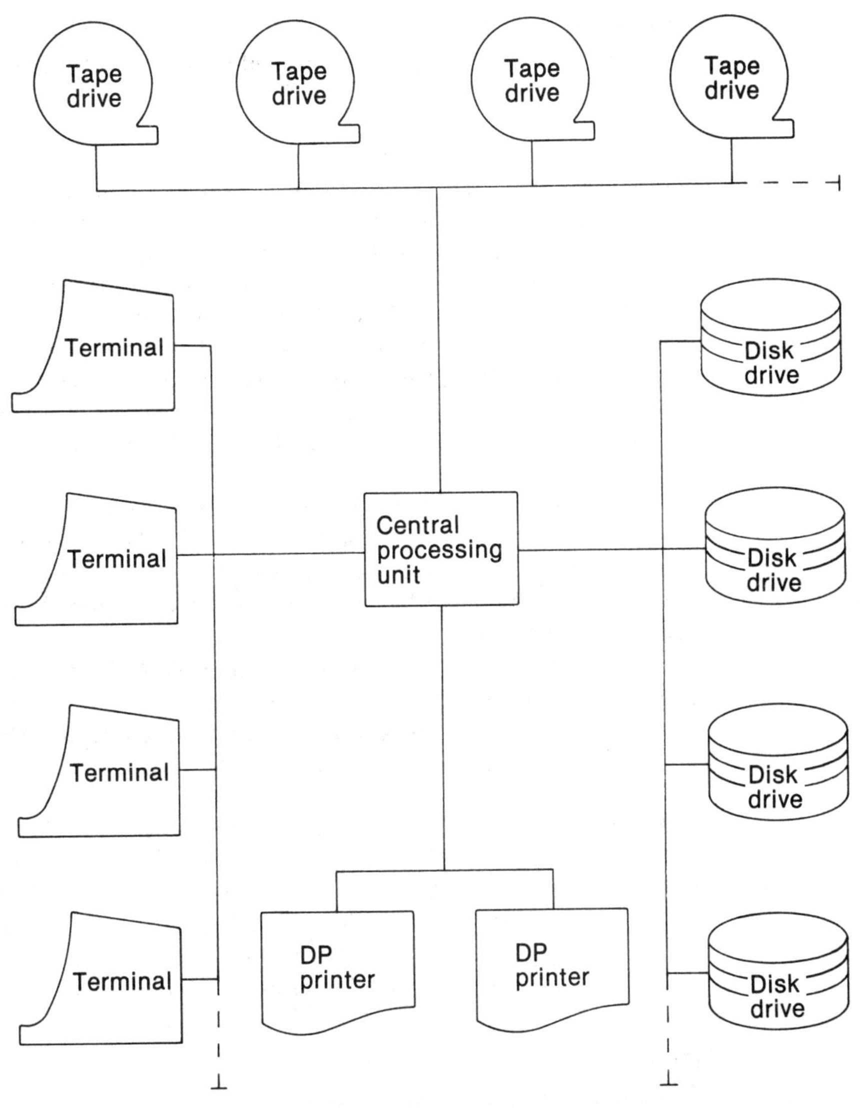


**Figure 1-5** A typical configuration for a mainframe

## Terminology

hardware
software
processor
central processing unit
CPU
main storage
main memory
byte
K
KB
kilobyte
MB
megabyte
input/output device
I/O device
disk device
disk drive
disk pack
track
access mechanism
read/write head
gigabyte
GB
visual display terminal
terminal
VDT
CRT
printer
continuous form
tape drive
magnetic tape unit
magnetic tape
density
card reader
system configuration
microcomputer
monitor
keyboard
diskette drive
diskette
floppy disk
soft disk
cartridge disk
hard disk
minicomputer
multi-user system
mainframe
direct access storage device
DASD

## Objectives

1. In simple terms, describe what a *byte* is.

2. Find out what type of system you're going to be working on: microcomputer, minicomputer, or mainframe.

3. Find out what the configuration of your system is.

## Topic 2 An introduction to computer applications

When a computer is used for some purpose, that purpose is called a *computer application*, or just *application*. On microcomputers, for example, word processing is the most common application. On minicomputers and mainframes, applications like billing, payroll, inventory control, and accounts receivable are common.

When you develop a COBOL program, it's usually for some business application. That's why this topic introduces you to the operation of a typical business application. First, I'll explain how the data for a business application is organized. Then, I'll describe some of the types of programs required by a typical application. When you complete this topic, you should have some idea of what it is that your COBOL programs are going to be able to do.

### The data for a business application

The data for a business application is commonly organized into one or more *files*. On our system, for example, we have a customer file, an inventory file, a vendor file, an employee file, and so on.

If a file contains permanent data, it is referred to as a *master file*. If a file contains temporary data, it is referred to as a *transaction file*. For instance, an employee master file will contain permanent information such as employee names, social security numbers, and year-to-date payroll data. In contrast, a payroll transaction file will contain information that is used only one time, such as the number of hours each employee worked in a specific week.

Each file on a system is made up of *records*. In an employee file, for example, you will normally find one record for each employee. In an inventory file, you will normally find one record for each type of inventory item (or stock keeping unit).

Each record is made up of *fields*. In an employee record, for example, you will probably find a field for employee number, one for employee name, one for social security number, and so on. In an inventory record, you will probably find fields for item number, item description, unit cost, unit price, quantity on hand, and so on. Within each record within a file, the fields will be in a standard format. For example, the employee number in an employee record might always be in bytes 1-5, the employee name in bytes 6-31, and so on.

Figure 1-6 schematically illustrates the relationships between fields, records, and files. When a file is stored on a disk device, any record can be accessed and read into main memory in an instant. Then, once the record is in storage, any of its fields can be processed at electronic speeds.

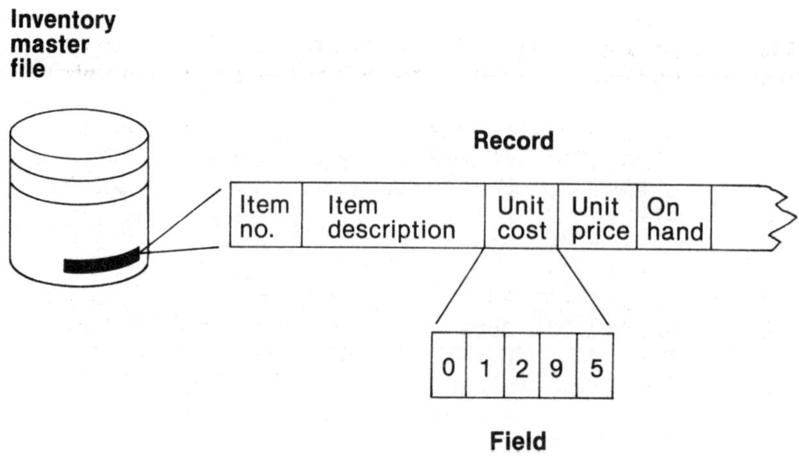


**Figure 1-6** Records and fields in an inventory master file

### File organizations

*File organization* refers to the way an application views a file's structure. For magnetic tape files, of course, data is organized sequentially because the records have to follow one another in sequence. When a file is stored on a disk device, though, it can be organized in more than one way. As a result, the person who designs an application has to decide what the best organization for a disk file is.

A COBOL program can process files in three different organizations: sequential, indexed, and relative. In this book, you'll learn how to use sequential and indexed files. So I'm going to introduce these organizations right now.

**Sequential organization** Like a tape file, a file on disk can be stored with *sequential organization*. In this case, its records are stored one after another in consecutive order. Usually, one field within each record contains a key value that's used to sequence the records in the file.

To illustrate, figure 1-7 presents a simple, 10-record employee file in sequence by social security number. In this example, the social security number field is the *key field*. Of course, the key field doesn't have to be the first field in a record. It can be located anywhere within the record.

On any computer system, many of the disk files have sequential organization. When a program has to read an entire file from beginning to end, sequential organization is the most efficient organization for the file. In this course, all of the programs you write will read at least one sequential disk file.

| Disk location | Social security number | First name | Middle initial | Last name | Employee number |
|---|---|---|---|---|---|
| 1 | 213-64-9290 | Thomas | T | Bluestone | 00008 |
| 2 | 279-00-1210 | William | J | Colline | 00002 |
| 3 | 334-96-8721 | Constance | M | Harris | 00007 |
| 4 | 498-27-6117 | Ronald | W | Westbrook | 00010 |
| 5 | 499-35-5079 | Stanley | L | Abbott | 00001 |
| 6 | 558-12-6168 | Marie | A | Littlejohn | 00005 |
| 7 | 559-35-2479 | E | R | Siebart | 00006 |
| 8 | 572-68-3100 | Jean | B | Glenning | 00009 |
| 9 | 703-47-5748 | Paul | M | Collins | 00004 |
| 10 | 899-16-9235 | Alice | | Crawford | 00003 |

**Figure 1-7** An employee file with sequential organization by social security number

**Indexed organization** When a file has *indexed organization*, a program can read the file in sequence by a key field, but it can also access any one of the records in the file on a direct basis. To make this possible, an indexed file consists of two parts: an *index component* and a *data component*. Within the index component, each entry contains a key field value and the location of the corresponding record in the data component of the file.

Figure 1-8 schematically illustrates how the sequential file in figure 1-7 would be organized if it were indexed. Here, if the employee's key value (employee number) is known, it's possible to access the record directly by getting its disk location from the index. This type of record retrieval is referred to as *direct*, or *random*, *access*. On the other hand, it's also possible to access the records sequentially by employee number using the index because the index entries are in sequence by employee number. When the records in an indexed file are accessed sequentially, the record retrieval is referred to as *sequential access*.

Actually, indexed organization is more complicated than the way I've just described it. For instance, to speed up processing, an indexed file is likely to have indexes at several different levels. Also, an indexed file can have more than one key field so the records in an employee file can be accessed by employee number or by social security number. For now, though, you only need to know the concept of an indexed file as presented in figure 1-8.

In practice, many of the significant data files of an application are likely to have indexed organization. That way, they can be processed sequentially or randomly by one or more key fields. In chapter 6 of this book, you'll learn how to process an indexed file with one key field on a sequential or random basis.

| **Index component** | | **Data component** | | | | | |
|---|---|---|---|---|---|---|---|
| **Employee number** | **Disk location** | **Disk location** | **Social security number** | **First name** | **Middle initial** | **Last name** | **Employee number** |
| 00001 | 5 | 1 | 213-64-9290 | Thomas | T | Bluestone | 00008 |
| 00002 | 2 | 2 | 279-00-1210 | William | J | Colline | 00002 |
| 00003 | 10 | 3 | 334-96-8721 | Constance | M | Harris | 00007 |
| 00004 | 9 | 4 | 498-27-6117 | Ronald | W | Westbrook | 00010 |
| 00005 | 6 | 5 | 499-35-5079 | Stanley | L | Abbott | 00001 |
| 00006 | 1 | 6 | 558-12-6168 | Marie | A | Littlejohn | 00005 |
| 00007 | 3 | 7 | 559-35-2479 | E | R | Siebart | 00006 |
| 00008 | 1 | 8 | 572-68-3100 | Jean | B | Glenning | 00009 |
| 00009 | 8 | 9 | 703-47-5748 | Paul | M | Collins | 00004 |
| 00010 | 4 | 10 | 899-16-9235 | Alice | | Crawford | 00003 |

**Figure 1-8** An employee file with indexed organization

**Blocked records** To improve the efficiency of a computer system, records within a sequential file are often *blocked*. Sometimes, the records within an indexed file are blocked too. This simply means that more than one record is stored between gaps on a disk track or on a magnetic tape. In figure 1-9, for example, the records are blocked with five records to a block, so you can say that the *blocking factor* is 5. Blocking can improve processing efficiency, because an entire block of records is read or written at one time.

I mention blocking at this time because you sometimes have to be able to specify the blocking factor of disk files in your COBOL programs. From a conceptual point of view, though, it doesn't matter whether the records within a file are blocked or unblocked. Although blocking improves I/O efficiency, your program still processes only one record at a time.

### Typical programs within a batch application

A *batch application* is one in which a number of transactions are processed at once. This implies that the transactions are not processed on an interactive basis using terminals. Before the development of interactive systems, all applications were batch applications.

To illustrate a batch application, figure 1-10 presents a system flowchart for a simple inventory application. A *system flowchart* is a chart that shows the sequence of operations within an application. In the flowchart in figure 1-10, the four operations are numbered from 1 through 4. The first operation is a manual procedure as indicated by the trapezoid symbol for it. The next three operations are done by computer programs as indicated by the rectangular symbols. The

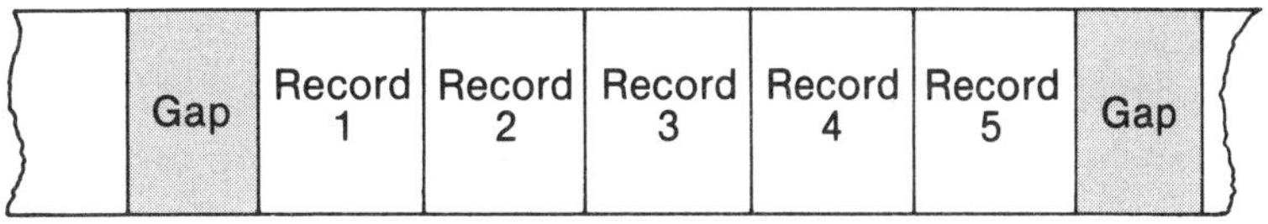

| | Gap | Record 1 | Record 2 | Record 3 | Record 4 | Record 5 | Gap | |
|---|---|---|---|---|---|---|---|---|

**Figure 1-9** The concept of blocked records on tape or disk

three programs represent the three functions required by any batch application: editing, updating, and document preparation.

**Edit programs** In operation 1 in figure 1-10, inventory transactions are keypunched into cards that can be read by the card reader of a computer system. Then, operation 2 is an edit operation done by an edit program. An *edit program* reads transaction records (in this case, punched cards) and checks the fields within the records for *validity*. If a record is valid, it is written on a tape or disk file of valid transactions. If a record contains one or more invalid fields, its data is printed on an error listing so the transaction can be corrected (in this case, keypunched into another card for processing later on).

Note that I didn't say an edit program checked the transaction data for accuracy. That would be impossible. An edit program can only check data for validity. For instance, it can check that a numeric field is numeric, that an alphabetic field is alphabetic, that a numeric field is within certain reasonable limits, and so on. After a transaction has been accepted as valid by an edit program, it is ready for further processing.

**Update and maintenance programs** *Update programs* play a primary role in almost all applications. An update program reads a file of valid transactions and updates one or more related master files. In operation 3 of figure 1-10, for example, the update program updates the inventory master file. If you check the line between the rectangle for operation 3 and the disk symbol, you can see that arrowheads point both to and from the disk file. After a transaction record is read, the update program reads the related master record. Then, it updates the affected fields in the master record based on the transaction data and writes the updated master record back on the disk file.

Some people use the terms "update" and "maintain" as general verbs that mean "keep the records in a file up-to-date." Others give these verbs more specific meanings. Then, they use the term "update" when a program changes the records in a file based on operational data such as sales, hours worked, or receipts to inventory. As a result, the program in operation 3 is an update program.

In contrast, a *maintenance program* processes transactions that contain maintenance data, such as an address change, rather than

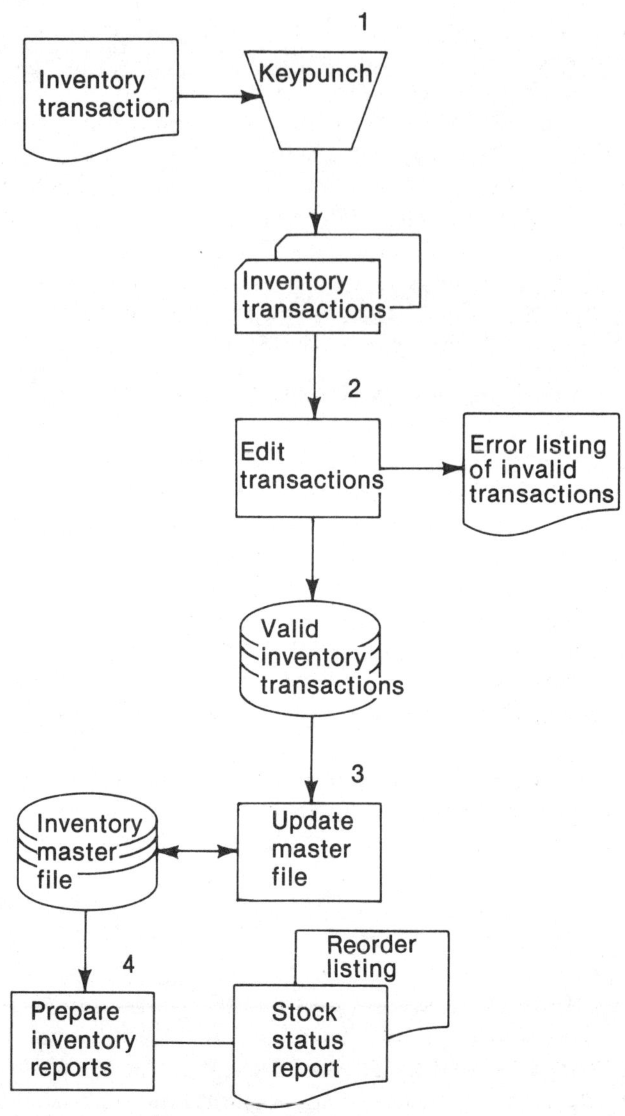


**Figure 1-10** A system flowchart for a batch inventory application

operational data. As a result, a maintenance program may add records to a file, delete records from a file, or change records in a file. To keep a file up-to-date, an application requires both update and maintenance programs.

**Document preparation programs** When files are up-to-date, they contain the data needed for the output documents of an application. A *document* is any printed output of a computer system, such as an invoice printed on a billing form, a payroll check printed on a check form, or a management report printed on a general-purpose form. A program that prepares one or more documents of a system can be called a *document preparation program*. If the program prepares one or more reports, it can also be called a *report preparation program*.

In figure 1-10, the program in operation 4 is a document, or report, preparation program. It prepares two reports: a stock status report that shows the status of all the items in inventory and a reorder listing that lists only those items in inventory that need to be reordered. In general, a document preparation program reads one or more input files so it can prepare one or more documents.

### Typical programs within an interactive application

An *interactive application* is one in which the transactions are entered into the system interactively through terminals. To illustrate, figure 1-11 presents a system flowchart for an interactive inventory application that performs the same functions as the application charted in figure 1-10. The second program in figure 1-11 is a *batch program* just like the one in figure 1-10. The other two programs, however, are *interactive programs*: an entry program and a display program. These programs, along with menu programs, are typical of the interactive programs in all interactive systems.

**Entry programs** An *entry program* is one during which transactions are entered into a system on an interactive basis. Sometimes, these programs are called *acceptance programs* because they actually accept the transactions that the operators enter through the keyboard of the terminal. More commonly, though, they're called entry programs.

Entry programs tend to be the most complicated programs in an interactive application because many of them do much more than accept the entered transactions. In figure 1-11, for example, the entry program gets a transaction from the terminal, edits it, and uses it to update the related inventory master record if the transaction is valid. If it isn't valid, the entry program sends messages back to the terminal screen so the operator can correct the transaction and try again to enter it. When an entry program edits all transactions, invalid transactions are never accepted by the system, so an error listing of invalid transactions isn't necessary.

In some applications, though, the entry programs don't do the updating, and sometimes they don't even do the editing. If an entry program doesn't do any editing, it simply accepts an unedited transaction from the terminal and writes it in a transaction file on disk for later processing. Then, the transaction file is edited on a batch basis later on just as in the system in figure 1-10.

**Display programs** A *display program* is one that displays information to a terminal operator on an interactive basis. In operation 3 of

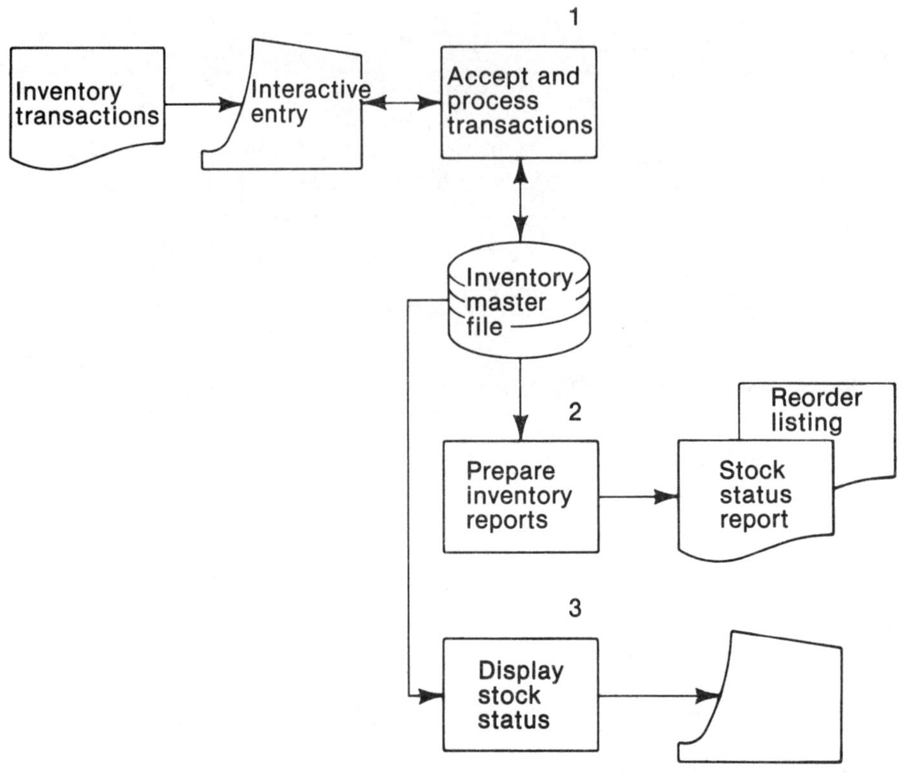


**Figure 1-11** A system flowchart for an interactive inventory application

figure 1-11, for example, the display program will display the stock status of any item in inventory. In a program like this, the operator enters the item code of the inventory item he is interested in. Then, the display program finds the record and displays the record's data on the terminal screen so the operator can review it. Display programs are sometimes called *inquiry programs* because they handle the inquiries made by the terminal operators.

**Menu programs** System flowcharts are useful when you're working with batch systems because they show the sequence in which programs must be executed if the system is to work. In an interactive system, though, system flowcharts are less useful because it's often better if the terminal operator decides on the sequence in which to execute programs. In figure 1-11, for example, programs 2 and 3 don't have to be performed in any particular sequence. The terminal operator can prepare inventory reports or inquire about the stock status of an item whenever he wants to.

A *menu program* is one that lets the operator select the program he wants to run next. Normally, a menu program displays the programs that can be run on a terminal screen, somewhat like a menu

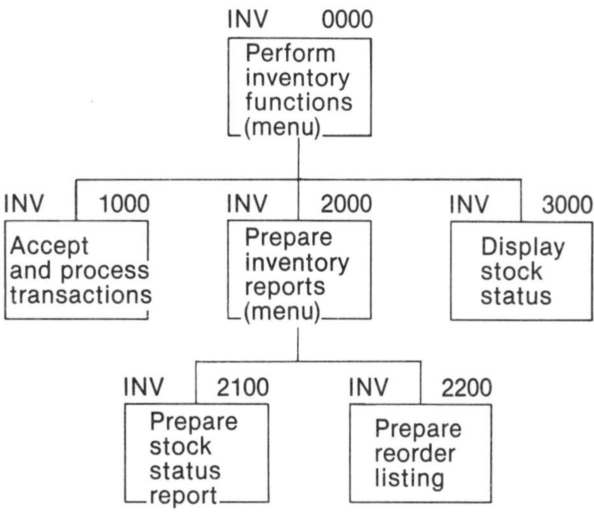


**Figure 1-12** A system structure chart for an interactive inventory application

in a restaurant. Then, the operator selects the program he wants and the computer system executes it. If you've ever used an interactive system, you know that menus are used extensively in most applications.

To show the menu structure of an interactive system, *system structure charts* like the one in figure 1-12 are useful. In figure 1-12, each box represents one program in the inventory application. The letters and numbers at the top of each box give the name of each program in the system. Thus, the top-level program is named INV0000, the leftmost box at the second level is named INV1000, and so on.

In this application, INV0000 and INV2000 are menu programs. INV0000 gives the operator three choices: the entry program (INV1000), the next menu program (INV2000), and the display program (INV3000). Then, the second menu program (INV2000) gives the operator two choices: prepare the stock status report (INV2100) or prepare the reorder listing (INV2200). If you compare the programs in this system structure chart with those in the flowchart in figure 1-11, you can see that they perform the same functions. However, there are two report preparation programs in the system in figure 1-12, while one program prepares both reports in the system in figure 1-10.

## Discussion

Needless to say, this topic is but a brief introduction to computer applications. But I wanted to give you some idea of the types of programs you're likely to develop using COBOL: menu programs, entry programs, edit programs, update and maintenance programs, document preparation programs, and display programs. In this introductory course, though, you'll only learn how to write document preparation programs.

At this time, I hope you understand the relationships between fields, records, and files. As you'll soon see, COBOL is specifically designed for processing the fields within the records within the files of a system.

## Terminology

computer application
application
file
master file
transaction file
record
field
file organization
sequential organization
key field
indexed organization
index component
data component
direct access
random access
sequential access
blocked records
blocking factor
batch application
system flowchart
edit program
field validity
update program
maintenance program
document
document preparation program
report preparation program
interactive application
batch program
interactive program
entry program
acceptance program
display program
inquiry program
menu program
system structure chart

## Objectives

1. Describe the relationships between files, records, and fields.

2. Explain the difference between sequential and indexed file organization.

3. Describe what blocked records are and what a blocking factor is.

4. Describe the differences between a batch application and an interactive application.

5. Describe the function of a document preparation program.

## Topic 3 An introduction to computer software

In the last topic, you were introduced to *application programs*. These are the programs that are visible to the user of a computer system: word processing programs, spreadsheet programs, programs that display management information, programs that print payroll checks, programs that keep accounts receivable records up-to-date, and so on. This is the *application software* of the system.

However, a modern computer system also requires *system programs*, or *system software*. These programs don't perform application functions, but they make it possible for application programs to be developed and used effectively. Collectively, the system programs that are used by a computer system are known as the *operating system* of the computer.

In this topic, I'm going to introduce you to some of the functions that are performed by the programs of an operating system. As you learn these functions, you'll also be introduced to some of the programs of an operating system. After I present these basic functions, I'll introduce you to the COBOL compilers that might be available to you as part of your operating system.

### The basic functions of an operating system

A modern operating system is likely to consist of hundreds of programs that perform system functions. As a result, I couldn't begin to present them all in a short introductory topic like this. Instead, I'm only going to present the ones that you need to understand in order to develop COBOL programs. These functions include job-to-job transition, file management, library management, and so on.

**Job-to-job transition** Before an application program can be *executed* by a computer system, it must be *loaded* into the main memory of the system. This loading is done by one of the programs of the operating system called a *supervisor program*, or just *supervisor*. The supervisor itself is loaded into main memory when the computer is turned on at the start of the day. After that, it stays in main memory at all times so it can load all of the programs that are to be run.

Figure 1-13 illustrates the contents of main memory after an application program has been loaded into main storage on a small, one-user system. As you can see, both the application program and the supervisor are in storage at the same time. In fact, the supervisor performs some functions during the execution of the application program that let the application program run more efficiently. In other words, loading programs isn't the only function of a supervisor.

**Figure 1-13** Main memory during the execution of an application program on a one-user system

At the bottom of the illustration in figure 1-13, you can see that some of the bytes of main storage are unused.

*Job-to-job transition* refers to the transition from one job to another during the operation of a computer system. Since a job is normally equivalent to the execution of one program, you can also think of this as program-to-program transition. As you would guess, the supervisor plays a key role in this transition from one program to another.

Figure 1-14 illustrates the contents of main memory during job-to-job transition on a small, one-user system. As you can see, this transition takes four steps. First, when program 1 finishes, it passes control to the supervisor. Second, the supervisor loads a system program called a *job control program* into storage and passes control to it. Third, the job control program gets the specifications for the next program to be executed. It may get these specifications interactively from the user's terminal, or it may get them from a file of job specifications (you'll learn more about this in chapter 8). After the job control program gets valid specifications, it passes control back to the supervisor. Then, the supervisor loads the next program to be executed and passes control to it. Although the entire process may take only a few seconds on a large system, job-to-job transition is an important function of an operating system.

**Multiprogramming** A common feature of minicomputers and mainframes is *multiprogramming*. When a system provides multiprogramming, it allows a single processor to execute more than one

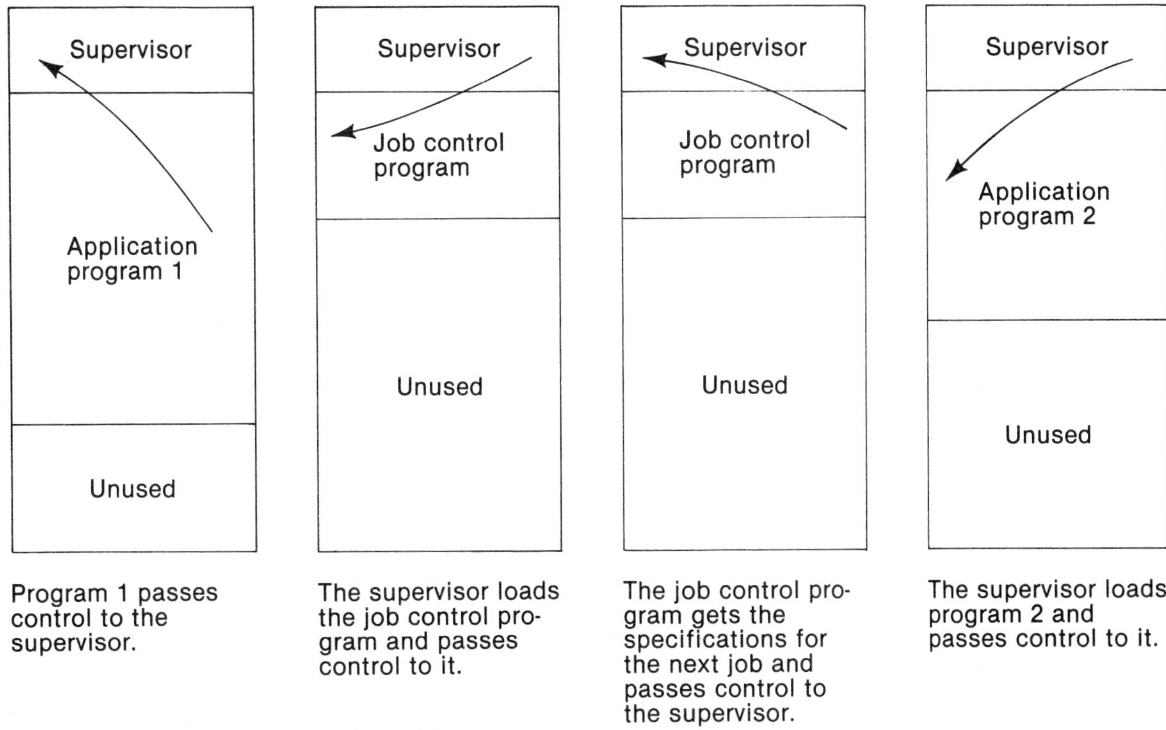


**Figure 1-14** Main memory during job-to-job transition on a one-user system

program at the same time. Actually, that's misleading, because only one program executes at any given time, even though more than one program is in main storage at the same time. The other programs wait for input or output operations to be completed, or simply wait for the supervisor to pass control back to them. Nevertheless, it looks to the users of the system as though multiple programs are executing at the same time.

Multiprogramming is important because it improves the overall productivity of a computer system. Because CPU operations such as arithmetic operations can be executed thousands of times faster than input or output operations, a processor that executes only one program at a time often has nothing to do while it's waiting for an I/O operation to finish. To make use of this idle time, multiprogramming systems allow additional programs to be in storage so their CPU operations can be executed while another program waits for its I/O operations to be completed.

Figure 1-15 is a conceptual illustration of the contents of main memory in a multiprogramming system. In this example, five programs plus the supervisor are in storage at the same time. When one program has to wait for an I/O operation to be completed, control is

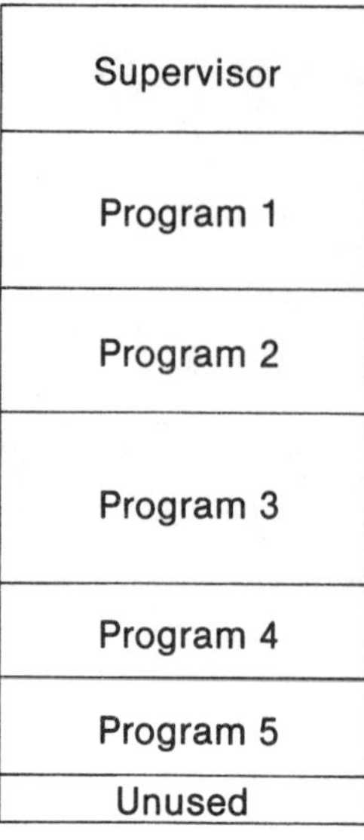


**Figure 1-15** Main memory during multiprogramming

automatically passed to the supervisor, which in turn passes control to another program in storage. In other words, the supervisor in a multiprogramming system decides which program it will pass control to next. In a system that is used only for batch applications, the supervisor passes control to the program in storage that has the highest priority, as long as that program isn't waiting for an I/O operation to finish.

If an interactive system provides for more than one user and lets each user do whatever jobs he or she wants to do, the system must provide for multiprogramming. For example, the illustration in figure 1-15 could represent an interactive system with five users. Then, user 1 is using program 1; user 2 is using program 2; and so on. In a system like this, the processor doesn't use a strict priority system. Instead, it makes sure that each user gets a fair share of the CPU time. That way, each user has the feeling that she has complete control of the computer system.

Although different systems handle multiprogramming and multi-users in different ways, you don't have to know the details in order to use a system. In fact, I've never bothered to find out how our Wang VS system provides for multiprogramming and multi-users, even though I've used the system for years. On some systems, though, you may have to learn how to specify the priority of your jobs.

**Spooling** If a system has only one printer, it can't print several documents at the same time. And that could mean that a multiprogramming system couldn't run more than one document

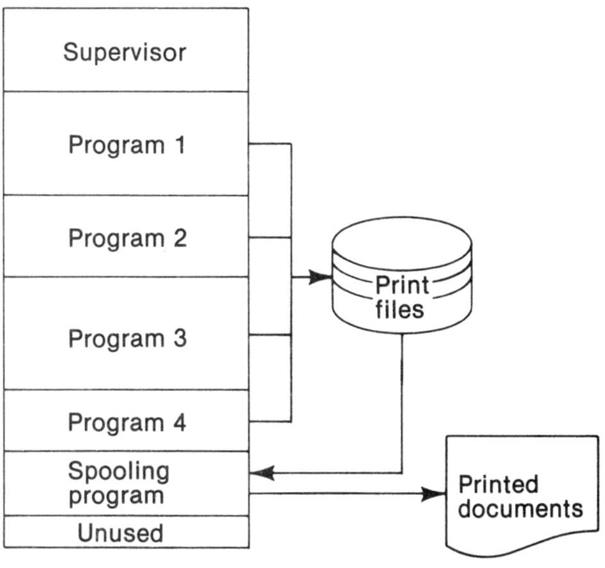


**Figure 1-16** The concept of spooling on a multi-user system

preparation program at a time. *Spooling*, however, makes it possible for several document preparation programs to run at the same time by writing the documents on disk files before actually printing them.

Figure 1-16 is a schematic illustration of the concept of spooling. Here, four document preparation programs are in storage along with the supervisor and a spooling program that is part of the operating system. As the document preparation programs are executed, they create *print files* on disk rather than printed documents. Then, when the printer finishes printing one document, the spooling program decides which document to print next based on print priorities or interactive operator instructions. Once it decides, the spooling program reads the selected print file and prints the output document.

Often, spooling takes place even though the programmer is completely unaware of it. In this case, the application programs are written as though they were using printer output, even though they are actually using disk output. Then, the operating system makes the necessary adjustments so that print spooling takes place automatically.

**File and library management** Even a small computer system is likely to use thousands of different files. As a result, one of the important functions of an operating system is *file management*. This includes finding space on disk devices for new files, locating old files, keeping expiration dates for all files so expired files can be deleted from disk devices, and so on.

To provide file management, an operating system lets you name disk packs with *volume names* and disk files with *file names*. These names are kept in *volume labels* and *file labels* that are actually records stored on the disk packs themselves. Then, if a user supplies the volume name and the file name for a file, the operating system can find it by searching through the file labels on the appropriate volume.

*Libraries* are collections of files. By using libraries, you can group related files as a means of organizing them. On our system, for example, we have several thousand files organized into a few dozen libraries: one library for system programs; one library for the programs of each application; one library for the data files of each application; one library for each user's word processing documents; and so on. By using libraries, we're able to keep better control of the files on our system so they don't proliferate unnecessarily.

*Library management* is the operating system function that lets you manage the libraries of a system. As a result, library management programs let you create libraries, delete them, modify any of the files within a library, and so on. If you're using a microcomputer, your operating system probably won't provide library management, but almost all other systems do provide it.

**Utilities** *Utilities* are routine system functions like copying files and sorting the records within a file. Functions like these are done repeatedly by a computer system. As a result, operating systems provide *utility programs* for these functions. To use a utility program, you supply parameters that tell the program what you want it to do. That way, you don't have to write a special program every time you need to perform a utility function.

**Program development** All operating systems provide programs that make it easier for you to develop application programs. To help you enter a new program into the computer system, an interactive system usually provides an *interactive editor*.

Before an application program can be executed by a system, it must be translated from the programming language into machine language. This is done by a *language translator* that is one of the programs of the operating system. Most systems, for example, have translators for languages like FORTRAN, COBOL, and BASIC.

Before a machine language program can be executed by a system, it must be combined with any subprograms that it requires. This is done by a *linkage editor* program, and the process is called *link editing*.

Although you'll learn more about interactive program entry, language translation, and link editing as you proceed through this course, figure 1-17 summarizes these development steps as they relate to COBOL. To start, you enter your COBOL program into the system under control of an interactive editor. The editor stores your program

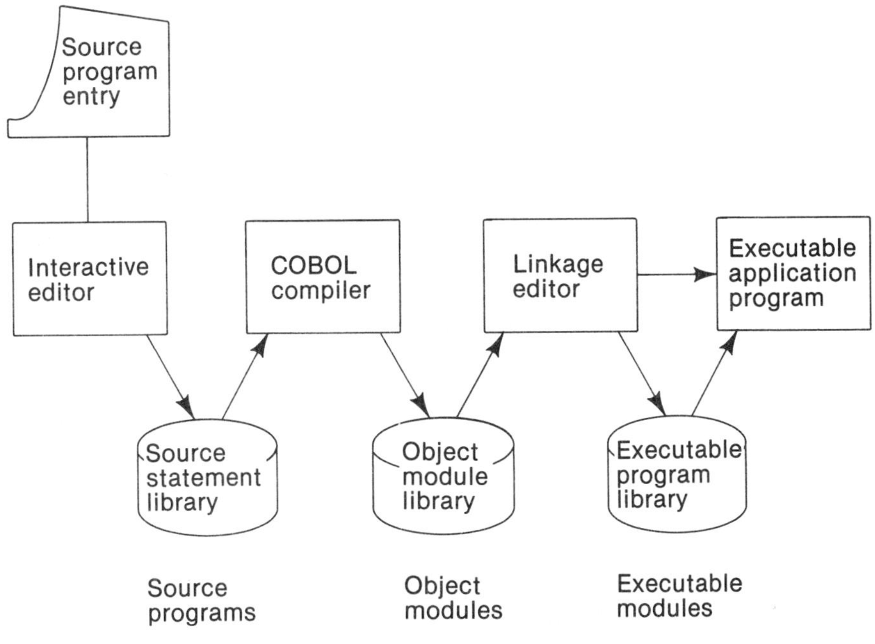


**Figure 1-17** Application development and the operating system

on disk in a library that can be called a *source statement library*. At this time, your program is called a *source program*.

Next, the computer system reads your COBOL source program from the source statement library and translates it into an *object program*, or *object module*. The program that does the translation is the *COBOL compiler*. The object program is stored on disk in a library that can be called an *object module library*.

Finally, the linkage editor program reads your object program and link edits it with any required subprograms into an *executable module*. This module can be stored in another library or it can be loaded directly into the computer system for execution.

Although figure 1-17 gives you a conceptual view of program development on a modern interactive system, keep in mind that there may be minor variations from one system to another. In particular, the terminology is likely to vary from one system to another. For instance, on an IBM mainframe, the object module libraries are called *relocatable libraries*, and the executable module libraries are called *core image libraries*. On our Wang system, we don't keep libraries of object modules; we only keep libraries of executable modules, which we call program libraries. And on an IBM PC, there are no libraries, so source programs, object programs, and executable modules are simply files.

## COBOL standards and COBOL compilers

Because you're going to learn how to develop COBOL programs in this course, I'd like now to tell you more about COBOL and COBOL compilers. To start, COBOL is an acronym that stands for COmmon Business Oriented Language. It was first introduced in 1959, so it's one of the oldest programming languages. By the mid-1960's, COBOL had become the most widely used language for business applications. Before 1968, however, there was no standard COBOL language. Although all computer manufacturers based their COBOL compilers on the same set of language specifications, there were major COBOL differences as you moved from one COBOL compiler to another.

Then, in 1968, the American National Standards Institute (ANSI) approved a set of *COBOL standards*. Theoretically, this meant that one standard language could be used on all types of computers. In practice, however, the 1968 standards didn't put an end to COBOL variations because the standards didn't provide for all of the capabilities that computer users wanted. In particular, they didn't provide for the use of indexed files. As a result, each computer manufacturer added *extensions* to the language that provided these additional capabilities. Furthermore, the 1968 standards allowed these extensions. As long as the rest of the language conformed to the standards, a manufacturer could refer to his version of COBOL as "standard," no matter how many extensions had been added.

In 1974, ANSI released another set of COBOL standards. These standards deleted some of the 1968 provisions, modified others, and, most important, added many of the capabilities that computer users had missed in the 1968 standards. As a result, ANS 74 COBOL led to far greater standardization than ANS 68 COBOL did. On the other hand, the 1974 standards didn't provide language for using terminals on an interactive basis, a major omission. Instead, any language for terminal use had to be provided as an extension to the standards. That's why it's fairly easy to convert a batch COBOL program from one 1974 compiler to another, but it can be a major effort to convert an interactive COBOL program from one compiler to another.

In 1985, ANSI released a third set of standards for COBOL. In general, these standards make only a few deletions or modifications to the 1974 standards, but they add a certain amount of new language to the old standards. In particular, the 1985 standards try to provide new language for structured programming as explained in chapter 7. On the other hand, these standards don't provide language for interactive terminal use, so we're still not going to see any kind of standardization when it comes to interactive COBOL programs.

Because it takes time to develop new compilers, a few years usually pass between the time a new set of standards is released and the time compilers that conform to these standards are available. For instance, IBM didn't release a 1974 ANS compiler for its most popular computer, the System/370, until 1977. And the first 1985 COBOL compilers aren't expected to be ready until the end of 1986. Then, after a new COBOL compiler becomes available, it usually takes another few years before computer users convert to it. In general, computer users delay the conversion until the new compiler gives them some capability that they don't have on their current compiler.

Today, early in 1986, almost all COBOL applications are developed using 1974 COBOL compilers. On microcomputers, you're likely to use the Microsoft or Microfocus 1974 COBOL compilers. On minicomputers, most manufacturers offer their own 1974 COBOL compiler. On IBM mainframes, the VS COBOL compiler is a 1974 COBOL compiler.

In the next few years, though, there will be a slow movement toward 1985 COBOL compilers. Already, IBM offers its mainframe users a COBOL compiler based on early drafts of the 1985 standards. It is called COBOL II, and we expect that it will eventually be modified so it is completely compatible with the 1985 standards. Similarly, other manufacturers will offer 1985 compilers to their customers, who will eventually convert to them. Perhaps by 1990, most COBOL programmers will be using 1985 COBOL compilers.

To provide for the future, this book teaches a subset of standard COBOL that will run on either 1974 or 1985 COBOL compilers. As I said, the 1985 compilers changed little in the 1974 standards, so it's no trick to learn and use a COBOL subset that will run on both 1974 and 1985 compilers. If you're using a 1974 compiler, this is the right way to learn COBOL, because you want to make sure that everything you code today will be compatible with the 1985 standards so you won't have to change anything later on. In addition, chapter 7 teaches most of the significant new language of the 1985 standards.

Because neither the 1974 or 1985 standards provide for complete compatibility between compilers, we're going to point out some of the common variations between compilers as we go along. These variations are referred to as *compiler dependencies*. In other words, the code depends on the compiler you're using, not the standards you're using. To help you understand these dependencies, each COBOL chapter in this book ends with a topic called "Compiler Dependent Code" that points out some common compiler differences. Specifically, these topics point out the dependencies related to (1) the 1974 Microsoft COBOL compiler for microcomputers, (2) the 1974 Wang VS COBOL compiler for Wang VS minicomputers, (3) the 1974 IBM VS COBOL compilers that run on IBM mainframes, and (4) the 1985 COBOL II compiler for IBM mainframes.

**Discussion**

This topic is designed to introduce you to the operating system functions and programs that you'll be using as you develop COBOL programs. Keep in mind, though, that this is a simplified introduction to system software. It is also a general introduction. As a result, different terminology may be used on your system, and the functions may be implemented in a slightly different way on your system. Nevertheless, this topic should provide a solid conceptual background for whatever you encounter on your system, whether you work on a microcomputer, a minicomputer, or a mainframe.

## Terminology

application program
application software
system program
system software
operating system
executing a program
loading a program
supervisor program
supervisor
job-to-job transition
job control program
multiprogramming
spooling
print file
file management
volume name
file name
volume label
file label
library
library management
utility
utility program
interactive editor
language translator
linkage editor
link editing
source statement library
source program
object program
object module
COBOL compiler
object module library
executable module
relocatable library
core image library
COBOL standards
COBOL extension
compiler dependency

## Objectives

1. Describe each of these operating system functions:
   a. job-to-job transition
   b. multiprogramming
   c. spooling
2. Describe the purpose of each of these programs as they relate to program development:
   a. interactive editor
   b. COBOL compiler
   c. linkage editor
3. Find out the name of your COBOL compiler and find out what standards it conforms to.

Chapter 2

# A student's procedure for developing COBOL programs

If you're new to programming, you should realize right now that there's more to writing a program in COBOL than just coding the program. To give you some idea of what's involved, this chapter describes the tasks of a student's procedure for developing COBOL programs. When you finish this chapter, you'll be ready to learn COBOL itself.

When you write a program in COBOL, you should follow a standard development procedure. To some extent, this procedure will vary from one company or school to another. As a starting point, though, figure 2-1 lists the seven tasks of a student's procedure for developing COBOL programs. In most training environments, you'll use a procedure like this when you develop the case study programs for this course.

## Task 1: Get complete program specifications

As a programmer, it's your responsibility to make sure you know exactly what a program is supposed to do before you start to develop it. You must know not only what the inputs and outputs are, but also what processing is required to derive the desired output from the input. If you are assigned a programming problem that isn't adequately defined, be sure to question the person who assigned the

**Analysis**

1. Get complete program specifications.

**Design**

2. Design the program using a structure chart (chapters 11 and 12).
3. If necessary, plan the critical modules of the program using pseudocode (chapters 11 and 12).

**Implementation**

4. Code the program (chapters 3 through 7) and enter it into the system.
5. Compile the program and correct its diagnostics (chapters 8 and 9).
6. Test and debug the program (chapters 8 and 10).
7. Document the program.

**Figure 2-1** A student's procedure for developing COBOL programs

program until you're confident you know what the program is supposed to do.

Most companies have standards for what a complete program specification must include. In general, it should include at least three items: (1) some sort of program overview; (2) record layouts for all files used by the program; and (3) print charts for all printed output prepared by the program. Other documents may be required for specific programs, but these are the most common ones.

**The program overview** *Program overviews* can be prepared in many different forms. Most companies have their own standards. What's important is that a program overview must present a complete picture of what the program is supposed to do.

Figure 2-2 presents the kind of program overview we use in our shop. You will work with program overviews like this if you do the case studies for this course. As you can see, the form is divided into three parts. The top section is for identification. It gives the name and number of the program as specified by the system documentation, along with the name of the program designer and the date.

The middle part of the form lists and describes all of the files that the program requires. In addition, it tells what the program will do with each of those files: use them for input only, use them for output only, or use them for update.

The last section of the form is for processing specifications. It's this section, of course, that is the most critical. Here, you must make sure that all of the information you need to develop the program has been provided. If it isn't all there, you must develop it yourself.

| Program: INV3520 Prepare investment listing | Page: 1 |
|---|---|
| Designer: Anne Prince | Date: 4-3-86 |

Input/output specifications

| File | Description | Use |
|---|---|---|
| INVMAST | Inventory master file | Input |
| INVLIST | Print file: Investment listing | Output |

Process specifications

This program prepares an investment listing from a file of inventory records. The records are in sequence by item number and the report should be printed in the same sequence. If a record is found to be out of sequence, the program should end and an appropriate message should be printed.

The basic processing requirements for each inventory record follow:

1. Read the inventory record.
2. Calculate the investment amount. (Investment amount = on-hand balance x unit cost.)
3. Add the investment amount to the investment total.
4. Format and print a detail line.

After all records have been processed, prepare and print a total line.

**Figure 2-2** A program overview for an investment-listing program

| File name INVMAST | Record name Inventory master record | Date April 3, 1986 |
|---|---|---|
| Application Inventory control | Designer AMP | |
| Comments | | |

| Field Name | Item number | Item description | Unit cost | Unit price | Reorder point | On hand | On order | Last order date | Last month sales |
|---|---|---|---|---|---|---|---|---|---|
| Characteristics | 9(5) | X(20) | 999V99 | 999V99 | 9(5) | 9(5) | 9(5) | 9(6) | 9(5)V99 |
| Usage | | | | | | | | | |
| Position | 1-5 | 6-25 | 26-30 | 31-35 | 36-40 | 41-45 | 46-50 | 51-56 | 57-63 |

| Last year sales | Not used |
|---|---|
| 9(7)V99 | X(8) |
| | |
| 64-72 | 73-80 |

**Figure 2-3** A record layout for an inventory master record

**Record layouts** For each file used by a program, your specification should include a *record layout*. Figure 2-3 shows one type of record layout form. In general, a record layout shows what fields the record contains, what the format of each field is, and where each field is located in the record. In figure 2-3, for example, you can see that the item description occupies bytes 6-25 of the inventory master record. In the characteristics portion of the form, X(20) means that the field contains alphanumeric data (X) and that it has a length of 20 characters. Similarly, 9(5) means that a field contains numeric data (9) and that it is 5 digits long. In this example, the characteristics are given using COBOL notation, so you'll learn what a characteristic like 999V99 means in the next chapter.

**Print charts** A *print chart*, such as the one in figure 2-4, shows the layout of a printed report or other document. It indicates the print positions to be used for each item on the report. For example, on the print chart in figure 2-4, the heading INVENTORY INVESTMENT LISTING is to be printed in print positions 32-59 of the third line of the report; the column heading ITEM NO. is to be printed in print positions 1-4 of the fourth and fifth heading lines; and so on. Similarly, the item-number field for each *detail line* (as opposed to a *heading line*) is to be printed in print positions 1-5, and the amount invested is to be printed in positions 58-68. At the end of the report, one line is to be skipped and a *total line* showing the total amount invested in inventory is to be printed. This total is to be indicated by one asterisk printed in position 70. In this print chart, the formats of the fields are described using COBOL notation, so you'll learn what a format like ZZZZZ means in the next chapter or two.

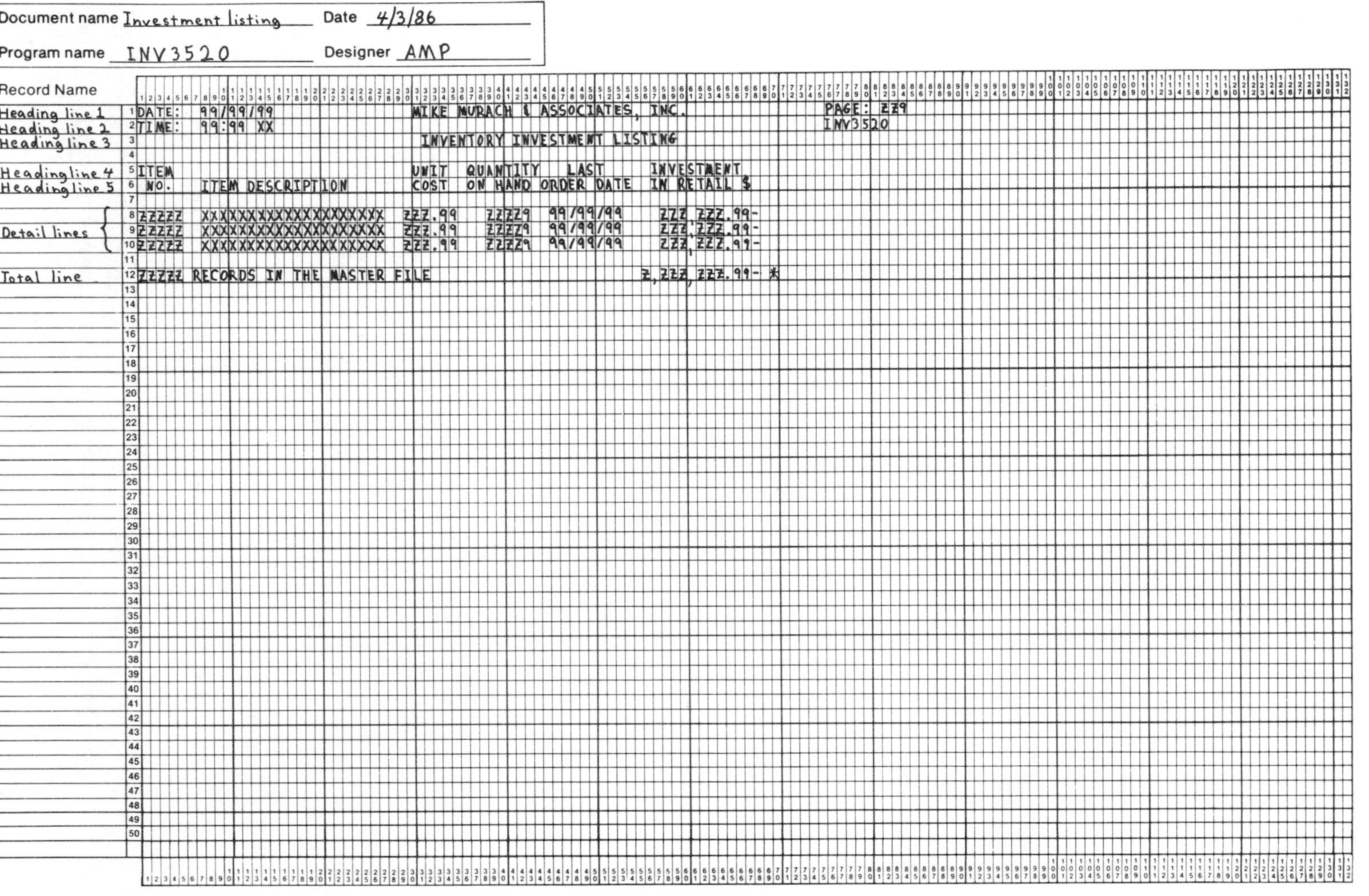

Document name Investment listing
Date 4/3/86
Program name INV3520
Designer AMP
Record Name
Heading line 1
Heading line 2
Heading line 3
Heading line 4
Heading line 5
Detail lines
Total line
DATE: 99/99/99 MIKE MURACH & ASSOCIATES, INC. PAGE: ZZ9
TIME: 99:99 XX INV3520
INVENTORY INVESTMENT LISTING
ITEM UNIT QUANTITY LAST INVESTMENT
NO. ITEM DESCRIPTION COST ON HAND ORDER DATE IN RETAIL $
ZZZZZ XXXXXXXXXXXXXXXXXXXX ZZZ.99 ZZZZ9 99/99/99 ZZZ,ZZZ.99-
ZZZZZ XXXXXXXXXXXXXXXXXXXX ZZZ.99 ZZZZ9 99/99/99 ZZZ,ZZZ.99-
ZZZZZ XXXXXXXXXXXXXXXXXXXX ZZZ.99 ZZZZ9 99/99/99 ZZZ,ZZZ.99-
ZZZZZ RECORDS IN THE MASTER FILE Z,ZZZ,ZZZ.99- *


**Figure 2-4** A print chart for an investment listing

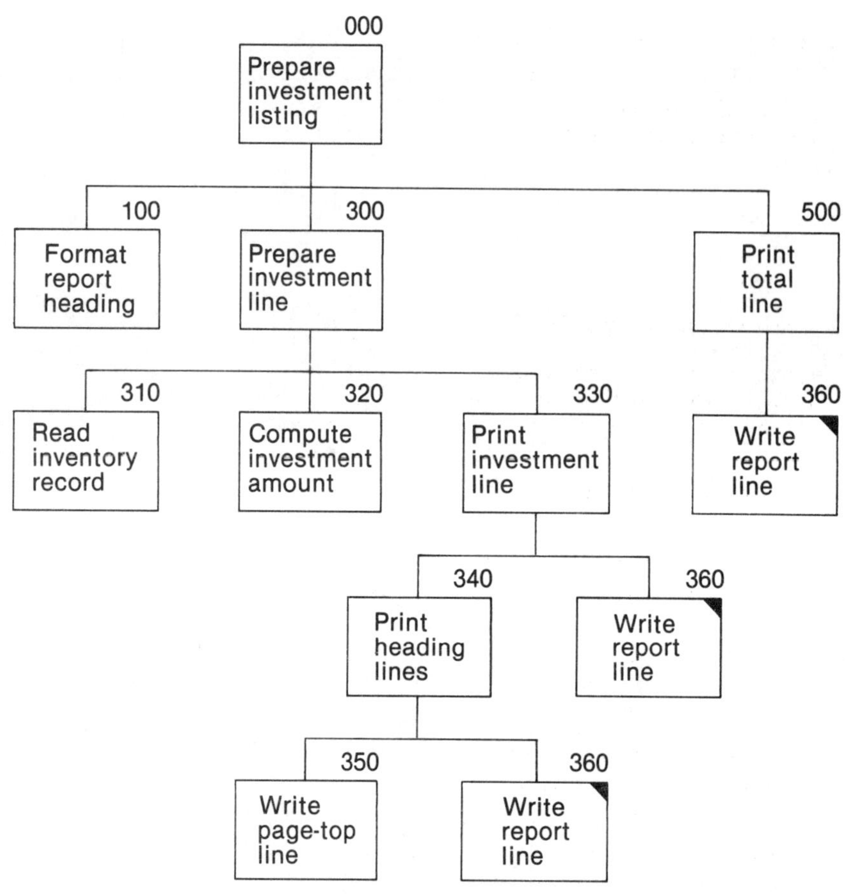


Figure 2-5 A structure chart for the investment-listing program

The report represented by the chart in figure 2-4 has five heading lines and one total line, but a document can have as many heading or total lines as needed. Note in the upper lefthand corner of the report that the date and time are printed as part of the heading. Similarly, the page number and program name are printed in the upper righthand corner of the report. This is a standard practice in many companies.

### Task 2: Design the program using a structure chart

To design a COBOL program, most programmers today use a technique called *structured design* to create a *structure chart* like the one in figure 2-5. In a structure chart, each box represents one COBOL module. The structure chart in figure 2-5 is for the program that is specified by the program overview, record layout, and print chart in figures 2-2 through 2-4. To create a chart like this, you start

```
000-prepare-investment-listing.

    Open files.
    DO 100-format-report-heading.
    DO 300-prepare-investment-line
        UNTIL invmast-eof.
    DO 500-print-total-line.
    Close files.
    Stop run.

300-prepare-investment-line.

    DO 310-read-inventory-record.
    IF not invmast-eof
        DO 320-compute-investment-amount
        DO 330-print-investment-line.

310-read-inventory-record.

    Read inventory master record
        AT END
            move 'Y' to invmast-eof-switch.
    IF NOT invmast-eof
        add 1 to record-count.
```

**Figure 2-6** Pseudocode for some of the critical modules of the investment-listing program

with the top-level module and work down. As a result, this design process is also referred to as *top-down design*.

Design is a critical task in the program development process because it affects the tasks that follow. If you create an effective design for a program, you can code and test the program with efficiency. If you don't design a program effectively, coding is likely to be inefficient and testing is often a nightmare. In chapters 11 and 12, you'll learn how to create effective designs for your COBOL programs.

## Task 3: If necessary, plan the critical modules of the program using pseudocode

In many cases, you'll be able to code and test your programs using only the program specifications and your structure charts. Sometimes, though, you'll want to plan the critical modules of a program before you code them. To do this, we recommend the use of *pseudocode* as illustrated in figure 2-6. This is the pseudocode for three of the modules in the structure chart in figure 2-5.

Pseudocode is useful because it corresponds closely to COBOL code, yet you can write it much more quickly. As a result, you can plan several modules of a program in a fraction of the time it would take you to actually code them. On the other hand, there's no sense in coding a program twice: once in pseudocode and once in COBOL. That's why we recommend the use of pseudocode only when

COBOL Coding Form

SYSTEM Inventory Control
PROGRAM INV3520
PROGRAMMER mm
DATE 4-3-86
PUNCHING INSTRUCTIONS — GRAPHIC: 1 Ø Z I; PUNCH: one zero zee eye
PAGE 1 OF 32

SEQUENCE (PAGE) (LINE) | A | B | COBOL STATEMENT | IDENTIFICATION

```
       IDENTIFICATION DIVISION.
       PROGRAM-ID.            INV3520.
      *AUTHOR.                MIKE MURACH.
      *
       ENVIRONMENT DIVISION.
       INPUT-OUTPUT SECTION.
       FILE-CONTROL.
           SELECT INVMAST ASSIGN TO "INVMAST" "DISK".
           SELECT INVLIST ASSIGN TO "INVLIST" "PRINTER".
      *
       DATA DIVISION.
       FILE SECTION.
      *
       FD  INVMAST
           LABEL RECORDS ARE STANDARD
           RECORD CONTAINS 80 CHARACTERS.
      *
```

Figure 2-7 The start of a COBOL program coded on a COBOL coding form

necessary. In chapters 11 and 12, you'll learn how to make effective use of pseudocode.

### Task 4: Code the program and enter it into the system

When you code a program in COBOL, you write a source program (*source code*) that must be translated into an object program (*object code*). As I explained in the last chapter, this translation is done by the COBOL compiler. It is called a *compilation*. Before the source program can be compiled, though, it must be entered into the computer system.

Since the major purpose of this book is to teach you how to code in COBOL, I won't try to introduce coding at this time. However, I will give you some idea of how you will enter your COBOL code into the system. Then, chapters 3 through 7 will teach you how to code in COBOL.

In the past, when you coded a COBOL program, you coded it on a special coding form like the one in figure 2-7. Then, when you were finished, you keypunched one 80-column *source card* for each line on

```
(1)DISP            (3)LAST          (5)NEXT              (7)UP    (8)FIND
(9)MOD  (10)CHNG  (11)INS  (12)DEL  (13)MOVE  (14)COPY  (15)COL  (16)MENU


000100  IDENTIFICATION DIVISION.
000200  PROGRAM-ID.        INV3520.
000300 *AUTHOR.            MIKE MURACH.
000400 *
000500  ENVIRONMENT DIVISION.
000600  INPUT-OUTPUT SECTION.
000700  FILE-CONTROL.
000800      SELECT INVMAST ASSIGN TO "INVMAST" "DISK".
000900      SELECT INVLIST ASSIGN TO "INVLIST" "PRINTER".
001000 *
001100  DATA DIVISION.
001200  FILE SECTION.
001300 *
001400  FD  INVMAST
001500      LABEL RECORDS ARE STANDARD
001600      RECORD CONTAINS 80 CHARACTERS.
001700 *
 ADD -
 ADD -
 ADD -
```

**Figure 2-8** The start of a COBOL program as entered into a terminal using an interactive editor

the coding form. After the cards were punched, they could be read into the computer system and stored in a source statement library.

Today, punched cards are nearly obsolete, so you will probably enter your source programs directly into the computer system on an interactive basis. In the system, the lines of code will be stored as 80-character records that you can think of as card images. For instance, figure 2-8 shows an entry screen for the interactive editor on a Wang VS system. Here, the programmer has entered the same 17 lines of code that are shown on the coding form in figure 2-7.

Although you may be asked to handcode your program on a coding form before you enter it into the system, this isn't really necessary. Instead, you can code your program as you enter it into the system using your structure chart and pseudocode as a guide for your entries. In fact, with a little practice, you'll find that you can enter your program directly into the system much faster than you can handcode your program and then enter it into the system.

When you enter a program directly into a system, you do it under the control of an interactive editor. As a result, you must learn how to use the editor for your system. Some editors, like the editor for the Wang VS system, are relatively easy to use, so training is minimal. For instance, you can see the function keys that are to be used for the different editing commands at the top of the screen in figure 2-8:

function key 9 to modify (MOD) one or more lines of code; function key 11 to insert (INS) one or more lines of code; function key 12 to delete (DEL) one or more lines of code; and so on. Because the commands are largely self-explanatory, you can learn how to use this editor in a short time with little or no use of the reference manuals available with it. In contrast, some editors are difficult to use. In any case, I'll make no attempt to show you how to use your interactive editor in this book since there are just too many to cover.

### Task 5: Compile the program and correct its diagnostics

After your program has been entered into the computer system, it can be compiled. In chapter 8, we'll show you how to start a compilation on a microcomputer or minicomputer. We'll also show you how to code the *job control procedures* you'll need for a compilation when you use an IBM mainframe under either the DOS/VSE operating system or the OS/MVS operating system.

During a compilation, a *compiler listing* is printed by the computer. The compiler listing is a listing of the source program as well as a listing of various reference tables. If any errors are caught by the compiler during the compilation (as is usually the case the first time you compile a program), one or more *diagnostic messages* (or *diagnostics*) are printed on a *diagnostic listing*, which is part of the compiler listing. Each diagnostic calls attention to one error in the source code.

If there are diagnostics, you must make the necessary corrections to the source code. Then, you recompile the program. You repeat this process until there are no more diagnostics in the compiler listing. At this point, the program is ready to be tested.

Chapter 9 will show you how to correct the diagnostics you encounter. It will also show you some of the optional output that can be part of the compiler listing. You can read chapter 9 any time after you've completed chapter 3. But you will certainly want to read it when you complete your first compilation and receive your first diagnostic messages.

### Task 6: Test and debug the program

Usually, an object program created by a compilation must be link edited by the linkage editor before it can be tested. The linkage editor converts the object program into an executable module. Then, you can *test* the executable module to see if it works.

In chapter 8, we'll show you how to link edit and test a program on a typical microcomputer or minicomputer. We'll also show you how to create the job control procedures you'll need on an IBM mainframe for compiling, link editing, and testing a program. These procedures must identify the test files your program is going to process.

The test data in your test files should be designed to try all of the conditions that may occur when your program is used. Before testing, you figure out what output your program should produce when it's run using that test data. After your program's been executed, you compare the actual output to the output you expected to get. If they agree, you can assume that the program does what you intended it to do.

More likely, however, the actual output and the intended output will not agree the first time the program is executed. If this is the case, you must *debug* the program. You must find the errors (*bugs*), make the necessary corrections to the source code using your interactive editor, recompile the source program, and make another test run. This process is continued until the program executes as intended.

In actual practice, rather than making just one test run on a new program, you make a series of test runs using different sets of test data. The test data for the first test run is usually low in volume, perhaps only a half-dozen records, and may be designed to test only the main processing functions of the program. After you have debugged the program using this data, you may test it on data that tries the exceptional conditions that may come up during the execution of the program. Finally, you may test your program for conditions that depend upon larger volumes of data, such as the page overflow condition when printing reports and other documents. Page overflow occurs when one page is full and a new one should be started.

In chapter 10, you will learn how to test and debug your COBOL programs. You can read chapter 10 any time after you complete chapter 3 of this book. But you will certainly want to read it when you get your first test run output and experience your first bugs.

Although chapter 10 shows you how to create the test data for your test runs, this book assumes that you will be given the test files you need to test your case study programs. As a result, you won't need to create your own test data until you start writing production programs. At that time, you should find out what your shop's standards are for planning test runs and creating test data.

### Task 7: Document the program

*Documentation* in data processing terminology refers to the collection of records that specify what is being done and what is going to be done within a data processing system. For each program in an installation, there should be a collection of documents referred to as *program documentation*. As a programmer, one of your jobs is to provide this documentation for each program you write.

Program documentation is important because it is almost inevitable that changes will be made to a production program.

Sometimes, the users of the program will discover that it doesn't work quite the way it was supposed to. Sometimes, the users will want the program to do more than they originally specified. Sometimes, a company will change the way it does some function, so the related programs have to be changed. No matter what the reason for the modifications, though, it is difficult indeed to modify or enhance a program that isn't adequately documented.

Fortunately, some of the most important components of program documentation are by-products of the program development process: the program overview, the record layouts, the print chart, and the structure chart. In addition, you should include the final compiler listing since it is the only document that shows the actual programming details. You may also be asked to include your listings of test data and test run output.

For production programs, your shop standards should specify what's required for program documentation. For your case study programs, you should provide (1) your structure chart, (2) your final compiler listing, and (3) listings of your test run output, plus any additional items your instructor requests.

## Discussion

This topic is designed to give you a better idea of what you must do to develop a COBOL program in a training environment. If you follow the procedure shown in figure 2-1, you should be able to do your case study assignments with relative efficiency. If you don't have a clear view of what the tasks in this procedure are right now, don't despair. The purpose of this course is to teach you how to do the tasks of this procedure.

In contrast to the procedure in figure 2-1, figure 2-9 presents a typical procedure for developing COBOL programs in a production environment. Here, you can see that the programmer should get related COPY members and subprograms as a task in the analysis phase. You'll learn more about this in chapter 5. In the implementation phase, you can see that the procedure suggests that you plan the testing, code the procedures for the test runs, and create the test data for the test runs before any coding is done. These tasks show how important it is to test a program in a carefully controlled manner. Finally, in step 8, the procedure suggests that you code and test the program a few modules at a time, using a technique called *top-down testing*. Chapter 11 introduces you to top-down testing so you can use it as you develop some of the case study programs for this course.

By now, you should realize that what I said about COBOL programming at the start of this chapter is true. There's a lot more to it than coding a program in COBOL. That's why we offer a book for experienced programmers called *How to Design and Develop COBOL Programs*. It assumes that you already know how to develop COBOL programs, so its purpose is to show you how to develop effec-

**Analysis**

1. Get complete program specifications.
2. Get related programs, COPY members, and subprograms.

**Design**

3. Design the program using a structure chart.
4. If necessary, plan the critical modules of the program using pseudocode.

**Implementation**

5. Plan the testing of the program by creating a test plan.
6. If necessary, code the job control procedures for the test runs.
7. If necessary, create the test data for the test runs.
8. Code and test the program using top-down testing.
9. Document the program.

Figure 2-9 A professional procedure for developing COBOL programs

tive programs more efficiently. As a result, it puts a major emphasis on design and testing techniques. After you complete *Part 1* and *Part 2* of this course, we recommend *How to Design and Develop COBOL Programs* as the next course in your COBOL training.

## Terminology

program overview
record layout
print chart
detail line
heading line
total line
structured design
structure chart
top-down design
pseudocode
source code
object code
compilation
source card
job control procedure
compiler listing
diagnostic message
diagnostic
diagnostic listing
testing
debugging
bug
documentation
program documentation
top-down testing

## Objective

List and describe the seven tasks of the student's development procedure presented in this chapter.

Section 2

# A professional subset of COBOL for report preparation

The five chapters in this section present a professional subset of COBOL. Once you have mastered it, you will be able to write COBOL programs for preparing reports and other documents.

The first chapter in this section introduces you to COBOL by presenting a complete program that uses only an introductory subset of COBOL. The next four chapters in this section expand upon this introductory subset. Each of these chapters also presents a program that uses the elements that have just been added to the subset.

The first chapter in this section is the most difficult one in this book. As a result, you should be prepared to put more time into this chapter than you do the other ones. When you complete this chapter, you should understand how the elements of a COBOL program are related and how the COBOL program relates to the specifications for the program. Once you understand these relationships, it should be relatively easy for you to learn the elements that are added to the introductory subset in the subsequent chapters.

Chapter 3

# An introduction to COBOL: The basic elements

This chapter introduces you to COBOL. It does this by presenting the specifications for a program along with the COBOL program that satisfies those specifications. After it presents one COBOL program in detail, it shows you other ways you could code the program so you can see that you can code a COBOL program in many different ways.

To make this introduction manageable, this chapter is divided into six topics. The first topic presents the program specifications and the working COBOL program. Then, topics 2, 3, and 4 present each of the four divisions of the COBOL program in detail. Next, topic 5 presents other ways in which the program could be written. Finally, topic 6 explains how the code in the program may vary from one system to the next, even though this book presents "standard" COBOL.

The purpose of this chapter is to get you to see the complete picture right away. That's why it shows you how the elements of COBOL work together in a complete program. When you finish this chapter, you should be able to write COBOL programs of considerable complexity. Then, chapters 4, 5, 6, and 7 will build on this base of COBOL knowledge.

This is the longest chapter in this book and it's probably the most difficult one, so be prepared to concentrate. If you can't read all six topics in one study session, at least try to read the first four topics in one session. As you read this chapter, remember that you're trying to understand the relationships between all the COBOL elements. Once you do that, it should be easy for you to learn new COBOL elements.

# Topic 1 The inventory-listing program

This topic presents the specifications and code for a report preparation program. This program reads an inventory master file and prints an inventory listing on the computer system's printer. We call it the inventory-listing program. Although it's a simple program, it illustrates many of the elements of COBOL.

## The program specifications

As I explained in chapter 2, program specifications should consist of (1) a program overview, (2) record layouts for the records of the input files, and (3) a print chart for each document that is to be printed. For the inventory-listing program, you'll find these items in figures 3-1 through 3-3.

**The program overview** Figure 3-1 presents the program overview for this program. As you can see, the program reads an inventory master file named INVMAST and prepares an inventory listing named INVLIST. For each record in the master file, the program prints one line on the inventory listing. The inventory master file is a sequential disk file in sequence by item number.

In COBOL, a printed document is considered to be a file. That's why the inventory listing is listed as a file on the program overview. Similarly, each line printed on a report is considered to be a record in the print file. As a result, you'll see file and record descriptions for the print file in the COBOL coding.

**The record layout and test data for the inventory master file** Figure 3-2 gives the record layout for the inventory master record. As you can see, the item number field is in positions 1-5 of the record; the item description field is in positions 6-25; the unit cost field is in positions 26-30; and so on. In the characteristics notation for the fields, an X indicates an alphanumeric character, a 9 indicates a decimal digit, and a V shows where a decimal point is assumed to be within the digits of a field. You'll learn more about this notation later on in this chapter. Although the last 30 positions of the master record are unused (at least by this program), they are a part of each master record, so they must be accounted for by the program.

If you review the test data for this program, you can see that it is consistent with the record format. Thus, the first record has an item number of 00001, an item description of GENERATOR, and a unit cost of 40.00. If you look at the last test record, you can see that the data is designed to test the size of each field, so all numeric fields are filled with 9's and all 20 positions in the alphanumeric field are filled with A's.

| Program: INV3510 Prepare inventory listing | Page: 1 |
|---|---|
| Designer: Anne Prince | Date: 3-11-86 |

Input/output specifications

| File | Description | Use |
|---|---|---|
| INVMAST | Inventory master file | Input |
| INVLIST | Print file: Inventory listing | Output |

Process specifications

```
The inventory master file is a sequential disk file in sequence by
item number.  This program reads the inventory master file
sequentially in order to prepare an inventory listing.  For each
record in the master file, the program prints one line on the
inventory listing.
```

**Figure 3-1** The program overview for the inventory-listing program

**Record layout**

| Field name | Item no. | Item description | Unit cost | Unit price | Reorder point | On hand | On order | Unused |
|---|---|---|---|---|---|---|---|---|
| Characteristics | 9(5) | X(20) | 999V99 | 999V99 | 9(5) | 9(5) | 9(5) | X(30) |
| Usage | | | | | | | | |
| Position | 1-5 | 6-25 | 26-30 | 31-35 | 36-40 | 41-45 | 46-50 | 51-80 |

**Test data**

| 1 5 | 6 25 | 26 30 | 31 35 | 36 40 | 41 45 | 46 50 |
|---|---|---|---|---|---|---|
| 00001 | GENERATOR | 04000 | 04900 | 00100 | 00070 | 00050 |
| 00103 | HEATER SOLENOID | 00330 | 00440 | 00050 | 00034 | 00000 |
| 03244 | GEAR HOUSING | 06500 | 07900 | 00000 | 00000 | 00000 |
| 03981 | PLUMB LINE | 00210 | 00240 | 00015 | 00035 | 00000 |
| 99999 | AAAAAAAAAAAAAAAAAAAA | 99999 | 99999 | 99999 | 99999 | 99999 |

**Figure 3-2** The record layout and test data for the inventory master file

**Print chart**

| Record Name | Line | |
|---|---|---|
| HEADING-LINE | 1 | ITEM NO. ITEM DESCRIPTION UNIT PRICE ON HAND REORDER POINT |
| | 2 | |
| INVENTORY-LINE | 3 | ZZZZZ XXXXXXXXXXXXXXXXXXXX ZZZ.99 ZZZZ9 ZZZZZ |
| | 4 | ZZZZZ XXXXXXXXXXXXXXXXXXXX ZZZ.99 ZZZZ9 ZZZZZ |
| | 5 | |
| | 6 | |
| | 7 | |
| | 8 | |
| | 9 | |
| | 10 | |
| | 11 | |
| | 12 | |

**Test run output**

```
ITEM NO.   ITEM DESCRIPTION              UNIT PRICE    ON HAND    REORDER POINT

      1    GENERATOR                          49.00         70              100
    103    HEATER SOLENOID                     4.40         34               50
   3244    GEAR HOUSING                       79.00          0
   3981    PLUMB LINE                          2.40         35               15
  99999    AAAAAAAAAAAAAAAAAAAA              999.99      99999            99999
```

**Figure 3-3** The print chart and test run output for the inventory listing

**The print chart and test run output for the inventory listing**
Figure 3-3 presents the print chart for the inventory listing. Here, you can see the format of the heading line as well as the format of the detail lines, which are called inventory lines. In the heading line, ITEM NO. is supposed to be printed in positions 1-8; ITEM DESCRIPTION in positions 11-26; and so on.

In the detail lines, a 9 means that a digit is supposed to be printed in a specific print position; an X means any character including a digit can be printed in a specific print position; and a Z is used in place of a 9 to show that an insignificant (lead) zero is to be suppressed. In each inventory line, then, the item number is to be printed with zero suppression in print positions 1-5; the item description is to be printed in positions 11-30; the unit price is to be printed in positions 38-43 with a decimal point in position 41 and zero suppression before the decimal point; and so on. You'll learn more about this notation later on in this chapter.

If you review the test run output for this program, you can see that it's consistent with the print chart. In the third inventory line, the on-hand field with its value of zero prints as a zero, but the reorder point field with its value of zero prints as a space. This is consistent with the print chart, because it doesn't specify zero suppression in the rightmost position of the on-hand field but it does specify zero suppression in the rightmost position of the reorder point field.

Because of space considerations, the print chart in figure 3-3 shows you only the first 76 characters of each print line. However, the actual line length is 132 characters—the number allowed by most printers. Throughout this book, you can assume that all print lines consist of 132 characters, even when fewer are shown on the print chart, and that all the positions not shown are blank.

### The structure chart

Figure 3-4 presents the structure chart for this program. As you can see, it consists of only six modules, which is an indication of how simple this program is. In fact, as you will see in topic 5, this program can be coded quite easily as a three-module program.

Although you aren't expected to be able to design structure charts right now, I present this chart so you'll be able to see how it relates to the COBOL program. Then, after you see a few structure charts and the related COBOL programs, you'll be able to start designing charts of your own.

### The COBOL listing

Figure 3-5 presents the complete COBOL listing for the inventory-listing program as it runs on an IBM mainframe using the DOS/VSE operating system. In the next three topics, I'll explain the code in this

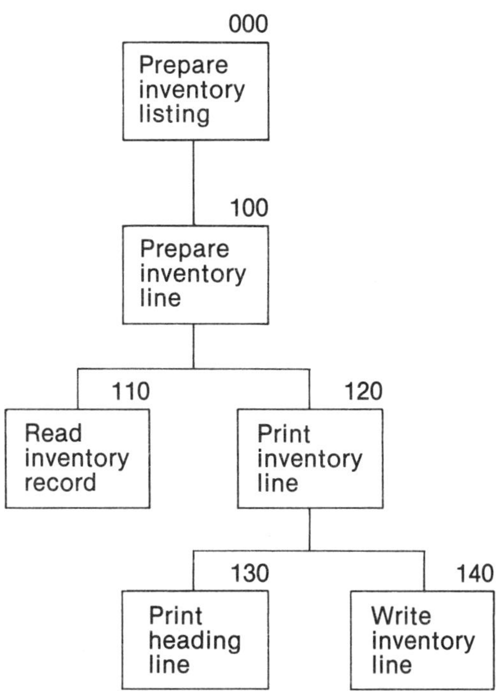


**Figure 3-4** The structure chart for the inventory-listing program

program in detail. Then, in topic 6, I'll show you the few modifications you might have to make to get this program to run on your system. For now, though, I just want you to understand some general characteristics of a COBOL program.

**The four COBOL divisions** If you read through the code for the program, you will find four *division headers*:

```
IDENTIFICATION DIVISION.
ENVIRONMENT DIVISION.
DATA DIVISION.
PROCEDURE DIVISION.
```

All COBOL programs are divided into these four divisions. If you omit a division header from your program by accident, your program will not compile successfully. As you will see later in this chapter, the first two divisions of a program are relatively trivial, while the last two divisions are the essence of a program.

**A and B margins in the COBOL code** If you review the COBOL coding form in figure 2-7 of the last chapter, you can see an *A margin* starting in column 8 of the form and a *B margin* starting in column 12.

```
000100 IDENTIFICATION DIVISION.
000200*
000300 PROGRAM-ID.        INV3510.
000400*AUTHOR.            MIKE MURACH.
000500*
000600 ENVIRONMENT DIVISION.
000700*
000800 CONFIGURATION SECTION.
000900*
001000 SOURCE-COMPUTER.   IBM-370.
001100 OBJECT-COMPUTER.   IBM-370.
001200*
001300 INPUT-OUTPUT SECTION.
001400*
001500 FILE-CONTROL.
001600     SELECT INVMAST ASSIGN TO SYS020-AS-INVMAST.
001700     SELECT INVLIST ASSIGN TO SYS006-UR-1403-S.
001800*
001900 DATA DIVISION.
002000*
002100 FILE SECTION.
002200*
002300 FD  INVMAST
002400     LABEL RECORDS ARE STANDARD
002500     RECORD CONTAINS 80 CHARACTERS.
002600*
002700 01  INVENTORY-MASTER-RECORD.
002800*
002900     05  IM-ITEM-NO           PIC 9(5).
003000     05  IM-ITEM-DESC         PIC X(20).
003100     05  IM-UNIT-COST         PIC 999V99.
003200     05  IM-UNIT-PRICE        PIC 999V99.
003300     05  IM-REORDER-POINT     PIC 9(5).
003400     05  IM-ON-HAND           PIC 9(5).
003500     05  IM-ON-ORDER          PIC 9(5).
003600     05  FILLER               PIC X(30).
003700*
003800 FD  INVLIST
003900     LABEL RECORDS ARE OMITTED
004000     RECORD CONTAINS 132 CHARACTERS.
004100*
004200 01  PRINT-AREA               PIC X(132).
004300*
```

**Figure 3-5** The COBOL listing for the inventory listing program (part 1 of 3)

As you will see, some COBOL statements have to begin in the A margin, and some have to begin in the B margin. In the remainder of this book, however, you won't see COBOL programs on coding forms; you'll see them as printed listings. So you have to be able to identify the A and B margins within a listing.

Figure 3-6 shows you how to interpret the code in a COBOL listing. From the left, the first 6 positions give sequence numbers for the coding lines. Then, the seventh position usually contains either a blank or an asterisk. The next 4 positions (8-11) make up the A

```
004400 WORKING-STORAGE SECTION.
004500*
004600 01  SWITCHES.
004700*
004800     05  INVMAST-EOF-SWITCH   PIC X        VALUE 'N'.
004900*
005000 01  PRINT-FIELDS.
005100*
005200     05  SPACE-CONTROL        PIC 9.
005300     05  LINES-ON-PAGE        PIC 99       VALUE 55.
005400     05  LINE-COUNT           PIC 99       VALUE 70.
005500*
005600 01  HEADING-LINE.
005700*
005800     05  FILLER               PIC X(8)     VALUE 'ITEM NO.'.
005900     05  FILLER               PIC X(2)     VALUE SPACE.
006000     05  FILLER               PIC X(16)    VALUE 'ITEM DESCRIPTION'.
006100     05  FILLER               PIC X(8).
006200     05  FILLER               PIC X(10)    VALUE 'UNIT PRICE'.
006300     05  FILLER               PIC X(5)     VALUE SPACE.
006400     05  FILLER               PIC X(7)     VALUE 'ON HAND'.
006500     05  FILLER               PIC X(5)     VALUE SPACE.
006600     05  FILLER               PIC X(13)    VALUE 'REORDER POINT'.
006700     05  FILLER               PIC X(58)    VALUE SPACE.
006800*
006900 01  INVENTORY-LINE.
007000*
007100     05  IL-ITEM-NO           PIC Z(5).
007200     05  FILLER               PIC X(5)     VALUE SPACE.
007300     05  IL-ITEM-DESC         PIC X(20).
007400     05  FILLER               PIC X(7)     VALUE SPACE.
007500     05  IL-UNIT-PRICE        PIC ZZZ.ZZ.
007600     05  FILLER               PIC X(7)     VALUE SPACE.
007700     05  IL-ON-HAND           PIC ZZZZ9.
007800     05  FILLER               PIC X(11)    VALUE SPACE.
007900     05  IL-REORDER-POINT     PIC Z(5).
008000     05  FILLER               PIC X(61)    VALUE SPACE.
008100*
```

**Figure 3-5** The COBOL listing for the inventory listing program (part 2 of 3)

margin. The next 61 positions (12-72) make up the B margin. And the last 8 positions can be used for other identifying information.

Since positions 1-6 are only used to give a unique number to each line in a program, they don't affect the operation of the program. Similarly, positions 73-80 don't affect the operation of the program; in fact, you normally don't use them when you develop programs on an interactive basis. As a result, most of the programs shown in this text won't include positions 1-6 or positions 73-80. When they are omitted, the leftmost position of a COBOL listing will be for position 7 of the code, the A margin will start in the next position, and so on.

**Comment lines** If you look again at the listing in figure 3-5, you can see that many of the lines have an asterisk in position 7. These

```
PROCEDURE DIVISION.
*
000-PREPARE-INVENTORY-LISTING.
*
    OPEN INPUT  INVMAST
         OUTPUT INVLIST.
    PERFORM 100-PREPARE-INVENTORY-LINE
        UNTIL INVMAST-EOF-SWITCH = 'Y'.
    CLOSE INVMAST
          INVLIST.
    STOP RUN.
*
100-PREPARE-INVENTORY-LINE.
*
    PERFORM 110-READ-INVENTORY-RECORD.
    IF INVMAST-EOF-SWITCH NOT = 'Y'
        PERFORM 120-PRINT-INVENTORY-LINE.
*
110-READ-INVENTORY-RECORD.
*
    READ INVMAST RECORD
        AT END
            MOVE 'Y' TO INVMAST-EOF-SWITCH.
*
120-PRINT-INVENTORY-LINE.
*
    IF LINE-COUNT > LINES-ON-PAGE
        PERFORM 130-PRINT-HEADING-LINE.
    MOVE IM-ITEM-NO           TO IL-ITEM-NO.
    MOVE IM-ITEM-DESC         TO IL-ITEM-DESC.
    MOVE IM-UNIT-PRICE        TO IL-UNIT-PRICE.
    MOVE IM-ON-HAND           TO IL-ON-HAND.
    MOVE IM-REORDER-POINT     TO IL-REORDER-POINT.
    MOVE INVENTORY-LINE       TO PRINT-AREA.
    PERFORM 140-WRITE-INVENTORY-LINE.
*
130-PRINT-HEADING-LINE.
*
    MOVE HEADING-LINE TO PRINT-AREA.
    WRITE PRINT-AREA
        AFTER ADVANCING PAGE.
    MOVE ZERO TO LINE-COUNT.
    MOVE 2 TO SPACE-CONTROL.
*
140-WRITE-INVENTORY-LINE.
*
    WRITE PRINT-AREA
        AFTER ADVANCING SPACE-CONTROL LINES.
    ADD 1 TO LINE-COUNT.
    MOVE 1 TO SPACE-CONTROL.
```

**Figure 3-5** The COBOL listing for the inventory listing program (part 3 of 3)

lines are called *comment lines*, and all comment lines are ignored by the COBOL compiler. As a result, comment lines don't affect the operation of a COBOL program.

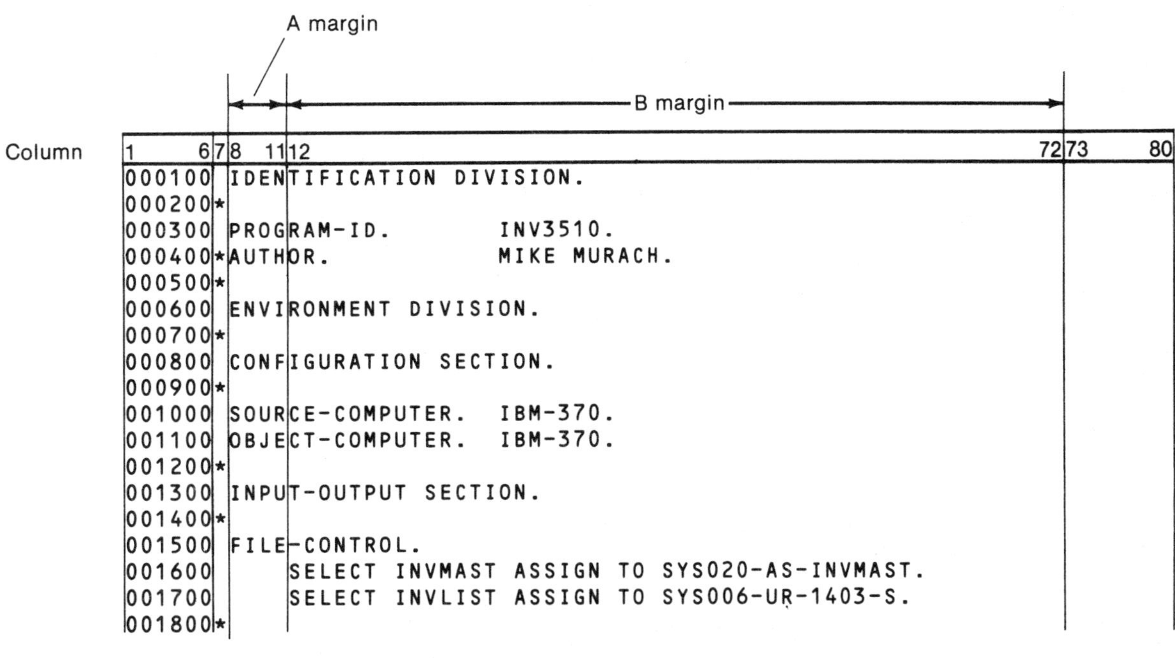


```
000100 IDENTIFICATION DIVISION.
000200*
000300 PROGRAM-ID.        INV3510.
000400*AUTHOR.            MIKE MURACH.
000500*
000600 ENVIRONMENT DIVISION.
000700*
000800 CONFIGURATION SECTION.
000900*
001000 SOURCE-COMPUTER.   IBM-370.
001100 OBJECT-COMPUTER.   IBM-370.
001200*
001300 INPUT-OUTPUT SECTION.
001400*
001500 FILE-CONTROL.
001600     SELECT INVMAST ASSIGN TO SYS020-AS-INVMAST.
001700     SELECT INVLIST ASSIGN TO SYS006-UR-1403-S.
001800*
```

**Figure 3-6** Source columns and the A and B margins

Sometimes, comment lines are used to give information about a program. This is illustrated by the first comment line in the program in figure 3-5, which gives the programmer's name. More often, though, comment lines are left blank.

**Blank comment lines** *Blank comment lines* are lines with an asterisk in position 7 and blanks in positions 8-72. They are used to give the program listing some vertical spacing. As a result, they don't affect the operation of the COBOL program. Although this spacing isn't so important in a short program like the one in figure 3-5, it can make a long program much easier to read.

**Spacing and punctuation** In COBOL, spaces are used to separate the elements of the language. Whenever a space is required, you can use one space or more than one space. As a result, you can use spacing to improve the readability of your COBOL code. In figure 3-5, for example, spacing is used to align all of the PICs in the Data Division. And spacing is used for indentation in the Procedure Division to make the coding easier to read.

Although you can use commas and semicolons in your COBOL code, the compiler ignores them. As a result, we recommend that you avoid using them. On the other hand, periods are critical to the operation of a COBOL program so you should make sure you use them in the right places, and always with a space after the period.

To show you the freedom that you have when coding a COBOL program, figure 3-7 shows you another way that lines 6300 through 8600 in figure 3-5 could be coded. The resulting program runs the same way as the program in figure 3-5. If you have to modify the program, though, I think you'll agree that the code in figure 3-5 is much easier to read and modify than the code in figure 3-7. So please use spacing to improve the readability of your programs, and avoid the use of commas and semicolons.

**Paragraph names in the Procedure Division** The names that start in the A margin in the Procedure Division are called paragraph names. If you design your programs using a structure chart as described in this book, you should have one paragraph in the Procedure Division for each module on the structure chart. Then, to relate the Procedure Division to the structure chart, you create the paragraph names from the module numbers and descriptions on the structure chart.

If, for example, you look at the top-level module in figure 3-4, you can see that it is module number 000 with a description of "Prepare inventory listing." As a result, the COBOL paragraph for this module is named:

```
000-PREPARE-INVENTORY-LISTING
```

In other words, the paragraph name consists of the module number followed by the module description, with all words and numbers separated by hyphens. When you code the paragraphs in the Procedure Division, you code them in sequence by module number.

## Discussion

With this as background, you're ready to learn about the COBOL coding that counts. In the next three topics, you'll learn how the critical code in each of the four divisions of the inventory-listing program works.

## Terminology

division header
A margin
B margin
comment line
blank comment line

```
 01   INVENTORY-LINE.
*
      05  IL-ITEM-NO, PIC Z(5).
      05  FILLER, PIC X(5), VALUE SPACE.
      05  IL-ITEM-DESC, PIC X(20).
      05  FILLER, PIC X(7), VALUE SPACE.
      05  IL-UNIT-PRICE, PIC ZZZ.99.
      05  FILLER, PIC X(7), VALUE SPACE.
      05  IL-ON-HAND, PIC ZZZZ9.
      05  FILLER, PIC X(11), VALUE SPACE.
      05  IL-REORDER-POINT, PIC Z(5).
      05  FILLER, PIC X(61), VALUE SPACE.
*
 PROCEDURE DIVISION.
*
 000-PREPARE-INVENTORY-LISTING.
*
      OPEN INPUT INVMAST; OUTPUT INVLIST.  PERFORM
      100-PREPARE-INVENTORY-LINE, UNTIL INVMAST-EOF-SWITCH
      = 'Y'.  CLOSE INVMAST, INVLIST.  STOP RUN.
*
```

**Figure 3-7** COBOL coding with ineffective spacing and punctuation

## Objectives

1. Given a COBOL listing, identify the following:

   a. the four divisions of the program
   b. the A margin
   c. the B margin
   d. the blank comment lines
   e. the comment lines
   f. the paragraph names in the Procedure Division

2. Explain how to create a paragraph name in the Procedure Division from the module number and description on a program structure chart.

## Topic 2 The Identification and Environment Divisions

Figure 3-8 shows the code for the Identification and Environment Divisions of the inventory-listing program. As you will soon see, these divisions are always short and relatively easy to code. In the Identification Division, you try to identify the program for others who may have to read or modify it later on. In the Environment Division, you identify the environment in which your program will be compiled and run.

### THE IDENTIFICATION DIVISION

The Identification Division doesn't cause any object code to be compiled and requires only two coding lines. In figure 3-8, the required lines are:

```
IDENTIFICATION DIVISION.
PROGRAM-ID.          INV3510.
```

Except for INV3510, which is the *program name* made up by the programmer, these two coding lines will be the same for all COBOL programs.

The COBOL standards allow a program name to be up to 30 characters long consisting of letters, the digits 0 through 9, and hyphens, provided that the name doesn't start or end with a hyphen. Based on these rules, the following are valid program names:

```
PREPARE-INVENTORY-LISTING
INV-3510
```

Many compilers, however, are more restrictive than the standards. On IBM mainframes, for example, it's best to create program names that (1) start with a letter, (2) use letters and digits only, and (3) use eight or fewer characters. If you don't do this, the compiler will convert your program name to one that obeys these rules. That's why the inventory-listing program uses the name INV3510. From a practical point of view, you are normally given a program name when you receive a production or training assignment, so you just code whatever name you're given.

Although the division name and PROGRAM-ID are the only lines required in the Identification Division, other identifying information can be given by using comment lines as shown in figure 3-9. Remember that comments are ignored by the compiler, so you can code whatever information you want in these lines. In figure 3-9, the

```
 IDENTIFICATION DIVISION.
*
 PROGRAM-ID.        INV3510.
*AUTHOR.            MIKE MURACH.
*
 ENVIRONMENT DIVISION.
*
 CONFIGURATION SECTION.
*
 SOURCE-COMPUTER.   IBM-370.
 OBJECT-COMPUTER.   IBM-370.
*
 INPUT-OUTPUT SECTION.
*
 FILE-CONTROL.
     SELECT INVMAST ASSIGN TO SYS020-AS-INVMAST.
     SELECT INVLIST ASSIGN TO SYS006-UR-1403-S.
*
```

**Figure 3-8** The Identification and Environment Divisions of the inventory-listing program

```
 IDENTIFICATION DIVISION.
*
 PROGRAM-ID.        INV3510.
*AUTHOR.            MIKE MURACH.
*INSTALLATION.      MIKE MURACH & ASSOCIATES, INC.
*DATE STARTED.      MARCH 18, 1986.
*DATE COMPLETED.    MARCH 18, 1986.
*SECURITY.          ANYONE MAY USE THIS PROGRAM.
*NARRATIVE.         THIS PROGRAM PREPARES AN INVENTORY LISTING
*                   FROM THE INVENTORY MASTER FILE.
*
```

**Figure 3-9** An expanded Identification Division

comments identify the author, the installation, the start and completion dates for the program, any security restrictions, and so on. Since most compiler listings show the compilation date at the top of the listing, there's usually no need to specify the date of the last compilation. But the other information can be useful in some shops.

The important thing is to find out what's expected of you. A professional COBOL shop will have standards for what you are expected to include in this division. In a class in industry or college, your instructor should tell you what to include to identify your programs.

## THE ENVIRONMENT DIVISION

The Environment Division of a COBOL program specifies the hardware components that are to be used for the compilation of the COBOL program and for the execution of the object program. As a result, the coding of this division varies from one compiler to another. In general, you have to change some of the code in this division when converting programs from one system to another. If you look at the code in figure 3-8, you can see that the Environment Division is divided into two sections: the Configuration Section and the Input-Output Section.

### The Configuration Section

The Configuration Section for the inventory-listing program is as follows:

```
ENVIRONMENT DIVISION.
CONFIGURATION SECTION.
SOURCE-COMPUTER.  IBM-370.
OBJECT-COMPUTER.  IBM-370.
```

Here, only the shaded words will change from one system to another. SOURCE-COMPUTER specifies the computer that will be used for the compilation. In most cases, this will be the same as the computer used for executing the object program, known as the OBJECT-COMPUTER. In the example, the computer specified is the IBM System/370 (or one of its successors).

On most compilers, the SOURCE-COMPUTER and OBJECT-COMPUTER paragraphs as shown here are ignored. In other words, they are treated as comments. When this is true, you can omit the entire Configuration Section, even though this section is required in the 1974 COBOL standards. As a result, I've omitted the Configuration Section from all of the other programs presented in this book. In the 1985 COBOL standards, this section is optional.

### The Input-Output Section

The Input-Output Section for the inventory-listing program is as follows:

```
INPUT-OUTPUT SECTION.
FILE-CONTROL.
    SELECT INVMAST ASSIGN TO SYS020-AS-INVMAST.
    SELECT INVLIST ASSIGN TO SYS006-UR-1403-S.
```

Here, only the shaded words in the SELECT statements will change from one system to another. When you write a program, you will code one SELECT statement for each file used by the program.

The format of a SELECT statement for a sequential file is as follows:

```
SELECT file-name ASSIGN TO system-name
```

Here, the capitalized words are always the same (they are part of the COBOL language), while the lowercase words represent names that are assigned by the programmer.

**File names** Using standard COBOL, you create a *file name* using these rules:

1. It must be 30 or fewer characters and consist entirely of letters, numbers, and hyphens.
2. It must not end or begin with a hyphen and cannot contain blanks.
3. It must contain at least one letter.

Thus, INVENTORY-MASTER-FILE is a valid file name.

You'll notice, though, that the file name for the inventory master file in figure 3-8 is INVMAST, a 7-character name with no hyphens. That's because I wanted to use the file name in the system name, too, and that put extra restrictions on me. In chapter 8, you'll see how this naming convention helps you coordinate the file names in your programs with the file names in your job control procedures if you're working on an IBM system. If you're working on a non-IBM system, check with your instructor or manager to find out if there are any extra rules you should follow when creating file names.

**System names** The *system name* given in a SELECT statement helps relate a file described in the COBOL program with an actual file on an I/O device of the system. Unfortunately, the rules for creating system names vary from one computer system to another. As a result, you must change the system names in the SELECT statements when you convert a program from one system to another. In topic 6, I'll show you how to create system names for some common COBOL compilers.

## DISCUSSION

With the exception of the system names in the SELECT statements, you should now be able to code the Identification Division and Environment Division for a report preparation program that reads a sequential disk file and prints a report from it. Then, in topic 6 of this chapter you'll learn how to code system names for some common compilers. You'll also learn how to code program and file names that are appropriate for your compiler.

## Terminology

program name
file name
system name

## Objectives

1. Describe the purpose of each of the following:

   a. the Identification Division
   b. the Configuration Section in the Environment Division

2. Given the specifications for a program that prepares a report from a sequential disk file, code the first two divisions of a COBOL program for it. For this objective, you are not expected to be able to code the system names in the SELECT statements. And you're not expected to know the best way to code program-IDs and file names for your system.

## Topic 3 The Data Division

The Data Division for the inventory-listing program consists of two sections: the File Section and the Working-Storage Section. These sections describe the files, records, and fields required by the Procedure Division.

### The File Section

Figure 3-10 presents the File Section for the inventory-listing program. If you review it, you can see that it contains two FD statements. When you code a File Section, you code one FD statement for each SELECT statement in the Environment Division (or one for each file used by the program). The FD statement begins with FD, which stands for File Description, and ends with a period. After the FD statement for a file, you code statements that describe the format of the records stored in the file.

**The FD statement for the inventory master file** The FD statement for the inventory master file follows:

```
FD  INVMAST
    LABEL RECORDS ARE STANDARD
    RECORD CONTAINS 80 CHARACTERS.
```

After FD, you code the file name that you created in the SELECT statement for the file. If, for example, you use INVMAST in the SELECT statement, you have to code INVMAST in the FD statement. Otherwise, the program will not compile without error.

The LABEL RECORDS clause is required in every FD statement when you use a 1974 compiler, but it's optional when you use a 1985 compiler. For disk files, you normally code STANDARD labels. This means that the file has labels in a standard format that identify the file to the operating system.

The RECORD CONTAINS clause gives the length of the records in the file. In this case, the length is 80 characters. Since disk files can be other lengths than 80, you have to adjust this coding from one program to the next to conform to the size of the records your program is processing.

For most minicomputer systems and mainframe systems, the FD statement I've just described will be adequate for the inventory master file. However, there are some variations that you may encounter. In particular, you may have to give the blocking factor for a file in a BLOCK CONTAINS clause like this:

```
BLOCK CONTAINS 100 RECORDS
```

```
 DATA DIVISION.
*
 FILE SECTION.
*
 FD  INVMAST
     LABEL RECORDS ARE STANDARD
     RECORD CONTAINS 80 CHARACTERS.
*
 01  INVENTORY-MASTER-RECORD.
*
     05  IM-ITEM-NO              PIC 9(5).
     05  IM-ITEM-DESC            PIC X(20).
     05  IM-UNIT-COST            PIC 999V99.
     05  IM-UNIT-PRICE           PIC 999V99.
     05  IM-REORDER-POINT        PIC 9(5).
     05  IM-ON-HAND              PIC 9(5).
     05  IM-ON-ORDER             PIC 9(5).
     05  FILLER                  PIC X(30).
*
 FD  INVLIST
     LABEL RECORDS ARE OMITTED
     RECORD CONTAINS 132 CHARACTERS.
*
 01  PRINT-AREA                  PIC X(132).
*
```

**Figure 3-10** The File Section in the Data Division of the inventory-listing program

This clause, of course, indicates that the records in the input file are blocked with 100 records per block. Often, though, you can omit this clause even if the records are blocked, because the operating system gets the blocking factor from the labels for the file. In topic 6, you'll learn how to handle compiler-dependent variations like this.

**The record description for the inventory master file** Immediately following the FD statement for a file, you code the format of the records in the file. For the inventory master file, the record layout for each master record along with the COBOL record description is given in figure 3-11.

To start, the 01 level number indicates that the name following is the name for an entire record. In other words, INVENTORY-MASTER-RECORD is the *record name*. The rules for forming a record name are the same as those for forming a file name. You can use up to 30 letters, numbers, or hyphens (but you can't start or end with a hyphen), and the name must contain at least one letter.

The 05 level numbers indicate that the lines describe fields within the 01 record. Following the 05 numbers are *data names*, which are made up using the rules for record names. When you use the word FILLER instead of a data name, it means that that field isn't going to

**Record layout**

| Field name | Item no. | Item description | Unit cost | Unit price | Reorder point | On hand | On order | Unused |
|---|---|---|---|---|---|---|---|---|
| Characteristics | 9(5) | X(20) | 999V99 | 999V99 | 9(5) | 9(5) | 9(5) | X(30) |
| Usage | | | | | | | | |
| Position | 1-5 | 6-25 | 26-30 | 31-35 | 36-40 | 41-45 | 46-50 | 51-80 |

**Record description in COBOL**

```
 01   INVENTORY-MASTER-RECORD.
*
      05   IM-ITEM-NO              PIC 9(5).
      05   IM-ITEM-DESC            PIC X(20).
      05   IM-UNIT-COST            PIC 999V99.
      05   IM-UNIT-PRICE           PIC 999V99.
      05   IM-REORDER-POINT        PIC 9(5).
      05   IM-ON-HAND              PIC 9(5).
      05   IM-ON-ORDER             PIC 9(5).
      05   FILLER                  PIC X(30).
*
```

**Figure 3-11** The record layout and the COBOL record description for the inventory file

be used by the program. Nevertheless, the field exists within each record in the file, so you must account for it.

In the record description for the inventory master record, the first two 05 lines give the data names IM-ITEM-NO and IM-ITEM-DESC to the item number and item description fields of the input records. Although I could have used names like S241 and B11 for item number and item description, I created names that reflect the contents of the fields. In these data names, IM refers to the Inventory Master record, so this prefix relates the fields to the record name. Thus, IM-ITEM-DESC identifies the item description field in the inventory master record. This is a common naming technique, one that you'll see throughout this book.

One point to remember when creating names such as file names, record names, or data names is that you must avoid duplicating COBOL *reserved words*. For example, the words SELECT, LABEL, RECORDS, ARE, and STANDARD are reserved words. Words like these are a part of the COBOL language. As a result, you cannot use any of these words for a name that you make up. If LABEL is used as a file name, for instance, the COBOL compiler will diagnose an error. Since you will use a prefix like IM for most of the names you create (as in IM-ITEM-NO), you normally have little chance of duplicating a reserved word. But you should be aware of this nonetheless.

The PIC clauses that follow the data names give the characteristics of the fields and correspond to the entries in the record layout form. The number or letter outside the parentheses tells what kind of data the field contains; the number inside parentheses tells how long the field is. For example, 9(5) means the field is numeric and consists of 5 digits. And X(20) means that the field is alphanumeric and consists of 20 characters. An alphanumeric field can contain letters, numbers, spaces, or special characters (like $ or &).

Do you understand so far? The data names give each of the fields in the record a symbolic name that can be used in the Procedure Division. The PIC clauses, which may start one or more spaces after the data names, indicate the nature of the data and the size of the field. Since PIC is short for PICTURE, a format like 9(5) is often referred to as the *picture* for a field.

Now, look a little further. The picture for the field named IM-UNIT-PRICE is 999V99. This means that the field is five digits long (there are five 9's) with a decimal point that is assumed to be two places from the right. In other words, a 9 indicates one digit and the V indicates the position of the assumed decimal point. The decimal point is not actually stored in the input record.

When the source program is compiled, the computer adds up the number of bytes indicated in the PIC clauses for a record (the V's do *not* count) and compares the sum to the character count in the RECORD CONTAINS clause. If they don't match, a diagnostic message is printed. For the INVENTORY-MASTER-RECORD, the sum of the pictures is 80. Since this is the count in the RECORD CONTAINS clause, no error is indicated.

**The FD statement for the inventory listing** The FD statement for the inventory listing follows:

```
FD  INVLIST
    LABEL RECORDS ARE OMITTED
    RECORD CONTAINS 132 CHARACTERS.
```

Here, INVLIST is the file name, which is the same as the file name in the second SELECT statement of the program. Then, the LABEL clause says that this file has no labels. This makes sense since this file is actually a report that should be printed by a printer. To complete the file description, the RECORD CONTAINS clause says that the records are 132 characters long. Since most printers have a print line that is 132 characters long, this clause will work for most printers.

**The record description for the inventory listing** The record description for the inventory listing consists of only one line:

```
01  PRINT-AREA                  PIC X(132).
```

As a result, it describes the entire record area, but it doesn't describe the fields within the lines of the inventory listing. Here, I gave the record description the general name of PRINT-AREA because it's used for more than one type of print line. As you will see in a moment, the record descriptions for the two types of lines printed in the inventory listing are described in the Working-Storage Section of the program.

In this record description, you can see that you can code a PIC clause at the 01 level if there are no field descriptions at lower levels. In fact, the PIC clause is required in this case. On the other hand, if there are lower levels, you can't code a PIC clause at the 01 level. This is illustrated by the coding for the INVENTORY-MASTER-RECORD in figure 3-11.

### The Working-Storage Section

Figure 3-12 shows the Working-Storage Section of the inventory-listing program. If you review this code, you can see that four 01 levels are used. The third 01 level and the 05 levels that follow it are the record description for the heading line of the inventory listing. The fourth 01 level and the 05 levels below it are the record description for the inventory line of the inventory listing. After I discuss these record descriptions, I'll talk about the other two 01 levels and the related field descriptions.

**The record description for the heading line** Figure 3-13 gives the print chart for the inventory listing along with the record descriptions for the lines in the listing. Since the inventory listing requires two different types of lines, the program requires two record descriptions, one for each line format. If you study this illustration, you should be able to figure out how the coding relates to the print lines.

In the record description for the heading line, I used HEADING-LINE for the record name. Then, each of the 05 levels describes one field of the heading line. For instance, the first field is eight alphanumeric characters, X(8); the second field is two characters, X(2); and so on. If you compare this coding with the print chart, you can see that each 05 level provides for either a column heading like ITEM NO. or the spacing between two column headings. Notice that I used FILLER instead of a data name for each 05 level because these heading fields won't be referred to in the Procedure Division.

After each PIC clause at the 05 level is a VALUE clause. A VALUE clause gives a starting or constant value to a field. Thus, the first field in the heading line has a value of ITEM NO.; the second field has a value of spaces; the third field has a value of ITEM DESCRIPTION; and so on.

To code a VALUE clause for an alphanumeric field, you enclose the value you want in quotation marks. This is called a *nonnumeric literal*. In this case, the quotation marks aren't part of the value, but they are part of the literal.

```
 WORKING-STORAGE SECTION.
*
 01  SWITCHES.
*
     05  INVMAST-EOF-SWITCH   PIC X        VALUE 'N'.
*
 01  PRINT-FIELDS.
*
     05  SPACE-CONTROL        PIC 9.
     05  LINES-ON-PAGE        PIC 99       VALUE 55.
     05  LINE-COUNT           PIC 99       VALUE 70.
*
 01  HEADING-LINE.
*
     05  FILLER               PIC X(8)     VALUE 'ITEM NO.'.
     05  FILLER               PIC X(2)     VALUE SPACE.
     05  FILLER               PIC X(16)    VALUE 'ITEM DESCRIPTION'.
     05  FILLER               PIC X(8)     VALUE SPACE.
     05  FILLER               PIC X(10)    VALUE 'UNIT PRICE'.
     05  FILLER               PIC X(5)     VALUE SPACE.
     05  FILLER               PIC X(7)     VALUE 'ON HAND'.
     05  FILLER               PIC X(5)     VALUE SPACE.
     05  FILLER               PIC X(13)    VALUE 'REORDER POINT'.
     05  FILLER               PIC X(58)    VALUE SPACE.
*
 01  INVENTORY-LINE.
*
     05  IL-ITEM-NO           PIC Z(5).
     05  FILLER               PIC X(5)     VALUE SPACE.
     05  IL-ITEM-DESC         PIC X(20).
     05  FILLER               PIC X(7)     VALUE SPACE.
     05  IL-UNIT-PRICE        PIC ZZZ.99.
     05  FILLER               PIC X(7)     VALUE SPACE.
     05  IL-ON-HAND           PIC ZZZZ9.
     05  FILLER               PIC X(11)    VALUE SPACE.
     05  IL-REORDER-POINT     PIC Z(5).
     05  FILLER               PIC X(61)    VALUE SPACE.
*
```

**Figure 3-12** The Working-Storage Section in the Data Division of the inventory-listing program

If you want to code a value of spaces, you can use the reserved word SPACE. As you will see in the next chapter, a word like SPACE is called a *figurative constant*. When you use SPACE, it gives a value of spaces to the entire field. As a result, this description

```
05  FILLER     PIC X(10)     VALUE '
```

and this description

```
05  FILLER     PIC X(10)     VALUE SPACE.
```

are equivalent.

**Print chart**

```
ITEM NO.  ITEM DESCRIPTION        UNIT PRICE     ON HAND     REORDER POINT

ZZZZZ     XXXXXXXXXXXXXXXXXXXX       ZZZ.99        ZZZZ9          ZZZZZ
ZZZZZ     XXXXXXXXXXXXXXXXXXXX       ZZZ.99        ZZZZ9          ZZZZZ
```

**Record descriptions for the print lines**

```
 01   HEADING-LINE.
*
      05   FILLER                PIC X(8)    VALUE 'ITEM NO.'.
      05   FILLER                PIC X(2)    VALUE SPACE.
      05   FILLER                PIC X(16)   VALUE 'ITEM DESCRIPTION'.
      05   FILLER                PIC X(8)    VALUE SPACE.
      05   FILLER                PIC X(10)   VALUE 'UNIT PRICE'.
      05   FILLER                PIC X(5)    VALUE SPACE.
      05   FILLER                PIC X(7)    VALUE 'ON HAND'.
      05   FILLER                PIC X(5)    VALUE SPACE.
      05   FILLER                PIC X(13)   VALUE 'REORDER POINT'.
      05   FILLER                PIC X(58)   VALUE SPACE.
*
 01   INVENTORY-LINE.
*
      05   IL-ITEM-NO            PIC Z(5).
      05   FILLER                PIC X(5)    VALUE SPACE.
      05   IL-ITEM-DESC          PIC X(20).
      05   FILLER                PIC X(7)    VALUE SPACE.
      05   IL-UNIT-PRICE         PIC ZZZ.99.
      05   FILLER                PIC X(7)    VALUE SPACE.
      05   IL-ON-HAND            PIC ZZZZ9.
      05   FILLER                PIC X(11)   VALUE SPACE.
      05   IL-REORDER-POINT      PIC Z(5).
      05   FILLER                PIC X(61)   VALUE SPACE.
```

**Figure 3-13** The print chart and the COBOL record descriptions for the inventory listing

**The record description for the inventory line** The record description for the inventory line in figure 3-13 contains variable fields as well as constant fields. If you study this figure, you can see that the record name for the inventory line is INVENTORY-LINE. Then, all data names within the line are given names that start with IL, so it's easy to see that they're part of the inventory line. If a field in the line isn't going to be referred to in the Procedure Division, FILLER is used instead of a data name. All of the FILLER fields are given a value of SPACE, because they represent the spacing between two fields in a line.

For the variable fields, you can see that the PIC clauses define the fields of the print line just as they did the fields of the inventory master record. However, two new symbols are used: the Z as in Z(5) and the decimal point as in ZZZ.99. As you might guess, Z(5) means that a five-digit numeric field is to be printed and the high-order zeros should be zero-suppressed. ZZZ.99 means that a five-digit numeric field is to be printed with two decimal places and a decimal point. In addition, the high-order zeros to the left of the decimal point are to be zero-suppressed. Thus, the number 00718 will print as 7.18; the number 00003 will print as .03.

Incidentally, when coding a PIC clause, 9(5) and 99999 are equivalent. Similarly, 9(3)V9(2) and 999V99 are equivalent as are Z(3).9(2) and ZZZ.99. In general, the programmer chooses the form that is easier for her to code or to understand. As a rule of thumb, use parentheses when four or more occurrences of the same character in a row are required.

**The switches and print fields** Now, look at the first two 01 levels in working storage and the 05 levels below them in figure 3-12. Unlike 01 levels for the heading and inventory lines, these 01 levels don't indicate the start of record descriptions. Instead, they're used to logically group the other fields that the program will need during the preparation of the inventory listing. As you will realize as you progress through this book, all report preparation programs require switches and print fields, so it's efficient to group them in this way. You'll also realize that these 01 levels are used as headers to help organize the Working-Storage Section; they aren't needed for the operation of the program.

We define a *switch* as a field that can have one of two possible values; these values indicate that the switch is either "off" or "on." In this book, a value of N is used to mean "off"; a value of Y is used to mean "on." In topic 4, you'll see how the value of a switch can be changed by statements in the Procedure Division.

The one switch in this program is coded as follows:

```
05  INVMAST-EOF-SWITCH  PIC X        VALUE 'N'.
```

It is named INVMAST-EOF-SWITCH. I created this name by coding the file name for the inventory master file (INVMAST), followed by EOF (which stands for End-Of-File), followed by SWITCH. The program uses this switch to indicate when all the records in the input file have been read.

Like all switches, INVMAST-EOF-SWITCH is described as a one-position alphanumeric field. Then, its VALUE clause gives it a starting value of N. When this value changes to Y during the execution of the program, it will indicate that there are no more records in the inventory master file. Switches are quite common in today's COBOL programs, so you'll learn more about how and when to use them as you go through this book.

The print fields used by this program are described as follows:

```
05  SPACE-CONTROL       PIC 9.
05  LINES-ON-PAGE       PIC 99       VALUE 55.
05  LINE-COUNT          PIC 99       VALUE 70.
```

When I describe the Procedure Division, I'll explain how these fields are used. For now, just concentrate on the coding for the fields.

The first field, SPACE-CONTROL, is a one-position numeric field that is *not* given a starting value. The second field, LINES-ON-PAGE, is a two-position numeric field, and its VALUE clause gives it a starting value of 55. In this case, 55 is a *numeric literal*. In contrast to a nonnumeric literal, you don't use quotation marks when you give a value to a numeric field. Similarly, LINE-COUNT is a two-digit numeric field that has a starting value of 70.

As you will see in the next topic, SPACE-CONTROL is used to control the spacing of the printed report; LINES-ON-PAGE determines how many inventory lines will be printed on each page of the inventory listing; and LINE-COUNT is used to keep track of the number of lines already printed on each page. LINE-COUNT is given a starting value that is higher than the one for LINES-ON-PAGE so the program will skip the printer to the start of a new page when it tries to print the first inventory line. You'll understand this after you read topic 4 on the Procedure Division.

### Discussion

At this point, you should understand in general how you code the file, record, and field descriptions for a sequential disk file or a printer file. You should also understand the coding for the switches and print fields of a program. In the next topic, you'll see how you refer to the descriptions of the Data Division in the statements of the Procedure Division. Then, you'll begin to realize why you have to code the Data Division in the first place.

### Terminology

record name
data name
reserved word
picture
nonnumeric literal
figurative constant
switch
numeric literal

## Objectives

1. Given a COBOL listing for a Data Division, identify the following:

   a. record names
   b. data names
   c. nonnumeric literals
   d. numeric literals

2. Given the specifications for a program that prepares a report like the inventory listing from a sequential disk file, code the Data Division for the program.

## Topic 4 The Procedure Division

Figure 3-14 shows the Procedure Division for the inventory-listing program. If you study this code, you will see that six of the lines start in the A margin (I'm not counting the division header). Each of these lines consists of only one name followed by a period. These names are called *procedure names*, or *paragraph names*. To form a paragraph name, you use the same rules as for record or data names with one exception: paragraph names don't have to contain a letter.

If you design your programs using a structure chart as described in section 4 of this book, you create your paragraph names from the names and descriptions you used in the chart. I explained this in topic 1. Then, in the Procedure Division, you code the paragraphs in sequence by module number. As a result, it's easy to locate a paragraph in a large program when you know its paragraph name.

The lines of coding that start in the B margin of the Procedure Division are COBOL statements that specify operations that are to take place on the fields, records, and files defined in the Data Division. These symbolic statements follow consistent formats.

In figure 3-15, you can see the formats of the statements used in figure 3-14. Here, three periods in a row are called an ellipsis, which means that you can code more than one of the preceding elements in a row. The braces ( { } ) mean that you use only one of the items in the stack. And the brackets ( [ ] ) mean that the coding is optional. As you read through this topic, you'll get a better idea of what the notation in figure 3-15 means.

To use any of the statements in figure 3-15, you substitute the file, record, or data names that are required by the formats. Or, you substitute a nonnumeric literal, a numeric literal, or an appropriate figurative constant where a literal is required. In contrast, the capitalized words in each statement are written just as they appear in the statement format. For instance, to execute a procedure named 110-READ-INVENTORY-RECORD, you code

```
PERFORM 110-READ-INVENTORY-RECORD.
```

In the remainder of this topic, I will explain the operation of each of the paragraphs in the inventory-listing program. Although this may be somewhat confusing at first, you should understand the operation of the inventory-listing program by the time you complete this topic.

### Module 000: Prepare inventory listing

The first paragraph in a program represents the entire program. Its primary function is to determine when each of the modules at the next level should be executed and how many times these modules should be

```
 PROCEDURE DIVISION.
*
 000-PREPARE-INVENTORY-LISTING.
*
     OPEN INPUT  INVMAST
          OUTPUT INVLIST.
     PERFORM 100-PREPARE-INVENTORY-LINE
         UNTIL INVMAST-EOF-SWITCH = 'Y'.
     CLOSE INVMAST
           INVLIST.
     STOP RUN.
*
 100-PREPARE-INVENTORY-LINE.
*
     PERFORM 110-READ-INVENTORY-RECORD.
     IF INVMAST-EOF-SWITCH NOT = 'Y'
         PERFORM 120-PRINT-INVENTORY-LINE.
*
 110-READ-INVENTORY-RECORD.
*
     READ INVMAST RECORD
         AT END
             MOVE 'Y' TO INVMAST-EOF-SWITCH.
*
 120-PRINT-INVENTORY-LINE.
*
     IF LINE-COUNT > LINES-ON-PAGE
         PERFORM 130-PRINT-HEADING-LINE.
     MOVE IM-ITEM-NO            TO IL-ITEM-NO.
     MOVE IM-ITEM-DESC          TO IL-ITEM-DESC.
     MOVE IM-UNIT-PRICE         TO IL-UNIT-PRICE.
     MOVE IM-ON-HAND            TO IL-ON-HAND.
     MOVE IM-REORDER-POINT      TO IL-REORDER-POINT.
     MOVE INVENTORY-LINE        TO PRINT-AREA.
     PERFORM 140-WRITE-INVENTORY-LINE.
*
 130-PRINT-HEADING-LINE.
*
     MOVE HEADING-LINE TO PRINT-AREA.
     WRITE PRINT-AREA
         AFTER ADVANCING PAGE.
     MOVE ZERO TO LINE-COUNT.
     MOVE 2 TO SPACE-CONTROL.
*
 140-WRITE-INVENTORY-LINE.
*
     WRITE PRINT-AREA
         AFTER ADVANCING SPACE-CONTROL LINES.
     ADD 1 TO LINE-COUNT.
     MOVE 1 TO SPACE-CONTROL.
```

**Figure 3-14** The Procedure Division of the inventory-listing program

**I/O statements**

```
OPEN INPUT  file-name-1 ...
     OUTPUT file-name-2 ...

READ file-name RECORD
    AT END
        imperative-statement ...

WRITE record-name
                        (PAGE                 )
    AFTER ADVANCING     {numeric-literal LINES}   .
                        (data-name LINES      )

CLOSE file-name ...
```

**Data-movement statements**

```
MOVE    {literal    }    TO data-name-2.
        {data-name-1}
```

**Arithmetic statements**

```
ADD    {literal    }    TO data-name-2.
       {data-name-1}
```

**Sequence-control statements**

```
IF condition
    statement-1 ...
[ELSE
    statement-2 ...].

PERFORM paragraph-name.

PERFORM paragraph-name
    UNTIL condition.
```

**Miscellaneous**

```
STOP RUN.
```

**Figure 3-15** Simplified formats for the statements used in the Procedure Division of the inventory-listing program

executed. Since there is only one module at the next level in this program, module 000 determines how many times module 100 should be executed. In addition, it gets the input and output files ready for processing at the start of the program, it deactivates the files when the processing has been completed, and it transfers control of the computer system to the supervisor at the end of the program so the next application program can be loaded and executed.

**The OPEN statement** The format for the OPEN statement as shown in figure 3-15 follows:

```
OPEN INPUT  file-name ...
     OUTPUT file-name ...
```

Here, the ellipses show that you can code a string of file names after the word INPUT and a string of file names after the word OUTPUT. But since the inventory-listing program only has one input file and one output file, the OPEN statement in module 000 is this:

```
OPEN INPUT  INVMAST
     OUTPUT INVLIST.
```

In this case, INVMAST and INVLIST are the file names originally created in the SELECT statements in the Environment Division and repeated in the FD statements in the Data Division.

An OPEN statement is required for each file that is to be read or written by a program. Therefore, the OPEN statements usually are found in the first paragraph of a program. For a disk file, the OPEN statement checks to make sure the required file is available for processing. For a printer file, the OPEN statement checks to make sure the device is ready for operation.

**The PERFORM UNTIL statement** The format of the PERFORM UNTIL statement as shown in figure 3-15 is this:

```
PERFORM paragraph-name
    UNTIL condition.
```

The PERFORM UNTIL statement in module 000 in figure 3-14 is this:

```
PERFORM 100-PREPARE-INVENTORY-LINE
    UNTIL INVMAST-EOF-SWITCH = 'Y'.
```

This statement causes the paragraph named 100-PREPARE-INVENTORY-LINE to be executed until INVMAST-EOF-SWITCH has a value of Y. When the value becomes Y, the program continues with the statement after the PERFORM UNTIL in module 000; that is, the CLOSE statement. In this statement, 'Y' is a nonnumeric

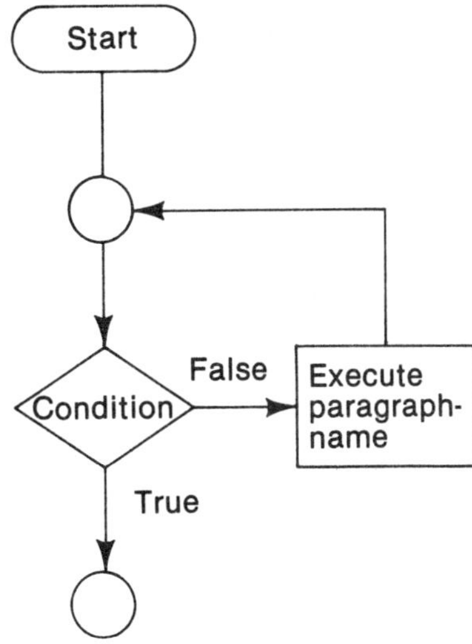


**Figure 3-16** A flowchart for the operation of the PERFORM UNTIL statement

literal, and it's coded just as nonnumeric literals are coded in the Data Division.

Since it's important that you understand how the PERFORM UNTIL statement works, its operation is flowcharted in figure 3-16. As you can see, when this statement is executed, it first tests the condition. If the condition is true, it does *not* perform the named paragraph. But, if the condition is false, it does perform the paragraph—and then it repeats the whole operation, starting with the condition test. As a result, the PERFORM UNTIL statement will continue to perform a paragraph until the condition becomes true.

In the inventory-listing program, the PERFORM UNTIL statement first tests the value of INVMAST-EOF-SWITCH to see whether the condition is true. But since this switch was given a starting value of N in working storage, it can't be true the first time. As a result, this statement will repeatedly execute paragraph 100 until the switch value is changed to Y.

Conditions are formed by using the general format shown in figure 3-17. In other words, two values can be compared to see whether value A is greater than value B, value A is equal to value B, or value A is less than value B. These values can be values stored in fields or values specified in the statement itself as literals. In the condition

```
INVMAST-EOF-SWITCH = 'Y'
```

the first value is the value stored in the field named INVMAST-EOF-SWITCH; the second value is the literal value Y.

NOT is an optional word in a condition. It is used to state the negative of a condition. Thus, the PERFORM UNTIL statement in

**Condition format**

```
              ⎧[IS  [NOT]]  GREATER THAN⎫
              ⎪[IS  [NOT]]  >           ⎪
{literal-1   }⎨[IS  [NOT]]  EQUAL TO    ⎬  {literal-2   }
{data-name-1 }⎪[IS  [NOT]]  =           ⎪  {data-name-2 }
              ⎪[IS  [NOT]]  LESS THAN   ⎪
              ⎩[IS  [NOT]]  <           ⎭
```

**Examples**

```
INVMAST-EOF-SWITCH IS NOT EQUAL TO 'N'
ITEM-CODE-1 IS GREATER THAN ITEM-CODE-2
SALES-AMOUNT IS LESS THAN 1000
2 < UPDATE-CODE
INVMAST-EOF-SWITCH = 'Y'
```

**Figure 3-17** Basic condition tests

module 000 could be written like this with the same results:

```
PERFORM 100-PREPARE-INVENTORY-LINE
    UNTIL INVMAST-EOF-SWITCH NOT = 'N'.
```

As you can see in figure 3-17, you can use either words or symbols to express a relationship like "greater than." Because the symbols are faster and easier to code, most professional COBOL programmers use them. And we use them in all the programs in this book.

**The CLOSE statement** Just as files must be opened at the start of a program, they must be closed at the end. As a result, module 000 uses this CLOSE statement:

```
CLOSE INVMAST
      INVLIST.
```

After a CLOSE statement is executed, the files are no longer available for processing.

**The STOP statement** STOP RUN means that the program has finished and the computer system should go on to the next program. It causes a branch to the supervisor so the next program can be loaded into storage and executed.

### Module 100: Prepare inventory line

The primary function of module 100 in figure 3-14 is to see that the modules it controls are executed properly. Each time module 100 is given control by module 000, it is executed one time; then, control passes back to the PERFORM UNTIL statement in module 000. Remember that the PERFORM UNTIL statement will cause module 100 to be executed again and again until INVMAST-EOF-SWITCH is equal to Y. Thus, module 100 will be executed once for each inventory master record.

**The PERFORM statement** The PERFORM statement causes one paragraph to be executed. The program then continues with the first statement following the PERFORM statement. As a result, the first statement in module 100 causes the paragraph named 110-READ-INVENTORY-RECORD to be executed. After this, the IF statement that follows the PERFORM statement is executed.

**The IF statement** The IF statement is the logical statement of the COBOL program. Its format as shown in figure 3-15 is this:

```
 IF condition
      statement-1 ...
[ELSE
      statement-2 ...]
```

As I mentioned earlier, the brackets around the ELSE clause mean that this clause is optional. As a result, it's legal to code an IF statement without an ELSE clause.

In paragraph 100 of the inventory-listing program, the IF statement is coded without an ELSE clause:

```
IF INVMAST-EOF-SWITCH NOT = 'Y'
    PERFORM 120-PRINT-INVENTORY-LINE.
```

As a result, the condition is:

```
INVMAST-EOF-SWITCH NOT = 'Y'
```

If this condition is true, the program executes the statement following the condition:

```
PERFORM 120-PRINT-INVENTORY-LINE
```

If the condition isn't true, the program continues with the next statement in sequence. In this case, since there is no other statement in module 100, the program goes back to the PERFORM UNTIL statement of module 000.

In terms of the complete program, this IF statement performs module 120 to print a line on the inventory listing. But it only performs module 120 if the end-of-file switch hasn't yet been turned on. In a moment, you'll see how this statement coordinates with the statements in module 110.

If you code an IF statement with an ELSE clause, the statements following the ELSE clause are executed if the condition is false. In the next chapter, you'll see examples of IF statements with ELSE clauses.

### Module 110: Read inventory record

**The READ statement** This module consists of only one statement, the READ statement:

```
READ INVMAST RECORD
    AT END
        MOVE 'Y' TO INVMAST-EOF-SWITCH.
```

When you code this statement, you use the file name for the disk file that you originally created in the SELECT statement for the file. This file name is coded after the word READ and before the word RECORD.

The READ statement in module 110 causes one inventory record to be read. When there are no more records in the inventory master file (AT END), the statements following the words AT END are executed. In this case, a MOVE statement is executed, which moves a value of Y into the field named INVMAST-EOF-SWITCH. Once the value of this switch field is changed, it affects the processing of both modules 100 and 000.

If you check the format for the READ statement in figure 3-15, you will see that AT END must be followed by an *imperative statement*. That means that conditional statements like IF statements are not allowed in the AT END clause. In most cases, you'll only use this clause to turn an end-of-file switch on so it can be tested by higher level modules.

You should understand that no record is available in the data area named INVENTORY-MASTER-RECORD once the AT END clause has been executed. That's why module 100 shouldn't perform module 120 if the end-of-file switch has been set to Y. If module 120 is executed after the AT END condition has occurred, the program is likely to be cancelled (but that depends on the system you're using).

### Module 120: Print inventory line

**The IF statement** Module 120 starts with this IF statement:

```
IF LINE-COUNT > LINES-ON-PAGE
    PERFORM 130-PRINT-HEADING-LINE.
```

In other words, if the value of LINE-COUNT is greater than the value of LINES-ON-PAGE, the program performs module 130 to print a heading line on the inventory listing. But LINE-COUNT was defined in the Data Division with an initial value of 70, and LINES-ON-PAGE was defined with an initial value of 55. As a result, module 130 will be performed the first time this IF statement is executed.

Although I defined LINE-COUNT with an initial value of 70 in the Data Division, any value greater than the value of LINES-ON-PAGE would have worked. As a general practice, though, it's good to use a value greater than the maximum number of lines that can be printed on a page (usually, 66). Then, if the program is changed later on so it prints more lines per page, you won't have to modify the VALUE clause for LINE-COUNT; you'll only have to modify the value for LINES-ON-PAGE.

**The MOVE statements** The next six statements in this module are MOVE statements:

```
MOVE IM-ITEM-NO          TO IL-ITEM-NO.
MOVE IM-ITEM-DESC        TO IL-ITEM-DESC.
MOVE IM-UNIT-PRICE       TO IL-UNIT-PRICE.
MOVE IM-ON-HAND          TO IL-ON-HAND.
MOVE IM-REORDER-POINT    TO IL-REORDER-POINT.
MOVE INVENTORY-LINE      TO PRINT-AREA.
```

The first five of these statements move the fields from the record area for the inventory master file to the record area for the inventory line in working storage. They also indicate the power of the MOVE statement in COBOL. If zero suppression or the insertion of a decimal point is necessary when a field is moved, the MOVE statement does it. For example, when IM-ITEM-NO is moved to IL-ITEM-NO, leading zeros are suppressed as follows:

| Field: | IM-ITEM-NO | IL-ITEM-NO |
|---|---|---|
| PICTURE: | 99999 | ZZZZZ |
| Value before: | 00103 | ????? |
| Value after: | 00103 | bb103<br>(b = one blank) |

When IM-UNIT-PRICE is moved to IL-UNIT-PRICE, a decimal point is inserted and the leading zeros before the decimal point are suppressed, as in this example:

| Field: | IM-UNIT-PRICE | IL-UNIT-PRICE |
|---|---|---|
| PICTURE: | 999V99 | ZZZ.99 |
| Value before: | 00449 | ?????? |
| Value after: | 00449 | bb4.49<br>(b = one blank) |

If 00005 were moved instead of 00449, IL-UNIT-PRICE would print as .05. As you can see, then, the result of a COBOL MOVE depends on the PICs given for each of the fields involved in the statement. In the next chapter, I'll cover MOVE statements in detail.

The last MOVE statement in this module moves the record named INVENTORY-LINE to the record named PRINT-AREA. As you will see in a moment, the data to be printed has to be moved to the record description area for the printer file before it can be printed. In other words, it must be moved to the record area for the printer file that is described in the File Section. And that, of course, is what this last MOVE statement does.

**The PERFORM statement** The last statement in module 120 is this PERFORM statement:

```
PERFORM 140-WRITE-INVENTORY-LINE.
```

As a result, it executes module 140. As you will see in a moment, module 140 contains the statements that cause the data in PRINT-AREA to be printed on the printer.

### Module 130: Print heading line

Module 130 consists of these statements:

```
MOVE HEADING-LINE TO PRINT-AREA.
WRITE PRINT-AREA
    AFTER ADVANCING PAGE.
MOVE ZERO TO LINE-COUNT.
MOVE 2 TO SPACE-CONTROL.
```

**The first MOVE statement** The first MOVE statement in this module moves the record for the heading line to the record area for the printer. As you'll see next, the WRITE statement can only print data from a print file's record area as defined in the File Section. So the heading data has to be moved to this area before it can be printed.

**The WRITE statement** The WRITE statement in this module causes one line to be printed on the printer. However, the printer prints the line AFTER ADVANCING PAGE. This means that the form in the printer will be skipped to the top of the next page before the line is printed. Because PRINT-AREA contains the heading line whenever this statement is executed, this statement will always print the heading line at the top of a new page.

Note in the format for the WRITE statement in figure 3-15 that you use the record name for the print area after the word WRITE. In contrast, you use the file name after the word READ in the READ statement. If you're aware of this COBOL inconsistency, it will help you code these statements correctly.

**The last MOVE statements** The next MOVE statement in this module moves a value of ZERO to LINE-COUNT. In this case, ZERO is a figurative constant like the word SPACE. As a result, it represents as many zeros as are necessary to fill the receiving field. In other words, this statement changes the initial value of LINE-COUNT from 70 to zero. Then, as module 140 is executed, LINE-COUNT will be increased by 1 each time an inventory line is printed.

The last MOVE statement moves a value of two to the field named SPACE-CONTROL. As you will see in a moment, this field is used to control the spacing of the printed output. In particular, it's used to single-space the inventory lines and to skip one line after each heading line is printed.

**Module 140: Write inventory line**

**The WRITE statement** The WRITE statement in module 140 is this:

```
WRITE PRINT-AREA
    AFTER ADVANCING SPACE-CONTROL LINES.
```

This statement causes one line to be printed from the record area named PRINT-AREA after advancing the form the number of lines indicated by the value in SPACE-CONTROL. If, for example, SPACE-CONTROL has a value of two, the form moves up two lines before the line is printed. If it has a value of one, the form is moved up one line, which is the equivalent of single-spacing.

If you relate this statement to the entire program, you can see that the form will be moved up two lines only after a heading line is printed. Otherwise, as you'll see in a moment, SPACE-CONTROL has a value of one, so the inventory lines are single-spaced.

**The ADD statement** The ADD statement that follows the WRITE statement in this module is this:

```
ADD 1 TO LINE-COUNT.
```

This statement uses a numeric literal (1) to add a value of one to LINE-COUNT. To relate this to the entire program, you should remember that LINE-COUNT is set to zero after the heading line is printed. After that, this statement increases the value of LINE-COUNT by one each time an inventory line is printed. Then, when LINE-COUNT exceeds the value of LINES-ON-PAGE (55), module 130 is executed again, a heading line is printed, and LINE-COUNT is reset to zero.

**The MOVE statement** The last statement in this module is this:

```
MOVE 1 TO SPACE-CONTROL.
```

This sets the value of SPACE-CONTROL to one so the program will single-space the inventory lines. In fact, the value of SPACE-CONTROL will be reset to one each time module 140 is executed, although this isn't really necessary. The only other time SPACE-CONTROL is changed in this program is when module 130 is executed to print a heading line.

## Discussion

I think the key to understanding the inventory-listing program is in following the flow of control from one module to another. So let me recap. First, the top module (module 000) is executed only once. However, control passes from module 000's PERFORM UNTIL statement to module 100 once for each record in the inventory master file until at last there are no more records in the file and Y is moved to INVMAST-EOF-SWITCH. Then, the program moves from the PERFORM UNTIL statement to the CLOSE statement that follows it.

Each time module 100 is executed, it causes module 110 to be executed. And as long as module 110 reads another data record, module 100 also causes module 120 to be executed. When module 120 is executed, it performs module 130 to skip to the next printer page and print a heading line, but only if LINE-COUNT is greater than LINES-ON-PAGE. Whether or not module 130 is performed, module 120 performs module 140 to write an inventory line on the printer.

## Terminology

procedure name
paragraph name
imperative statement

## Objective

Given test data and a COBOL listing that uses any of the statements in figure 3-15 in its Procedure Division, describe the operation of the program and the flow of control from one module to another.

## Topic 5 Shop standards for COBOL programs

As I said when I introduced the inventory-listing program in topic 1 of this chapter, you can write a working COBOL program in many different ways. In fact, some people think that COBOL lets you do things in too many different ways. That's why, in the mid-1970's, *structured programming* became popular. Structured programming refers to a collection of methods that impose some limits on how programs (non-COBOL programs included) can be designed, coded, and tested. Its purpose is to make programs easier to create and keep up-to-date.

Structured programming is kind of a catchall term, though, because the use of structured methods varies from shop to shop. For example, some COBOL shops use structure charts like the ones in this book to design programs; some use charts that give data names as well as paragraph names; some use different types of numbering systems for the program modules; and some don't have any guidelines for design at all, though they might have rules for writing structured code. While some of the differences are trivial, others actually defeat the purpose of structured programming. So the resulting COBOL programs aren't easy to create or change.

In this book, all of the programs have been developed using the structured design and coding methods that are part of our own *installation standards*, or *shop standards* (that is, the rules we've established for developing COBOL programs in our shop). We've published these standards in a book called *The COBOL Programmer's Handbook*, and they're used in thousands of shops throughout the country. To give you some idea of how they can affect your programs, let me present some other ways in which the inventory-listing program can be written.

### An unstructured Working-Storage Section for the inventory-listing program

Figure 3-18 presents part of an unstructured Working-Storage Section for the inventory-listing program. Here, the switch and print fields are coded with 77 level numbers. A 77 level means that the field is unrelated to any of the other fields in the program. As a result, the 01 levels named SWITCHES and PRINT-FIELDS are dropped from the program. Since they weren't referred to by any of the statements in the Procedure Division, they weren't really needed.

In a short program like this, coding an unstructured Working-Storage Section isn't much of a problem, if any at all. But a typical production program requires dozens of fields that can be treated as 77 levels. Then, it's important to group related fields and similar fields

```
WORKING-STORAGE SECTION.
*
77  INVMAST-EOF-SWITCH    PIC X        VALUE 'N'.
77  SPACE-CONTROL         PIC 9.
77  LINES-ON-PAGE         PIC 99       VALUE 55.
77  LINE-COUNT            PIC 99       VALUE 70.
```

**Figure 3-18** Unstructured working-storage fields for the inventory-listing program

under 01 levels so they're easier to find and modify. That's why we *never* use 77 levels in our own shop. And that's why we won't show you any programs in this book that use 77 levels.

### An unstructured Procedure Division for the inventory-listing program

The Procedure Division in figure 3-19 produces the same output as the Procedure Division in figure 3-14. If you study this code, you can see that it uses GOTO statements to loop through the MAINLINE-ROUTINE and to branch out of it. We consider a program like this to be "unstructured."

Here again, the use of GOTO statements isn't a serious problem in a short program like this. In fact, you may find that this program is easier to read and follow than the program in figure 3-14. If so, by all means study this code so you get a better understanding of the inventory-listing program.

Unfortunately, GOTOs become more and more of a problem as a program gets longer. So GOTOS are a serious problem in production programs of 1000 lines or more. As a general rule, the more GOTOs a program uses, the worse it is. That's why we don't use GOTO statements in our shop. And that's why we won't show you how to use them in this book.

### A Procedure Division for the inventory-listing program with inadequate structure

If you look at the Procedure Division in figure 3-14, you may question why it uses six paragraphs. After all, the longest module requires only nine coding lines. So couldn't this structure be simplified? Of course, it could be.

One Procedure Division with a simpler structure is shown in figure 3-20. In fact, I think this program is easier to read and understand than the coding in figure 3-14. So, here again, if you find this coding manageable, by all means study it so you get a better understanding of the inventory-listing program.

Although the structure in figure 3-20 is acceptable for a short program like this, the structure we've shown in figure 3-14 is adaptable to

```
PROCEDURE DIVISION.
HOUSEKEEPING-ROUTINE.
    OPEN INPUT  INVMAST
         OUTPUT INVLIST.
MAINLINE-ROUTINE.
    READ INVMAST RECORD
        AT END
            GO TO END-OF-JOB-ROUTINE.
    IF LINE-COUNT > LINES-ON-PAGE
        MOVE HEADING-LINE TO PRINT-AREA
        WRITE PRINT-AREA
            AFTER ADVANCING PAGE
        MOVE ZERO TO LINE-COUNT
        MOVE 2 TO SPACE-CONTROL.
    MOVE IM-ITEM-NO TO IL-ITEM-NO.
    MOVE IM-ITEM-DESC TO IL-ITEM-DESC.
    MOVE IM-UNIT-PRICE TO IL-UNIT-PRICE.
    MOVE IM-ON-HAND TO IL-ON-HAND.
    MOVE IM-REORDER-POINT TO IL-REORDER-POINT.
    MOVE INVENTORY-LINE TO PRINT-AREA.
    WRITE PRINT-AREA
        AFTER ADVANCING SPACE-CONTROL LINES.
    ADD 1 TO LINE-COUNT.
    MOVE 1 TO SPACE-CONTROL.
    GO TO MAINLINE-ROUTINE.
END-OF-JOB-ROUTINE.
    CLOSE INVMAST
          INVLIST.
    STOP RUN.
```

**Figure 3-19** An unstructured Procedure Division for the inventory-listing program

a wider range of problems. I think you'll appreciate this after you read the next chapter, which presents a more complicated report preparation program. In summary, you can use a simple structure for simple, classroom problems. But what we're trying to teach in this book is a structure that is applicable to a wide range of production programs.

## Discussion

To become an effective COBOL programmer, you have to do more than just learn the language. You have to learn how to use the language so your programs are easy to create and maintain. In other words, you have to learn standards for design and coding that will raise the quality of your programs to a professional level.

As you read this book, then, you must learn to distinguish between COBOL requirements and our recommendations for shop standards. As you have seen, our standards are more restrictive than the rules of COBOL. They may also be more restrictive than those of your shop or training program. On the other hand, if you adhere to our standards, you can be sure that your programs will be relatively easy to test, debug, and modify.

```
PROCEDURE DIVISION.
*
000-PREPARE-INVENTORY-LISTING.
*
     OPEN INPUT  INVMAST
          OUTPUT INVLIST.
     PERFORM 100-PREPARE-INVENTORY-LINE
         UNTIL INVMAST-EOF-SWITCH = 'Y'.
     CLOSE INVMAST
           INVLIST.
     STOP RUN.
*
100-PREPARE-INVENTORY-LINE.
*
     READ INVMAST RECORD
         AT END
             MOVE 'Y' TO INVMAST-EOF-SWITCH.
     IF INVMAST-EOF-SWITCH NOT = 'Y'
         PERFORM 110-PRINT-INVENTORY-LINE.
*
110-PRINT-INVENTORY-LINE.
*
     IF LINE-COUNT > LINES-ON-PAGE
         MOVE HEADING-LINE TO PRINT-AREA
         WRITE PRINT-AREA
             AFTER ADVANCING PAGE
         MOVE ZERO TO LINE-COUNT
         MOVE 2 TO SPACE-CONTROL.
     MOVE IM-ITEM-NO         TO IL-ITEM-NO.
     MOVE IM-ITEM-DESC       TO IL-ITEM-DESC.
     MOVE IM-UNIT-PRICE      TO IL-UNIT-PRICE.
     MOVE IM-ON-HAND         TO IL-ON-HAND.
     MOVE IM-REORDER-POINT   TO IL-REORDER-POINT.
     MOVE INVENTORY-LINE     TO PRINT-AREA.
     WRITE PRINT-AREA
         AFTER ADVANCING SPACE-CONTROL LINES.
     ADD 1 TO LINE-COUNT.
     MOVE 1 TO SPACE-CONTROL.
```

**Figure 3-20** A Procedure Division for the inventory-listing program with inadequate structure

## Terminology

structured programming
installation standards
shop standards

## Objective

Explain how shop standards can affect the quality of a COBOL program.

## Topic 6 Compiler dependent code

Although COBOL is a standard language, some of the code in each program depends on the system that's being used. For instance, the system names that are acceptable in SELECT statements usually vary as you move from one system to another. As a result, system names can be referred to as *compiler dependent code* (or *system dependent code*).

Fortunately, only a few COBOL elements are system dependent. As a result, with only a couple of changes, the inventory-listing program presented in this chapter will run on any system that uses 1974 or 1985 ANS COBOL.

In this topic, I'd like to make you aware of the elements in the inventory-listing program that may be different on your system. Then, you can find out how to code them on your system. Since all of them are relatively trivial, you shouldn't have any trouble coding them once you find out what the coding rules are.

### Identification Division code

**Program name** Although the COBOL standards say that a program name can be up to 30 characters long with embedded hyphens, some compilers don't accept names like that. For instance, the Microsoft COBOL compiler wants names of 6 or fewer characters consisting of only letters and digits with a letter as the first character, and the Wang VS compiler wants names of 8 or fewer letters and digits. Similarly, the IBM VS compiler will use only the first 8 characters of a program name that is longer than 8 characters. In addition, it will convert a leading digit to a letter, and it will convert all hyphens to zeros. Then, the compiler uses the abridged name to identify compiler listings, object modules, and so on. When you work with a compiler that converts long program names to shorter forms, you can eliminate confusion by coding your program names in the form the compiler wants.

### Environment Division code

**The Configuration Section** As I said in topic 2, many compilers treat the Configuration Section as comments, and this section is optional in the 1985 standards. As a result, you can omit this section on many systems. From this point on, all Configuration Sections will be omitted in the programs in this book. However, you will have to code this section if you use the COBOL debugging feature or the SPECIAL-NAMES paragraph, neither of which is covered in this book.

**Microsoft COBOL**

Disk file: `"DISK"`

Printer file: `"PRINTER"`

**Wang VS COBOL**

Disk file: `"parameter-reference-name" "DISK"`

Printer file: `"parameter-reference-name" "PRINTER"`

Note: The *parameter-reference-name* must be eight or fewer letters or digits, starting with a letter. For consistency, this can be the same name as the file name.

**IBM VS COBOL on a DOS/VSE system**

Disk file: `SYSnnn-UT-device-S-name`
(for a non-VSAM sequential file)

`SYSnnn-AS-name`
(for a VSAM sequential file)

Examples: `SYS020-UT-3350-S-INVMAST`
(for a non-VSAM sequential file)

`SYS020-AS-INVMAST`
(for a VSAM sequential file)

Printer file: `SYSnnn-UR-device-S`

Example: `SYS006-UR-1403-S`

Notes:

1. The SYS number is a number between SYS000 and SYS240 that is used to identify a specific I/O device. Find out what numbers you should use on your system.
2. The *device* is a number like 3350 for the 3350 disk drive or 1403 for the 1403 printer. Find out what device numbers you should use on your system.
3. The *name* consists of from three to seven letters or digits, starting with a letter. For consistency, this can be the same name as the file name. This name is used to relate the file description in the program with a file on a disk.
4. UT stands for utility device, UR stands for unit record device, S stands for sequential organization, and AS stands for sequential organization in a VSAM file.

**Figure 3-21** The formats of system names for some common COBOL compilers (part 1 of 2)

**IBM VS COBOL or COBOL II on an OS/MVS system**

Disk file: `[comments-] [S-] ddname`
(for a non-VSAM sequential file)

`[comments-] AS-ddname`
(for a VSAM sequential file)

Examples: `INVMAST`
(for a non-VSAM sequential file)

`AS-INVMAST`
(for a VSAM sequential file)

Printer file: `[comments-] [S-] ddname`

Example: INVLIST

Notes:

1. The brackets ( [ ] ) mean that an item is optional. Thus, the system name for a non-VSAM sequential file could be written as UT-S-INVMAST (where UT is a comment), S-INVMAST, or just INVMAST.
2. The *ddname* is made up of eight or fewer letters or digits, starting with a letter. For consistency, this can be the same name as the file name. This name is used to relate the file description in the program with a file on a disk.

**Figure 3-21** The formats of system names for some common COBOL compilers (part 2 of 2)

**System names in SELECT statements in the Input-Output Section**
Figure 3-21 gives the format of system names for sequential disk files and printer files when you're using the Microsoft, Wang VS, IBM VS, or IBM COBOL II compilers. In general, the names are relatively simple when you're using compilers on microcomputers and minicomputers, and they're more complicated when you're using a mainframe compiler.

On an IBM mainframe, there can be two kinds of sequential files: VSAM and non-VSAM. As you can see in figure 3-21, the format of a system name for a VSAM file is different than for a non-VSAM file. If you check the system name for the inventory master file in figure 3-5, you can see that it is for a VSAM sequential file. In this book, all the programs are written for VSAM disk files.

## Data Division code

Technically speaking, all of the code in the Data Division is standard so there shouldn't be differences as you go from one system to another. Nevertheless, there are some minor differences that relate to the way FD statements are coded for disk and printer files. These differences in turn relate to the way the systems handle different types of files.

**FD statements for disk files** Figure 3-22 presents FD statements for the inventory master file in the inventory-listing program as implemented on some common COBOL systems. As you can see, some systems require the BLOCK CONTAINS clause to give the blocking factor for the file on disk. And some require the VALUE clause to identify the actual file on disk.

The first example is the one taken from the inventory-listing program of this chapter. Although it will compile and run on most minicomputer and mainframe systems, it will affect different systems in different ways. On a Wang system, for example, this coding means that the system will assume 2K blocks of records.

On an IBM mainframe, the interpretation of the coding in the first example depends on whether the file is a VSAM or non-VSAM file. If it's a VSAM file, this coding is adequate for any sequential file, because blocking has no meaning for VSAM file organizations. In contrast, for non-VSAM sequential files, the VS compiler assumes unblocked records when the FD statement is coded this way. As a result, since disk records in a sequential file are normally blocked, you will usually code a BLOCK CONTAINS clause for a non-VSAM sequential file on an IBM system.

This is illustrated in example 2 by the code for a VS COBOL compiler on a DOS/VSE system. Here, the BLOCK CONTAINS clause specifies a blocking factor of 100 for the non-VSAM file.

The third example is for a VS COBOL or COBOL II compiler on an OS/MVS system when processing a non-VSAM sequential disk file. Here, the BLOCK CONTAINS clause specifies zero records. This means that the blocking factor will be given outside of the COBOL program. This is useful because it means that the blocking factor can be changed without changing the COBOL program. As a result, this is the way you'll code most FD statements for non-VSAM sequential files on an OS/MVS system. In this book, though, all of the example programs process VSAM files, so you won't see the BLOCK CONTAINS clause used in them.

Because the FD statements in the first three examples don't identify the files to the operating system, the files must be identified outside the program. In chapter 8, you'll learn how to do this on some common systems. In particular, you'll learn how to identify the actual files to be processed by using job control procedures on an IBM mainframe.

On some systems, though, you have to identify the file to the operating system in the FD statement. This is illustrated in example 4 of figure 3-22. It's for a disk file when using Microsoft COBOL on an IBM PC. For this compiler, you must use the VALUE clause to identify the disk file to be used. In this example, the file is named INVMAST.DAT and it resides on disk drive B.

The fifth example is for a disk file when using Wang VS COBOL to identify the disk file to be used. On the Wang system, you identify a disk file by giving its name, the library it's in, and the disk volume it's

**Example 1: Wang VS COBOL, IBM VS COBOL, or IBM COBOL II**

```
FD  INVMAST
    LABEL RECORDS ARE STANDARD
    RECORD CONTAINS 80 CHARACTERS.
```

Notes:
1. In Wang VS COBOL, the compiler assumes records in 2K blocks.
2. For VSAM files in IBM VS COBOL or COBOL II, the concept of blocking has no meaning, so this file description is adequate for any sequential VSAM file.
3. For non-VSAM files in IBM VS COBOL or COBOL II, the compiler assumes an unblocked file.

**Example 2: IBM VS COBOL on a DOS/VSE system for a non-VSAM sequential file with blocked records**

```
FD  INVMAST
    LABEL RECORDS ARE STANDARD
    BLOCK CONTAINS 100 RECORDS
    RECORD CONTAINS 80 CHARACTERS.
```

**Example 3: IBM VS COBOL or COBOL II on an OS/MVS system for a non-VSAM sequential file with blocked records**

```
FD  INVMAST
    LABEL RECORDS ARE STANDARD
    BLOCK CONTAINS 0 RECORDS
    RECORD CONTAINS 80 CHARACTERS.
```

Note: When zero records per block is specified, the blocking factor must be defined outside of the program.

**Example 4: Microsoft COBOL on an IBM PC**

```
FD  INVMAST
    LABEL RECORDS ARE STANDARD
    VALUE OF FILENAME IS "B:INVMAST.DAT"
    RECORD CONTAINS 80 CHARACTERS.
```

**Example 5: Wang VS COBOL to identify the file on disk**

```
FD  INVMAST
    LABEL RECORDS ARE STANDARD
    VALUE OF FILENAME IS "INVMAST"
             LIBRARY  IS "INVDATA"
             VOLUME   IS "SYS1"
    RECORD CONTAINS 80 CHARACTERS.
```

**Figure 3-22** FD statements for a sequential disk file using some common COBOL compilers

on. And, if you want to, you can supply this information in a VALUE clause in the FD statement for the file. On the other hand, if you omit the VALUE clause, you can supply this information interactively when the program is executed or as part of the procedure language that initiates program execution. If you omit the VALUE clause, the FD statement for a Wang sequential disk file is the same as the FD statement in example 1.

In the 1985 COBOL standards, the LABEL RECORDS clause is optional. If it's omitted, standard labels are assumed. Also, VALUE clauses in the FD statement have been dropped from these standards. As a result, you most likely won't code LABEL RECORDS or VALUE clauses when you use a 1985 compiler.

In this book, all of the FD statements for sequential disk files will be coded as they are for the inventory master file in the inventory-listing program in figure 3-5. This will work on (1) the Wang VS compiler, (2) the IBM VS compilers when using VSAM sequential files, and (3) the IBM COBOL II compiler when using VSAM sequential files. You should realize, however, that you may have to modify these statements to meet the requirements of your compiler or your shop standards.

**FD statements for printer files** Figure 3-23 gives FD statements for a print file when using some common COBOL compilers. Here, the primary variation is in the LABEL RECORDS clause since some compilers expect OMITTED for print files, some expect STANDARD, and some accept both. In addition, for print files on an OS/MVS system when using the VS or COBOL II compiler, you may have to code the BLOCK CONTAINS clause.

The first example is the one you've already seen. Here, LABEL RECORDS are OMITTED.

The second example is similar, but it specifies STANDARD labels, which will work on most compilers. On a system that provides spooling, a print file is actually written on disk before it is printed, so STANDARD labels make sense. Note that either OMITTED or STANDARD will work for a print file when using the Wang VS compiler.

The third example is for the IBM VS or COBOL II compiler when using an OS/MVS system. Here, the print file is described just as you would describe a sequential disk file on this system. You code a print file in this way because the system actually creates a disk file for each printed document before it prints it. This is an automatic part of the system's spooling capability. Then, by specifying blocks of zero records, you can assign an efficient blocking factor for the print file on disk later on. Although all spooling systems write print files on disk before they print them, you don't have to be aware of it on most systems. It's done automatically for you. On the MVS system, though, you should be aware of it so you can describe your print files as shown in figure 3-23.

**Example 1: Microsoft COBOL, Wang VS COBOL, or IBM VS COBOL on a DOS/VSE system**

```
FD  INVLIST
    LABEL RECORDS ARE OMITTED
    RECORD CONTAINS 132 CHARACTERS.
```

**Example 2: Wang VS COBOL, IBM VS COBOL on an OS/MVS system, or IBM COBOL II on an OS/MVS system**

```
FD  INVLIST
    LABEL RECORDS ARE STANDARD
    RECORD CONTAINS 132 CHARACTERS.
```

Note: On an OS/MVS system, the compiler assumes unblocked records for the print file on disk.

**Example 3: IBM VS COBOL or COBOL II on an OS/MVS system**

```
FD  INVLIST
    LABEL RECORDS ARE STANDARD
    BLOCK CONTAINS 0 RECORDS
    RECORD CONTAINS 132 CHARACTERS.
```

Note: The blocking factor for the print file on disk must be defined outside of the program.

**Figure 3-23** FD statements for a printer file using some common COBOL compilers

Beyond these variations, you will sometimes have to adjust the RECORD CONTAINS clause to your system. In many IBM mainframe shops, for example, a print record is coded as 133 characters. Then, the system uses the first character in each record for space control. By setting a compiler option, the VS compiler can be used for print records of either 132 or 133 characters.

Here again, the LABEL RECORDS clause is optional in the 1985 standards. If it's omitted, standard labels are assumed. Since almost all files on modern systems have standard labels (even print files), you can expect to see this clause de-emphasized by future compilers.

### Quotation marks

When you code a nonnumeric literal in a COBOL program, you enclose a value in quotation marks. For most systems, this means the double quotation mark ("), which is what the standards specify. On IBM mainframes, though, it is common to use the single quotation mark (') for this purpose. Although the IBM compilers will accept either single or double quotation marks based on an option that you can set at compile time, you should use the mark that is used in your shop. In this book, we've used the single quotation mark (or apostrophe) in all the IBM programs.

### The inventory-listing program as implemented on some common computer systems

Consistent with the intent of this book, I'd now like to show you how the compiler dependent code is implemented on five different systems: Microsoft COBOL on an IBM PC, VS COBOL on a Wang VS system, VS COBOL on an IBM mainframe under DOS/VSE, VS COBOL on an IBM mainframe under OS/MVS, and COBOL II on an IBM mainframe under OS/MVS. As a result, figures 3-24 through 3-26 present the first page of the inventory-listing program as implemented on each of the systems not illustrated by the program in figure 3-5. In each case, I've shaded the differences between the new listing and the VS COBOL listing for a DOS/VSE system in figure 3-5. As you will see, the differences are trivial.

**Microsoft COBOL on the IBM PC** Figure 3-24 gives the first page of the inventory-listing program as implemented on the Microsoft COBOL compiler on an IBM PC. Primarily, you should realize that you must identify the name of each disk file used by your program in the VALUE clause of the FD statement for the file.

**VS COBOL on the Wang VS system** Figure 3-25 gives the first page of the inventory-listing program as implemented on the Wang VS COBOL compiler. In this case, the file on disk isn't identified by the VALUE clause in the FD statement for the file because we think it's better to identify disk files outside of the program.

**VS COBOL or COBOL II on an IBM mainframe under OS/MVS** Figure 3-26 gives the first page of the inventory-listing program as implemented using VS COBOL or COBOL II on an IBM mainframe under OS/MVS. Here, the differences between this code and the code in figure 3-5 are (1) the system names for the disk and printer files, (2) the LABEL RECORDS clause for the print file, and (3) the BLOCK CONTAINS clause for the print file.

### Discussion

If you're using one of the five systems described in this book, you can figure out the compiler dependent code for your system by using the examples presented in this topic. If you're not using one of these systems, you must find out what code is acceptable on your system. You can do this by asking your instructor or an associate. Or, you can consult the manuals for your system.

```
 IDENTIFICATION DIVISION.
*
 PROGRAM-ID.          IN3510.
*AUTHOR.              MIKE MURACH.
*
 ENVIRONMENT DIVISION.
*
 INPUT-OUTPUT SECTION.
*
 FILE-CONTROL.
     SELECT INVMAST ASSIGN TO "DISK".
     SELECT INVLIST ASSIGN TO "PRINTER".
*
 DATA DIVISION.
*
 FILE SECTION.
*
 FD  INVMAST
     LABEL RECORDS ARE STANDARD
     VALUE OF FILENAME IS "B:INVMAST.DAT"
     RECORD CONTAINS 80 CHARACTERS.
*
 01  INVENTORY-MASTER-RECORD.
*
     05  IM-ITEM-NO              PIC 9(5).
     05  IM-ITEM-DESC            PIC X(20).
     05  IM-UNIT-COST            PIC 999V99.
     05  IM-UNIT-PRICE           PIC 999V99.
     05  IM-REORDER-POINT        PIC 9(5).
     05  IM-ON-HAND              PIC 9(5).
     05  IM-ON-ORDER             PIC 9(5).
     05  FILLER                  PIC X(30).
*
 FD  INVLIST
     LABEL RECORDS ARE OMITTED
     RECORD CONTAINS 132 CHARACTERS.
*
 01  PRINT-AREA                  PIC X(132).
*
 WORKING-STORAGE SECTION.
*
 01  SWITCHES.
*
     05  INVMAST-EOF-SWITCH      PIC X        VALUE "N".
*
 01  PRINT-FIELDS.
*
     05  SPACE-CONTROL           PIC 9.
     05  LINES-ON-PAGE           PIC 99       VALUE 55.
     05  LINE-COUNT              PIC 99       VALUE 70.
*
 01  HEADING-LINE.
*
     05  FILLER                  PIC X(8)     VALUE "ITEM NO.".
     05  FILLER                  PIC X(2)     VALUE SPACE.
```

**Figure 3-24** The first page of the inventory-listing program using Microsoft COBOL on an IBM PC

```
 IDENTIFICATION DIVISION.
*
 PROGRAM-ID.         INV3510.
*AUTHOR.             MIKE MURACH.
*
 ENVIRONMENT DIVISION.
*
 INPUT-OUTPUT SECTION.
*
 FILE-CONTROL.
     SELECT INVMAST ASSIGN TO "INVMAST" "DISK".
     SELECT INVLIST ASSIGN TO "INVLIST" "PRINTER".
*
 DATA DIVISION.
*
 FILE SECTION.
*
 FD  INVMAST
     LABEL RECORDS ARE STANDARD
     RECORD CONTAINS 80 CHARACTERS.
*
 01  INVENTORY-MASTER-RECORD.
*
     05  IM-ITEM-NO            PIC 9(5).
     05  IM-ITEM-DESC          PIC X(20).
     05  IM-UNIT-COST          PIC 999V99.
     05  IM-UNIT-PRICE         PIC 999V99.
     05  IM-REORDER-POINT      PIC 9(5).
     05  IM-ON-HAND            PIC 9(5).
     05  IM-ON-ORDER           PIC 9(5).
     05  FILLER                PIC X(30).
*
 FD  INVLIST
     LABEL RECORDS ARE OMITTED
     RECORD CONTAINS 132 CHARACTERS.
*
 01  PRINT-AREA                PIC X(132).
*
 WORKING-STORAGE SECTION.
*
 01  SWITCHES.
*
     05  INVMAST-EOF-SWITCH    PIC X       VALUE "N".
*
 01  PRINT-FIELDS.
*
     05  SPACE-CONTROL         PIC 9.
     05  LINES-ON-PAGE         PIC 99      VALUE 55.
     05  LINE-COUNT            PIC 99      VALUE 70.
*
 01  HEADING-LINE.
*
     05  FILLER                PIC X(8)    VALUE "ITEM NO.".
     05  FILLER                PIC X(2)    VALUE SPACE.
     05  FILLER                PIC X(16)   VALUE "ITEM DESCRIPTION".
```

**Figure 3-25** The first page of the inventory-listing program using VS COBOL on a WANG VS system

```
 IDENTIFICATION DIVISION.
*
 PROGRAM-ID.          INV3510.
*AUTHOR.              MIKE MURACH.
*
 ENVIRONMENT DIVISION.
*
 INPUT-OUTPUT SECTION.
*
 FILE-CONTROL.
     SELECT INVMAST ASSIGN TO AS-INVMAST.
     SELECT INVLIST ASSIGN TO INVLIST.
*
 DATA DIVISION.
*
 FILE SECTION.
*
 FD  INVMAST
     LABEL RECORDS ARE STANDARD
     RECORD CONTAINS 80 CHARACTERS.
*
 01  INVENTORY-MASTER-RECORD.
*
     05  IM-ITEM-NO          PIC 9(5).
     05  IM-ITEM-DESC        PIC X(20).
     05  IM-UNIT-COST        PIC 999V99.
     05  IM-UNIT-PRICE       PIC 999V99.
     05  IM-REORDER-POINT    PIC 9(5).
     05  IM-ON-HAND          PIC 9(5).
     05  IM-ON-ORDER         PIC 9(5).
     05  FILLER              PIC X(30).
*
 FD  INVLIST
     LABEL RECORDS ARE STANDARD
     BLOCK CONTAINS 0 RECORDS
     RECORD CONTAINS 132 CHARACTERS.
*
 01  PRINT-AREA              PIC X(132).
*
 WORKING-STORAGE SECTION.
*
 01  SWITCHES.
*
     05  INVMAST-EOF-SWITCH  PIC X        VALUE 'N'.
*
 01  PRINT-FIELDS.
*
     05  SPACE-CONTROL       PIC 9.
     05  LINES-ON-PAGE       PIC 99       VALUE 55.
     05  LINE-COUNT          PIC 99       VALUE 70.
*
 01  HEADING-LINE.
*
     05  FILLER              PIC X(8)     VALUE 'ITEM NO.'.
     05  FILLER              PIC X(2)     VALUE SPACE.
```

**Figure 3-26** The first page of the inventory-listing program using VS COBOL or COBOL II on an IBM mainframe under OS/MVS with a VSAM inventory master file

When you're first introduced to compiler dependent code, it may seem like there's a lot of it. However, if you look at the shaded code in figures 3-24 through 3-26, you can see that only a few lines need to be changed as you move from one computer system or compiler to another. Then, once you master the compiler dependent code for your system, you will use it in program after program. As a result, the compiler dependent code shouldn't present any problems for you.

## Terminology

compiler dependent code
system dependent code

## Objectives

1. Find out how to code the compiler dependent COBOL elements for your compiler.

2. Given program specifications and a structure chart for a COBOL program that can be developed using only the elements in this chapter, code an acceptable program.

Chapter 4

# Building on the COBOL basics

In chapter 3, you were introduced to a simple report preparation program. In practice, though, you probably won't ever write a program as simple as the one in figure 3-5. At the least, all production programs should print the date of preparation in the heading of a report. And almost all reports have one or more total lines at the end.

In this chapter, you will learn more COBOL elements so you can write more complex programs. Topic 1 presents elements that you need to code in the Data Division, and topic 2 presents elements that you need in the Procedure Division. After you learn these elements, topic 3 shows you how to use them in a more realistic report preparation program. Finally, topic 4 explains the compiler dependent code that is related to the COBOL elements presented in this chapter.

The elements in this chapter plus those in chapter 3 make up an introductory subset of COBOL. By using just the elements in this subset, you will be able to write most report preparation programs. Also, it will be easy for you to add elements to this introductory subset as you continue with your COBOL training.

## Topic 1 Data Division elements

In chapter 3, you were introduced to some basic ways of describing records and fields in the Data Division of a program. This topic expands on that base. When you complete this topic, you should be able to code data entries for any of the fields required by a report preparation program. In fact, this is the last topic in this book that presents entries for the Data Division.

Figure 4-1 gives the formats for the Data Division elements presented in this topic. Here, as in all COBOL manuals, the braces mean that you should use one item in a stack; the brackets mean that a word, phrase, or clause is optional. If a word is underlined, it means that it's required; otherwise, it's optional.

If you study figure 4-1, you can see that a PICTURE clause can be written like this:

```
PICTURE IS character-string
```

In the last chapter, though, all PICTURE clauses were coded as:

```
PIC character-string
```

In other words, IS is an optional word and PIC is an acceptable abbreviation for PICTURE. In the programs in this book, you'll see all Data Division clauses written as efficiently as possible. As a result, most optional words will be omitted and abbreviations will be used whenever they're allowed.

You're already familiar with all the clauses shown in the FD statement format in figure 4-1. So now let's go on to the elements you can use for data descriptions.

### Level numbers

In chapter 3, 01 and 05 *level numbers* were used in the inventory-listing program. In addition, however, level numbers from 01 through 49 can be used to describe fields within fields within records. To illustrate, consider the record layout and record description in figure 4-2. Here, the 13 fields in the record are divided into four 05 levels. In addition, one of the fields at the 10 level is divided into three 15 level fields.

Notice that PICTUREs are used only for *elementary items*; that is, data fields that are not broken down any further. In contrast, *group items* have fields within them so they can't have PICTURE clauses. To find the total length of a record like INVENTORY-MASTER-RECORD, you add the lengths of all the elementary fields within the record.

```
DATA DIVISION.

FILE SECTION.

FD      file-name
        LABEL RECORDS ARE {OMITTED }
                          {STANDARD}

        [BLOCK CONTAINS integer RECORDS]

        [RECORD CONTAINS integer CHARACTERS].

01-49   {data-name}
        {FILLER   }

        [ {PICTURE}   IS character-string]
          {PIC    }

        [BLANK WHEN ZERO]

                     {DISPLAY         }
                     {COMPUTATIONAL   }
        [USAGE IS    {COMP            } ] .
                     {COMPUTATIONAL-3 }
                     {COMP-3          }

01-49   data-name-1 REDEFINES data name-2.

88      condition-name VALUE IS literal.

WORKING-STORAGE SECTION.

01-49   {data-name}
        {FILLER   }

        [ {PICTURE}   IS character-string]
          {PIC    }

        [BLANK WHEN ZERO]

        [VALUE IS literal]

                     {DISPLAY         }
                     {COMPUTATIONAL   }
        [USAGE IS    {COMP            } ] .
                     {COMPUTATIONAL-3 }
                     {COMP-3          }

01-49   data-name-1 REDEFINES data-name-2.

88      condition-name VALUE IS literal.
```

**Figure 4-1** Basic formats for Data Division entries

**Record layout**

| Field name | Item no. | Item description | Unit cost | Unit price | Reorder point | On hand | On order | Last order date | | | Last month sales | Last year sales |
|---|---|---|---|---|---|---|---|---|---|---|---|---|
| | | | | | | | | MO | DA | YR | | |
| Characteristics | 9(5) | X(20) | 999V99 | 999V99 | S9(5) | S9(5) | S9(5) | 99 | 99 | 99 | S9(5)V99 | S9(7)V99 |
| Usage | | | | | | | | | | | | |
| Position | 1-5 | 6-25 | 26-30 | 31-35 | 36-40 | 41-45 | 46-50 | 51-56 | | | 57-63 | 64-72 |

| Unused | |
|---|---|
| X(8) | |
| | |
| 73-80 | |

**COBOL description**

```
 01   INVENTORY-MASTER-RECORD.
*
      05   IM-DESCRIPTIVE-DATA.
           10   IM-ITEM-NO                PIC 9(5).
           10   IM-ITEM-DESC              PIC X(20).
           10   IM-UNIT-COST              PIC 999V99.
           10   IM-UNIT-PRICE             PIC 999V99.
      05   IM-INVENTORY-DATA.
           10   IM-REORDER-POINT          PIC S9(5).
           10   IM-ON-HAND                PIC S9(5).
           10   IM-ON-ORDER               PIC S9(5).
      05   IM-SALES-DATA.
           10   IM-LAST-ORDER-DATE.
                15   IM-LAST-ORDER-MONTH  PIC 99.
                15   IM-LAST-ORDER-DAY    PIC 99.
                15   IM-LAST-ORDER-YEAR   PIC 99.
           10   IM-LAST-MONTH-SALES       PIC S9(5)V99.
           10   IM-LAST-YEAR-SALES        PIC S9(7)V99.
      05   FILLER                         PIC X(8).
```

**Figure 4-2** Using level numbers to organize the fields within a record

Although you can use 01, 02, 03, and so on for level numbers, it's a common practice to use level numbers that are multiples of 5 (05, 10, 15, and so on). By leaving a gap between the level numbers, it's easier to insert levels into a record later on. As long as one level number is larger than a preceding level number, it is considered to be part of the group item that precedes it.

## PICTURE clauses

As figure 4-3 shows, PICTURE clauses can be written for five different types of data items in the Data Division. These are referred to

| Item type | Allowable characters in PICTURE clauses | Examples |
|---|---|---|
| Alphabetic | A | AAA<br>A(5)<br>A(20) |
| Alphanumeric | X | XXX<br>X(5)<br>X(20) |
| Numeric | 9 S V | 9999<br>99V9<br>S9(5)<br>S9(3)V99 |
| Alphanumeric edited | X B / | XXBXX<br>XX/XX/XX |
| Numeric edited | B / Z 9 , . * + -<br>$ CR DB | 99B99<br>99/99/99<br>ZZZ.99CR<br>ZZ,ZZZ.99DB<br>**,***.99<br>--,---,---<br>+++,+++.99<br>$$$,$$$,$$$.99CR |

**Figure 4-3** Data types and PICTURE clauses

as alphabetic, alphanumeric, numeric, alphanumeric edited, and numeric edited. Although this figure doesn't give every allowable character for each type of item, it does give you a working subset of picture characters.

**Alphabetic items** If an item is described with A's, it is an *alphabetic item* and can only be used to store alphabetic data. This data can consist only of the letters (A through Z) and the space. However, this is too limiting for most fields. As a result, you should avoid using alphabetic items in your programs.

**Alphanumeric items** An *alphanumeric item* can be used to store any characters allowed on a computer system. Thus, it can store letters (A through Z), digits (0 through 9), and any of the special characters (period, comma, #, $, and so on). As a result, you should use alphanumeric items for name fields, address fields, etc.

**Numeric items** In the last chapter, you saw *numeric items* that consisted of 9's or 9's and V's. When a field can be positive or negative, though, you must also include an S to show that the field carries a

| Value of sending field | Picture of receiving field | Edited result |
|---|---|---|
| 0321 | XXBXX | 03 21 |
| 392380401 | XXXBXXBXXXX | 392 38 0401 |
| 032185 | XX/XX/XX | 03/21/85 |
| ABCDEF | XXXBXXX | ABC DEF |

**Figure 4-4** Alphanumeric editing

sign, as in these examples:

```
05  ON-HAND              PIC S9(5).
05  NET-PAY              PIC S999V99.
```

On most systems, the S doesn't require an extra storage position.

If S isn't specified in the picture for a field and the field becomes negative as the result of a calculation, the minus sign is removed. Thus, -200 is converted to an unsigned 200, which is treated as +200. In most cases, of course, you wouldn't want this to happen.

In general, you should use an S on all numeric fields in working storage unless you deliberately intend to remove plus or minus signs that may occur during the execution of the program. For numeric input fields, though, you should only use S for fields that may carry a sign.

**Alphanumeric edited items** When an alphanumeric field is prepared for output, you will sometimes want to edit it. To do this, you move the alphanumeric field to an *alphanumeric edited field*. As a result of this move, *alphanumeric editing* takes place.

Figure 4-4 illustrates alphanumeric editing using the *insertion characters* B and /. As you can see, the insertion characters are inserted into the sending field as indicated by the picture of the alphanumeric edited item. The primary use for this type of editing in many shops is inserting slashes (/) or spaces into a date field. (Incidentally, a slash is called a *stroke* in COBOL manuals.)

**Numeric edited items** When numeric data is moved to a *numeric edited item*, the data is normally converted to a more readable form. This is called *numeric editing* (or just *editing*), and it is illustrated by the examples in figure 4-5.

In group 1 of figure 4-5, you can see that the insertion characters B and / can be used in numeric edited items in a way that is similar to their use in alphanumeric edited items. In addition, zeros can be used as insertion characters. This is useful when you want to expand a number representing thousands or millions into its full value.

In group 2, the numbers 12345 and 00123 are converted to 123.45 and 1.23 by using PICTURE clauses consisting of Z's, 9's, and decimal

| Group | Value of sending field | Picture of receiving field | Edited result |
|---|---|---|---|
| 1 | | | |
| Insertion | 0321 | 99B99 | 03 21 |
| characters | 032185 | 99/99/99 | 03/21/85 |
| (B / 0) | 125 | 999000 | 125000 |
| 2 | | | |
| Zero | 12345 | ZZZ.99 | 123.45 |
| suppression | 00123 | ZZZ.99 | 1.23 |
| | 00123- | ZZZ.99 | 1.23 |
| 3 | | | |
| Comma | 142090 | Z,ZZZ.99 | 1,420.90 |
| insertion | 001242 | Z,ZZZ.99 | 12.42 |
| | 000009 | Z,ZZZ.99 | .09 |
| 4 | | | |
| Sign | 001234 | ZZZ,ZZZCR | 1,234 |
| control | 001234- | ZZZ,ZZZCR | 1,234CR |
| (CR, DB, −, and +) | 001234 | ZZZ,ZZZDB | 1,234 |
| | 001234- | ZZZ,ZZZDB | 1,234DB |
| | 001234 | ZZZ,ZZZ- | 1,234 |
| | 001234- | ZZZ,ZZZ- | 1,234- |
| | 001234 | ZZZ,ZZZ+ | 1,234+ |
| | 001234- | ZZZ,ZZZ+ | 1,234- |
| 5 | | | |
| Fixed | 001234 | $ZZZ,ZZZ | $   1,234 |
| dollar | 123456 | $ZZZZ.99 | $1234.56 |
| sign | 000012- | $ZZZZ.99CR | $     .12CR |
| 6 | | | |
| Floating | 142090 | $$,$$$.99 | $1,420.90 |
| dollar | 001242 | $$,$$$.99 | $12.42 |
| sign | 000009- | $$,$$$.99CR | $.09CR |
| 7 | | | |
| Asterisk | 142090 | $*,***.99 | $1,420.90 |
| check | 001242 | $*,***.99 | $***12.42 |
| protection | 123456 | **,***.99 | *1,234.56 |
| 8 | | | |
| Floating | 142090 | ++,+++.99 | +1,420.90 |
| plus | 142090- | ++,+++.99 | -1,420.90 |
| sign | 001242 | ++,+++.99 | +12.42 |
| | 001242- | ++,+++.99 | -12.42 |
| 9 | | | |
| Floating | 001242 | --,---.99 | 12.42 |
| minus | 001242- | --,---.99 | -12.42 |
| sign | 1234 | ---.99 | 12.34 |
| | 1234- | ---.99 | -12.34 |

**Figure 4-5** Numeric editing

points. This is simple *zero suppression* as illustrated by the program in chapter 3.

To further refine numeric data, picture characters such as the comma and the CR symbol are used. For example, commas are normally used when editing a field that has four or more digits to the left of the decimal point. In group 3, since the numbers 001242 and 000009 do not have four or more significant digits to the left of the decimal point, the comma is suppressed along with the insignificant zeros. Otherwise, the comma is inserted as desired. If a field can have a value in the millions or billions, additional commas may be used as in this picture: ZZ,ZZZ,ZZZ,ZZZ.99.

In the examples in group 2, a negative field moved to a numeric edited item is stripped of its sign and treated as if it were positive. As shown in group 4, though, the credit symbol (CR) or the debit symbol (DB) can be used to indicate that a field is negative. When these symbols are used in a numeric edited item, the symbols become two spaces if the value is positive. Similarly, the minus (−) or plus (+) sign can be used for sign control. When a minus sign is used in an editing picture, it becomes one space if the value is positive. When a plus sign is used, it prints as a plus sign if the value is zero or positive; as a minus sign if the value is negative.

Group 5 illustrates the use of a fixed dollar sign. Here, one dollar sign is used as the leftmost character of an editing picture. When data is moved to this numeric edited field, editing takes place as usual with the dollar sign remaining unchanged in the leftmost position of the field.

Group 6 represents the use of the floating dollar sign. Here, the dollar signs replace the Z's that would otherwise be used and one additional dollar sign is placed to the left of the field. Since there are four digit positions to the left of the decimal point in the values in the examples, five dollar signs and one comma are used. When numeric data is moved to a field described with a floating dollar sign, the dollar sign is placed just to the left of the leftmost digit in the edited result.

The asterisk (*), illustrated in group 7, is often used when printing checks to make sure that no one changes the amount printed. In this case, a fixed dollar sign is often used at the far left of the field, but it may be omitted. At least one asterisk is used for each digit position to the left of the decimal point in the sending value. When data with insignificant zeros is moved to a field like this, asterisks replace the lead zeros, and, if necessary, the commas.

A floating plus (+) or minus (−) sign may be used in place of the CR or DB symbol to indicate whether a field is positive or negative. Groups 8 and 9 give some examples. In either case, the number of signs used in the numeric edited item is one more than the number of digit positions to the left of the decimal point in the sending item. Since there are four digit positions to the left of the decimal point in all of the examples in group 8 and in the first two examples in group 9, five plus or minus signs appear in the picture for each corresponding receiving field. When the floating plus sign is used (group 8), it is placed to the left of the result if the value is zero or positive; a minus sign is placed to the left if the value is negative. When the floating minus sign is used (group 9), no sign appears if the value is positive; the minus sign is placed to the left of the value if the value is negative.

Although there are other ways in which numeric fields can be edited, those just illustrated satisfy the requirements of most business programs. When coding these pictures, always try to have the same number of decimal places in the sending and the receiving fields. In other words, you should align decimal points. Otherwise, your program may not run as efficiently as it could. By the same token, you should try to have as many Z's and 9's in the receiving field as there are 9's in the sending field. When using floating characters, there should be one more $, +, or − than would be used if coding Z's.

### The BLANK WHEN ZERO clause

The BLANK WHEN ZERO clause causes a field to be set to all blanks (spaces) if it is zero. If, for example, a value of zero is moved to a field with this picture:

```
$$,$$$.99CR
```

the edited result will normally be $.00. However, if the BLANK WHEN ZERO clause is coded for it, the edited result becomes all spaces.

You code the BLANK WHEN ZERO clause just as you do any clause in a field description. Here's an example:

```
05  SALES-AMOUNT                PIC ZZZ,ZZZ.99
                                BLANK WHEN ZERO.
```

Although you won't need to code this clause often, you'll probably find it useful on occasion.

### VALUE clauses

When you code a VALUE clause, it must be consistent with the picture of the field for which you code it. As a result, an alphanumeric item requires a nonnumeric literal in the VALUE clause; a numeric item requires a numeric literal.

Figure 4-6 shows the allowable characters for each type of literal. Quite simply, you can code any characters within the single or double quotation marks of a nonnumeric literal. However, if you want a quotation mark to be part of the literal value, you have to code two quotation marks in a row for each quotation mark you want. This is illustrated in the last example for nonnumeric literals.

To code a numeric literal, you code the numeric value you want using the digits 0 through 9, the decimal point, and the plus or minus

| Type | Allowable characters | Literals | Literal values |
|---|---|---|---|
| Nonnumeric | Any | 'Y'<br>'N'<br>'ITEM NO.'<br>'O''CLOCK' | Y<br>N<br>ITEM NO.<br>O'CLOCK |
| Numeric | 0-9 + − . | 1.23<br>-100<br>+55.1 | 1.23<br>-100<br>+55.1 |

**Figure 4-6** Literals as used in VALUE clauses or Procedure Division statements

sign. If you code the literal with a sign, though, you must code an S in the picture of the field. Similarly, the number of decimal positions in the literal must be consistent with the picture for the field.

If you refer back to the Data Division formats in figure 4-1, you can see that you can't code a VALUE clause in a data description at the 01 through 49 level in the File Section of the division. The assumption here is that you're describing fields that will be read into the program and written out from the program so they should be variable. As a result, a VALUE clause shouldn't be needed in this section. In a moment, though, you'll be introduced to 88 level descriptions that are legal in the File Section and that do require VALUE clauses.

### Figurative constants

In chapter 3, I introduced you to the *figurative constants* ZERO and SPACE. The complete list of figurative constants for ANS COBOL is given in figure 4-7. Except for the words ZERO, ZEROS, and ZEROES, these figurative constants act as if they were nonnumeric literals. If, for example, a field is described as

```
05  FILLER  PIC X(5)  VALUE ALL '-'.
```

the effect is the same as if it were described as

```
05  FILLER  PIC X(5)  VALUE '-----'.
```

Similarly,

```
05  QUOTE-EXAMPLE   PIC XX   VALUE QUOTE.
```

describes a field of two bytes that contains two quotation marks.

The figurative constants HIGH-VALUE and LOW-VALUE represent a computer's highest and lowest values. This means that a

| Constant | Represents |
|---|---|
| ZERO<br>ZEROS<br>ZEROES | One or more zeros |
| SPACE<br>SPACES | One or more spaces (blanks) |
| ALL 'literal' | One or more occurrences of the value within the quotation marks |
| QUOTE<br>QUOTES | One or more occurrences of the quotation mark |
| HIGH-VALUE<br>HIGH-VALUES | One or more occurrences of the highest value that can be stored in a byte of CPU storage |
| LOW-VALUE<br>LOW-VALUES | One or more occurrences of the lowest value that can be stored in a byte of CPU storage |

**Figure 4-7** Figurative constants

field that is given a value of HIGH-VALUE contains the highest possible value that can be stored in a field of that size. Similarly, a field with a value of LOW-VALUE is given the lowest possible value that can be stored in a field of that size. In general, these figurative constants are used when you want to force an unequal comparison between two fields (HIGH-VALUE will never be less than another value, and LOW-VALUE will never be more). On most compilers, only an alphanumeric field can be given one of these values.

Although you can use either the singular or plural forms of figurative constants, we suggest you stick to the singular forms (SPACE, ZERO, etc.). Because both the singular and plural forms mean the same thing, the plurals are unnecessary.

## USAGE clauses

Most computers can store data in two or more different forms. When you write a COBOL program, you can specify the form of storage you want for a data item by coding a USAGE clause. If you check the format for the USAGE clause in figure 4-1, you can see that an item's usage can be DISPLAY, COMPUTATIONAL (abbreviated COMP), or COMPUTATIONAL-3 (abbreviated COMP-3). Although some systems provide for other usages, you probably won't ever need to use them, so they aren't covered in this book.

Although you don't have to code USAGE clauses in a COBOL program, they can affect the efficiency of the object program that is compiled. In addition, USAGE clauses can allow you to reduce the lengths of fields and records so storage devices like tape and disk drives can be used more efficiently. But that depends on the system you're using. On some systems, data can only be stored in one form, so USAGE clauses have no effect on system efficiency. More about this in topic 4.

**DISPLAY usage** When the DISPLAY form of storage is used, one character of data is stored in each byte of storage. If you check the format for the USAGE clause in figure 4-1, you can see that it's optional. If a field is described without a USAGE clause, DISPLAY usage is assumed. That in turn means that all of the fields described in the inventory-listing program in chapter 3 had DISPLAY usage.

Since DISPLAY usage is assumed when the USAGE clause is omitted, most programmers don't bother to code USAGE clauses for DISPLAY fields. As a result, USAGE IS DISPLAY is never used in the programs illustrated in this book. And you should never have to code this form of the USAGE clause.

**COMP usage** In addition to the DISPLAY form of usage, most computer systems also have one or more computational forms. These computational forms of data storage are used when arithmetic operations are performed. According to the standards for 1974 or 1985 ANS COBOL, the primary computational usage should be called COMPUTATIONAL (abbreviated COMP).

When you describe a field that is going to be used in arithmetic computations, you can code it like this:

```
05  SALES-TOTAL     PIC S9(5)     COMP.
```

Here again, because the words USAGE and IS are optional, most programmers omit them. And programmers generally use the abbreviated form of the word COMPUTATIONAL.

**COMP-3 usage** If you check the format of the USAGE clause in figure 4-1, you can see that COMPUTATIONAL-3 (or COMP-3) usage is shaded. This means that it is an extension to the COBOL standards. Strictly speaking, then, it is non-standard COBOL. As a result, it is valid on some systems, but invalid on others.

Even though COMP-3 usage is an extension to the COBOL standards, it is the preferred form of computational usage on many systems. That's why I present it in this book. For instance, COMP-3 is the preferred computational usage on IBM mainframes as well as on the IBM PC when using Microsoft COBOL. So on some systems you'll use COMP-3 usage for most computational fields, while on others you'll use COMP usage. More about this in topic 4.

When you code COMP-3 usage, you code it just as you code COMP usage:

```
05  SALES-TOTAL     PIC S9(5)V99    COMP-3.
```

Here again, you omit the words USAGE and IS, and you use the abbreviated form of COMPUTATIONAL-3.

**When to code computational usages** When you develop a report preparation program, you can code computational usage for two types of fields: (1) fields within a record of an input file and (2) fields in working storage. When describing the fields for an input record, however, you have no choice. You must code the USAGE clauses so they are consistent with the specifications for the input record. If, for example, the monthly sales total field in an input record was created with computational usage, you have to code the same usage when you describe the field in your program. Otherwise, your program won't run properly.

On the other hand, when you code numeric fields in working storage, you have a choice as to what usage you should code. So the rule of thumb is this: If a field is going to be involved in arithmetic operations or in arithmetic comparisons, code the field with the primary computational usage for your system. On some systems, this usage will be COMP; on others, it will be COMP-3. You'll see this principle illustrated in the program in topic 3 of this chapter, and I'll give you more background on usages for different systems in topic 4.

In general, all of the other fields in a program are DISPLAY usage. This includes all alphanumeric, alphanumeric edited, and numeric edited items, which can only be DISPLAY usage. And it includes numeric fields like some date fields that aren't operated upon or compared arithmetically. As a result, assigning usages normally isn't much of a problem when coding a COBOL program.

**USAGE clauses at the group level** Although you can't code a PICTURE clause for a group item, you can code a USAGE clause for one. If, for example, all of the items in a group are COMP usage, you can code the group like this:

```
 01  TOTAL-FIELDS          COMP.
*
     05  MONTHLY-TOTAL     PIC S9(5)V99.
     05  YEARLY-TOTAL      PIC S9(7)V99.
```

In this case, both MONTHLY-TOTAL and YEARLY-TOTAL are assigned COMP usage. Since all group items are classified as alphanumeric fields and you can only code COMP usage for a numeric item, this isn't that logical. But it is acceptable COBOL, and it's common to code computational groups in this fashion.

### The REDEFINES clause

The REDEFINES clause can be used to define a field in two or more different ways. This is illustrated by the example in figure 4-8. Here, a

```
 01  TRANSACTION-RECORD.
*
     05  TR-TRANSACTION-CODE   PIC X.
     05  TR-DATE               PIC X(6).
     05  TR-INVOICE-NO         PIC 9(6).
     05  TR-ORDER-NO REDEFINES TR-INVOICE-NO
                               PIC X(6).
     05  TR-ITEM-NO            PIC X(5).
     05  TR-QUANTITY           PIC 9(5).
*
```

**Figure 4-8** Using the REDEFINES clause in a record description

field in an input record is defined and redefined as follows:

```
05  TR-INVOICE-NO     PIC 9(6).
05  TR-ORDER-NO REDEFINES TR-INVOICE-NO
                      PIC X(6).
```

When the field is coded in this way, it can be referred to by two different names by the statements in the Procedure Division. When it's called TR-INVOICE-NO, it's treated as numeric. When it's called TR-ORDER-NO, it's treated as alphanumeric.

If order number was a five-position numeric field in positions 8-12 and invoice number was a six-position numeric field in positions 8-13, REDEFINES could be used in this way:

```
05  TR-INVOICE-NO     PIC 9(6).
05  TR-ORDER-NO-X REDEFINES TR-INVOICE-NO.
    10  TR-ORDER-NO   PIC 9(5).
    10  FILLER        PIC X.
```

As you can see, then, REDEFINES can be used in a group item.

You can also redefine a data area more than once. If, for example, the same field or group of fields can have more than two possible forms, you can redefine the first form more than once as in this example:

```
05  TR-INVOICE-NO                PIC 9(6).
05  TR-ORDER-NO-X REDEFINES TR-INVOICE-NO.
    10  TR-ORDER-NO              PIC 9(5).
    10  FILLER                   PIC X.
05  TR-RETURN-NO REDEFINES TR-INVOICE-NO
                                 PIC X(6).
```

As you can see in figure 4-1, the format of the REDEFINES clause is this:

```
01-49 data-name-1 REDEFINES data-name-2
```

When it is used, it must be the first clause following data-name-1 and must have the same level number as the data name it is redefining (data-name-2).

Because two or more data names are assigned to the same storage area when REDEFINES is used, VALUE clauses cannot be used *after* the REDEFINES clause. As a result, the following code is illegal:

```
05  WS-EXAMPLE-1    PIC X(4)   VALUE 'ABCD'.
05  WS-EXAMPLE-2 REDEFINES WS-EXAMPLE-1
                    PIC 9(4)   VALUE 100.
```

This is also illogical and impossible, since two different values cannot be stored in the same storage positions. On the other hand, a VALUE clause can be used on the field that is being redefined. So the following code is legal:

```
05  WS-EXAMPLE-1    PIC X(4)   VALUE 'ABCD'.
05  WS-EXAMPLE-2 REDEFINES WS-EXAMPLE-1
                    PIC 9(4).
```

The REDEFINES clause has two main uses. One, as we have already seen, is to allow a single field to contain two or more types of data. The second is to get around some limitation of COBOL. You'll see an example of this second use in the program in topic 3.

### Condition names

The 88 level in the Data Division can be used to give *condition names* to the values that a field can contain. To illustrate, look at the example in figure 4-9. This shows how a condition name can be used to represent the end-of-file condition for an input file named INVMAST. The 88 level description says a condition named INVMAST-EOF should be turned on when INVMAST-EOF-SWITCH has a value of Y. Then, in the Procedure Division, the PERFORM statement uses the condition name INVMAST-EOF to express the condition rather than expressing the condition directly as:

```
INVMAST-EOF-SWITCH = 'Y'
```

When you refer to a condition name in a Procedure Division statement, you can also use NOT with it. Then, it expresses the negative of a condition. For instance,

```
NOT INVMAST-EOF
```

is equivalent to

```
INVMAST-EOF-SWITCH NOT = 'Y'
```

when INVMAST-EOF is defined as in figure 4-9.

```
 DATA DIVISION.
*
 WORKING-STORAGE SECTION.
*
 01  SWITCHES.
*
     05  INVMAST-EOF-SWITCH        PIC X  VALUE 'N'.
         88  INVMAST-EOF                  VALUE 'Y'.
*
 01  FLAGS.
*
     05  COMMISSION-LEVEL-FLAG     PIC X.
         88  COMMISSION-LEVEL-1           VALUE '1'.
         88  COMMISSION-LEVEL-2           VALUE '2'.
         88  COMMISSION-LEVEL-3           VALUE '3'.
         88  COMMISSION-LEVEL-4           VALUE '4' 'D' THRU 'F'.
     .
     .
*
 PROCEDURE DIVISION.
*
 000-PREPARE-INVENTORY-LISTING.
*
     .
     .
     PERFORM 300-PREPARE-INVENTORY-LINE
         UNTIL INVMAST-EOF.
     .
     .
*
 310-READ-INVENTORY-MASTER.
*
     READ INVMAST
         AT END
             MOVE 'Y' TO INVMAST-EOF-SWITCH.
*
     .
     .
*
 390-DETERMINE-SALES-COMMISSION.
*
     IF COMMISSION-LEVEL-1
         MOVE L1-PCT TO COMMISSION-PCT.
     IF COMMISSION-LEVEL-2
         MOVE L2-PCT TO COMMISSION-PCT.
     IF COMMISSION-LEVEL-3
         MOVE L3-PCT TO COMMISSION-PCT.
     IF COMMISSION-LEVEL-4
         MOVE L4-PCT TO COMMISSION-PCT.
     .
     .
```

**Figure 4-9** Using condition names for switches and flags

More than one condition name can be assigned to a field by using more than one 88 level for the name:

```
05  VALID-TRAN-SWITCH   PIC X.
    88  VALID-TRAN                  VALUE 'Y'.
    88  INVALID-TRAN                VALUE 'N'.
```

Also, the word THRU can be used to assign a sequence of values to one condition name:

```
05  TRAN-CODE     PIC X.
    88  ISSUE         VALUE '1'.
    88  RECEIPT       VALUE '2'.
    88  RETURN        VALUE 'R'.
    88  SCRAP         VALUE '3' THRU '9'.
```

Here, the condition name SCRAP can be used in the Procedure Division to mean the equivalent of "TRAN-CODE is equal to 3, 4, 5, 6, 7, 8, or 9."

When condition names are used to give more than just off or on values to a field, we refer to the field as a *flag*, not a switch. In figure 4-9, for example, COMMISSION-LEVEL-FLAG has four names assigned to it representing seven different values. In our terms, then, it's a flag.

Condition names can be used in either the File Section or the Working-Storage Section of the Data Division. Also, the field being described can be numeric or alphanumeric. Note that an 88 level description doesn't have a PICTURE clause; it only has a VALUE clause.

To make your condition names easy to understand, they should be related to the data names whenever practical. If, for example, a switch is named VALID-TRAN-SWITCH, a good condition name is VALID-TRAN. This is simply the data name without the suffix, -SWITCH. Similarly, if a flag named COMMISSION-LEVEL can have four values, the condition names can be COMMISSION-LEVEL-1, COMMISSION-LEVEL-2, and so on.

Sometimes, though, it doesn't make sense to relate the condition names of a flag to the data name. Take, for example, a flag named SALESMAN-STATUS that can have four values. For a flag like this, condition names like TRAINEE, ASSOCIATE, SENIOR-ASSOCIATE, and MANAGER may be more practical than condition names related to the data name.

Condition names are valuable because they can make a program easier to read and understand. Also, they can make it easier to modify a program when codes are changed. Without condition names, you have to change every statement in the Procedure Division that refers to the codes. With condition names, only the 88 level statements in the Data Division need to be changed.

## Discussion

You can't understand Data Division entries completely until you see how they relate to the Procedure Division code of a program. As a result, you'll see all of the entries described in this topic in a complete COBOL program in topic 3. Once you understand this program, you shouldn't have much trouble coding Data Division entries.

To some extent, though, Data Division entries vary depending on the system you're using. This is particularly true for computational usages. In topic 4, then, I'll describe the code in this topic that is compiler dependent.

## Terminology

level number
elementary item
group item
alphabetic item
alphanumeric item
numeric item
alphanumeric edited item
alphanumeric editing
insertion character
stroke
numeric edited item
numeric editing
editing
zero suppression
figurative constant
condition name
flag

## Objective

Given a program specification, code the Data Division entries for any of the fields required by the program.

# Topic 2 Procedure Division elements

In chapter 3, you were introduced to some basic Procedure Division statements. This topic expands upon that base. When you complete this topic, you should be able to code most of the Procedure Division statements you will ever need for report preparation programs.

## Figurative constants

All of the figurative constants in figure 4-7 can be used in the Procedure Division as well as in the Data Division. These constants have the same meaning in both divisions. Some examples of their use in the Procedure Division follow:

```
MOVE ZERO TO CUSTOMER-TOTAL.
MOVE ALL '*' to PRINT-AREA.
MOVE HIGH-VALUE TO TR-CUSTOMER-NO.
```

In example 1, the value of CUSTOMER-TOTAL is set to zero. In example 2, one asterisk is moved to each storage position in PRINT-AREA. In example 3, the highest value for the computer system is moved to TR-CUSTOMER-NO.

## The ACCEPT DATE/DAY/TIME/DAY-OF-WEEK statement

On modern computer systems, the current date and time are entered into storage when the system is started. This date and time are then kept current by the system as long as it's in continuous operation. As a result, the date and time can be accessed by application programs so they can be printed on reports.

The standard statement for getting the date, day, or time from the system has this format:

```
                          {DATE}
ACCEPT data-name FROM     {DAY }
                          {TIME}
```

When executed, the current date, day, or time is moved to a field described in the user's program. The field must be an elementary item with the proper picture.

The picture of the standard DATE field is 9(6), and its form is YYMMDD (two-digit year, month, and day). As a result, July 1, 1986 is stored as 860701. Similarly, the picture of the standard DAY field is 9(5), and its form is YYDDD, where DDD represents three digits that indicate what number day in the year it is. Thus, July 1, 1986 is stored as 86182 (the 182nd day of 1986).

The picture of the standard TIME field is 9(8), and its form is HHMMSSHH (two-digit hours, minutes, seconds, and hundredths of seconds). This assumes a 24-hour clock, so 2:00 p.m. is hour 14. As a result, 2:41 p.m. is stored as 14410000. The minimum value of TIME is 00000000; the maximum is 23595999.

Figure 4-10 shows you how you can access DATE and TIME using the ACCEPT statement. Note that REDEFINES clauses are used in the Data Division for both the PRESENT-DATE and PRESENT-TIME fields. This is done so they can be defined with the standard pictures of 9(6) and 9(8), but their component fields can still be referred to by the statements of the program. Since many programs require the date in the form of MM/DD/YY and the form of the standard date field is YYMMDD, the coding in this example moves the month, day, and year components from PRESENT-DATE to EDITED-DATE. In so doing, the components are rearranged and slashes are inserted between the month, day, and year. In the program in topic 3 of this chapter, you'll see the ACCEPT statement used in a complete program.

In 1985 COBOL, you can also get the day of the week using an ACCEPT statement with this format:

```
ACCEPT data-name FROM DAY-OF-WEEK
```

In this case, the data name must be defined as a one-digit elementary item. After the statement has been executed, a value of 1 in the receiving field represents Monday; a value of 2, Tuesday; and so on.

### The DISPLAY statement

The DISPLAY statement can be used to send operational messages to a user's screen, to the computer system's operational console, or to a printer...it depends on the system you're using. If, for example, you want to send a message at the end of a program to let the user or operator know the program has run to completion, you can use the DISPLAY statement.

The format of the DISPLAY statement follows:

```
DISPLAY {data-name} ...
        {literal  }
```

Therefore, these are valid DISPLAY statements:

```
DISPLAY OUTPUT-DATA.
DISPLAY 'END OF JOB'.
DISPLAY 'RECORD NUMBER ' INV-ITEM-NUMBER
    ' IS IN ERROR.'.
```

In example 1, the contents of the field named OUTPUT-DATA are displayed. In example 2, END OF JOB (a literal) is displayed. In

```
 WORKING-STORAGE SECTION.
*
      .
      .
*
 01   DATE-AND-TIME-FIELDS.
*
      05   PRESENT-DATE              PIC 9(6).
      05   PRESENT-DATE-X REDEFINES PRESENT-DATE.
           10   PD-YEAR              PIC 99.
           10   PD-MONTH             PIC 99.
           10   PD-DAY               PIC 99.
      05   PRESENT-TIME              PIC 9(8).
      05   PRESENT-TIME-X REDEFINES PRESENT-TIME.
           10   PT-HOURS             PIC 99.
           10   PT-MINUTES           PIC 99.
           10   FILLER               PIC X(4).
      05   EDITED-DATE.
           10   ED-MONTH             PIC 99.
           10   FILLER               PIC X      VALUE '/'.
           10   ED-DAY               PIC 99.
           10   FILLER               PIC X      VALUE '/'.
           10   ED-YEAR              PIC 99.
      .
      .
 PROCEDURE DIVISION.
      .
      .
*
 110-GET-CURRENT-DATE.
*
      ACCEPT PRESENT-DATE FROM DATE.
      MOVE PD-MONTH TO ED-MONTH.
      MOVE PD-DAY   TO ED-DAY.
      MOVE PD-YEAR  TO ED-YEAR.
      .
      .
*
 120-GET-CURRENT-TIME.
*
      ACCEPT PRESENT-TIME FROM TIME.
      .
      .
```

**Figure 4-10** Using the ACCEPT statement

example 3, a series of a literal, a data name, and another literal are displayed. As a result, if INV-ITEM-NUMBER contains 7904, this line is displayed:

```
RECORD NUMBER 7904 IS IN ERROR.
```

When a numeric field with some kind of computational usage is displayed, the program first converts it to DISPLAY usage. If the field has a sign, though, it may be difficult for you to interpret the displayed data. For instance, a + 184 might display as 18D; a − 184 might display as 18M. Of course, if S's aren't used in the pictures of the fields that are displayed, the fields will not carry signs.

In general, the DISPLAY statement is used to display messages about the operation of a program during its execution. However, DISPLAY statements can also be useful when testing and debugging a program, as you'll learn in chapter 10.

In the next topic, you'll see the use of the DISPLAY statement within a complete program. Then, in topic 4, you'll learn how DISPLAY statements operate on different types of systems. On most microcomputers and minicomputers, DISPLAY statements display the named literals and fields on the user's screen. But on mainframes, DISPLAY statements usually print the output on one of the system's printers.

### The MOVE statement

As you learned in the last chapter, the MOVE statement converts data from the picture of the sending field to the picture of the receiving field. Now that you know something about usages, you should realize that the MOVE statement also converts data from the usage of the sending field to the usage of the receiving field.

**Items in a series** The format of the MOVE statement is this:

```
MOVE {literal-1   } TO  data-name-2  ...
     {data-name-1 }
```

As a result, you can move one field or literal value to a series of receiving fields as in this statement:

```
MOVE ZERO TO CUSTOMER-TOTAL
             SALESMAN-TOTAL
             BRANCH-TOTAL.
```

Most of the time, though, you will code MOVE statements with only one receiving field.

**Valid MOVE statements** When you code a MOVE statement, you have to know the type of data item you're using in the sending and receiving fields. For instance, it's illegal to move a numeric item to an alphabetic item. It's also illogical. When you code an illegal move, the compiler should identify the statement in its diagnostic listing so you can correct it before testing your program.

Figure 4-11 is a table that shows the types of MOVE statements you are likely to code. It also identifies the types of moves that are illegal. As you can see, it's illegal to move a numeric field to an alphabetic field, and vice versa. When you move a numeric field to an

| Sending item | Receiving item | | | | |
|---|---|---|---|---|---|
| | Alphabetic | Alphanumeric | Numeric | Alphanumeric edited | Numeric edited |
| Alphabetic | Yes | Yes | No | Yes | No |
| Alphanumeric | Alphabetic only | Yes | Integer only | Yes | Integer only |
| Numeric | No | Integer only | Yes | Integer only | Yes |

**Figure 4-11** The common uses of MOVE statements

alphanumeric or alphanumeric edited field, you must be sure that it contains *integers* (whole numbers) only. And when you move an alphanumeric field to an alphabetic, numeric, or numeric edited field, you must be sure that the sending field is sending data that is acceptable to the receiving field. Since an alphanumeric field can contain any characters, it can contain numeric data, alphabetic data, or other data. In short, when you code MOVE statements, you must know your data so you won't send invalid data to a receiving field.

**Field sizes in editing moves** When you move an alphanumeric field to an alphanumeric edited field, alphanumeric editing takes place. When you move a numeric field to a numeric edited field, numeric editing takes place. In either case, it's important to coordinate the size of the sending field with the size of the receiving field.

More specifically, in a numeric editing operation, you should try to have the same number of decimal positions in the sending and the receiving fields. You should try to have as many Z's, 9's, and asterisks (*) in the receiving field as there are 9's in the sending field. And when using the floating characters $, +, and −, you should use one more character than you would if you were coding Z's, 9's, or asterisks.

If you don't coordinate the size and number of decimal positions during numeric editing moves, editing will still take place properly...under some conditions. However, the program won't execute as efficiently as it would otherwise. And in either type of editing, if the receiving field isn't large enough to accommodate all of the characters of the sending field, *truncation* will take place. This means that some of the characters of the sending field will be dropped, which in turn means inaccurate results. In most cases, then, you will want to coordinate your sending and receiving fields as illustrated by the examples in figures 4-4 and 4-5 in topic 1.

| | Sending field A | | Receiving field B | |
|---|---|---|---|---|
| | Picture | Value | Picture | Value |
| Alphanumeric A < B | X(5) | ABCDE | X(10) | ABCDEbbbbb (b = blank) |
| Alphanumeric A > B | X(10) | ABCDEFGHIJ | X(5) | ABCDE |
| Numeric A < B | 9(5) | 12345 | 9(9) | 000012345 |
| Numeric A > B | 9(9) | 123456789 | 9(5) | 56789 or ? |

**Figure 4-12** The operation of the MOVE statement when the sending field isn't the same size as the receiving field

**Field sizes in non-editing moves** When you move a field of one type to a field of the same type, editing doesn't take place. Then, if the size of the sending field is equal to the size of the receiving field, the sending field is simply duplicated in the receiving field. In some cases, though, you may want to code moves with fields of unequal sizes. As a result, you should know what happens when statements like this are executed.

Figure 4-12 shows the results of four MOVE statements that involve fields of unequal sizes. To understand this, you must distinguish between alphanumeric and numeric moves. When you move an alphanumeric field of one size to an alphanumeric field of a larger size, the receiving field is filled out with spaces to the right of the original data. Thus, a sending field of ABCDE becomes ABCDE followed by five spaces in a 10-character receiving field. In contrast, when you move an alphanumeric field of one size to an alphanumeric field of a smaller size, the original data is truncated in the receiving field. Thus, a sending field of ABCDEFGHIJ becomes ABCDE in a five-character receiving field. As you get more programming experience, you'll realize that there are times when you'll want to code both types of moves.

When you move a numeric field of one size to a larger receiving field, the original data is filled out on the left with zeros. Thus, 12345 sent to a nine-digit receiving field becomes 000012345. In contrast, when you move a numeric field of one size to a smaller receiving field, the data is usually truncated on the left. Thus, a sending field of 123456789 might become 56789 in a five-digit receiving field (I say "might" because, depending on factors that are beyond the scope of this book, the result could be something else). Anyway, that's not what you want in most programs. As a result, you may move numeric fields to larger receiving fields, but you should avoid moving them to smaller receiving fields.

## Arithmetic statements

In chapter 3, you were introduced to one of the COBOL arithmetic statements, the ADD statement. Now, I'd like to present the four most common arithmetic statements in detail. They are the ADD, SUBTRACT, MULTIPLY, and DIVIDE statements, and their formats are given in figure 4-13.

In general, there are two formats for each type of arithmetic statement. In the first format, the result of the arithmetic operation replaces the contents of the field or fields named after the word TO, FROM, BY, or INTO. In the second format, the result of the arithmetic operation replaces the contents of the field or fields named in the GIVING clause. This is illustrated by the examples in figure 4-14.

If you study figure 4-14, you can see that all of the statements operate on two fields named FIELD-A and FIELD-B. When the GIVING clause isn't used, the result of the arithmetic operation is stored in FIELD-B; in this case, FIELD-A isn't changed. When the GIVING clause is used, the result is stored in FIELD-C; in this case, neither FIELD-A nor FIELD-B is changed.

As you can see by the examples, COBOL arithmetic operations take place just as you would expect them to. When one or more fields in an operation carry a sign, the sign of the result field is determined using normal algebraic rules. If, for example, you multiply a negative field by a positive field, the result is negative.

When coding arithmetic statements, you should make sure that the receiving fields are large enough to store the results. To do this well, you have to understand the data you're working with. If, for example, you're multiplying a three-digit field by a five-digit field, the result can have eight digits. However, you may know that the resulting value will never exceed six digits. As a result, you can code the receiving field with only six digits. You should realize, though, that digits will be lost in the result field if the size of the result requires more positions than provided for by the receiving field.

**Items in a series** As you can tell by the formats in figure 4-13, you can code items in a series in all of the arithmetic statements. For instance, you can code a series of GIVING fields in all of the statements. And you can code a series of fields to be added in an ADD statement as in this example:

```
ADD FIELD-1 FIELD-2 FIELD-3 FIELD-4
    GIVING FIELD-5.
```

Here, four fields are added together and the result is stored in FIELD-5.

In most cases, though, you won't want to code a series of items in arithmetic statements. And you can always accomplish the same thing without using a series. In the programs in this book, then, you won't

**The ADD statement**

**Format 1**

```
ADD {literal-1   } ... TO data-name-m [ROUNDED] ...
    {data-name-1 }

    [ON SIZE ERROR imperative-statement]
```

**Format 2**

```
ADD {literal-1   } {literal-2   } ...
    {data-name-1 } {data-name-2 }

    GIVING data-name-m [ROUNDED] ...

    [ON SIZE ERROR imperative-statement]
```

**The SUBTRACT statement**

**Format 1**

```
SUBTRACT {literal-1   } ... FROM data-name-m [ROUNDED] ...
         {data-name-1 }

    [ON SIZE ERROR imperative-statement]
```

**Format 2**

```
SUBTRACT {literal-1   } ... FROM {literal-m   }
         {data-name-1 }          {data-name-m }

    GIVING data-name-n [ROUNDED] ...

    [ON SIZE ERROR imperative-statement]
```

**Figure 4-13** The formats of the COBOL arithmetic statements (part 1 of 2)

see a series of items used in arithmetic statements. I just want you to realize that a series of items is legal in case you encounter a series when reviewing someone else's code.

**Numeric edited GIVING fields** You can combine an arithmetic operation with numeric editing by using a numeric edited item in a GIVING clause. Then, the program edits the result field before storing it in the GIVING field. In other words, the statement has the effect of an arithmetic statement followed by a MOVE statement for editing.

**The MULTIPLY statement**

**Format 1**

```
MULTIPLY {literal-1   }  BY  data-name-2 [ROUNDED]  ...
         {data-name-1 }

      [ON SIZE ERROR  imperative-statement]
```

**Format 2**

```
MULTIPLY {literal-1   } BY { literal-2  }
         {data-name-1 }    {data-name-2 }

      GIVING data-name-3 [ROUNDED]  ...

      [ON SIZE ERROR  imperative-statement]
```

**The DIVIDE statement**

**Format 1**

```
DIVIDE   {literal-1   }  INTO  data-name-2 [ROUNDED]  ...
         {data-name-1 }

      [ON SIZE ERROR  imperative-statement]
```

**Format 2**

```
DIVIDE   {literal-1   } INTO { literal-2  }
         {data-name-1 }      {data-name-2 }

      GIVING data-name-3 [ROUNDED]  ...

      [REMAINDER data-name-4]

      [ON SIZE ERROR  imperative-statement]
```

**Format 3**

```
DIVIDE   {literal-1   }  BY  {literal-2   }
         {data-name-1 }      {data-name-2 }

      GIVING data-name-3 [ROUNDED]  ...

      [REMAINDER data-name-4]

      [ON SIZE ERROR  imperative-statement]
```

Note: You can't code a series of GIVING fields when you use the REMAINDER clause in either format 2 or 3.

**Figure 4-13** The formats of the COBOL arithmetic statements (part 2 of 2)

| | FIELD-A | FIELD-B | FIELD-C | FIELD-D |
|---|---|---|---|---|
| **ADD FIELD-A TO FIELD-B.** | | | | |
| Picture: | S9(5) | S9(5) | | |
| Contents before: | 00050 | 00070 | | |
| Contents after: | 00050 | 00120 | | |
| **ADD FIELD-A TO FIELD-B GIVING FIELD-C.** | | | | |
| Picture: | S9(5) | S9(5) | S9(5) | |
| Contents before: | 00050 | 00070 | N/A | |
| Contents after: | 00050 | 00070 | 00120 | |
| **SUBTRACT FIELD-A FROM FIELD-B.** | | | | |
| Picture: | S9(5) | S9(5) | | |
| Contents before: | 01000 | 00250 | | |
| Contents after: | 01000 | 00750- | | |
| **SUBTRACT FIELD-A FROM FIELD-B GIVING FIELD-C.** | | | | |
| Picture: | S9(5) | S9(5) | S9(5) | |
| Contents before: | 01000 | 01250 | N/A | |
| Contents after: | 01000 | 01250 | 00250 | |
| **MULTIPLY FIELD-A BY FIELD-B.** | | | | |
| Picture: | S9(3) | S9(5) | | |
| Contents before: | 100 | 00250 | | |
| Contents after: | 100 | 25000 | | |
| **MULTIPLY FIELD-A BY FIELD-B GIVING FIELD-C.** | | | | |
| Picture: | S9(3) | S9(5) | S9(7) | |
| Contents before: | 100- | 12500 | N/A | |
| Contents after: | 100- | 12500 | 1250000- | |
| **DIVIDE FIELD-A INTO FIELD-B ROUNDED.** | | | | |
| Picture: | S9(3) | S9(5) | | |
| Contents before: | 100 | 00250 | | |
| Contents after: | 100 | 00003 | | |
| **DIVIDE FIELD-A INTO FIELD-B GIVING FIELD-C REMAINDER FIELD-D.** | | | | |
| Picture: | S9(3) | S9(5) | S9(3) | S9(3) |
| Contents before: | 100- | 00175 | N/A | N/A |
| Contents after: | 100- | 00175 | 001- | 075 |

**Figure 4-14** The operation of typical arithmetic statements

You will sometimes want to code an arithmetic statement in this way when the result isn't going to be used in other arithmetic operations. However, if the result field is going to be reused, it's better to code the result field as a numeric field. Then, the field can be moved to a numeric edited field later on.

**The ROUNDED clause** The ROUNDED clause simply says that the result should be rounded before it's placed in the result field. This is illustrated by the first DIVIDE example in figure 4-14. Here, the actual result is 2.5, but the result field is described with a picture of S9(3). As a result, 2.5 is rounded up to the next whole number, so a value of 3 is placed in the result field. If ROUNDED hadn't been specified, the decimal position would have been truncated so a value of 2 would have been placed in the result field.

You should consider using the ROUNDED clause whenever the result of a calculation will have more decimal places than is specified in the picture of the result field. However, for efficiency, you should avoid using this clause if there's no need for rounding. In fact, most compilers will issue a warning diagnostic if you code a ROUNDED clause when there's no need for it.

**The ON SIZE ERROR clause** When the result field isn't large enough to hold the result of an arithmetic operation, a size error occurs. Then, if the arithmetic statement has used the ON SIZE ERROR clause, the imperative statements within it are executed. For instance, this clause can be coded as follows:

```
MULTIPLY HOURS-WORKED BY HOURLY-RATE
    GIVING NET-PAY
    ROUNDED
    ON SIZE ERROR
        PERFORM 330-PRINT-ERROR-MESSAGE.
```

This means that the program will perform paragraph 330 if the result of the calculation has more digits than are specified in the picture of the result field. If, for example, NET-PAY has a picture of 999V99 and the result of the multiplication is 2125.90, a size error has occurred. Without the ON SIZE ERROR clause, the computer would continue to execute the program without notifying the user that a size error had occurred.

In general, you should avoid using the ON SIZE ERROR clause whenever possible. As you might guess, it affects the efficiency of the program because a test for size overflow must be made each time a calculation is performed. As a more efficient alternative, data should be checked before it is used in arithmetic statements. That way the program knows that the result won't lead to a size error before the arithmetic statements are ever executed. This is the type of checking that is done in an efficient business system.

**The REMAINDER clause** When you want to keep the remainder in a divide operation, you use the REMAINDER clause as shown in the second DIVIDE example in figure 4-14. The program then places the remainder in the field you specify.

As shown in the formats in figure 4-13, you can combine the ROUNDED and ON SIZE ERROR clauses with the REMAINDER clause. Be aware, though, that rounding is done *after* the remainder has been stored. As a result, if the second DIVIDE example in figure 4-14 had included the ROUNDED clause, the final value in FIELD-C would have been -002, but FIELD-D would still have contained 075.

As for the ON SIZE ERROR clause, it applies to *both* the quotient and remainder fields. So, since a remainder can never be bigger than the divisor, we recommend that you always make sure your remainder field is as large as the divisor field. Then, if a size error occurs, you'll know it applies to the quotient field.

### Nested IF statements

In chapter 3, you were introduced to simple IF statements. In many programs, however, you will want to code IF statements within IF statements. For instance, this code consists of one IF statement within another:

```
IF NOT INVTRAN-EOF
    IF IM-UNIT-PRICE > 100.00
        PERFORM 330-PRINT-INVENTORY-LINE.
```

Here, module 330 will be performed only if the condition named INVTRAN-EOF is *not* true and the field named IM-UNIT-PRICE has a value of more than 100.00. When IF statements are coded this way, they are referred to as *nested IF statements*.

Figure 4-15 gives the format and flowchart for one form of nested IF statements. In this case, an IF-ELSE statement is coded within the IF portion of an earlier IF statement, and another IF-ELSE statement is coded within the ELSE portion. To continue with further levels of nesting, IF statements could also be coded within statement groups A through D.

Because nested IF statements can become quite confusing if they're coded carelessly, you should use indentation to indicate the levels of nesting. In figure 4-16, for example, you can see the indentation we recommend for some common nesting structures. In brief, each level of nesting is indented four more spaces than the preceding level. And the statements to be performed when a condition is met are indented four spaces to the right of the related IF or ELSE.

One key point to remember when coding nested IF statements is this: *The compiler will pair each ELSE with the first IF that precedes it that doesn't already have an ELSE.* This happens no matter what your indentation indicates. In figure 4-17, for example, the compiler

**Coding**

```
IF condition-1
    IF condition-2
        statement-group-a
    ELSE
        statement-group-b
ELSE
    IF condition-3
        statement-group-c
    ELSE
        statement-group-d.
```

**Logic flow**

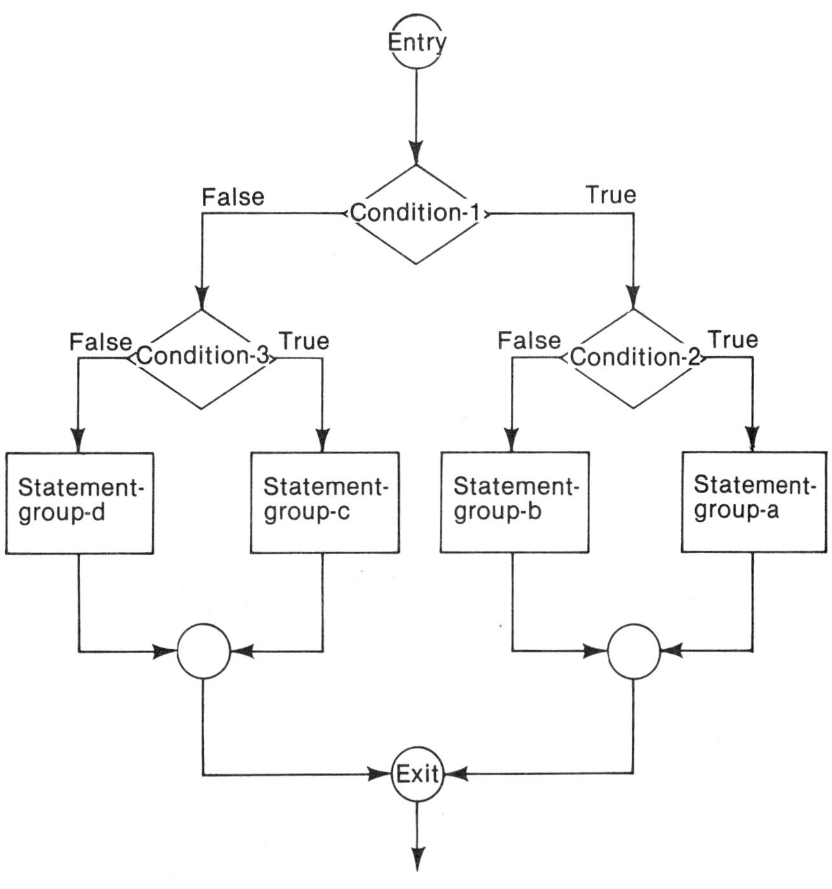


**Figure 4-15** Nested IF statements: Coding and logic

interprets the code differently than the programmer indicates through his indentation. So remember that a COBOL compiler ignores spaces; the indentation is only meant to make your code more readable.

**Example 1**

```
IF condition-a
    statement-group-a
    IF condition-b
        statement-group-b
        IF condition-c
            statement-group-c.
```

**Example 2**

```
IF condition-a
    statement-group-a
    IF condition-b
        statement-group-b
        IF condition-c
            statement-group-c
        ELSE
            statement-group-d
    ELSE
        statement-group-e
ELSE
    statement-group-f.
```

**Example 3**

```
IF condition-a
    statement-group-a
ELSE
    IF condition-b
        statement-group-b
    ELSE
        IF condition-c
            statement-group-c
        ELSE
            statement-group-d.
```

**Figure 4-16** Proper use of indentation in some common forms of nested IF statements

To eliminate coding errors, you should be sure that each IF statement has a corresponding ELSE statement if it requires one. You should also use indentation to make sure you have properly paired your IFs and ELSEs, as well as to show the logical structure of your nesting. If you do both of these things, several levels of nesting can be used with limited confusion.

**Indentation error**

```
IF condition-a
    PERFORM paragraph-1
    IF condition-b
        PERFORM paragraph-2
ELSE<-------------------------- Improperly aligned ELSE clause
    IF condition-c
        PERFORM paragraph-3
    ELSE
        PERFORM paragraph-4.
```

**Indentation corresponds to compilation**

```
IF condition-a
    PERFORM paragraph-1
    IF condition-b
        PERFORM paragraph-2
    ELSE
        IF condition-c
            PERFORM paragraph-3
        ELSE
            PERFORM paragraph-4.
```

**Figure 4-17** Improper and proper use of indentation in nested IF statements

## Discussion

In the next topic, you will see a complete program that uses the statements presented in this topic. Then, I think you'll get a better understanding of how these statements work and how they should be coded.

## Terminology

integer
truncation
nested IF statements

## Objective

Given a program specification, a program structure chart, and the first three divisions of the program, code the Procedure Division statements for the program.

## Topic 3 The investment-listing program

To show you how the COBOL elements presented in topic 1 and 2 work together, this topic presents a complete program that uses most of the elements. This program is a bit more complicated than the program presented in chapter 3, but you shouldn't have much trouble understanding it. So I'll simply try to describe the important points as I present the program.

### The program overview

Figure 4-18 presents the program overview for this program, which I'll call the investment-listing program. As you can see, it prepares an investment listing from an inventory master file. On the investment listing, one line is printed for each inventory master record that has an investment amount of more than $10,000. The investment amount is calculated by multiplying the on-hand quantity of an inventory item by its unit price.

### The record description for the inventory master file

Most of the time, it's easier to create a COBOL description for a record layout of a file than it is to create a record layout using a record layout form. In addition, a COBOL description is easier to change, and it can be reused in all the programs that process the related file. That's why we recommend COBOL descriptions, rather than hand-written layouts on forms, as the documentation for record layouts. And from now on, we'll use COBOL descriptions to document the record layouts for the example programs.

In figure 4-19, you can see the COBOL record description for the inventory master file. Here, the first seven fields are the same as those in the inventory master file described in chapter 3. However, S's are used in the pictures of those fields that could become negative due to an error in a processing routine (obviously, you can't actually have negative on-hand, on-order, or reorder point fields). And I've grouped the fields under general 05 level headings.

In addition, the record description provides for four new fields at the 10 level. In these descriptions, you can see REDEFINES used so the last order date field can be described both as 9(6) and as a group field with lower-level month, day, and year fields. By describing IM-LAST-ORDER-DATE as 9(6), it can be edited by moving it to a numeric edited field described as 99/99/99. You can also see that last month sales and last year sales are signed fields, because it's possible for a sales field to be negative.

| Program: INV3520 PREPARE INVESTMENT LISTING | Page: 1 |
|---|---|
| Designer: Anne Prince | Date: 04-03-86 |

Input/output specifications

| File | Description | Use |
|---|---|---|
| INVMAST | Inventory master file | Input |
| INVLIST | Print file: Investment listing | Output |

Process specifications

This program prepares an investment listing from a sequential file of inventory master records. The records are in sequence by item number, and the report should be printed in the same sequence. For each master record, a line should be printed on the investment listing only if the investment amount is greater than $10,000.

The basic processing requirements for each inventory master record follow:

1. Read the master record.

2. Calculate the investment amount.
   (Investment amount = on-hand balance x unit price)

3. If the investment amount is greater than $10,000, add the investment amount to the investment total and format and print an investment line. To figure the number of months inventory on hand, divide the investment amount by last month's sales.

After all records have been processed, prepare and print the total lines.

**Figure 4-18** The program overview for the investment-listing program

```
 01   INVENTORY-MASTER-RECORD.
*
      05   IM-DESCRIPTIVE-DATA.
           10   IM-ITEM-NO               PIC 9(5).
           10   IM-ITEM-DESC             PIC X(20).
           10   IM-UNIT-COST             PIC 999V99.
           10   IM-UNIT-PRICE            PIC 999V99.
      05   IM-INVENTORY-DATA.
           10   IM-REORDER-POINT         PIC S9(5).
           10   IM-ON-HAND               PIC S9(5).
           10   IM-ON-ORDER              PIC S9(5).
      05   IM-SALES-DATA.
           10   IM-LAST-ORDER-DATE       PIC 9(6).
           10   IM-LAST-ORDER-DATE-R REDEFINES IM-LAST-ORDER-DATE.
                15   IM-LAST-ORDER-MONTH PIC 99.
                15   IM-LAST-ORDER-DAY   PIC 99.
                15   IM-LAST-ORDER-YEAR  PIC 99.
           10   IM-LAST-MONTH-SALES      PIC S9(5)V99.
           10   IM-LAST-YEAR-SALES       PIC S9(7)V99.
      05   FILLER                        PIC X(8).
```

**Figure 4-19** The COBOL description for the inventory master record

### The print chart and test run output for the investment listing

Figure 4-20 gives the print chart and some test run output for the investment listing. In the top line of the listing, you can see that the current date and the page number are printed. In the second line, you can see that the current time and the program name (INV3520) are printed. In the investment line, you can see that floating minus signs are used to indicate the sign of a field. And, in the total lines, you can see that floating dollar signs are used with no provision for negative values.

In actual practice, of course, this is the way most reports are prepared. All reports should have standard heading lines that indicate the current date, the current time, the page number, the program that prepares the report, and the title of the report. And most reports have one or more total lines that summarize the data of the report. As you will see, the other programs in this book also prepare reports with complete headings and useful total lines.

### The structure chart

Figure 4-21 presents the structure chart for the investment-listing program. In this case, the upper righthand corner of module 360 is shaded because it is used in more than one place in the chart. A module like this is called a *common module*.

In the second level of the chart, module 300 is the module that is repeatedly executed while the program prepares the investment

**Print chart**

```
DATE:  99/99/99                                            MIKE MURACH & ASSOCIATES, INC.                                       PAGE: ZZ9
TIME:  99:99 XX                                                                                                                 INV3520
                                          INVENTORY INVESTMENT LISTING -- ITEMS WITH RETAIL VALUE OVER $10,000

ITEM                                      UNIT   QUANTITY    LAST     LAST MONTH           INVESTMENT     NO. OF MONTHS
 NO.    ITEM DESCRIPTION                 PRICE   ON HAND ORDER DATE  SALES IN $           IN RETAIL $   INVENTORY ON HAND

ZZZZZ  XXXXXXXXXXXXXXXXXXXX             ZZZ.99  -----9   99/99/99    ---,---.99         --,---,---.99         ----.9


ZZZZZ RECORDS IN THE MASTER FILE                                $$$$,$$$,$$$.99 *  $$$$,$$$,$$$.99 *        ZZZ.9 *
ZZZZZ RECORDS IN THIS SELECTED LISTING
```

**Test run output**

```
DATE: 04/15/86                                    MIKE MURACH & ASSOCIATES, INC.                                       PAGE:    1
TIME: 04:30 PM                                                                                                         INV3520
                                   INVENTORY INVESTMENT LISTING -- ITEMS WITH RETAIL VALUE OVER $10,000

ITEM                               UNIT  QUANTITY    LAST      LAST MONTH           INVESTMENT    NO. OF MONTHS
 NO.    ITEM DESCRIPTION          PRICE  ON HAND ORDER DATE   SALES IN $           IN RETAIL $  INVENTORY ON HAND

  103   HEATER SOLENOID            1.25    11000   03/19/86    -1,000.00             13,750.00         -13.8
 3981   PLUMB LINE               900.00      100   03/19/86                          90,000.00         999.9
99999   AAAAAAAAAAAAAAAAAAAA     999.99    99999   99/99/99    99,999.99            SIZE ERROR           N/A

    5 RECORDS IN THE MASTER FILE                               $98,999.99 *        $103,750.00 *         1.0 *
    3 RECORDS IN THIS SELECTED LISTING
```

**Figure 4-20** The print chart and the test run output for the investment listing

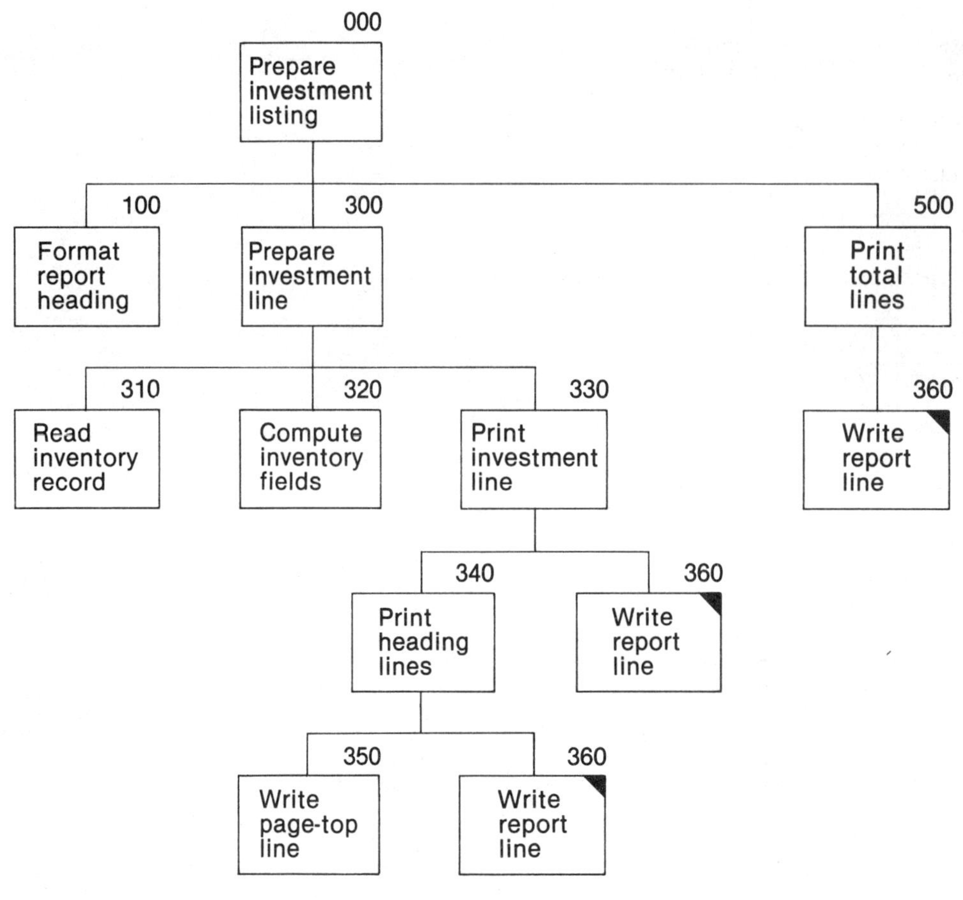


**Figure 4-21** The structure chart for the investment-listing program

listing. In contrast, module 100 is executed only once, before the program starts executing module 300. And module 500 is executed only once, after the program stops executing module 300. You'll understand this better after you study the COBOL listing for the program.

### The COBOL listing

Like the other program listings in this book, the one in figure 4-22 is for an IBM mainframe using the VS COBOL compiler under the DOS/VSE operating system. Since the first part of the program is similar to the first part of the inventory-listing program, you shouldn't have any questions until you reach the Working-Storage Section. So let me start there.

```
 IDENTIFICATION DIVISION.
*
 PROGRAM-ID.        INV3520.
*AUTHOR.            MIKE MURACH.
*
 ENVIRONMENT DIVISION.
*
 INPUT-OUTPUT SECTION.
*
 FILE-CONTROL.
     SELECT INVMAST ASSIGN TO SYS020-AS-INVMAST.
     SELECT INVLIST ASSIGN TO SYS006-UR-1403-S.
*
 DATA DIVISION.
*
 FILE SECTION.
*
 FD  INVMAST
     LABEL RECORDS ARE STANDARD
     RECORD CONTAINS 80 CHARACTERS.
*
 01  INVENTORY-MASTER-RECORD.
*
     05  IM-DESCRIPTIVE-DATA.
         10  IM-ITEM-NO              PIC 9(5).
         10  IM-ITEM-DESC            PIC X(20).
         10  IM-UNIT-COST            PIC 999V99.
         10  IM-UNIT-PRICE           PIC 999V99.
     05  IM-INVENTORY-DATA.
         10  IM-REORDER-POINT        PIC S9(5).
         10  IM-ON-HAND              PIC S9(5).
         10  IM-ON-ORDER             PIC S9(5).
     05  IM-SALES-DATA.
         10  IM-LAST-ORDER-DATE      PIC 9(6).
         10  IM-LAST-ORDER-DATE-R REDEFINES IM-LAST-ORDER-DATE.
             15  IM-LAST-ORDER-MONTH PIC 99.
             15  IM-LAST-ORDER-DAY   PIC 99.
             15  IM-LAST-ORDER-YEAR  PIC 99.
         10  IM-LAST-MONTH-SALES     PIC S9(5)V99.
         10  IM-LAST-YEAR-SALES      PIC S9(7)V99.
     05  FILLER                      PIC X(8).
*
 FD  INVLIST
     LABEL RECORDS ARE OMITTED
     RECORD CONTAINS 132 CHARACTERS.
*
 01  PRINT-AREA              PIC X(132).
*
 WORKING-STORAGE SECTION.
*
 01  SWITCHES.
*
     05  INVMAST-EOF-SWITCH              PIC X       VALUE 'N'.
         88  INVMAST-EOF                             VALUE 'Y'.
     05  INVESTMENT-SIZE-ERROR-SWITCH    PIC X       VALUE 'N'.
```

Figure 4-22 The COBOL listing for the investment-listing program (part 1 of 7)

```
           88  INVESTMENT-SIZE-ERROR                          VALUE 'Y'.
*
 01   PRINT-FIELDS              COMP-3.
*
      05  SPACE-CONTROL         PIC S9.
      05  LINES-ON-PAGE         PIC S999 VALUE +55.
      05  LINE-COUNT            PIC S999 VALUE +99.
      05  PAGE-COUNT            PIC S999 VALUE ZERO.
*
 01   DATE-AND-TIME-FIELDS.
*
      05  PRESENT-DATE              PIC 9(6).
      05  PRESENT-DATE-R REDEFINES PRESENT-DATE.
          10  PRESENT-YEAR          PIC 99.
          10  PRESENT-MONTH         PIC 99.
          10  PRESENT-DAY           PIC 99.
      05  TODAYS-DATE               PIC 9(6).
      05  TODAYS-DATE-R REDEFINES TODAYS-DATE.
          10  TODAYS-MONTH          PIC 99.
          10  TODAYS-DAY            PIC 99.
          10  TODAYS-YEAR           PIC 99.
      05  PRESENT-TIME              PIC 9(8).
      05  PRESENT-TIME-R REDEFINES PRESENT-TIME.
          10  PRESENT-HOURS         PIC 99.
          10  PRESENT-MINUTES       PIC 99.
          10  FILLER                PIC X(4).
*
 01   COUNT-FIELDS                  COMP-3.
*
      05  RECORD-COUNT              PIC S9(5)      VALUE ZERO.
      05  SELECTED-RECORD-COUNT     PIC S9(5)      VALUE ZERO.
*
 01   CALCULATED-FIELDS             COMP-3.
*
      05  INVESTMENT-AMOUNT         PIC S9(7)V99.
      05  NO-OF-MONTHS-STOCK        PIC S9(3)V9.
*
 01   TOTAL-FIELDS                      COMP-3.
*
      05  SELECTED-LM-SALES-TOTAL       PIC S9(9)V99    VALUE ZERO.
      05  SELECTED-INVESTMENT-TOTAL     PIC S9(9)V99    VALUE ZERO.
*
 01   HEADING-LINE-1.
*
      05  FILLER                PIC X(7)   VALUE 'DATE:   '.
      05  HDG1-DATE             PIC 99/99/99.
      05  FILLER                PIC X(36)  VALUE SPACE.
      05  FILLER                PIC X(20)  VALUE 'MIKE MURACH & ASSOCI'.
      05  FILLER                PIC X(20)  VALUE 'ATES, INC.          '.
      05  FILLER                PIC X(31)  VALUE SPACE.
      05  FILLER                PIC X(6)   VALUE 'PAGE: '.
      05  HDG1-PAGE-NO          PIC ZZ9.
      05  FILLER                PIC X      VALUE SPACE.
*
 01   HEADING-LINE-2.
*
```

**Figure 4-22** The COBOL listing for the investment-listing program (part 2 of 7)

```
          05  HDG2-TIME-DATA.
              10  FILLER              PIC X(7)    VALUE 'TIME:   '.
              10  HDG2-HOURS          PIC 99.
              10  FILLER              PIC X       VALUE ':'.
              10  HDG2-MINUTES        PIC 99.
              10  FILLER              PIC X       VALUE SPACE.
              10  HDG2-TIME-SUFFIX    PIC X(2).
          05  FILLER                  PIC X(107)  VALUE SPACE.
          05  HDG2-REPORT-NUMBER      PIC X(10)   VALUE 'INV3520   '.
*
 01   HEADING-LINE-3.
*
          05  FILLER    PIC X(20)    VALUE '                    '.
          05  FILLER    PIC X(20)    VALUE '           INVENTOR'.
          05  FILLER    PIC X(20)    VALUE 'Y INVESTMENT LISTING'.
          05  FILLER    PIC X(20)    VALUE ' -- ITEMS WITH RETAI'.
          05  FILLER    PIC X(20)    VALUE 'L VALUE OVER $10,000'.
          05  FILLER    PIC X(20)    VALUE '                    '.
          05  FILLER    PIC X(12)    VALUE '            '.
*
 01   HEADING-LINE-4.
*
          05  FILLER    PIC X(20)    VALUE 'ITEM                '.
          05  FILLER    PIC X(20)    VALUE '         UNIT   QUAN'.
          05  FILLER    PIC X(20)    VALUE 'TITY    LAST      LAST'.
          05  FILLER    PIC X(20)    VALUE ' MONTH          INVEST'.
          05  FILLER    PIC X(20)    VALUE 'MENT     NO. OF MONTH'.
          05  FILLER    PIC X(20)    VALUE 'S                   '.
          05  FILLER    PIC X(12)    VALUE '            '.
*
 01   HEADING-LINE-5.
*
          05  FILLER    PIC X(20)    VALUE ' NO.    ITEM DESCRIPT'.
          05  FILLER    PIC X(20)    VALUE 'ION        PRICE  ON H'.
          05  FILLER    PIC X(20)    VALUE 'AND ORDER DATE  SALE'.
          05  FILLER    PIC X(20)    VALUE 'S IN $         IN RET'.
          05  FILLER    PIC X(20)    VALUE 'AIL $  INVENTORY ON '.
          05  FILLER    PIC X(20)    VALUE 'HAND                '.
          05  FILLER    PIC X(12)    VALUE '            '.
*
 01   INVESTMENT-LINE.
*
          05  IL-ITEM-NO               PIC Z(5).
          05  FILLER                   PIC X(2)    VALUE SPACE.
          05  IL-ITEM-DESC             PIC X(20).
          05  FILLER                   PIC X(2)    VALUE SPACE.
          05  IL-UNIT-PRICE            PIC ZZZ.99.
          05  FILLER                   PIC X(2)    VALUE SPACE.
          05  IL-ON-HAND               PIC -----9.
          05  FILLER                   PIC X(2)    VALUE SPACE.
          05  IL-LAST-ORDER-DATE       PIC 99/99/99.
          05  FILLER                   PIC X(3)    VALUE SPACE.
          05  IL-LAST-MONTH-SALES      PIC ---,---.99
                                       BLANK WHEN ZERO.
          05  FILLER                   PIC X(6)    VALUE SPACE.
          05  IL-INVESTMENT-AMOUNT     PIC --,---,---.99.
```

**Figure 4-22** The COBOL listing for the investment-listing program (part 3 of 7)

```
     05  IL-INVESTMENT-AMT-MESSAGE REDEFINES IL-INVESTMENT-AMOUNT
                                 PIC X(13).
     05  FILLER                  PIC X(6)    VALUE SPACE.
     05  IL-NO-OF-MONTHS-STOCK PIC ----.9.
     05  IL-NO-OF-MONTHS-STOCK-MESSAGE
             REDEFINES IL-NO-OF-MONTHS-STOCK
                                 PIC X(6).
     05  FILLER                  PIC X(35)   VALUE SPACE.
*
 01  TOTAL-LINE-1.
*
     05  TL1-RECORD-COUNT        PIC Z(5).
     05  FILLER                  PIC X(15)   VALUE ' RECORDS IN THE'.
     05  FILLER                  PIC X(12)   VALUE ' MASTER FILE'.
     05  FILLER                  PIC X(19)   VALUE SPACE.
     05  TL1-SEL-LM-SALES-TOTAL      PIC $$$$,$$$,$$$.99.
     05  FILLER                  PIC X(2)    VALUE ' *'.
     05  FILLER                  PIC X(2)    VALUE SPACE.
     05  TL1-SEL-INVESTMENT-TOTAL    PIC $$$$,$$$,$$$.99.
     05  FILLER                  PIC X(2)    VALUE ' *'.
     05  FILLER                  PIC X(5)    VALUE SPACE.
     05  TL1-SEL-NO-OF-MONTHS-STOCK PIC ZZZ.9.
     05  FILLER                  PIC X(2)    VALUE ' *'.
     05  FILLER                  PIC X(33)   VALUE SPACE.
*
 01  TOTAL-LINE-2.
*
     05  TL2-SEL-RECORD-COUNT    PIC Z(5).
     05  FILLER              PIC X(15)   VALUE ' RECORDS IN THI'.
     05  FILLER              PIC X(18)   VALUE 'S SELECTED LISTING'.
     05  FILLER              PIC X(94)   VALUE SPACE.
*
 PROCEDURE DIVISION.
*
 000-PREPARE-INVESTMENT-LISTING.
*
     OPEN INPUT  INVMAST
          OUTPUT INVLIST.
     PERFORM 100-FORMAT-REPORT-HEADING.
     PERFORM 300-PREPARE-INVESTMENT-LINE
         UNTIL INVMAST-EOF.
     PERFORM 500-PRINT-TOTAL-LINES.
     CLOSE INVMAST
           INVLIST.
     DISPLAY 'INV3520   I   1   NORMAL EOJ'.
     STOP RUN.
*
 100-FORMAT-REPORT-HEADING.
*
     ACCEPT PRESENT-DATE FROM DATE.
     MOVE PRESENT-MONTH TO TODAYS-MONTH.
     MOVE PRESENT-DAY   TO TODAYS-DAY.
     MOVE PRESENT-YEAR  TO TODAYS-YEAR.
     MOVE TODAYS-DATE   TO HDG1-DATE.
     ACCEPT PRESENT-TIME FROM TIME.
     IF PRESENT-HOURS < 1
```

Figure 4-22 The COBOL listing for the investment-listing program (part 4 of 7)

```
          MOVE 12 TO HDG2-HOURS
      ELSE
          IF PRESENT-HOURS < 13
              MOVE PRESENT-HOURS TO HDG2-HOURS
          ELSE
              SUBTRACT 12 FROM PRESENT-HOURS
                  GIVING HDG2-HOURS.
      MOVE PRESENT-MINUTES TO HDG2-MINUTES.
      IF PRESENT-HOURS < 12
          MOVE 'AM' TO HDG2-TIME-SUFFIX
      ELSE
          MOVE 'PM' TO HDG2-TIME-SUFFIX.
*
 300-PREPARE-INVESTMENT-LINE.
*
      PERFORM 310-READ-INVENTORY-RECORD.
      IF NOT INVMAST-EOF
          PERFORM 320-COMPUTE-INVENTORY-FIELDS
          IF INVESTMENT-AMOUNT > 10000
              PERFORM 330-PRINT-INVESTMENT-LINE.
*
 310-READ-INVENTORY-RECORD.
*
      READ INVMAST RECORD
          AT END
              MOVE 'Y' TO INVMAST-EOF-SWITCH.
      IF NOT INVMAST-EOF
          ADD 1 TO RECORD-COUNT.
*
 320-COMPUTE-INVENTORY-FIELDS.
*
      MULTIPLY IM-ON-HAND BY IM-UNIT-PRICE
          GIVING INVESTMENT-AMOUNT
          ON SIZE ERROR
              MOVE 9999999.99 TO INVESTMENT-AMOUNT
              MOVE 'Y' TO INVESTMENT-SIZE-ERROR-SWITCH.
      IF NOT INVESTMENT-SIZE-ERROR
          IF IM-LAST-MONTH-SALES > ZERO
              DIVIDE INVESTMENT-AMOUNT BY IM-LAST-MONTH-SALES
                  GIVING NO-OF-MONTHS-STOCK
                  ROUNDED
                  ON SIZE ERROR
                      MOVE 999.9 TO NO-OF-MONTHS-STOCK
          ELSE
              MOVE 999.9 TO NO-OF-MONTHS-STOCK
      ELSE
          MOVE 999.9 TO NO-OF-MONTHS-STOCK.
*
 330-PRINT-INVESTMENT-LINE.
*
      IF LINE-COUNT > LINES-ON-PAGE
          PERFORM 340-PRINT-HEADING-LINES.
      MOVE IM-ITEM-NO                TO IL-ITEM-NO.
      MOVE IM-ITEM-DESC              TO IL-ITEM-DESC.
      MOVE IM-UNIT-PRICE             TO IL-UNIT-PRICE.
      MOVE IM-ON-HAND                TO IL-ON-HAND.
```

**Figure 4-22** The COBOL listing for the investment-listing program (part 5 of 7)

```
    MOVE IM-LAST-ORDER-DATE        TO IL-LAST-ORDER-DATE.
    MOVE IM-LAST-MONTH-SALES       TO IL-LAST-MONTH-SALES.
    ADD IM-LAST-MONTH-SALES        TO SELECTED-LM-SALES-TOTAL.
    IF NOT INVESTMENT-SIZE-ERROR
        MOVE INVESTMENT-AMOUNT     TO IL-INVESTMENT-AMOUNT
        ADD INVESTMENT-AMOUNT      TO SELECTED-INVESTMENT-TOTAL
        MOVE NO-OF-MONTHS-STOCK TO IL-NO-OF-MONTHS-STOCK
    ELSE
        MOVE '    SIZE ERROR'      TO IL-INVESTMENT-AMT-MESSAGE
        MOVE '    N/A'             TO IL-NO-OF-MONTHS-STOCK-MESSAGE
        MOVE 'N'                   TO INVESTMENT-SIZE-ERROR-SWITCH.
    MOVE INVESTMENT-LINE           TO PRINT-AREA.
    PERFORM 360-WRITE-REPORT-LINE.
    MOVE 1 TO SPACE-CONTROL.
    ADD 1 TO SELECTED-RECORD-COUNT.
*
 340-PRINT-HEADING-LINES.
*
    ADD 1 TO PAGE-COUNT.
    MOVE PAGE-COUNT TO HDG1-PAGE-NO.
    MOVE HEADING-LINE-1 TO PRINT-AREA.
    PERFORM 350-WRITE-PAGE-TOP-LINE.
    MOVE HEADING-LINE-2 TO PRINT-AREA.
    MOVE 1 TO SPACE-CONTROL.
    PERFORM 360-WRITE-REPORT-LINE.
    MOVE HEADING-LINE-3 TO PRINT-AREA.
    PERFORM 360-WRITE-REPORT-LINE.
    MOVE HEADING-LINE-4 TO PRINT-AREA.
    MOVE 2 TO SPACE-CONTROL.
    PERFORM 360-WRITE-REPORT-LINE.
    MOVE HEADING-LINE-5 TO PRINT-AREA.
    MOVE 1 TO SPACE-CONTROL.
    PERFORM 360-WRITE-REPORT-LINE.
    MOVE 2 TO SPACE-CONTROL.
*
 350-WRITE-PAGE-TOP-LINE.
*
    WRITE PRINT-AREA
        AFTER ADVANCING PAGE.
    MOVE 1 TO LINE-COUNT.
*
 360-WRITE-REPORT-LINE.
*
    WRITE PRINT-AREA
        AFTER ADVANCING SPACE-CONTROL LINES.
    ADD SPACE-CONTROL TO LINE-COUNT.
*
 500-PRINT-TOTAL-LINES.
*
    MOVE RECORD-COUNT TO TL1-RECORD-COUNT.
    MOVE SELECTED-LM-SALES-TOTAL TO TL1-SEL-LM-SALES-TOTAL.
    MOVE SELECTED-INVESTMENT-TOTAL
        TO TL1-SEL-INVESTMENT-TOTAL.
    DIVIDE SELECTED-INVESTMENT-TOTAL BY SELECTED-LM-SALES-TOTAL
        GIVING TL1-SEL-NO-OF-MONTHS-STOCK
        ROUNDED
```

Figure 4-22 The COBOL listing for the investment-listing program (part 6 of 7)

```
        ON SIZE ERROR
            MOVE 999.9 TO TL1-SEL-NO-OF-MONTHS-STOCK.
    MOVE TOTAL-LINE-1 TO PRINT-AREA.
    MOVE 3 TO SPACE-CONTROL.
    PERFORM 360-WRITE-REPORT-LINE.
    MOVE SELECTED-RECORD-COUNT TO TL2-SEL-RECORD-COUNT.
    MOVE TOTAL-LINE-2 TO PRINT-AREA.
    MOVE 1 TO SPACE-CONTROL.
    PERFORM 360-WRITE-REPORT-LINE.
```

**Figure 4-22** The COBOL listing for the investment-listing program (part 7 of 7)

**The Working-Storage Section** In the Working-Storage Section, you can see a number of groupings that weren't in the inventory-listing program. Specifically, you can see groups for date-and-time fields, count fields, calculated fields, and total fields. As you become more familiar with report preparation programs, you'll realize that groups like these are found in most programs.

At first, it may seem like there are more date fields than you really need. So let me briefly describe the purpose of each. PRESENT-DATE is the field that will be used in the ACCEPT statement (remember, it has to be an elementary item). It's redefined so the individual date fields can be moved into the proper format in TODAYS-DATE-R. Then, TODAYS-DATE will be moved as a single field into the first heading line. I could have coded the month, day, and year fields in HEADING-LINE-1 and moved the PRESENT-DATE-R fields directly there (this is how I handled PRESENT-TIME). Then, I could have dropped out the TODAYS-DATE fields entirely. But in many programs, you'll need to use the date in some of your processing modules, so it's a good practice to keep the date in the proper format in working storage.

Note, as you review the groups in working storage, that four of them specify COMP-3 usage at the group level. That means that all of the fields in the group have that usage. When arithmetic fields have COMP-3 usage on an IBM mainframe, the program runs more efficiently. On the other hand, if the usage specifications were omitted, the program would still work.

If you check the descriptions for heading lines 3 through 5, you can see that all of them are described using the same coding technique. Here, each 05 level describes a 20-character or 12-character FILLER field. Then, I've filled in the nonnumeric literals to correspond to the specifications on the print chart. This technique, which can be used for most heading lines, makes it easy to code the headings initially, and it also makes them easy to modify later on.

In the descriptions for INVESTMENT-LINE and for the total lines, you can see some editing pictures that weren't used in the program in chapter 3. Also, you can see the BLANK WHEN ZERO clause used for one of the fields in the investment line. In actual practice, you probably wouldn't use this clause, but I wanted you to see it in a complete program.

In the descriptions for two of the INVESTMENT-LINE fields, you can see the use of REDEFINES. The investment amount is redefined so the message "SIZE ERROR" can be moved to an alphanumeric field rather than a numeric edited field. Similarly, the number-of-months-stock field is redefined so the literal "N/A" can be moved to an alphanumeric field rather than a numeric edited field. This is consistent with the rules for MOVE statements.

**The Procedure Division** If you study the Procedure Division, you should be able to figure out the flow of control from one paragraph to another. Since this program is similar to the one explained in detail in the preceding chapter, it shouldn't be too difficult for you. But it will take some concentration. If necessary, create some test data for the program and follow the statements of the program as it processes your test data.

After module 000 opens the two files used by the program, it performs module 100 to format the heading of the investment listing. Then, it calls module 300 to prepare the investment lines of the listing until there are no more inventory master records:

```
PERFORM 300-PREPARE-INVESTMENT-LINE
    UNTIL INVMAST-EOF.
```

Here, a condition name (INVMAST-EOF) is used to mean the same thing as INVMAST-EOF-SWITCH = 'Y'. The condition name is described in working storage with an 88 level description.

After module 300 has prepared all investment lines for the program, module 000 performs module 500 to print the total lines. Then, it closes the files and issues a DISPLAY statement that prints or displays this message:

```
INV3520  I  1  NORMAL EOJ
```

This means that the message is for information only (I), that it is the first message of the program (1), and that the program ran to a normal completion (End Of Job). On an IBM mainframe under DOS/VSE, this message will be printed at the end of the report, but on other systems it might be printed separately or displayed as you will learn in the next topic.

Module 100 uses the ACCEPT statement to get the date and time for the heading of the investment listing. Notice how it uses IF-ELSE statements to move the time to the heading in a readable format.

After module 300 performs module 310 to read an inventory master record, it uses nested IF statements to direct the execution of modules 320 and 330:

```
IF NOT INVMAST-EOF
    PERFORM 320-COMPUTE-INVENTORY-FIELDS
    IF INVESTMENT-AMOUNT > 10000
        PERFORM 330-PRINT-INVESTMENT-LINE.
```

First, it says to perform module 320 if the end of the inventory master file hasn't been detected. Here again, the condition name INVMAST-EOF is used for the condition. After module 320 has been executed, the second IF statement says to perform module 330 if the investment amount (calculated in module 320) is over $10,000. Remember that you can't use dollar signs or commas when coding a numeric literal, so $10,000 in the COBOL statement is simply 10000.

Module 310 reads an inventory record just as module 110 did in the program in chapter 3. However, the RECORD-COUNT field is increased by one each time a record is read before the end of the file has been reached. When counting the records in a file, we recommend that you put the counting code in the read module for the file.

Module 320 calculates the fields required for each investment line. In the MULTIPLY statement, it uses the ON SIZE ERROR clause to move a value of Y to a field named INVESTMENT-SIZE-ERROR-SWITCH. Then, it uses nested IF statements to put a proper value in NO-OF-MONTHS-STOCK. To start, it checks to see whether a size error on the investment field has occurred. If so, it skips down to the final ELSE clause and puts a value of 999.9 in NO-OF-MONTHS-STOCK. Otherwise, if the last month's sales are greater than zero, the program calculates the number of months stock on hand for the item; if the last month's sales are less than or equal to zero (ELSE), it moves 999.9 to the result field. This routine also moves 999.9 to the result field if a size error occurs during the execution of the DIVIDE statement.

Module 320 illustrates the importance of knowing what valid field sizes are. It also illustrates the importance of having valid data in all master file fields. If, for example, the programmer knows that the investment amount field size won't be exceeded, he can simplify this module considerably. On the other hand, valid data or not, it's relatively easy to exceed a field size during a DIVIDE operation, so it's worth coding an ON SIZE ERROR clause for the DIVIDE statement.

After module 330 checks to see whether the heading lines need to be printed on a new page, it arranges the data for an investment line using MOVE statements. Because a size error during the calculation for the investment amount affects the format of the printed output, this module uses the INVESTMENT-SIZE-ERROR condition in an IF statement to determine the printing of two of the fields. Within this IF statement, the switch is reset to N so it will work for the next record.

To accumulate the totals for the report, two ADD statements are used within module 330. Also, to count the number of records listed, a third ADD statement adds one to SELECTED-RECORD-COUNT. To write the investment line, module 330 calls module 360.

Module 340 simply moves data to PRINT-AREA and performs either module 350 or 360 to print it. Note the use of the SPACE-CONTROL field to control the spacing of the heading lines. Also, note how the PAGE-COUNT field is increased by one each time this module is performed.

Module 350 writes one line on the printer after advancing to the start of a new page. Then, it resets the LINE-COUNT field to a value of one (because one line has been printed on the page).

Module 360 writes one line on the printer after advancing SPACE-CONTROL lines. Then, it adds SPACE-CONTROL to the LINE-COUNT field so LINE-COUNT will represent the actual number of lines printed on a page including all heading lines and blank lines. This is a more sophisticated way to count print lines than the program in chapter 3 used.

Module 500, like any print module, moves the fields that are going to be printed to PRINT-AREA. Then, it writes a line using module 360. Here again, note the use of SPACE-CONTROL to control the spacing of the total lines.

## Discussion

Although I could describe the execution of this program in more detail, you should be able to figure out how this program works by yourself. It may not be easy when you first start studying COBOL listings. You may have to refer back to topics 1 and 2 to remind yourself what certain coding elements mean or how certain statements work. You may have to refer back to chapter 3, too. But you have to master this information by yourself if you want to become an effective COBOL programmer. So you must study this program until it makes sense to you.

## Terminology

common module

## Objectives

1. Given the program specifications, structure chart, and COBOL listing for a program, describe the operation of the program and the flow of control from one module to another. The program will use only the elements presented in chapters 3 and 4.

2. Given program specifications and a structure chart for a program that can be developed using only the COBOL elements presented in chapters 3 and 4, code an acceptable program.

## Topic 4 Compiler dependent code

The program in figure 4-22 is written for an IBM mainframe using the VS COBOL compiler running under DOS/VSE. However, because the COBOL code in the program is standard, it should run with only a couple of changes on any system that uses 1974 or 1985 ANS COBOL.

As I explained in chapter 3, you should code the program name, the Configuration Section, the system names in the SELECT statements, and the FD statements to conform to your compiler and your computer system. In addition, though, you may have to code the computational usage clauses shown in figure 4-22 in a different way. You may have to code your programs differently to provide for the way signs are handled by your system. And you should know how simple DISPLAY statements work on your system. In this topic, then, I will try to give you an idea of what you should know about usages, signs, and DISPLAY statements as they are implemented on your system.

To understand the compiler dependent code presented in this chapter, it helps to have some familiarity with the forms in which data can be stored in a computer. This is referred to as *data representation*. That's why I'll start by introducing you to the most common forms of data representation. After that, I'll show you how this information is related to usages, signs, and DISPLAY statements.

### Data representation

Most COBOL programs use one data format for character data and another format or two for numeric data. These formats can be referred to as alphanumeric, zoned decimal, packed decimal, and binary.

**Alphanumeric format** In *alphanumeric* (or *character*) *format*, one character of data is stored in each byte of storage. To be more specific, within a single byte of storage, any one of 256 different characters (letters, numbers, and special characters) can be represented. The codes used to represent these characters are called *EBCDIC* or *ASCII*, depending on the system you're using. On IBM systems, the code is EBCDIC; on most other systems, the code is ASCII.

When you're writing COBOL programs, you don't need to know what the codes for the characters are. Just realize that this is the data format that's used when the usage is DISPLAY. One character of data is stored in one byte of storage.

**Zoned decimal format** *Zoned decimal format* is alphanumeric representation as it applies to numeric fields. In this case, one digit is stored in one byte of storage. So a five-digit number requires five bytes of storage. On most systems, this is the way numeric fields are stored when the usage is DISPLAY. On some systems, you'll see zoned decimal format referred to as *external decimal format*.

When a signed number is stored in a zoned decimal field, the sign is normally carried in the rightmost byte of the field along with the rightmost digit of the field. In other words, the sign of the field doesn't require an extra byte of storage. This means, however, that the rightmost byte of a negative number has a different code than the rightmost byte of a positive number. And both have a different code than the rightmost byte of an unsigned number.

That explains why a DISPLAY statement won't always display a signed number in a readable form. If, for example, the number 184 in a three-byte field is to be displayed, it will be displayed as 184 if it is unsigned, as 18D if it is a signed positive number, and as 18M if it is a signed negative number. In other words, the code for + 4 is the same as for the character D; the code for − 4 is the same as for the character M.

Once again, in terms of COBOL programming, you don't need to know the exact codes for unsigned, positive, and negative numbers. But you should realize that they're different. Then, if you encounter problems related to signs, you'll know how to handle them.

**Packed decimal format** *Packed decimal format* is a compressed form of storage for numeric fields. It can also be referred to as *internal decimal format*. With the exception of the rightmost storage position, two digits are stored in each byte of a packed decimal field. The rightmost byte stores only one digit, but it also stores the sign of the field. Thus, a one-digit packed decimal field requires one byte of storage; a three-digit field requires two bytes; a five-digit field requires three bytes; and so on.

Because packed decimal fields on most systems lead to efficient editing, arithmetic, and comparison operations, they should be used for most of the fields that are involved in these operations. That's why specifying usages in a COBOL program can improve program efficiency. Because a packed decimal field always contains an odd number of digits, the picture for a packed decimal field should also carry an odd number of digits. This too can improve the efficiency of the program.

**Binary format** When *binary format* is used, as many digits as possible are stored in a single byte of storage. On an IBM mainframe, for example, a binary field occupies two, four, or eight bytes of storage depending on the number of digits in the field. If the field has from one to four digits in its picture, it occupies two bytes of storage. If from five to nine digits, it occupies four bytes. If from ten to eighteen digits, it occupies eight bytes. In any of these cases, the sign is included with the digits.

When arithmetic operations are performed on binary fields, the operations are likely to be executed faster than if packed decimal fields are used. However, more time is likely to be spent converting data from one form to another. For example, when a field is displayed, it has to be in alphanumeric format, and it's faster to convert from packed decimal to alphanumeric than from binary to alphanumeric. In brief, whatever you gain by using binary format in arithmetic operations is lost in data conversion and editing operations. As a result, when a computer provides for both packed decimal and binary formats, packed decimal is usually the preferred form for most of the fields in a business program.

I only mention binary format for those of you who use systems that support both packed decimal and binary data representation. Users of other systems won't have to choose between the two. In either case, you don't need to know the exact format of binary data. Just realize that it's available on some systems.

### USAGE clauses

On an IBM mainframe, a COBOL programmmer normally uses three different usages: DISPLAY, COMP-3, and COMP. On most other systems, a programmer normally uses only two different usages: DISPLAY and COMP or DISPLAY and COMP-3. And on some systems, you don't ever have to use anything but DISPLAY usage because the system provides for only one form of data representation.

Now that you know something about the forms of data representation, you should have a better idea of what USAGE clauses do. In general, they specify that a field should be stored in alphanumeric, zoned decimal, packed decimal, or binary format. By making these specifications correctly, you can improve the efficiency of the program. So let me describe again the three usages that you are likely to find on your system.

**DISPLAY usage** When you specify DISPLAY usage or you omit the USAGE clause, an alphabetic or alphanumeric field is stored in alphanumeric form. Similarly, a numeric field is stored in zoned decimal form. In either case, one character (letter, digit, or special character) is stored in one byte of storage.

**COMP usage** When you specify COMP usage for a numeric field, you either get packed decimal or binary format. This depends on the system you're using. On the Wang VS system, for example, you get packed decimal format. On an IBM mainframe, you get binary format.

**COMP-3 usage** Remember that COMP-3 usage is an IBM extension to the COBOL standards. As a result, it isn't available on all systems. When you specify COMP-3 on an IBM mainframe, you get packed decimal format.

When COMP-3 is available on other systems, it is usually for compatibility with programs written for IBM mainframes. So it will probably lead to packed decimal format. For instance, COMP-3 is supported in Microsoft COBOL for the IBM PC, and it leads to packed decimal fields on this system.

**Coding USAGE clauses on your system** On IBM mainframes, COMP-3 is commonly used for numeric fields. This leads to packed decimal format. Similarly, COMP-3 is the preferred numeric usage on the IBM PC when using Microsoft COBOL. So on either of these systems, you should code usages as shown in the investment-listing program in figure 4-22.

On most non-IBM systems, though, COMP is the preferred usage for numeric fields. On the Wang VS system, for example, COMP is the preferred usage and it leads to packed decimal format. On some non-IBM systems, COMP is likely to be the preferred usage even though it leads to binary format.

With this as background, you should find out what usages are available on your system and what the preferred usage for numeric fields is. On most systems, you will use only one computational usage for numeric fields, and it will either be COMP or COMP-3. But for some systems, you may have to get guidelines on using two or more computational usages.

On IBM systems, for example, you should eventually learn when to use COMP-3 and when to use COMP usage for a field. Fortunately, there are only a few cases in which you should use COMP. In this book, though, none of these special cases are covered, because they aren't required for most report preparation programs. As a result, all of the programs in this book use only COMP-3 usage for numeric fields.

### Signed fields

Most systems today handle signed fields the way I just described them when I presented the forms of data representation. In other words, when an S is specified in the picture of a zoned decimal field, the sign is carried in the rightmost byte of the field along with the rightmost digit of the field. Similarly, when an S is specified in the picture of a packed decimal field, the sign is carried in the rightmost byte along with the rightmost digit.

On some systems, though, the sign of a numeric field in DISPLAY usage is carried in a separate byte of storage. Since this can affect the size of the records you store on tape or disk devices, you should know how your system handles signs. On the other hand, the sign of a packed decimal field is always carried within the field so it never affects the size of a record.

**Example 1: Signs included in the rightmost bytes of zoned decimal fields**

```
 FD   INVMAST
      LABEL RECORDS ARE STANDARD
      RECORD CONTAINS 80 CHARACTERS.
*
 01   INVENTORY-MASTER-RECORD.
*
      .
      .
      05   INVENTORY-DATA.
           10   IM-REORDER-POINT         PIC S9(5).
           10   IM-ON-HAND               PIC S9(5).
           10   IM-ON-ORDER              PIC S9(5).
      05   SALES-DATA.
           .
           .
           10   IM-LAST-MONTH-SALES      PIC S9(5)V99.
           10   IM-LAST-YEAR-SALES       PIC S9(7)V99.
      05   FILLER                        PIC X(8).
```

**Example 2: Signs stored in separate bytes in zoned decimal fields**

```
 FD   INVMAST
      LABEL RECORDS ARE STANDARD
      RECORD CONTAINS 85 CHARACTERS.
*
 01   INVENTORY-MASTER-RECORD.
*
      .
      .
      05   INVENTORY-DATA.
           10   IM-REORDER-POINT         PIC S9(5).
           10   IM-ON-HAND               PIC S9(5).
           10   IM-ON-ORDER              PIC S9(5).
      05   SALES-DATA.
           .
           .
           10   IM-LAST-MONTH-SALES      PIC S9(5)V99.
           10   IM-LAST-YEAR-SALES       PIC S9(7)V99.
      05   FILLER                        PIC X(8).
```

**Figure 4-23** The effect of signs and usages on record sizes (part 1 of 2)

To illustrate, look at the examples in figure 4-23. In example 1, which could be for an IBM mainframe, the record description includes five signed fields in DISPLAY (zoned decimal) format. In this case, the computer system stores the sign along with one digit in the rightmost byte of a field, so the record is 80 bytes long. In example 2, which could be for a Wang VS system, the same record description requires 85 bytes because the computer stores the sign as a separate byte in each signed field. Finally, in example 3, which could be for an IBM mainframe, the five signed fields in examples 1 and 2 are all in

**Example 3: Signs included in the rightmost bytes of packed decimal fields**

```
 FD    INVMAST
       LABEL RECORDS ARE STANDARD
       RECORD CONTAINS 67 CHARACTERS.
*
 01    INVENTORY-MASTER-RECORD.
*
       .
       .
       05   INVENTORY-DATA               COMP-3.
            10   IM-REORDER-POINT        PIC S9(5).
            10   IM-ON-HAND              PIC S9(5).
            10   IM-ON-ORDER             PIC S9(5).
       05   SALES-DATA.
            .
            .
            10   IM-LAST-MONTH-SALES     PIC S9(5)V99     COMP-3.
            10   IM-LAST-YEAR-SALES      PIC S9(7)V99     COMP-3.
       05   FILLER                       PIC X(8).
```

**Figure 4-23** The effect of signs and usages on record sizes (part 2 of 2)

packed decimal format. In this case, since two digits are stored in each byte and the sign is included in the rightmost byte of each packed decimal field, the records are 67 bytes long.

To complicate matters, the Wang VS system can treat the sign of a zoned decimal field as either a separate byte or as an inclusion in the rightmost byte of a field. How the sign is treated is determined by an option that you can set when a program is compiled. Then, if a program that creates a disk file is compiled with the option set one way and a program that reads the file is compiled with the option set the other way, debugging problems will result. In other words, the second program will try to read a record that is shorter or longer than the actual record on disk.

I mention this only so you're aware that different systems handle signs in different ways. And these differences can affect the operation of a program. As a result, you should find out how signs are handled on your system. If they don't require separate bytes, they shouldn't affect any of your programs ever. If they do, you should keep this fact in the back of your mind so you will recognize situations in which signs may affect your coding.

### DISPLAY statements

As I mentioned in topic 2, DISPLAY statements can be used for occasional messages to the user or operator of the system. Since the form of a DISPLAY statement is standard, the statement in the program in

```
*** MESSAGE DISP BY COBOL
                    INFORMATION REQUIRED BY  PROGRAM  INVLIST
                              TO DEFINE DISPLAY

PRESS ENTER KEY TO CONTINUE PROGRAM

INV3520  I  1  NORMAL EOJ
```

**Figure 4-24** The screen displayed by the DISPLAY statement when executed on a Wang VS system

figure 4-22 should compile on any standard COBOL compiler. How it executes, though, will depend on the system.

On an IBM PC when using Microsoft COBOL, the DISPLAY statement in the investment-listing program will display upon the user's screen. Thus, this message will be displayed:

```
INV3520  I  1  NORMAL EOJ
```

After the message is displayed, the program will continue with the next statement in sequence, the STOP statement. Then, control will be passed back to the operating system, which will start the execution of the next program in sequence. And this may display a new screen, so the END OF JOB message won't stay on the screen for long.

In contrast, on the Wang VS system, the DISPLAY statement displays the screen shown in figure 4-24. In this case, the program waits until the user presses the ENTER key on the keyboard. Then, it continues with the next statement in sequence, the STOP statement, so the program ends.

Under DOS/VSE on an IBM mainframe, the DISPLAY messages are commonly interspersed with the printer output that comes from the WRITE statement. For the DISPLAY statement in figure 4-22, then, the message prints after the last total line of the investment report.

```
 IDENTIFICATION DIVISION.
*
 PROGRAM-ID.            INV3520.
*AUTHOR.                MIKE MURACH.
*
 ENVIRONMENT DIVISION.
*
 INPUT-OUTPUT SECTION.
*
 FILE-CONTROL.
     SELECT INVMAST ASSIGN TO SYS020-AS-INVMAST.
     SELECT INVLIST ASSIGN TO SYS006-UR-1403-S.
*
 DATA DIVISION.
*
 FILE SECTION.
*
 FD  INVMAST
     LABEL RECORDS ARE STANDARD
     RECORD CONTAINS 80 CHARACTERS.
*
 01  INVENTORY-MASTER-RECORD.
*
     .
     .
 FD  INVLIST
     LABEL RECORDS ARE OMITTED
     RECORD CONTAINS 132 CHARACTERS.
*
 01  PRINT-AREA                   PIC X(132).
*
```

**Figure 4-25** Compiler dependent code in the investment-listing program (part 1 of 2)

On an IBM mainframe under OS/MVS, the displayed messages can be printed as a separate listing. To do this, you direct the DISPLAY output to a separate print file through a statement in the job control procedure for running the program. I'll describe this in topic 3 of chapter 8.

As you can see, then, a DISPLAY statement works differently on different systems. You'll have to find out how these statements work on your system so you'll know where to find the output they produce.

## Discussion

This topic has presented some of the differences that you encounter when you move a program from one system to another. Keep in mind, though, that these differences are relatively trivial. For instance, the only changes that you would have to make to the program in figure

```
 WORKING-STORAGE SECTION.
*
 01  SWITCHES.
*
     .
     .
 01  PRINT-FIELDS                          COMP-3.
*
     05  SPACE-CONTROL                     PIC S9.
     05  LINES-ON-PAGE                     PIC S999        VALUE +55.
     05  LINE-COUNT                        PIC S999        VALUE +99.
     05  PAGE-COUNT                        PIC S999        VALUE ZERO.
*
 01  DATE-AND-TIME-FIELDS.
*
     .
     .
 01  COUNT-FIELDS                          COMP-3.
*
     05  RECORD-COUNT                      PIC S9(5)       VALUE ZERO.
     05  SELECTED-RECORD-COUNT             PIC S9(5)       VALUE ZERO.
*
 01  CALCULATED-FIELDS                     COMP-3.
*
     05  INVESTMENT-AMOUNT                 PIC S9(7)V99.
     05  NO-OF-MONTHS-STOCK                PIC S9(3)V9.
*
 01  TOTAL-FIELDS                          COMP-3.
*
     05  SELECTED-LM-SALES-TOTAL           PIC S9(9)V99    VALUE ZERO.
     05  SELECTED-INVESTMENT-TOTAL         PIC S9(9)V99    VALUE ZERO.
*
 01  HEADING-LINE-1.
*
     .
     .
```

**Figure 4-25** Compiler dependent code in the investment-listing program (part 2 of 2)

4-22 to get it to run on your system are highlighted in figure 4-25. In addition to the compiler dependent code described in chapter 3, you might have to change the four instances of COMP-3 usage to COMP usage. Also, depending on how your system handles signs, you may have to change the size given for INVMAST in the RECORD CONTAINS clause.

If you want a more complete understanding of how data is stored in your system and how USAGE clauses and signs can affect the efficiency of your programs, it helps to learn the assembler language for your system. This is particularly true for COBOL programmers on

IBM mainframes, because the architecture of these systems is quite complicated. In contrast, COBOL programmers on non-IBM systems will benefit less from a knowledge of assembler language.

If you're working on an IBM mainframe and you're interested in assembler language, we offer two books on the subject: *DOS/VSE Assembler Language* for DOS users and *OS/MVS Assembler Language* for OS users. If you read just the first eight chapters of one of these books, you'll find the answers to many of the questions you might have about the operation of your COBOL programs.

## Terminology

data representation
alphanumeric format
character format
EBCDIC code
ASCII code
zoned decimal format
external decimal format
packed decimal format
internal decimal format
binary format

## Objectives

1. Find out how to code usages, signs, and DISPLAY statements for your compiler and system.

2. Given program specifications and a structure chart for a program that can be developed using only the COBOL elements in chapters 3 and 4, code an acceptable program for your system.

Chapter 5

# COBOL elements the professionals use

In this chapter, you will learn more COBOL elements so you can write more complex programs. Topic 1 presents elements that you can code in the Procedure Division. Topic 2 shows you how to reuse code that has already been written and stored in a COPY library. Topic 3 shows you how to reuse code that has already been coded, compiled, tested, and stored in a subprogram library. Topic 4 presents a complete program that uses the elements of topics 1 through 3. And topic 5 presents two compiler dependencies that you should be aware of.

## Topic 1 Procedure Division elements

This topic presents some new code that you can use in the Procedure Division of your COBOL programs. Specifically, it presents advanced forms of the READ and WRITE statements. It presents one new statement, the COMPUTE statement. And it presents some advanced ways to code the conditions within IF or PERFORM statements.

### The READ INTO form of the READ statement

Figure 5-1 presents the complete format of a READ statement for a sequential file. When the INTO clause is used, the READ statement first reads a record into the area of storage defined after the FD statement for the file. In figure 5-1, that area is named RECORD-AREA. Then, the READ statement moves the record into the area specified by the INTO clause. In figure 5-1, that area is named INVENTORY-MASTER-RECORD. Thus, the READ INTO form of the READ statement is the equivalent of a READ statement followed by a MOVE statement.

The main reason for using the INTO option is that the data from the last record in a file is available after the AT END clause for that file has been executed. In contrast, if the data for the last input record hasn't been moved to working storage, it isn't available to the program after the AT END clause has been executed. Since many report preparation programs need to process the data in the last record in a file after the AT END clause has been executed, the READ INTO form of the READ statement is useful in many programs. You'll see READ INTO illustrated in the program in topic 4.

### The WRITE FROM form of the WRITE statement

Figure 5-2 presents the complete format of a WRITE statement for a print file. If the FROM option is used, the WRITE statement first moves the record in the area specified in the FROM clause to the area defined after the FD statement for the file. In figure 5-2, that means the WRITE statement moves HEADING-LINE-1 to PRINT-AREA. Then, it writes (or prints) the record. As a result, the WRITE FROM statement is the equivalent of a MOVE statement followed by a WRITE statement.

The FROM option is useful when a file has only one record format. Then, the WRITE FROM statement can be used to move the record into the output area and to write it. However, when a file consists of records with more than one record format, using the FROM option results in more than one WRITE statement for the file (one for

**Statement format**

```
READ file-name RECORD [INTO record-name]

    AT END imperative-statement
```

**Example**

```
 DATA DIVISION.
*
 FILE SECTION.
*
 FD  INVMAST
     LABEL RECORDS ARE STANDARD
     RECORD CONTAINS 80 CHARACTERS.
*
 01  RECORD-AREA                  PIC X(80).
*
     .
     .
*
 WORKING-STORAGE SECTION.
*
     .
     .
*
 01  INVENTORY-MASTER-RECORD.
*
     05  IM-ITEM-CODE             PIC X(5).
     05  IM-ITEM-DESCRIPTION      PIC X(20).
     .
     .
*
 PROCEDURE DIVISION.
*
     .
     .
     READ INVMAST INTO INVENTORY-MASTER-RECORD
         AT END
             MOVE 'Y' TO INVMAST-EOF-SW.
     .
     .
```

**Figure 5-1** The READ INTO statement for a sequential file

each record format). Since this causes your program to run less efficiently, you usually shouldn't use the FROM option of the WRITE statement for print files, except for the first heading line of a report when using the AFTER ADVANCING PAGE clause. It's usually okay to use the FROM option to print the first line on each page of a report because that line usually has only one format. This is illustrated in figure 5-2.

**Statement format**

```
WRITE record-name [FROM record-name]

    AFTER ADVANCING  {literal     [LINE ]}
                     {data-name   [LINES]}
                     {PAGE               }
```

**Example**

```
 DATA DIVISION.
*
 FILE SECTION.
*
      .
      .
*
 FD   INVLIST
      LABEL RECORDS ARE OMITTED
      RECORD CONTAINS 132 CHARACTERS.
*
 01   PRINT-AREA                   PIC X(132).
*
      .
      .
*
 WORKING-STORAGE SECTION.
*
      .
      .
*
 01   HEADING-LINE-1.
*
      05   FILLER                  PIC X(7)   VALUE 'DATE:'.
      05   HDG1-DATE               PIC 99/99/99.
      .
      .
*
 PROCEDURE DIVISION.
*
      .
      .
      WRITE PRINT-AREA FROM HEADING-LINE-1
          AFTER ADVANCING PAGE.
      .
      .
```

Figure 5-2 The WRITE FROM statement for a print file

## The COMPUTE statement

The format of the COMPUTE statement is given in figure 5-3. It can be used to express arithmetic calculations in a form that is reasonably

**Statement format**

```
COMPUTE data-name-1 [ROUNDED] [data-name-2 [ROUNDED]] ...

    = arithmetic-expression

    ON SIZE ERROR imperative-statement
```

**Examples**

```
COMPUTE TOTAL-HOURS = ZERO.

COMPUTE RECORD-COUNT = RECORD-COUNT + 1.

COMPUTE TOTAL-HOURS = YTD-HOURS + CURRENT-HOURS.

COMPUTE GROSS-PAY ROUNDED
    = HOURLY-RATE * CURRENT-HOURS
    ON SIZE ERROR
        PERFORM 560-PRINT-ERROR-MESSAGE.

COMPUTE MONTHLY-INTEREST MONTHLY-INTEREST-PAID ROUNDED
    = PRINCIPAL * RATE * DAYS / 365.
```

**Figure 5-3** The COMPUTE statement

close to normal arithmetic notation. For example,

```
COMPUTE NET-PAY ROUNDED = HOURS * RATE - DEDUCTIONS
```

can be used to indicate that the contents of the field named HOURS should be multiplied (*) by the contents of the field named RATE and the contents of the field named DEDUCTIONS should be subtracted (−) from the product. The result should be rounded and placed in the field named NET-PAY.

**Arithmetic expressions** In the format in figure 5-3, you can see that an *arithmetic expression* follows the equals sign in a COMPUTE statement. To form an arithmetic expression in COBOL, you use the *arithmetic operators* shown in figure 5-4. When an arithmetic operator is used within an expression, it must be preceded and followed by one or more spaces.

As you can see in figure 5-4, ** indicates exponentiation, which means "raise to the power of." Thus, X ** 2 is equivalent to the arithmetic expression $X^2$.

**The sequence of operations in an arithmetic expression** When a series of operations is given in an arithmetic expression, it's important

| Arithmetic operator | Meaning | Sequence |
|---|---|---|
| + | Addition | 3 |
| - | Subtraction | 3 |
| * | Multiplication | 2 |
| / | Division | 2 |
| ** | Exponentiation | 1 |

**Examples of arithmetic expressions**

```
7.5

FIELD-X + 1.5

PRINCIPAL * RATE * DAYS / 365

GROSS-PAY - FIT - SIT - FICA - OTHER-DEDUCTIONS

3.14 * (GM-RADIUS * GM-RADIUS)

((IM-UNIT-SALES * 50) / (IM-UNIT-COST * .30)) ** .5
```

**Figure 5-4** The arithmetic operators in arithmetic expressions

to know the order in which the operations will be executed. For example, the expression

```
H * R - D
```

will have different values depending on whether the multiplication or the subtraction is done first. If H = 40, R = 2, and D = 5.00, the value of the expression is 75.00 if the multiplication is done first or -120.00 if the subtraction is done first.

In COBOL, the order in which arithmetic operations are executed is this: (1) exponentiation, (2) multiplication and division, and (3) addition and subtraction. This is shown by the sequence codes in figure 5-4. If the same sequence level is used more than once in an expression, the sequence is from left to right for each level. For example, in the expression

```
H * R - D
```

multiplication takes place first. In the expression

```
A * B + C * D
```

first A and B are multiplied, next C and D are multiplied, and then the two products are added together to give the final result.

**Using parentheses to dictate the sequence of operations in an arithmetic expression** Sometimes an expression is so complex that it's hard to figure out the sequence of operations. In a case like this, you should use parentheses to dictate the sequence in which the operations should be done. When you use parentheses, the compiler performs operations within parentheses before operations outside parentheses. When there are parentheses within parentheses, the compiler performs the operations in the innermost set of parentheses first and works its way outward.

To illustrate, consider this expression:

```
A + B ** 3 / C - D * E * F
```

If no parentheses are used, the compiler will execute it using the sequence of operations indicated by the parentheses in this expression:

```
A + ((B ** 3) / C) - (D * E * F)
```

This means exponentiation will be done first, followed by multiplication and division from left to right, and finally addition and subtraction from left to right. But suppose that isn't the sequence of operations you want. To change the sequence you can use parentheses as in this example:

```
((A + B) ** 3) / ((C - D) * E) * F
```

In this case, the compiler performs the expressions (A + B) and (C − D) first; next, it takes the cube of (A + B) and multiplies (C − D) by E; then, it performs the final division and multiplication. Because parentheses can dictate as well as clarify the order in which an expression will be evaluated, you should use them frequently in your COMPUTE statements.

**Result fields in a COMPUTE statement** When the arithmetic expression in a COMPUTE statement is evaluated, intermediate results are produced. For instance, in the expression A * B / C, the computer multiplies A * B to produce an intermediate result before dividing this result by C to produce the final result.

The COBOL compiler determines the sizes of any intermediate result fields based on the sizes of the fields in the intermediate computation. If, for example, A and B are both two digits (PIC 99) in the computation A * B, the intermediate result field should provide for four digits (PIC 9999) because that's the maximum size that the result may be. You should realize, then, that an intermediate result field may provide for more digits than the final result field does.

As a programmer, your job is to make sure that the sizes of your intermediate result fields don't exceed the maximum size allowed by your system. This size varies from one system to another. If the size of an intermediate result field does exceed the maximum size allowed by your system, you should get a diagnostic message that alerts you to the problem. Then, to correct the problem, you can divide the COMPUTE statement into two or more other statements.

You should also realize that the ON SIZE ERROR clause in a COMPUTE statement applies only to the final result field, not to any intermediate results. Also, the ON SIZE ERROR clause will always be executed if an attempt is made to divide by zero, whether or not it occurred during an intermediate computation.

In the format in figure 5-3, you can see that a series of result fields is acceptable. They can be numeric or numeric edited fields. For instance,

```
COMPUTE FIELD-A FIELD-B ROUNDED =
    1.23 * FIELD-X + (FIELD-Y - FIELD-Z)
```

is an acceptable statement. Here, the result of the arithmetic expression is moved to FIELD-A and FIELD-B, but only the result in FIELD-B is rounded. A statement like this is useful when you need a rounded result for something like interest for the current month as well as an unrounded result for ongoing calculations.

## Condition tests in IF and PERFORM statements

In the last two chapters, you were introduced to simple *condition tests* as used in IF and PERFORM statements. In these statements, a condition is tested to determine whether it's true or false. Then, if it's true, the statement does one thing; if it's false, it does another.

Now you're going to learn how to code conditions that are far more complex than the ones you've seen thus far. In addition to relation tests, you can code sign and class tests; you can use arithmetic expressions within condition tests; and you can code compound conditions with or without implied subjects and relational operators.

**Relation tests** The top part of figure 5-5 presents the format of a *relation test*. That's the type of test you've been coding thus far. Note in the format, however, that a relation test can compare fields, literals, or arithmetic expressions.

In a simple test between two numeric fields, the fields are evaluated based on their numeric value; the picture or usage of the fields does not affect the results. Thus, 30.5 is less than 40 and 58 is greater than 40.00.

When a relation test compares alphanumeric data, the evaluation is made in a different way. The fields are evaluated character by character, from left to right. Since the computer considers A to have the least value and Z to have the greatest, it's fairly easy to compare purely alphabetic fields. For example, JONES comes before (is less than) THOMAS. However, when special characters and numbers are mixed in with letters, an alphanumeric test becomes difficult to evaluate. For instance, it's hard to say whether X-12-13 is less than or greater than X1213.

When an alphanumeric relation test is done, it is based on the *collating sequence* of a computer. In general, a system that uses EBCDIC

**Relation test**

```
                                      ⎧GREATER THAN⎫
                                      ⎪>           ⎪
⎧data-name-1            ⎫             ⎪EQUAL TO    ⎪  ⎧data-name-2            ⎫
⎨literal-1              ⎬  IS [NOT]   ⎨=           ⎬  ⎨literal-2              ⎬
⎩arithmetic-expression-1⎭             ⎪LESS THAN   ⎪  ⎩arithmetic-expression-2⎭
                                      ⎩<           ⎭
```

**Sign test**

```
                                       ⎧POSITIVE⎫
⎧data-name            ⎫   IS [NOT]     ⎨ZERO    ⎬
⎩arithmetic-expression⎭                ⎩NEGATIVE⎭
```

**Class test**

```
data-name IS [NOT]   ⎧NUMERIC   ⎫
                     ⎩ALPHABETIC⎭
```

**Figure 5-5** Condition tests that can be used in IF or PERFORM statements

code has one collating sequence, and a system that uses ASCII code has another one. In EBCDIC, for example, the special characters have the lowest values, followed by the letters A through Z, followed by the digits 0 through 9. As a result, the hyphen (-) has a lower value than the digits, so X-12-13 is less than X1213.

In general, you don't need to know the collating sequence for your computer, because most of your alphanumeric relation tests will be for equal or not equal conditions. You usually won't need to know whether one alphanumeric field like H&R has a higher value than another one like H-R. If, by chance, you do need to know the collating sequence, though, it should be available in one of your system's reference manuals.

One thing to remember when coding relation tests is to compare numeric items with numeric items and alphanumeric items with alphanumeric items. It's illegal to compare an alphabetic item with a numeric item, and, although an alphanumeric item can be compared with a numeric item of DISPLAY usage, the comparison takes place based on collating sequence instead of on the numeric value of the fields. Also, to make your programs run more efficiently, you should compare numeric items with items that have the same number of decimal places, and alphanumeric items with items that have the same number of characters.

**Sign tests** The middle part of figure 5-5 gives the format for a *sign test*. This simply tests whether a numeric item or an arithmetic expression is greater than, equal to, or less than zero. In this case, zero is considered to be neither positive nor negative. As you would expect, a sign test can be used on numeric data items of any usage.

Sign tests aren't that useful, because you can do the same comparison with a relation test. In some cases, though, the use of sign tests can simplify your coding.

**Class tests** The last part of figure 5-5 gives the format for a *class test*. The alphabetic form of this test can be performed on an elementary alphabetic or alphanumeric field. If the field consists entirely of the letters A through Z and blanks (SPACE), the field is considered to be alphabetic.

The numeric form of this test can be performed on an elementary item that is (1) alphanumeric or (2) numeric with DISPLAY usage. An alphanumeric item is considered numeric if all bytes consist of the digits 0 through 9. Likewise, an *unsigned* numeric item of DISPLAY usage is considered numeric if it contains only digits and does not contain a sign. A *signed* numeric item is considered numeric if it contains all digits along with a valid sign.

Because a class test can only be used on an elementary item, you will occasionally want to use a REDEFINES clause in conjunction with a class test. This is illustrated by the example in figure 5-6. Here, the REDEFINES clause is used to redefine INVOICE-DATE. Then, INVOICE-DATE-R can be tested with a single class test as in this statement:

```
IF INVOICE-DATE-R IS NUMERIC
    MOVE 'Y' TO VALID-DATE-SW
ELSE
    MOVE 'N' TO VALID-DATE-SW.
```

Otherwise, each of the three fields within INVOICE-DATE would have to be tested individually for numeric validity.

As you might guess, class tests aren't too useful in report preparation programs. So you'll rarely, if ever, need to use them in the programs you write for this course.

**Using arithmetic expressions within conditions** As I've mentioned, you can use arithmetic expressions in some condition tests. As you can see in figure 5-5, arithmetic expressions can be used in relation or sign tests, but not in class tests. If necessary, parentheses can be used within the arithmetic expression to dictate the order of operations, and they should always be used if they make the expression easier to understand.

In general, though, you should avoid using arithmetic expressions in condition tests. Instead, you should do the calculation in one statement and the condition test in a second statement. Then, if the program specifications change and the result of the calculation is needed in another part of the program, you don't have to code the calculation in two different places. This can also make your program run more efficiently.

```
 DATA DIVISION.
*
       .
       .
       05  INVOICE-DATE.
           10  INVOICE-MONTH                          PIC 99.
           10  INVOICE-DAY                            PIC 99.
           10  INVOICE-YEAR                           PIC 99.
       05  INVOICE-DATE-R REDEFINES INVOICE-DATE      PIC X(6).
       .
       .
*
 PROCEDURE DIVISION.
*
       .
       .
       IF INVOICE-DATE-R IS NUMERIC
           MOVE 'Y' TO VALID-DATE-SW
       ELSE
           MOVE 'N' TO VALID-DATE-SW.
       .
       .
```

**Figure 5-6** A class test used with REDEFINES that checks a date field to make sure it's numeric

**Compound conditions** A *compound condition* is created by using the words AND and OR as shown in figure 5-7. Compound conditions can be used in either PERFORM or IF statements. Relation, sign, or class tests can be used to express the conditions within a compound condition, and arithmetic expressions can be used within the relation or sign tests.

In a compound condition, AND means "both" and OR means "either or both." In other words, when using AND, both conditions must be true before the compound condition is true. When using OR, the compound condition is true if either condition or both conditions are true.

When a compound condition is evaluated, the NOT conditions are evaluated first, followed next by the AND conditions, and then by the OR conditions. Because compound conditions can be confusing, parentheses should be used whenever appropriate to dictate the sequence of evaluation and to improve clarity.

To illustrate, how do you think your compiler would evaluate this expression based on the rules of sequence:

```
A > B OR A = C AND D NOT POSITIVE
```

Confusing, isn't it? However, the sequence can be shown by using parentheses in this way:

```
(A > B) OR (A = C AND (D NOT POSITIVE))
```

**Proper indentation when using compound conditions**

```
PERFORM paragraph-name
    UNTIL condition-1
      AND condition-2
       OR condition-3
      AND condition-4.

IF         condition-1
       OR condition-2
      AND condition-3
    statement-group-1
ELSE
    statement-group-2.
```

**Examples**

```
IF         EM-HOURS IS NUMERIC
      AND EM-RATE IS NUMERIC
    PERFORM 320-CALCULATE-EMPLOYEE-PAY.


IF         AP-CODE < 18
       OR AP-CODE = 1
    PERFORM 380-PRINT-ERROR-MESSAGE
ELSE
    PERFORM 330-LOOKUP-INSURANCE-RATE.


PERFORM 430-SEARCH-STATE-TABLE
    UNTIL STATE-CODE = TABLE-STATE-CODE
       OR TABLE-STATE-CODE = ZZ.


IF         (CM-TIMES-DUNNED < 4
            AND CM-CUST-YEARS > 2)
      AND CM-OVER-60-BAL-OWED = ZERO
    PERFORM 550-PREPARE-SHIPPING-ORDER
ELSE
    IF         (CM-TIMES-DUNNED > 3
                OR CM-CUST-YEARS NOT > 2)
          AND CM-OVER-60-BAL-OWED > ZERO
        PERFORM 560-PRINT-REFUSE-CREDIT-LINE
    ELSE
        PERFORM 570-PRINT-REFER-TO-MGR-LINE.
```

**Figure 5-7** The use of compound conditions in PERFORM or IF statements

As in arithmetic expressions, conditions within parentheses are evaluated first.

Figure 5-7 shows the proper use of indentation when coding compound conditions. In the first three examples, no parentheses are necessary because the indentation makes the meaning clear. In the last example, indentation is combined with parentheses to make the coding clear, even though the example is a nested IF statement with compound conditions at two different levels.

Although COBOL allows compound conditions of great complexity, it's best to keep them relatively simple. Then, programming errors are less likely to occur, and program changes can be made more easily.

If you encounter problems when using compound conditions in an IF statement, remember that you can write any compound condition as a series of nested IF statements. For instance,

```
IF          condition-1
        AND condition-2
       PERFORM ROUTINE-A
```

is the same as

```
IF condition-1
    IF condition-2
        PERFORM ROUTINE-A
```

So don't hesitate to use nested IFs if they improve the clarity of your code.

**Implied subjects and relational operators** If you want to compare a single field to two or more values in a condition, you can code the comparison like this:

```
    AP-AGE < 60
AND AP-AGE > 18
```

Or you can write it this way:

```
AP-AGE < 60 AND > 18
```

In the AND portion of this example, AP-AGE is the *implied subject*, since it's not written out. In other words, it's implied that AP-AGE is to be compared to 18 because AP-AGE is the most recently stated subject.

You can also use *implied relational operators*. For example,

```
    AP-AGE < 60
AND AP-AGE > 18
AND AP-AGE > PREVIOUS-AGE
```

can be written

```
    AP-AGE < 60
AND AP-AGE > 18 AND PREVIOUS-AGE
```

Here, since there's no relational operator given right before PREVIOUS-AGE, the last-stated operator is assumed to still be in effect. To make this example even more brief, you can combine an implied subject with an implied operator as follows:

```
    AP-AGE < 60
AND > 18 AND PREVIOUS-AGE
```

The word NOT can also be used in conjunction with implied subjects and relational operators. For instance,

```
AP-AGE NOT > 18 OR PREVIOUS-AGE
```

is equivalent to

```
   AP-AGE NOT > 18
OR AP-AGE NOT > PREVIOUS-AGE
```

Often, however, the use of NOT can lead to confusion within compound conditions.

When should you use implied subjects and relational operators? I think common sense is your best guide. If your code is easy to understand even though you've used implied subjects and operators, by all means use them. But if the code becomes confusing, you should state the complete condition using indentation and parentheses. And check out your compiler, too. In our shop, we avoid the use of implied subjects and operators because two of the compilers we've used have had bugs related to this code.

### Discussion

You probably won't understand or appreciate all of the code presented in this topic until you see how it's used in a complete program. As a result, topic 4 presents a complete program that includes most of the code in this topic.

### Terminology

arithmetic expression
arithmetic operator
condition test
relation test
collating sequence
sign test
class test
compound condition
implied subject
implied relational operator

### Objective

Apply the COBOL elements presented in this topic to your application programs.

## Topic 2 How to use the COPY library

As you have already seen, a large portion of a typical COBOL program consists of routine descriptions for files, records, and fields. Since a file is normally processed by several programs, a lot of effort would be wasted if each programmer had to code the same descriptions for each program. Also, there would probably be minor differences in the way each programmer defined the files and records...differences that could lead to errors.

Fortunately, though, segments of COBOL code can be written just once and stored in a *source statement library*. Then, you can copy the segments of code into your programs using COPY statements. This will save coding time, promote consistency between programs, and reduce errors.

### The COPY library

Normally, you can have one or more source statement libraries for each language you use on your system. These libraries are stored on disk devices so the segments of code within them can be accessed rapidly. Since you use the COPY statement in COBOL to copy segments of code from a library into your program, a COBOL source statement library is often referred to as a *COPY library*. From now on, I'll refer to COBOL source statement libraries as COPY libraries.

Each segment of code in the COPY library can be called a *COPY member*. On IBM mainframes, COPY members are also called *COPY books*. And on other systems, they may be called by other names.

Each COPY member in a library is identified by a unique name that can be called a *member name*, *book name*, or *text name*. In this chapter, we'll use the term *text name* to refer to the name that identifies a COPY member. That is consistent with most COBOL manuals.

### The COPY statement

Figure 5-8 illustrates the use of a COPY library. Here, a COPY member contains the record and field descriptions for a transaction record. The text name for this COPY member is TRANREC. In the Data Division, the following COPY statement specifies that the member named TRANREC should be copied into the program:

```
COPY TRANREC.
```

Then, when the source program is compiled, the statements from the COPY library are copied into the program and printed on the source

**TRANREC member in the COPY library**

```
*
 01  INVENTORY-TRANSACTION-RECORD.
*
     05  TR-CODE                PIC X.
     05  TR-ITEM-NO             PIC 9(5).
     05  TR-QUANTITY            PIC 9(5).
     05  TR-REF-NO              PIC X(6).
     05  TR-REF-DATE            PIC X(6).
```

**COPY statement in the Data Division**

```
COPY TRANREC.
```

**Resulting source code as printed on the source listing**

```
            COPY TRANREC.
C          *
C           01  INVENTORY-TRANSACTION-RECORD.
C          *
C               05  TR-CODE                PIC X.
C               05  TR-ITEM-NO             PIC 9(5).
C               05  TR-QUANTITY            PIC 9(5).
C               05  TR-REF-NO              PIC X(6).
C               05  TR-REF-DATE            PIC X(6).
```

**Figure 5-8** Using the COPY statement to copy a record description into the Data Division of a program

listing. Usually, the letter C or some other character like a plus sign is printed to the left of each copied statement on the source listing to show that it has been copied into the program.

A COPY statement can be used wherever a programmer-defined word (name), a reserved word, a literal, a PICTURE character string, or a comment entry can be used. It can also be used wherever a separator like a space or a period can be used. In other words, a COPY statement can generally be used in any logical place within a program. Its format is simply the word COPY followed by the text name of the member that you want to copy into the program.

Once a COPY member has been copied into a program, it is treated as a part of the program. In the case of a record description like the one in figure 5-8, the programmer can use any of the names in the COPY member in statements in the Procedure Division. For instance, she can use the name INVENTORY-TRANSACTION-RECORD to refer to the entire record, and she can use TR-CODE and TR-ITEM-NO to refer to two of the fields within the record.

### Guidelines for using the COPY library

So far, I've shown you how to use the COPY library and COPY statement. Now, let me give you some ideas about where in a program you should use COPY statements.

**File and record descriptions** Storing file and record descriptions is the most important job of the COPY library. Besides saving programmer time by eliminating repetitious coding, this ensures that all the programs within an installation will use the same names for the records and fields within a file. This, in turn, reduces confusion, program bugs, and interface problems between programs written by different programmers.

At the least, then, the COPY library should contain a COPY member for each record description used within each file of a system. And you should always copy these descriptions into your programs. Then, if a change must be made to a description, a change to one COPY member makes it possible for all programs using the COPY member to be changed simply by recompiling them. In addition, unless system limitations make this impossible, you may want to use COPY members for the SELECT and FD statements of the files within your system.

If you're writing the first program that processes a file, you should see to it that the file and record descriptions are stored in the COPY library. On the other hand, if your program is going to use files that have already been stored in the COPY library, you should get listings of the members so you'll know what code is going to be copied into your program.

**Tables** Another common use of the COPY library is to store commonly used tables that aren't subject to a lot of change. For example, suppose a table contains the names of the 50 states as well as their two-letter abbreviations. This table shouldn't ever need to be changed, and it should be used frequently by programmers who want to convert a state code to the expanded state name or vice versa.

**Procedure Division paragraphs** In general, you shouldn't use COPY members for code in the Procedure Division because the paragraph names and data names usually have to be changed to suit your program. Although there is a REPLACING clause that you can use with the COPY statement to modify code as it's copied into your program, it's hard to use it efficiently. That's why we don't recommend using it, and that's why we haven't presented it in this book.

Instead, we recommend that you copy the Procedure Division code you want from a previous program using the copy facility of your system's editor. Or, you can copy the code you need by entering it into the system manually. Then, you can change the names to suit your program, and the code becomes a permanent part of your program. In contrast, the COPY statement copies code into your program every time the program is compiled.

### Discussion

A professional programmer uses COPY statements in almost every program. Usually, right after you get complete specifications for a program, you should get listings of all the COPY members that might be applicable to your program. In fact, in a modern COBOL shop, the program specifications should include listings of the COPY members that define the files and records that the program uses.

### Terminology

source statement library
COPY library
COPY member
COPY book
member name
book name
text name

### Objective

Given program specifications and listings of related members in a COPY library, use the COPY statement to copy the members into your program.

## Topic 3 How to use subprograms

Some processing routines are so general that they can be used in many different programs. In our shop, for example, all of our edit programs check state codes and zip codes to make sure that they're valid. And all our report preparation programs get the date and time so they can be printed in the report headings. Needless to say, it would be a waste of programming effort to develop routines like this from scratch each time they were needed.

Fortunately, though, a commonly used routine can be coded, compiled, and tested, after which it can be stored in a *subprogram library*. Then, this *subprogram* can be called by any COBOL programs that need to use its function. This saves coding, compiling, and testing time, and it reduces programming errors.

### The subprogram library

Normally, you can have one or more subprogram libraries on your system. These libraries are stored on disk devices so the segments of code within them can be accessed rapidly. On IBM systems, these libraries are called *relocatable libraries* because the modules within them must be relocated by the linkage editor before they can be executed. On other systems, these libraries are called *object libraries* to distinguish them from source libraries.

The subprograms in a subprogram library have already been compiled and tested, so they consist of object code. As a result, each subprogram can also be called an *object module*. Before a subprogram can be executed, the linkage editor must link it with the program that uses it.

Each subprogram in a library is identified by a unique name that can be called a *subprogram name*. On IBM mainframes, you'll also hear these names referred to as *module names*.

### The CALL statement

To execute a subprogram, a COBOL program issues a CALL statement, as shown in figure 5-9. The program that contains the CALL statement is referred to as the *calling program* (or *calling module*). When it passes control to the subprogram, it *calls* the subprogram. Sometimes, you'll hear the subprogram referred to as the *called module*, or the *called program*.

As you can see in the CALL statement format in figure 5-9, the name of the subprogram can be followed by a USING clause that identifies one or more data items that are *passed* to the subprogram. If more than one data item is used, the order in which they are listed

**Statement format**

```
CALL 'subprogram-name' [USING data-name ...]
```

**Example**

```
 DATA DIVISION.
*
      .
      .
      05   DEVIATION-TOTAL               PIC 9(5)      COMP.
      05   DEVIATION-TOTAL-SQ-ROOT       PIC 9(5)V99   COMP.
      .
      .
*
 PROCEDURE DIVISION.
*
      .
      .
      CALL 'SQROOT' USING DEVIATION-TOTAL
                          DEVIATION-TOTAL-SQ-ROOT.
      MOVE DEVIATION-TOTAL-SQ-ROOT TO SL-DEVIATION-TOTAL-SQ-ROOT.
      .
      .
```

**Figure 5-9** Calling a subprogram that takes the square root of the first field passed to it and puts the result in the second field

must correspond to the order in which the subprogram expects to receive them. Also, the pictures and usages of the fields must correspond to the expectations of the subprogram. As a result, you must get detailed specifications about the subprogram so you can pass it the fields it needs in the order and with the formats it expects.

In figure 5-9, the subprogram calculates the square root of the number in the first field that is passed to it and puts the result in the second field. As a result, the CALL statement in the calling program is coded as follows:

```
CALL 'SQROOT' USING DEVIATION-TOTAL
                    DEVIATION-TOTAL-SQ-ROOT.
```

Here, the name of the subprogram is SQROOT; the name of the field to be operated upon is DEVIATION-TOTAL; and the name of the field that should receive the result is DEVIATION-TOTAL-SQ-ROOT. After the subprogram has calculated the square root of DEVIATION-TOTAL, it moves the result to DEVIATION-TOTAL-SQ-ROOT and returns control to the first statement after the CALL statement in the calling program. In figure 5-9, that statement is a MOVE statement.

Notice that nothing has been said about the language in which the subprogram is written. It may have been written in COBOL, but it may also have been written in another language. Since the object module for the calling program is linked with the object module for the subprogram, it doesn't matter what language the subprogram was written in.

### Testing and debugging problems

When you write a program that calls one or more subprograms, you should get the specifications for each subprogram before you code your program. That way you'll know how to define the records or fields that each subprogram requires. You'll also know in what sequence to code the data names in the USING portion of the CALL statement.

When you're testing a program that calls one or more subprograms, you may encounter some problems that are difficult to debug. If, for example, a program is cancelled during the execution of one of the subprograms, which module caused the problem: the calling program or the subprogram?

When a subprogram fails or returns incorrect data to the calling program, the first thing to do is make sure that the fields were passed to the subprogram in the right sequence and with the right formats. Most of the time, you'll find that the calling program passed data in a form that wasn't expected by the subprogram. This is particularly true if the subprogram has been used so long that it has been thoroughly tested.

If you're sure that your program has passed data to the subprogram properly and you're not sure that the subprogram has been thoroughly tested, it's possible that the problem is in the subprogram. In this case, you should pass the problem on to the person who is responsible for maintaining the subprogram. In *Part 2* of this course, you will learn how to write and maintain COBOL subprograms yourself.

### Discussion

A professional programmer uses CALL statements in almost every program. Usually, right after you get complete specifications for a program, you should check your subprogram library to see whether it offers any functions that you might find useful in your program. Then, when you design the structure chart for your program, you draw a striped box on the chart for each subprogram that you'll use. You'll see this illustrated in the next topic.

### Terminology

subprogram library
subprogram
relocatable library
object library
object module
subprogram name
module name
calling program
calling module
calling a subprogram
called module
called program
passing data to a subprogram

### Objective

Given program specifications and subprogram specifications, use CALL statements to call the required subprograms whenever needed by your program.

## Topic 4 The investment-listing program

In the last chapter, I presented an investment-listing program to show you how the COBOL elements work together. In this topic, I'll present that same program again, but I'll use the elements presented in the first three topics of this chapter whenever they're appropriate. Keep in mind that the investment-listing program in this topic executes in exactly the same way that the program in the last chapter does. However, the program in this topic is written in a more professional style using COPY and CALL statements.

If you want to review the specifications for the investment-listing program, you'll find them in figures 4-18, 4-19, and 4-20 in the last chapter. The program reads a sequential inventory master file and prints a listing of all items in inventory that have an investment amount of over $10,000. To develop the program in this chapter, though, the programmer has two COPY members and two subprograms available to her.

### The structure chart

Figure 5-10 presents the structure chart for the investment-listing program of this chapter. This chart is just like the chart in figure 4-21, except that two subprogram modules have been added to it. Each subprogram module has a stripe at its top to show that it represents a subprogram and not a COBOL module.

Within each subprogram stripe, the name of the subprogram is given. In other words, this program will call two subprograms named SYSDATE and SYSTIME. SYSDATE will be used to get the current date in its proper format for use in the heading line for the investment listing. SYSTIME will be used to get the current time and place it in its proper format in the heading line.

### The COBOL listing

Figure 5-11 presents the COBOL listing for the new version of the investment-listing program. Like the other program listings in this book, this one is for an IBM mainframe using the VS COBOL compiler under the DOS/VSE operating system. Since this program is so much like the one in the last chapter, some of the repeated code isn't shown in figure 5-11. Within the code that is shown, I have shaded the code that differs from the code in figure 4-22.

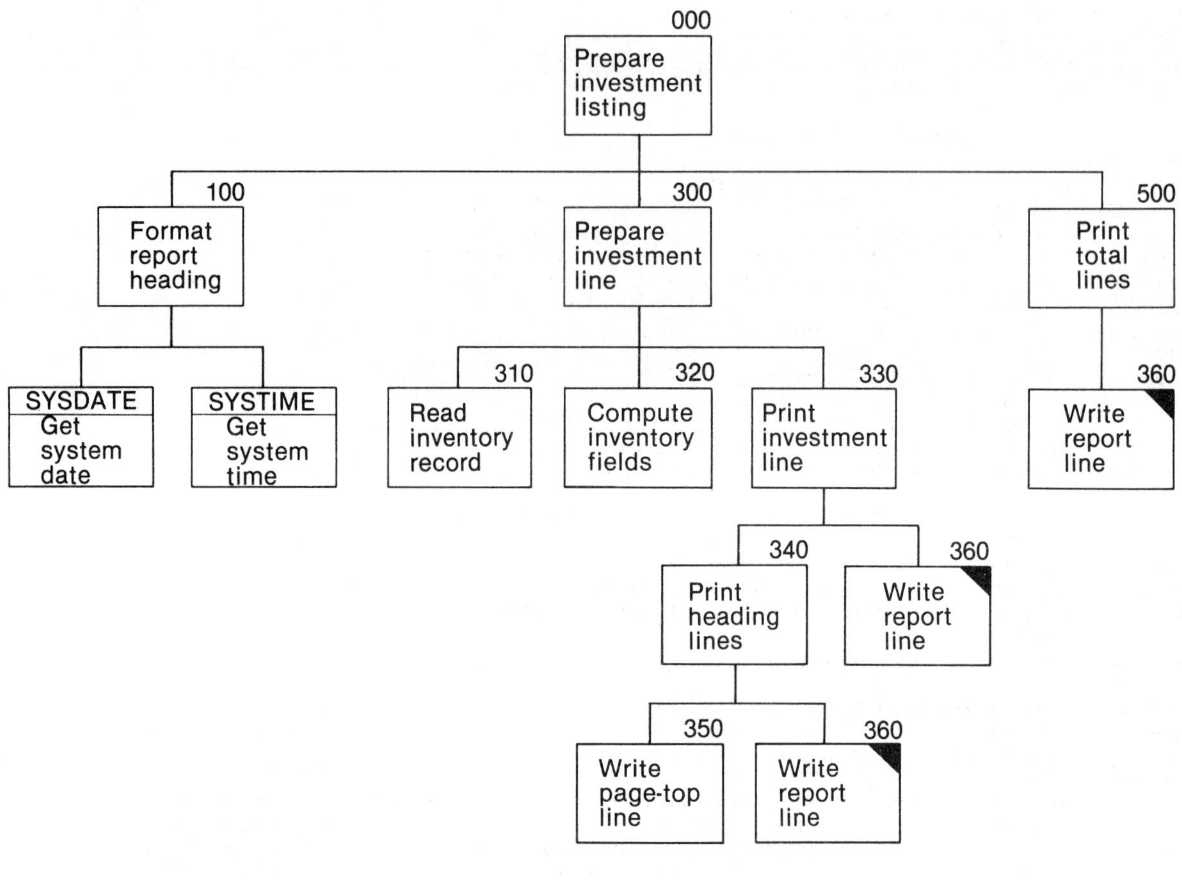


**Figure 5-10** The structure chart for the investment-listing program using two subprograms

**The Data Division** In the Data Division, you can see that two COPY statements are used to copy members from the COPY library into this program. The first one copies a member named INVMAST into the program. This is the record description for the inventory master record. Notice that this description is copied into the Working-Storage Section and that the record description after the FD statement for the file simply defines the record area with a length of 80 bytes. Later on, you'll see how the READ INTO statement works in conjunction with these record descriptions.

The second COPY statement copies a member named RPTHDG14 into the program. This member defines the first two heading lines of the report. Since it defines them in our company's standard report heading format, it is used in all of our report preparation programs for 14-inch wide reports. For narrower reports, we use other COPY members named RPTHDG11 (for 11-inch reports) and RPTHDG85 (for 8-and-one-half-inch reports).

```
000100 IDENTIFICATION DIVISION.
000200*
000300 PROGRAM-ID.        INV3520.
000400*AUTHOR.            MIKE MURACH.
000500*
000600 ENVIRONMENT DIVISION.
000700*
000800 INPUT-OUTPUT SECTION.
000900*
001000 FILE-CONTROL.
001100     SELECT INVMAST ASSIGN TO SYS020-AS-INVMAST.
001200     SELECT INVLIST ASSIGN TO SYS006-UR-1403-S.
001300*
001400 DATA DIVISION.
001500*
001600 FILE SECTION.
001700*
001800 FD  INVMAST
001900     LABEL RECORDS ARE STANDARD
002000     RECORD CONTAINS 80 CHARACTERS.
002100*
002200 01  INVENTORY-MASTER              PIC X(80).
002300*
002400 FD  INVLIST
002500     LABEL RECORDS ARE OMITTED
002600     RECORD CONTAINS 132 CHARACTERS.
002700*
002800 01  PRINT-AREA                    PIC X(132).
002900*
003000 WORKING-STORAGE SECTION.
003100*
003200 01  SWITCHES.
003300*
003400     05  INVMAST-EOF-SWITCH                PIC X       VALUE 'N'.
003500         88  INVMAST-EOF                               VALUE 'Y'.
003600     05  INVESTMENT-SIZE-ERROR-SWITCH      PIC X       VALUE 'N'.
003700         88  INVESTMENT-SIZE-ERROR                     VALUE 'Y'.
003800*
003900 01  PRINT-FIELDS                  COMP-3.
004000*
004100     05  SPACE-CONTROL             PIC S9.
004200     05  LINES-ON-PAGE             PIC S999 VALUE +55.
004300     05  LINE-COUNT                PIC S999 VALUE +99.
004400     05  PAGE-COUNT                PIC S999 VALUE ZERO.
004500*
004600 01  DATE-FIELDS.
004700*
004800     05  TODAYS-DATE                 PIC 9(6).
004900     05  TODAYS-DATE-R REDEFINES TODAYS-DATE.
005000         10  TODAYS-MONTH            PIC 99.
005100         10  TODAYS-DAY              PIC 99.
005200         10  TODAYS-YEAR             PIC 99.
005300*
005400 01  COUNT-FIELDS                    COMP-3.
005500*
005600     05  RECORD-COUNT                PIC S9(5)      VALUE ZERO.
005700     05  SELECTED-RECORD-COUNT       PIC S9(5)      VALUE ZERO.
005800*
005900 01  CALCULATED-FIELDS               COMP-3.
```

**Figure 5-11** Highlights of the COBOL listing for the investment-listing program using two COPY and two CALL statements (part 1 of 4)

```
  006000*
  006100        05  INVESTMENT-AMOUNT        PIC S9(7)V99.
  006200        05  NO-OF-MONTHS-STOCK       PIC S9(3)V9.
  006300*
  006400 01  TOTAL-FIELDS                         COMP-3.
  006500*
  006600        05  SELECTED-LM-SALES-TOTAL      PIC S9(9)V99    VALUE ZERO.
  006700        05  SELECTED-INVESTMENT-TOTAL    PIC S9(9)V99    VALUE ZERO.
  006800*
  006900 COPY INVMAST.
C            01  INVENTORY-MASTER-RECORD.
C            *
C                05  IM-DESCRIPTIVE-DATA.
C                    10  IM-ITEM-NO                PIC 9(5).
C                    10  IM-ITEM-DESC              PIC X(20).
C                    10  IM-UNIT-COST              PIC 999V99.
C                    10  IM-UNIT-PRICE             PIC 999V99.
C                05  IM-INVENTORY-DATA.
C                    10  IM-REORDER-POINT          PIC S9(5).
C                    10  IM-ON-HAND                PIC S9(5).
C                    10  IM-ON-ORDER               PIC S9(5).
C                05  IM-SALES-DATA.
C                    10  IM-LAST-ORDER-DATE        PIC 9(6).
C                    10  IM-LAST-ORDER-DATE-R REDEFINES IM-LAST-ORDER-DATE.
C                        15  IM-LAST-ORDER-MONTH PIC 99.
C                        15  IM-LAST-ORDER-DAY   PIC 99.
C                        15  IM-LAST-ORDER-YEAR  PIC 99.
C                    10  IM-LAST-MONTH-SALES       PIC S9(5)V99.
C                    10  IM-LAST-YEAR-SALES        PIC S9(7)V99.
C                05  FILLER                        PIC X(8).
  007000*
  007100 COPY RPTHDG14.
C            01  HEADING-LINE-1.
C            *
C                05  FILLER           PIC X(7)      VALUE 'DATE:'.
C                05  HDG1-DATE        PIC 99/99/99.
C                05  FILLER           PIC X(36)     VALUE SPACE.
C                05  FILLER           PIC X(20)     VALUE 'MIKE MURACH & ASSOCI'.
C                05  FILLER           PIC X(20)     VALUE 'ATES, INC.          '.
C                05  FILLER           PIC X(31)     VALUE SPACE.
C                05  FILLER           PIC X(6)      VALUE 'PAGE:'.
C                05  HDG1-PAGE-NO     PIC ZZ9.
C                05  FILLER           PIC X         VALUE SPACE.
C            *
C            01  HEADING-LINE-2.
C            *
C                05  HDG2-TIME-DATA.
C                    10  FILLER              PIC X(7)     VALUE 'TIME:'.
C                    10  HDG2-HOURS          PIC 99.
C                    10  FILLER              PIC X        VALUE ':'.
C                    10  HDG2-MINUTES        PIC 99.
C                    10  FILLER              PIC X        VALUE SPACE.
C                    10  HDG2-TIME-SUFFIX    PIC X(8).
C                05  FILLER                  PIC X(101)   VALUE SPACE.
C                05  HDG2-REPORT-NUMBER      PIC X(10)    VALUE 'XXXX9999'.
  007200*
  007300 01  HEADING-LINE-3.
  007400*
              .
              .
```

**Figure 5-11** Highlights of the COBOL listing for the investment-listing program using two COPY and two CALL statements (part 2 of 4)

```
 PROCEDURE DIVISION.
*
 000-PREPARE-INVESTMENT-LISTING.
*
     OPEN INPUT  INVMAST
          OUTPUT INVLIST.
     PERFORM 100-FORMAT-REPORT-HEADING.
     PERFORM 300-PREPARE-INVESTMENT-LINE
         UNTIL INVMAST-EOF.
     PERFORM 500-PRINT-TOTAL-LINES.
     CLOSE INVMAST
           INVLIST.
     DISPLAY 'INV3520   I   1   NORMAL EOJ'.
     STOP RUN.
*
 100-FORMAT-REPORT-HEADING.
*
     CALL 'SYSDATE' USING TODAYS-DATE.
     MOVE TODAYS-DATE TO HDG1-DATE.
     CALL 'SYSTIME' USING HDG2-TIME-DATA.
     MOVE 'INV3520' TO HDG2-REPORT-NUMBER.
*
 300-PREPARE-INVESTMENT-LINE.
*
     PERFORM 310-READ-INVENTORY-RECORD.
     IF NOT INVMAST-EOF
         PERFORM 320-COMPUTE-INVENTORY-FIELDS
         IF INVESTMENT-AMOUNT > 10000
             PERFORM 330-PRINT-INVESTMENT-LINE.
*
 310-READ-INVENTORY-RECORD.
*
     READ INVMAST RECORD INTO INVENTORY-MASTER-RECORD
         AT END
             MOVE 'Y' TO INVMAST-EOF-SWITCH.
     IF NOT INVMAST-EOF
         ADD 1 TO RECORD-COUNT.
*
 320-COMPUTE-INVENTORY-FIELDS.
*
     COMPUTE INVESTMENT-AMOUNT = IM-ON-HAND * IM-UNIT-PRICE
         ON SIZE ERROR
             MOVE 9999999.99 TO INVESTMENT-AMOUNT
             MOVE 'Y' TO INVESTMENT-SIZE-ERROR-SWITCH.
     IF         NOT INVESTMENT-SIZE-ERROR
            AND IM-LAST-MONTH-SALES POSITIVE
         COMPUTE NO-OF-MONTHS-STOCK ROUNDED =
             INVESTMENT-AMOUNT / IM-LAST-MONTH-SALES
             ON SIZE ERROR
                 MOVE 999.9 TO NO-OF-MONTHS-STOCK
     ELSE
         MOVE 999.9 TO NO-OF-MONTHS-STOCK.
*

          :

 340-PRINT-HEADING-LINES.
*
     ADD 1 TO PAGE-COUNT.
     MOVE PAGE-COUNT TO HDG1-PAGE-NO.
     PERFORM 350-WRITE-PAGE-TOP-LINE.
```

**Figure 5-11** Highlights of the COBOL listing for the investment-listing program using two COPY and two CALL statements (part 3 of 4)

```
           MOVE HEADING-LINE-2 TO PRINT-AREA.
           MOVE 1 TO SPACE-CONTROL.
           PERFORM 360-WRITE-REPORT-LINE.
           MOVE HEADING-LINE-3 TO PRINT-AREA.
           PERFORM 360-WRITE-REPORT-LINE.
           MOVE HEADING-LINE-4 TO PRINT-AREA.
           MOVE 2 TO SPACE-CONTROL.
           PERFORM 360-WRITE-REPORT-LINE.
           MOVE HEADING-LINE-5 TO PRINT-AREA.
           MOVE 1 TO SPACE-CONTROL.
           PERFORM 360-WRITE-REPORT-LINE.
           MOVE 2 TO SPACE-CONTROL.
      *
       350-WRITE-PAGE-TOP-LINE.
      *
           WRITE PRINT-AREA FROM HEADING-LINE-1
               AFTER ADVANCING PAGE.
           MOVE 1 TO LINE-COUNT.
      *
       360-WRITE-REPORT-LINE.
      *
           WRITE PRINT-AREA
               AFTER ADVANCING SPACE-CONTROL LINES.
           ADD SPACE-CONTROL TO LINE-COUNT.
      *
       500-PRINT-TOTAL-LINES.
      *
           MOVE RECORD-COUNT TO TL1-RECORD-COUNT.
           MOVE SELECTED-LM-SALES-TOTAL TO TL1-SEL-LM-SALES-TOTAL.
           MOVE SELECTED-INVESTMENT-TOTAL
               TO TL1-SEL-INVESTMENT-TOTAL.
           COMPUTE TL1-SEL-NO-OF-MONTHS-STOCK ROUNDED =
               SELECTED-INVESTMENT-TOTAL / SELECTED-LM-SALES-TOTAL
               ON SIZE ERROR
                   MOVE 999.9 TO TL1-SEL-NO-OF-MONTHS-STOCK.
           MOVE TOTAL-LINE-1 TO PRINT-AREA.
           MOVE 3 TO SPACE-CONTROL.
           PERFORM 360-WRITE-REPORT-LINE.
           MOVE SELECTED-RECORD-COUNT TO TL2-SEL-RECORD-COUNT.
           MOVE TOTAL-LINE-2 TO PRINT-AREA.
           MOVE 1 TO SPACE-CONTROL.
           PERFORM 360-WRITE-REPORT-LINE.
```

**Figure 5-11** Highlights of the COBOL listing for the investment-listing program using two COPY and two CALL statements (part 4 of 4)

**The Procedure Division** In the Procedure Division, you can see the use of the READ INTO, WRITE FROM, COMPUTE, and CALL statements. You can also see the use of sign tests and compound conditions. But let's go through the program changes one module at a time.

In module 100, you can see how two CALL statements are used to get the current date and time and format them properly. In the CALL statement for SYSDATE, the USING clause specifies TODAYS-DATE, a field in working storage where the formatted date will be available for processing throughout the program. Then, the next statement moves this field into the first heading line. In the

CALL statement for SYSTIME, the USING clause specifies HDG2-TIME-DATA, a field that's copied into the program as part of the COPY member named RPTHDG14. If you compare this module with module 100 in the program in figure 4-22, you can see how the use of subprograms can reduce coding.

Also note the last statement in module 100. It's required because the COPY member for the first two heading lines is a general one that can be used by any program. So the report number is no longer coded as a literal value in the second heading line.

In module 310, you can see how the READ INTO statement is used. When the statement is executed, the next inventory master record in the file is first read into the area named INVENTORY-MASTER that is defined in the File Section. Then, this record is moved from INVENTORY-MASTER to the area named INVENTORY-MASTER-RECORD in the Working-Storage Section. Although the record could be processed in the File Section in this program, that wouldn't work in some programs because the last record isn't available after the AT END clause in the READ statement has been executed. As a result, reading functions for disk files are often coded as shown in this program.

Module 320 shows how COMPUTE statements can be used instead of ADD, SUBTRACT, MULTIPLY, and DIVIDE statements. In fact, the standards for some shops say that the COMPUTE statement should be used for all arithmetic operations because one COMPUTE statement is often easier to understand than a series of other arithmetic statements. When using COMPUTE statements, though, remember that intermediate results can be a problem, so it's sometimes better to code a series of COMPUTE statements instead of just one.

Module 320 also illustrates the use of a compound condition and a sign test within an IF statement. If you compare this with the related coding in module 320 of the program in figure 4-22, you can see that COBOL lets you code most logical operations in several different ways. In this case, the code in figure 4-22 is acceptable, and so is the code in figure 5-11. Your goal, of course, is to code each logical operation in the way that is easiest to understand.

Module 350 uses the WRITE FROM statement to write the first heading line of the investment listing on the print file. Since this statement is the equivalent of a move and a write function, one less MOVE statement is required in module 340. As I explained in topic 1, this is acceptable coding for the printing of the first heading line with the AFTER ADVANCING PAGE option, but it isn't acceptable for the other report lines. If you compare this coding with the coding in module 350 in figure 4-22, you can see that the difference is trivial. As a result, either way of coding this module is acceptable.

Module 500 also illustrates the use of the COMPUTE statement. Since the statement requires division, the program could check

SELECTED-LM-SALES-TOTAL to make sure that it isn't zero before executing the COMPUTE statement. However, this doesn't seem necessary in this module because this field shouldn't ever be zero when the module is executed.

## Discussion

Although this program doesn't do anything that the program in chapter 4 didn't do, it does illustrate some professional coding practices. In particular, a professional programmer uses COPY and CALL statements in almost every program. In addition, she uses the READ INTO statement for reading many disk files. And she uses the COMPUTE statement and compound conditions whenever they can simplify coding and make it easier to understand.

## Objective

Apply the COBOL elements presented in this chapter to your application programs.

## Topic 5 Compiler dependent code

The program in figure 5-11 is written for an IBM mainframe using the VS COBOL compiler running under DOS/VSE. However, because the COBOL code in the program is standard, it should run with only a couple of changes on any system that uses 1974 or 1985 ANS COBOL. As I explained in chapter 3, you should code the program name, the Configuration Section, the system names in the SELECT statements, and the FD statements to conform to your compiler and your computer system. As I explained in chapter 4, you should code computational usages so they meet the requirements of your system and you should know how simple DISPLAY statements work on your system.

As for the code presented in this chapter, it should run on all systems. Nevertheless, there are two compiler dependencies that you should be aware of just in case they apply to your system. These involve COMPUTE statements and COPY statements.

### COMPUTE statements

Your compiler may put limitations on the COMPUTE statement that aren't defined in the standards. In fact, the standards are rather general, so it's acceptable for a compiler to place limitations on the expressions that may be coded within a COMPUTE statement.

For instance, the COBOL II compiler for IBM mainframes doesn't allow exponentiation. Similarly, the Wang VS compiler, which conforms to the 1974 standards, doesn't allow fractional exponents, so this COMPUTE statement won't compile properly:

```
COMPUTE FIELD-A = FIELD-B ** (.5)
```

Since the standards say nothing about fractional exponents, this is an acceptable limitation. On the other hand, this code does compile and execute properly on an IBM mainframe when using the VS compiler. When it compiles properly, it takes the square root of a number because a number raised to the one-half power is the same as the square root of a number. At any rate, when you use the COMPUTE statement on your system, you may discover limitations that are peculiar to your compiler.

### COPY statements

On some systems, you will want to use this expanded format of the COPY statement:

```
COPY text-name {OF} library-name
               {IN}
```

This can be used when an installation has more than one COPY library, as is often the case. Then, the COPY statement specifies the library name as well as the text name. As a result, a single program can copy members from more than one library. We sometimes use this facility on our Wang VS system because we keep COBOL COPY members in several different libraries. It isn't necessary on the Wang system, though, because you can identify the libraries you're using in other ways.

On most systems, in fact, this facility isn't needed. On an IBM PC, for example, libraries aren't supported at all, so the text name in a COPY statement identifies a file that contains one COPY member. In contrast, on IBM mainframes, you don't need to identify the libraries in your COPY statements because you can use job control language to set up a chain of COPY libraries to be searched.

### Discussion

When it comes to COMPUTE statements, be aware that you may run into some limitations when you try to specify complex combinations of operations. This is particularly true when using compilers on small systems. For this reason, your shop standards or your COBOL manuals may have something to say about the limitations of COMPUTE statements on your system.

As for COPY statements, check your shop standards. In some shops, you may be expected to identify the libraries you're using in the COPY statements. In other shops, you may be prohibited from identifying them, even if this facility is available to you.

### Objective

Find out what your shop standards say about the use of COMPUTE and COPY statements.

Chapter 6

# Completing the professional subset

In this chapter, you will learn how to use the elements that complete a professional subset of COBOL. Topic 1 shows you how to use the COBOL elements for handling one-level tables. Topic 2 shows you how to read records in indexed, rather than sequential, files. Topic 3 presents a complete program that uses the elements of topics 1 and 2. And topic 4 presents two minor compiler dependencies that you should be aware of.

# Topic 1 How to handle one-level tables using indexes

Many programs require the use of tables. That's why the COBOL standards provide language for handling tables. In fact, the 1974 COBOL standards provide language for tables of up to three levels, and the 1985 standards provide for tables of up to seven levels.

In most report preparation programs, though, you only need to work with *one-level tables*. Those are tables that tabulate data based on only one variable factor. So that's what I'm going to cover in this topic. Then, in *Part 2* of this series, you can learn how to handle more complicated tables.

## The COBOL elements for table handling

Figure 6-1 presents a subset of the COBOL elements for table handling. These are the only elements you'll need for the vast majority of tables that your programs will operate upon. As you can see, the table handling elements include four new clauses for defining a table in the Data Division. They provide two new statements: the SET and the SEARCH statements. And they provide an expanded form of the PERFORM statement.

**Data Division code for table definitions**

**Format 1**

```
level-number  data-name-1  OCCURS integer TIMES

                           [ {ASCENDING }  KEY IS data-name-2]
                             {DESCENDING}

                           INDEXED BY index-name
```

**Format 2 (for a binary search of a variable-length table)**

```
level-number  data-name-1  OCCURS integer-1 TO integer-2 TIMES

                           DEPENDING ON data-name-2

                           [ {ASCENDING }  KEY IS data-name-3]
                             {DESCENDING}

                           INDEXED BY index-name
```

**Figure 6-1** A subset of the COBOL elements for table handling (part 1 of 2)

**Procedure Division code for referring to an entry in a table**

```
data-name  {(index-name)                 }
           {(literal-occurrence-number)  }
```

**The SET statement**

**Format 1**

```
                              {data-name-2 }
SET  {data-name-1 }   TO      {index-name-2}
     {index-name-1}           {literal-1   }
```

**Format 2**

```
SET  index-name    {UP BY  }   {data-name}
                   {DOWN BY}   {literal  }
```

**The SEARCH statement**

**Format 1 (sequential search)**

```
SEARCH data-name
     [AT END imperative-statement-1]
     WHEN condition-1   {imperative-statement-2}
                        {NEXT SENTENCE         }
     [WHEN condition-2  {imperative-statement-3}  ] ...
                        {NEXT SENTENCE         }
```

**Format 2 (binary search)**

```
SEARCH ALL data-name
     [AT END imperative-statement-1]
     WHEN equal-condition
        {imperative-statement-2}
        {NEXT SENTENCE         }
```

**The PERFORM VARYING statement**

```
PERFORM paragraph-name
                                 {data-name-1 }
     VARYING   index-name-1  FROM {index-name-2}  BY  {data-name-2}
                                 {literal-1   }      {literal-2  }
     UNTIL  condition
```

**Figure 6-1** A subset of the COBOL elements for table handling (part 2 of 2)

As you read through this topic, please refer to the formats in figure 6-1. I'll explain each of them as I present examples of table handling code. By the time you complete this topic, you should be able to use any of the elements in figure 6-1.

## How to define a table in the Data Division

Figures 6-2 and 6-3 present two tables and their COBOL definitions. Both tables are defined by using the OCCURS clause and the INDEXED BY clause. For most tables, those are the only new clauses you'll need. To put constant values in the table in figure 6-2, the REDEFINES clause is also used.

Although the tables in figures 6-2 and 6-3 are similar in form, you can see that I coded them differently. In the COBOL code, the month table has only one field that is repeated, but the price table has two fields that are repeated. In figure 6-2, I didn't code the month numbers as part of the table because they are simply the numbers from 1 through 12. By the time you complete this topic, you should understand why it isn't necessary to code the month numbers in this table.

**The OCCURS clause** The OCCURS clause can be used to describe any data item that is not at an 01 level. It can be used with an elementary item as in figure 6-2. It can be used with a group item as in figure 6-3.

The integer in the OCCURS clause tells how many times a field or group of fields is to be repeated in storage. As a result, the table in figure 6-2 requires 108 bytes of storage since the 9-byte field is repeated 12 times. Similarly, the table in figure 6-3 requires 112 bytes of storage since the 7-byte group consisting of item number and item price is repeated 16 times.

**The INDEXED BY clause** The INDEXED BY clause follows the OCCURS clause and assigns an *index name* to the *index* for the table entries. In figure 6-2, MONTH-INDEX is the index for the 12 MONTH-NAME entries. To refer to any of the 12 entries in the Procedure Division, you code the data name followed by the index name in parentheses as in this statement:

```
MOVE MONTH-NAME (MONTH-INDEX) TO HDG3-MONTH-NAME.
```

Here, the value of MONTH-INDEX determines which of the 12 month values will be moved to HDG3-MONTH-NAME. If, for example, the value is 3, the third MONTH-NAME in the table is moved to HDG3-MONTH-NAME.

In figure 6-3, PRICE-TABLE-INDEX is the index name for the 16 occurrences of PRICE-GROUP. Then, either of the fields within

**Month table**

| Number | Month | Number | Month |
|---|---|---|---|
| 1 | JANUARY | 7 | JULY |
| 2 | FEBRUARY | 8 | AUGUST |
| 3 | MARCH | 9 | SEPTEMBER |
| 4 | APRIL | 10 | OCTOBER |
| 5 | MAY | 11 | NOVEMBER |
| 6 | JUNE | 12 | DECEMBER |

**Table definition in COBOL**

```
 01   MONTH-TABLE.
*
      05   MONTH-NAME                PIC X(9)
                                     OCCURS 12 TIMES
                                     INDEXED BY MONTH-INDEX.
```

**Table definition in COBOL with constant values**

```
 01   MONTH-TABLE-VALUES.
*
      05   FILLER                    PIC X(9)   VALUE 'JANUARY'.
      05   FILLER                    PIC X(9)   VALUE 'FEBRUARY'.
      05   FILLER                    PIC X(9)   VALUE 'MARCH'.
      05   FILLER                    PIC X(9)   VALUE 'APRIL'.
      05   FILLER                    PIC X(9)   VALUE 'MAY'.
      05   FILLER                    PIC X(9)   VALUE 'JUNE'.
      05   FILLER                    PIC X(9)   VALUE 'JULY'.
      05   FILLER                    PIC X(9)   VALUE 'AUGUST'.
      05   FILLER                    PIC X(9)   VALUE 'SEPTEMBER'.
      05   FILLER                    PIC X(9)   VALUE 'OCTOBER'.
      05   FILLER                    PIC X(9)   VALUE 'NOVEMBER'.
      05   FILLER                    PIC X(9)   VALUE 'DECEMBER'.
*
 01   MONTH-TABLE REDEFINES MONTH-TABLE-VALUES.
*
      05   MONTH-NAME                PIC X(9)
                                     OCCURS 12 TIMES
                                     INDEXED BY MONTH-INDEX.
```

**Statement that refers to an entry in the month table**

```
MOVE MONTH-NAME (MONTH-INDEX) TO HDG3-MONTH-NAME.
```

**Figure 6-2** A month table and its COBOL definitions

each of the 16 groups can be referred to using this index name as in these examples:

```
ITEM-NUMBER (PRICE-TABLE-INDEX)
ITEM-PRICE (PRICE-TABLE-INDEX)
```

**Price table**

| Item number | Price | Item number | Price |
|---|---|---|---|
| 101 | 12.50 | 277 | 1.11 |
| 107 | 50.00 | 297 | 7.77 |
| 111 | 7.70 | 305 | .10 |
| 158 | 5.55 | 341 | 15.00 |
| 161 | 62.50 | 342 | 57.50 |
| 192 | 25.00 | 343 | 65.00 |
| 201 | .40 | 347 | 22.50 |
| 213 | 6.66 | 351 | .35 |

**Table definition in COBOL**

```
 01   PRICE-TABLE.
*
      05   PRICE-GROUP              OCCURS 16 TIMES
                                    INDEXED BY PRICE-TABLE-INDEX.
           10   ITEM-NUMBER         PIC 9(3).
           10   ITEM-PRICE          PIC 99V99.
*
```

**Statement that refers to a price in the price table**

```
MULTIPLY TR-QUANTITY BY ITEM-PRICE (PRICE-TABLE-INDEX)
    GIVING LINE-ITEM-EXTENSION ROUNDED.
```

Figure 6-3 A price table and its COBOL definition

Here again, the actual entries referred to depend upon the value of PRICE-TABLE-INDEX at the time of the referral. If, for example, the index value is 10, the coding above refers to the tenth item number (297) and the tenth price (7.77).

You can also use the index name to refer to PRICE-GROUP as a whole:

```
PRICE-GROUP (PRICE-TABLE-INDEX)
```

In most cases, though, you'll want to refer to the individual fields, not to the group item.

When you index a table as illustrated in figures 6-2 and 6-3, you don't define the index as a field in storage elsewhere in the program. Instead, the INDEXED BY clause automatically defines the index, giving it a size and usage that is appropriate for the system you're using.

**The REDEFINES clause** When a table isn't likely to be changed, you will often code its values in the Data Division. This is illustrated by the second table definition in figure 6-2. Since the month values aren't going to change, they may as well be coded as part of the program.

To code constant values for a table in the Data Division, you need to use the REDEFINES clause as shown in figure 6-2. Because VALUE clauses are illegal in statements that redefine a storage area, you must first code the values of the table. Then, you redefine the storage area as a table by using the REDEFINES, OCCURS, and INDEXED BY clauses.

Since a price table like the one in figure 6-3 is likely to change, you normally wouldn't code its values as part of the Data Division. Instead, you would read the values into storage at the start of any program that used the table. Nevertheless, figure 6-4 shows you two ways to define the data in the price table within a program. Although this table has data that's likely to be changed, other tables with the same form may have data that won't be changed.

In the first method in figure 6-4, one VALUE clause is used for each of the 32 fields within the table. First, an item number; next, an item price; then, another item number; and so on. In the second method, one VALUE clause gives the values for a group of values consisting of one item number and one item price. You could also define more than one group in a single VALUE clause, but the more you combine fields and groups, the more difficult your coding is to read.

If you define your table fields with computational usages, you have to code one VALUE clause for each field as shown in method 1 in figure 6-4, or the values won't be stored properly. Also, if some of the fields in the table have signs, you have to use method 1. In most cases, though, you will probably use unsigned fields with DISPLAY usages in the tables that you give values to in the Data Division.

## How to refer to the entries in a table

I've already shown you the most common way to refer to entries in a table. That is, you code the name of the field you want to refer to followed by the index name for the table, as in this example:

```
ITEM-PRICE (PRICE-TABLE-INDEX)
```

Then, the value of the index determines the specific table element that the code refers to.

Sometimes, however, you may know which entry you want to refer to at the time that you code the program. If so, you can code the index value as a literal, as in this example:

```
MONTH-NAME (1)
```

Here, the code refers to the first month in the table.

**Method 1**

```
 01   PRICE-TABLE-VALUES.
*
      05   FILLER                PIC 9(3)         VALUE 101.
      05   FILLER                PIC 99V99        VALUE 12.50.
      05   FILLER                PIC 9(3)         VALUE 107.
      05   FILLER                PIC 99V99        VALUE 50.00.
      .
      .
      05   FILLER                PIC 9(3)         VALUE 351.
      05   FILLER                PIC 99V99        VALUE .35.
*
 01   PRICE-TABLE REDEFINES PRICE-TABLE-VALUES.
*
      05   PRICE-GROUP           OCCURS 16 TIMES
                                 INDEXED BY PRICE-TABLE-INDEX.
           10   ITEM-NUMBER      PIC 9(3).
           10   ITEM-PRICE       PIC 99V99.
*
```

**Method 2**

```
 01   PRICE-TABLE-VALUES.
*
      05   FILLER                PIC 9(7)         VALUE 1011250.
      05   FILLER                PIC 9(7)         VALUE 1075000.
      .
      .
      05   FILLER                PIC 9(7)         VALUE 3510035.
*
 01   PRICE-TABLE REDEFINES PRICE-TABLE-VALUES.
*
      05   PRICE-GROUP           OCCURS 16 TIMES
                                 INDEXED BY PRICE-TABLE-INDEX.
           10   ITEM-NUMBER      PIC 9(3).
           10   ITEM-PRICE       PIC 99V99.
*
```

**Figure 6-4** Two ways to define the price table in figure 6-3 with constant values

When you use a literal instead of an index name, it represents an *occurrence number*. As a result, it must be an integer between 1 and the number of times the element occurs in the table. For the month table, the occurrence number must be from 1 through 12; for the price table, the occurrence number must be from 1 through 16.

Although you can use either an index name or an occurrence number to identify an entry in a table, you should realize that the values aren't the same. In contrast to an occurrence number, an index represents a *displacement value* from the start of the table. For instance, the index value for the first month in the month table is a displacement value of 0 (the first month is 0 positions from the start of the table), but the occurrence number is 1. Similarly, the index value is 9 for the second month and 18 for the third month, but the corresponding occurrence numbers are 2 and 3. Fortunately, you don't have to worry about this when you handle tables in COBOL, because the compiler handles the conversions between occurrence numbers and displacement values. In fact, as you'll see in a moment, you use occurrence numbers rather than displacement values to assign a value to an index.

### How to load a fixed-length table into storage

When the values in a table are likely to change, you normally load the table into storage from a disk file at the start of any program that uses the table. As a result, you normally load a price table like the one in figure 6-3 from a disk file.

A routine for loading this table is illustrated in figure 6-5. This routine assumes that each group of table entries is stored in one record in a sequential file that contains all of the values for the table. If you study this code, you should be able to understand it without too much trouble. The only new statement is the PERFORM VARYING statement.

**The PERFORM VARYING statement** To load a table, a PERFORM VARYING statement is often useful. This is illustrated by the statement in figure 6-5:

```
PERFORM 110-LOAD-PRICE-TABLE-ENTRY
    VARYING PRICE-TABLE-INDEX FROM 1 BY 1
    UNTIL PTABLE-EOF
       OR PRICE-TABLE-INDEX > 16.
```

This statement executes module 110 until the end of the table file has been reached or until the occurrence value represented by the index is greater than 16 (the number of entries defined for the table). The VARYING clause in this statement gives the index a starting value equivalent to an occurrence value of one (FROM 1). That means that the index points to the first price group in the table the first time module 110 is executed. Then, each time module 110 is executed, the index is increased by an occurrence value of one (BY 1).

Figure 6-6 illustrates the flow of control for the PERFORM VARYING statement. Note that the index is increased by the BY value right after the called module is performed but before the condition is tested again. And, as always when the UNTIL clause is used, the condition is tested *before* the called module is performed.

With this as background, I hope you can understand the OR portion of the condition in the PERFORM VARYING statement in figure 6-5:

```
OR PRICE-TABLE-INDEX > 16
```

```
 WORKING-STORAGE SECTION.
*
 01   SWITCHES.
*
      05   PTABLE-EOF-SWITCH  PIC X          VALUE 'N'.
           88   PTABLE-EOF                   VALUE 'Y'.
*
 01   PRICE-TABLE.
*
      05   PRICE-GROUP          OCCURS 16 TIMES
                                INDEXED BY PRICE-TABLE-INDEX.
           10   ITEM-NUMBER     PIC 9(3).
           10   ITEM-PRICE      PIC 99V99.
*
 01   PRICE-TABLE-RECORD.
*
      05   PT-ITEM-NUMBER       PIC 9(3).
      05   PT-ITEM-PRICE        PIC 99V99.
      05   FILLER               PIC X(13).
*
      .
      .
*
 PROCEDURE DIVISION.
*
      .
      .
 100-LOAD-PRICE-TABLE.
*
      PERFORM 110-LOAD-PRICE-TABLE-ENTRY
          VARYING PRICE-TABLE-INDEX FROM 1 BY 1
          UNTIL PTABLE-EOF
             OR PRICE-TABLE-INDEX > 16.
*
 110-LOAD-PRICE-TABLE-ENTRY.
*
      PERFORM 120-READ-PRICE-TABLE-RECORD.
      IF NOT PTABLE-EOF
          MOVE PT-ITEM-NUMBER TO ITEM-NUMBER (PRICE-TABLE-INDEX)
          MOVE PT-ITEM-PRICE  TO ITEM-PRICE (PRICE-TABLE-INDEX).
*
 120-READ-PRICE-TABLE-RECORD.
*
      READ PTABLE RECORD INTO PRICE-TABLE-RECORD
          AT END
              MOVE 'Y' TO PTABLE-EOF-SWITCH.
      .
      .
```

**Figure 6-5** Loading a price table with 16 entries

This stops the loading of the table if the number of entries in the table file is greater than the number of entries provided for by the OCCURS

**Statement format**

```
PERFORM paragraph-name
    VARYING index-name FROM value-1 BY value-2
    UNTIL condition
```

**Flow of control**

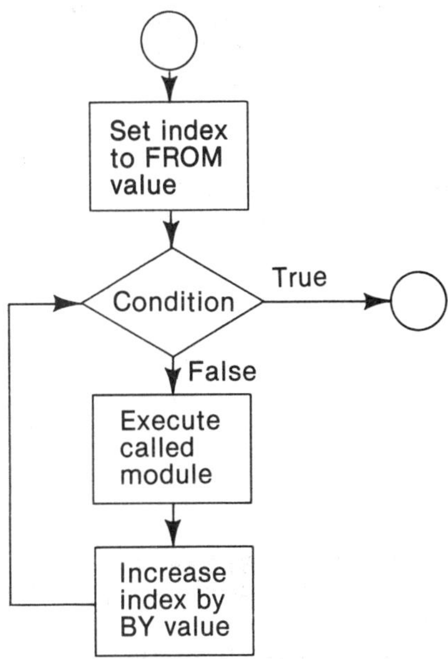


**Figure 6-6** Flowchart for the logic of the PERFORM VARYING statement

clause for the table. The condition isn't coded as

```
PRICE-TABLE-INDEX = 16
```

because the index is increased by a value of one after each execution of module 110 but *before* the condition is checked. So PRICE-TABLE-INDEX will be increased to a value of 16 right after the fifteenth entry is loaded into the table. As a result, a greater-than condition has to be used, or the program will exit the PERFORM statement without loading the sixteenth table entry.

One final point I want to mention is that I've simplified this routine to illustrate the essential table handling elements. In a production program, you'd have to do some kind of error processing if the end of the PTABLE file were reached before 16 values had been loaded into the table.

### How to load a variable-length table into storage

In actual practice, the number of entries in a table like the price table is usually variable. As new items are added to the product line, the number increases. As items are dropped, the number decreases. Normally, then, a table like this is loaded as a variable-length table.

Figure 6-7 illustrates the code for loading a variable-length price table into storage. Here, the OCCURS clause for the table gives an occurrence value of 100. That means that the table may hold a maximum of 100 groups of item number and item price. However, the actual number of entries loaded into this table will depend upon the number of entries in the table file. This number will be stored in a count field named PT-ENTRY-COUNT.

The PERFORM VARYING statement in figure 6-7 is much like the one in figure 6-5. This time, the statement says that module 110 should be repeatedly executed until the end of the table file has been reached or until the index value represents an occurrence number greater than 100. After each time that module 110 is executed, the occurrence number represented by the index is increased by one.

**The SET statement** In module 110, two SET statements are used:

```
SET PRICE-TABLE-INDEX DOWN BY 1
SET PT-ENTRY-COUNT TO PRICE-TABLE-INDEX.
```

They are executed when the end of the table file has been reached (PTABLE-EOF). The first one reduces the index for the table by the equivalent of one occurrence number. The second one sets PT-ENTRY-COUNT equal to the occurrence number represented by the index value.

Remember that index values are not the same as occurrence numbers. That's why you have to use SET statements when you operate upon indexes. They make the appropriate conversions between displacement values and occurrence numbers.

Do you understand why the index value had to be reduced by an occurrence number of one before it represented the number of entries in the table? Remember that the index value is increased after the called module is performed. As a result, if 16 values have been loaded into the table, the index is increased to an occurrence value of 17 before module 110 is executed again. So when the end-of-file condition for the table file occurs during the execution of module 110, no new values are loaded into the table, and the index value represents an occurrence number that is one more than the number of table entries. That's why it has to be reduced before the value of PT-ENTRY-COUNT can be set.

### How to search a table in sequence

Once a table has been loaded into storage, you can search it to find the entries your program requires. For a simple table like the month

```
WORKING-STORAGE SECTION.
*
01  SWITCHES.
*
    05  PTABLE-EOF-SWITCH   PIC X        VALUE 'N'.
        88  PTABLE-EOF                   VALUE 'Y'.
*
01  COUNT-FIELDS            COMP-3.
*
    05  PT-ENTRY-COUNT      PIC 9(3).
*
01  PRICE-TABLE.
*
    05  PRICE-GROUP         OCCURS 100 TIMES
                            INDEXED BY PRICE-TABLE-INDEX.
        10  ITEM-NUMBER     PIC 9(3).
        10  ITEM-PRICE      PIC 99V99.
*
01  PRICE-TABLE-RECORD.
*
    05  PT-ITEM-NUMBER      PIC 9(3).
    05  PT-ITEM-PRICE       PIC 99V99.
    05  FILLER              PIC X(13).
*
    .
    .
*
PROCEDURE DIVISION.
*
    .
    .
100-LOAD-PRICE-TABLE.
*
    PERFORM 110-LOAD-PRICE-TABLE-ENTRY
        VARYING PRICE-TABLE-INDEX FROM 1 BY 1
        UNTIL PTABLE-EOF
           OR PRICE-TABLE-INDEX > 100.
*
110-LOAD-PRICE-TABLE-ENTRY.
*
    PERFORM 120-READ-PRICE-TABLE-RECORD.
    IF NOT PTABLE-EOF
        MOVE PT-ITEM-NUMBER TO ITEM-NUMBER (PRICE-TABLE-INDEX)
        MOVE PT-ITEM-PRICE  TO ITEM-PRICE (PRICE-TABLE-INDEX)
    ELSE
        SET PRICE-TABLE-INDEX DOWN BY 1
        SET PT-ENTRY-COUNT TO PRICE-TABLE-INDEX.
*
120-READ-PRICE-TABLE-RECORD.
*
    READ PTABLE RECORD INTO PRICE-TABLE-RECORD
        AT END
            MOVE 'Y' TO PTABLE-EOF-SWITCH.
    .
    .
```

**Figure 6-7** Loading a price table with a variable number of entries

table, you can find the entry you want by setting the index to the appropriate value. If, for example, you want to move the name of the current month into a heading line, you can code statements like this:

```
SET MONTH-INDEX TO CURRENT-MONTH.
MOVE MONTH-NAME (MONTH-INDEX) TO HDG3-MONTH-NAME.
```

Here, the SET statement sets the index value to the equivalent of the occurrence value represented by CURRENT-MONTH. This assumes, of course, that CURRENT-MONTH is a value from 01 through 12. Technically, this isn't a search, because the program gets the entry you want without searching through the other entries in the table first. Nevertheless, this code has the same effect as a search.

To illustrate a true search, figure 6-8 illustrates a routine that searches the variable-length price table that was loaded by the code in figure 6-7. This assumes that the code in figure 6-7 and figure 6-8 are parts of the same program. First, the table is loaded into storage. Then, it is searched as part of the processing of the program. You should be able to understand this routine without too much difficulty because the only new statement it presents is the SEARCH statement.

**The SEARCH statement** The SEARCH statement in figure 6-8 is coded as follows:

```
SEARCH PRICE-GROUP
    AT END
        MOVE 'N' TO PRICE-FOUND-SWITCH
    WHEN ITEM-NUMBER (PRICE-TABLE-INDEX) = TR-ITEM-NO
        MOVE ITEM-PRICE (PRICE-TABLE-INDEX) TO UNIT-PRICE
        MOVE 'Y' TO PRICE-FOUND-SWITCH
    WHEN PRICE-TABLE-INDEX > PT-ENTRY-COUNT
        MOVE 'N' TO PRICE-FOUND-SWITCH.
```

When this statement is executed, it searches the item numbers in the table until the item number in the table is equal to TR-ITEM-NO or until the occurrence value represented by the index is greater than the number of occurrences in the table (PT-ENTRY-COUNT). In other words, the search ends when the condition in either WHEN clause becomes true. If neither condition ever becomes true, the search ends when all 100 entries in the table have been searched (AT END).

In figure 6-8, the SET statement sets the index to the equivalent of an occurrence value of one before the SEARCH statement is executed. As a result, the search starts with the first item number in the table. Then, it continues in sequence from the first item to the last. Note that a SET statement must always give a starting value to an index before a sequential SEARCH statement is executed, but the value doesn't have to be one.

Since the SEARCH statement searches the entries in sequence from the first to the last, the entries themselves don't have to be in sequence. In the price table, for example, the item numbers could be

```
 WORKING-STORAGE SECTION.
*
 01  SWITCHES.
*
     .
     .
     05  PRICE-FOUND-SWITCH          PIC X.
         88  PRICE-FOUND                             VALUE 'Y'.
*
 01  COUNT-FIELDS           COMP-3.
*
     05  PT-ENTRY-COUNT     PIC 9(3).
*
 01  PRICE-TABLE.
*
     05  PRICE-GROUP        OCCURS 100 TIMES
                            INDEXED BY PRICE-TABLE-INDEX.
         10  ITEM-NUMBER    PIC 9(3).
         10  ITEM-PRICE     PIC 99V99.
*
 01  WORK-FIELDS            COMP-3.
*
     05  UNIT-PRICE         PIC 99V99.
*
 01  TRANSACTION-RECORD.
*
     05  TR-REFERENCE-CODE  PIC X(6).
     05  TR-REFERENCE-DATE  PIC X(6).
     05  TR-CUSTOMER-NO     PIC X(5).
     05  TR-ITEM-NO         PIC 9(3).
     .
     .
*
 PROCEDURE DIVISION.
*
     .
     .
 350-SEARCH-PRICE-TABLE.
*
     SET PRICE-TABLE-INDEX TO 1.
     SEARCH PRICE-GROUP
         AT END
             MOVE 'N' TO PRICE-FOUND-SWITCH
         WHEN ITEM-NUMBER (PRICE-TABLE-INDEX) = TR-ITEM-NO
             MOVE ITEM-PRICE (PRICE-TABLE-INDEX) TO UNIT-PRICE
             MOVE 'Y' TO PRICE-FOUND-SWITCH
         WHEN PRICE-TABLE-INDEX > PT-ENTRY-COUNT
             MOVE 'N' TO PRICE-FOUND-SWITCH.
*
     .
     .
```

**Figure 6-8** Searching a price table with a variable number of entries

in reversed sequence or in no sequence at all and the search in figure 6-8 would still work.

However, the sequence of the entries can have a major effect on the processing efficiency of the program. Since you usually search a table from the first entry to the last, the most used entries should be the first ones in the table and the least used entries should be the last ones. If, for example, 60 percent of the transactions in the price table involve item numbers 305, 347, and 351, these entries should be the first ones in the table.

Since the search routine in figure 6-8 is for a variable-length table, the SEARCH statement uses two WHEN clauses and an AT END clause. You should realize, though, that coding a SEARCH statement is simpler when the table has a fixed number of entries. If, for example, the price table always had 16 occurrences, the SEARCH statement could be coded as follows:

```
SEARCH PRICE-GROUP
    AT END
        MOVE 'N' TO PRICE-FOUND-SWITCH
    WHEN ITEM-NUMBER (PRICE-TABLE-INDEX) = TR-ITEM-NO
        MOVE ITEM-PRICE (PRICE-TABLE-INDEX) TO UNIT-PRICE
        MOVE 'Y' TO PRICE-FOUND-SWITCH.
```

Here, the search either finds the right item number in the table or it ends when it has searched all of the item numbers in the table.

### How to search a table with a binary search

Figure 6-9 shows how you can use a *binary search* to search the variable-length price table. For a binary search, the item numbers have to be in sequence in the table. Then, the search starts with an item number near the middle of the table, and that number's compared to the desired item number. Based on this comparison, the search continues in either the first half or the second half of the table. The next comparison is near the middle of the half just selected, and the search continues by successively halving the portion of the table remaining. Eventually, the condition in the WHEN clause of the SEARCH statement is satisfied or the AT END clause is executed.

The advantage of a binary search is its speed. In a table of 16 occurrences, any entry can be found with a maximum of just 4 comparisons. In contrast, a sequential search requires an average of 8 comparisons to find an entry if the frequency of use is distributed evenly over the 16 entries. For large tables, say tables of 128 or more entries, a binary search is likely to be far more efficient than a sequential search.

If you study the coding in figure 6-9, you can see that it's just like the coding in figure 6-8 with a few exceptions: (1) the OCCURS clause specifies a range of values; (2) the DEPENDING ON clause and the ASCENDING KEY clause are used to define the table; (3) no SET is required; and (4) a SEARCH ALL statement is used.

```
 WORKING-STORAGE SECTION.
*
 01  SWITCHES.
*
     .
     .
     05  PRICE-FOUND-SWITCH          PIC X.
         88  PRICE-FOUND                          VALUE 'Y'.
*
 01  COUNT-FIELDS            COMP-3.
*
     05  PT-ENTRY-COUNT      PIC 9(3).
*
 01  PRICE-TABLE.
*
     05  PRICE-GROUP         OCCURS 1 TO 100 TIMES
                             DEPENDING ON PT-ENTRY-COUNT
                             ASCENDING KEY IS ITEM-NUMBER
                             INDEXED BY PRICE-TABLE-INDEX.
         10  ITEM-NUMBER     PIC 9(3).
         10  ITEM-PRICE      PIC 99V99.
*
 01  WORK-FIELDS             COMP-3.
*
     05  UNIT-PRICE          PIC 99V99.
*
 01  TRANSACTION-RECORD.
*
     05  TR-REFERENCE-CODE   PIC X(6).
     05  TR-REFERENCE-DATE   PIC X(6).
     05  TR-CUSTOMER-NO      PIC X(5).
     05  TR-ITEM-NO          PIC 9(3).
     .
     .
*
 PROCEDURE DIVISION.
*
     .
     .
 350-SEARCH-PRICE-TABLE.
*
     SEARCH ALL PRICE-GROUP
         AT END
             MOVE 'N' TO PRICE-FOUND-SWITCH
         WHEN ITEM-NUMBER (PRICE-TABLE-INDEX) = TR-ITEM-NO
             MOVE ITEM-PRICE (PRICE-TABLE-INDEX) TO UNIT-PRICE
             MOVE 'Y' TO PRICE-FOUND-SWITCH.
*
```

**Figure 6-9** Searching a variable-length price table with a binary search

**The OCCURS clause** When you use a binary search with a variable-length table, the OCCURS clause gives the range of occurrences that can be searched. Normally, this clause is coded so the range is from the first occurrence to the last, as in figure 6-9:

```
OCCURS 1 TO 100 TIMES
```

Here, the first integer says that the search should include the entries of the table starting with the first occurrence. The second integer says that the table may have a maximum of 100 occurrences. Then, as you will see in a moment, the DEPENDING ON clause names a field that specifies the actual number of occurrences to be searched.

This clause can be coded so the range of the search doesn't include all of the entries in the table, but you'll rarely, if ever, want to do this. If, for example, the clause in figure 6-9 were coded as

```
OCCURS 11 to 100 TIMES
```

the first ten entries in the table wouldn't be included in the search. Usually, though, if you didn't want to include these entries in the search, you wouldn't bother to define them or load them into the table.

**The DEPENDING ON clause** Because the price table is variable in length, the DEPENDING ON clause must be used. It tells the SEARCH ALL statement how many entries to search. In contrast, the second integer in the OCCURS clause gives the maximum number of entries that might be in the table. For the SEARCH ALL statement to work properly, the proper value must be moved into the field named in the DEPENDING ON clause before the SEARCH statement is executed. Thus, PT-ENTRY-COUNT must have the proper occurrence value in figure 6-9. If a table has a fixed number of occurrences or you're not using a binary search, you don't have to code this clause when you define it.

**The ASCENDING/DESCENDING KEY clause** In the price table, the item number is the *key* for the search. In a binary search, the keys must be in either ascending or descending sequence in the table. As a result, this clause tells the SEARCH statement what the *key field* is and what sequence it's in.

**The SEARCH ALL statement** When the SEARCH ALL statement is executed, it performs a binary search on the key field defined for the table. Since the binary search figures out its own starting point, you don't have to set the index value using a SET statement before the SEARCH ALL statement is executed.

If you compare the SEARCH ALL statement in figure 6-9 with the SEARCH statement in figure 6-8, you can see that the second WHEN clause isn't used in the SEARCH ALL statement. It isn't needed, because the DEPENDING ON clause limits the binary search to the actual number of entries in the table. If you check the format for the SEARCH ALL statement in figure 6-1, you can see that two

WHEN clauses are illegal in a SEARCH ALL statement. In addition, you can only code equal conditions in the one WHEN clause; greater-than or less-than conditions are illegal.

## Discussion

By using the table handling elements presented in this chapter, you should be able to handle the tables required by most of the report preparation programs you are assigned. You should realize, however, that there are a few more table handling elements, even though they aren't used that often. Also, you should realize that tables of two or three levels are fairly common in business programs. As a result, *Part 2* in this series presents all of the table handling elements of COBOL as well as the techniques for handling two- and three-level tables.

When you code table handling routines, you should be on guard for debugging problems. Two of the most common coding errors are (1) failing to set an index to a starting value before a SEARCH statement is executed, and (2) using an index that is beyond the acceptable number of occurrences for a table. Both errors can lead to program cancellation and difficult debugging problems, so it's best to avoid these problems by watching for these errors when you code.

As you might guess, commonly used tables are often supplied as COPY members. For instance, a constant table like the month table is likely to be available as a COPY member. Similarly, a routine for loading a commonly used table like the price table may be available as a subprogram. Then, you can load the table by issuing a single CALL statement.

## Terminology

one-level table
index name
index
occurrence number
displacement value
binary search
key
key field

## Objective

Given program specifications involving a one-level table, code the required COBOL routines.

## Topic 2 How to read records in indexed files

In chapter 1, I introduced you to the concept of *indexed file organization*. When a file has indexed organization, a program can read the file in sequence by *key field*. This is called *sequential access* of the file. However, a program can also access any one of the records in the file on a direct basis. This is called *random access*. To access a file on a random basis, the program must supply the *key* of the record to be accessed. If, for example, one of the key fields for a file is the customer number field, one key for a record is its customer number. If you want to refresh your memory about indexed files, please refer back to chapter 1 and figure 1-8.

In this topic I'll show you how to write programs that read indexed files with only one key field on either a sequential or random basis. As you'll see, this is relatively easy to do. Then, in *Part 2* of this series, you'll learn how to write, rewrite, and delete the records in an indexed file. You'll also learn how to process indexed files that have more than one key field.

### The COBOL elements for reading indexed files

Figure 6-10 presents a subset of the COBOL elements for reading indexed files. However, these are the only elements you'll need for reading the files in the vast majority of report preparation programs that you'll ever write. As you can see, you need to learn some new clauses for SELECT statements. You also need to learn the format for a READ statement that reads the records in an indexed file on a random basis.

The SELECT statement for an indexed file gives the method of file organization (INDEXED), the access method (SEQUENTIAL or RANDOM), and the name of the key field (RECORD KEY). For sequential access, you can omit the ACCESS MODE clause because sequential access is assumed, but it's a good practice to code the clause so it's clear that sequential access is being used.

The RECORD KEY clause gives the name of the key field for the file, and this field must be coded in the File Section, not the Working-Storage Section. The standards say that this field should be an alphanumeric item. However, most compilers allow you to define this field as a numeric item with DISPLAY usage. What's most important, though, is that you define the key field the same way in all the programs that access the file.

For sequential access of an indexed file, you code the READ statement just as you do a READ statement for a sequential file. As

### The COBOL elements for sequential access

#### The SELECT statement for sequential access

```
SELECT   file-name   ASSIGN TO system-name
                     ORGANIZATION IS INDEXED
                     [ACCESS MODE IS SEQUENTIAL]
                     RECORD KEY IS data-name.
```

Note: The RECORD KEY field must be defined in the File Section within the record area description that comes right after the FD statement for the file.

#### The READ statement for sequential access

```
READ file-name RECORD
     [INTO record-name]
     AT END imperative-statement.
```

### The COBOL elements for random access

#### The SELECT statement for random access

```
SELECT   file-name   ASSIGN TO system-name
                     ORGANIZATION IS INDEXED
                     ACCESS MODE IS RANDOM
                     RECORD KEY IS data-name.
```

Note: The RECORD KEY field must be defined in the File Section within the record area description that comes right after the FD statement for the file.

#### The READ statement for random access

```
READ file-name RECORD
     [INTO record-name]
     INVALID KEY imperative-statement.
```

**Figure 6-10** A subset of the COBOL elements for reading indexed files

consecutive READ statements are executed, the file is read in sequence from start to finish, one record at a time. When there are no more records in the file, the AT END clause is executed.

For random access of an indexed file, you code an INVALID KEY clause instead of an AT END clause. Before the READ statement is executed, though, the key of the record that is to be read must be placed in the key field identified by the RECORD KEY clause in the SELECT statement. Then, if the program finds a record in the file with a key equal to the key in the RECORD KEY field, the record is read into storage. If the program can't find the record, the INVALID KEY clause of the READ statement is executed.

### How to read an indexed file on a sequential basis

Figure 6-11 gives an example of the coding you need when your program reads an indexed file sequentially. In the SELECT statement, you can see the three new clauses for the file. They specify the organization, the access method, and the name of the key field for the file.

In the File Section, you can see that you code the FD statement for an indexed file just as you code the FD statement for a sequential file. If the records are blocked, you can use the BLOCK CONTAINS clause. However, on most modern systems, indexed files are either unblocked or the system determines an efficient blocking factor for each file, so you usually don't need this clause.

In the record description after the FD statement, the RECORD KEY field is coded. Since the READ INTO form of the READ statement is used in this example, only the key field is defined in this area. Note that its name is the same as the name in the RECORD KEY clause in the SELECT statement for the file. Note also that this key field has the same picture and the same location within the record description in the File Section as IM-ITEM-NO does within the record description in the Working-Storage Section.

In the Working-Storage Section, the end-of-file switch and the complete record description for the file are defined. This is done just as if the file had sequential organization. Then, in the Procedure Division, the READ statement for sequential access operates just like a READ statement for a sequential file.

### How to read an indexed file on a random basis

Figure 6-12 gives an example of the coding you need when your program reads an indexed file on a random basis. Here again, the SELECT statement for the file gives the organization, the access method, and the name of the key field. Also, only the RECORD KEY field is coded in the record description after the FD statement in the File Section.

**The SELECT statement in the Environment Division**

```
SELECT INVMAST ASSIGN TO SYS020-INVMAST
               ORGANIZATION IS INDEXED
               ACCESS IS SEQUENTIAL
               RECORD KEY IS ITEM-NUMBER.
```

**The FD statement and record description in the File Section of the Data Division**

```
 FD  INVMAST
     LABEL RECORDS ARE STANDARD
     RECORD CONTAINS 100 CHARACTERS.
*
 01  INVENTORY-MASTER.
*
     05  ITEM-NUMBER                  PIC X(5).
     05  FILLER                       PIC X(95).
*
```

**The EOF switch and the record description in the Working-Storage Section of the Data Division**

```
 01  SWITCHES.
*
     05  INVMAST-EOF-SWITCH           PIC X         VALUE 'N'.
         88  INVMAST-EOF                            VALUE 'Y'.
*
 01  INVENTORY-MASTER-RECORD.
*
     05  IM-ITEM-NO                   PIC X(5).
     05  IM-ITEM-DESCRIPTION          PIC X(20).
     .
     .
*
```

**The sequential read module in the Procedure Division**

```
 310-READ-INVENTORY-MASTER.
*
     READ INVMAST RECORD INTO INVENTORY-MASTER-RECORD
         AT END
             MOVE 'Y' TO INVMAST-EOF-SWITCH.
*
```

**Figure 6-11** Reading an indexed master file using sequential access

In the Working-Storage Section, a different kind of switch is used for the indexed file because it's going to be read on a random basis. This switch is named RECORD-FOUND-SWITCH in this example, but it could be named something like MASTER-FOUND-SWITCH or INVMAST-FOUND-SWITCH. After a READ statement is executed for the file, this switch should have a value of Y if the record has been found or a value of N if the INVALID KEY clause has been executed.

**The SELECT statement in the Environment Division**

```
SELECT INVMAST ASSIGN TO SYS020-INVMAST
               ORGANIZATION IS INDEXED
               ACCESS IS RANDOM
               RECORD KEY IS ITEM-NUMBER.
```

**The FD statement and record description in the File Section of the Data Division**

```
 FD   INVMAST
      LABEL RECORDS ARE STANDARD
      RECORD CONTAINS 100 CHARACTERS.
*
 01   INVENTORY-MASTER.
*
      05   ITEM-NUMBER                     PIC X(5).
      05   FILLER                          PIC X(95).
*
```

**The record-found switch and the record description in the Working-Storage Section of the Data Division**

```
 01   SWITCHES.
*
      05   RECORD-FOUND-SWITCH             PIC X.
           88   RECORD-FOUND                         VALUE 'Y'.
*
 01   INVENTORY-MASTER-RECORD.
*
      05   IM-ITEM-NO                      PIC 9(5).
      05   IM-ITEM-DESCRIPTION             PIC X(20).
      .
      .
*
```

**The random read module in the Procedure Division**

```
 310-READ-INVENTORY-MASTER.
*
     MOVE TR-ITEM-NUMBER TO ITEM-NUMBER.
     MOVE 'Y' TO RECORD-FOUND-SWITCH.
     READ INVMAST RECORD INTO INVENTORY-MASTER-RECORD
         INVALID KEY
             MOVE 'N' TO RECORD-FOUND-SWITCH.
*
```

**Figure 6-12** Reading an indexed master file using random access

In the Procedure Division, you can see how a read module for random access of an indexed file is coded. First, the key of the record to be read is moved into the RECORD KEY field. In this example, a transaction item number (TR-ITEM-NUMBER) is moved into ITEM-

NUMBER. Second, the RECORD-FOUND-SWITCH is turned on. Third, the READ statement is executed, and a value of N is moved to RECORD-FOUND-SWITCH if the INVALID KEY clause is executed. As a result, this switch has a value of N if the record can't be found and a value of Y if it has been found.

### Discussion

As I promised, it's relatively easy to code reading operations for indexed files. It gets quite a bit more complicated when you use more than one key, when you switch from one access mode to another within a single program, and when you write, rewrite, and delete records in a file. Nevertheless, indexed file handling isn't that difficult. In *Part 2*, you'll learn all of the COBOL elements for processing indexed files as well as the techniques for handling them efficiently.

Perhaps you've noticed the similarities between the terminology for table handling and the terminology for indexed file handling. To search a table, you vary the *indexes* that identify the entries in the table. Also, for a binary search, the *keys* must be in sequence. Similarly, indexed files are controlled by *indexes*, and you access records on a random basis by supplying the *keys* of the records you want. These similarities shouldn't confuse you, though. You just have to keep in mind that the indexes and keys for tables are one thing, and the indexes and keys for files are another.

### Terminology

indexed file organization
key field
sequential access
random access
key

### Objective

Given program specifications that require one or more indexed input files, code the required COBOL routines.

## Topic 3 The investment-listing program

In this topic, I'll show you another version of the investment-listing program that I presented in chapters 4 and 5. It illustrates the use of table handling elements and indexed files. It reads an inventory master file with indexed organization on a sequential basis. And it reads an inventory extension file with indexed organization on a random basis. At the end of this topic, I'll show you how you could modify this program so it reads both files sequentially.

### The program overview

Figure 6-13 presents the program overview for this program. It prepares an investment listing from an inventory master file and an inventory extension file. Both files are indexed by the item number field. In other words, the item number field is the key field.

Otherwise, this program is much like the previous version of the investment-listing program. It prints a line on the investment listing when the investment amount is over $10,000. However, it derives one of the fields on the listing from data in the extension record.

### The record description for the inventory extension file

Figure 6-14 is a listing of the COPY member that describes the records in the inventory extension file. This COPY member is named INVEXT. As you can see, each extension record contains 12 occurrences of monthly sales data. Each of these occurrences gives the sales for one month in both units and dollars. You can assume that these records are updated at the end of each month, so the data for occurrence 12 is for the most recent month, while the data for occurrence 1 is for the twelfth month before the current month.

Because data like this isn't used by every program that requires the inventory master record, it's not uncommon to keep it in an extension record, rather than in the master record itself. Then, the master file is smaller so it can be read more efficiently, and the extension file is only used when its data is needed. In any event, the use of the extension file in this example will serve to illustrate the use of indexed files.

### The print chart for the investment listing

Figure 6-15 gives the print chart for the revised investment listing. As the shaded data indicates, only one column of data is different than the data in the investment listings of the previous chapters. Instead of

| Program: | INV3520 Prepare investment listing | Page: 1 |
|---|---|---|
| Designer: | Anne Prince | Date: 04-03-86 |

Input/output specifications

| File | Description | Use |
|---|---|---|
| INVMAST | Inventory master file | Input |
| INVEXT | Inventory extension file | Input |
| INVLIST | Print file: Investment listing | Output |

Process specifications

```
This program prepares an investment listing from an indexed file of
inventory master records and an indexed file of inventory extension
records.  Both files are indexed by the item number field.

The investment listing should be printed in item number sequence.  For
each master record, a line should be printed on the investment listing
only if the investment amount is greater than $10,000.

The basic processing requirements for each inventory master record
follow:

1.  Read the master record.

2.  Calculate the investment amount.
    (Investment amount = on-hand balance x unit price)

3.  If the investment amount is greater than $10,000:
    a.  read the inventory extension record on a random basis
    b.  calculate the required output fields
    c.  format and print an investment line.  To figure the number of
        months inventory on hand, divide the investment amount by the
        average of the last three months' sales.

After all records have been processed, prepare and print the total
lines.
```

**Figure 6-13** The revised program overview for the investment-listing program

```
 01   INVENTORY-EXTENSION-RECORD.
*
     05  IE-ITEM-NO                  PIC 9(5).
     05  IE-MONTHLY-SALES-DATA       OCCURS 12 TIMES
                                     INDEXED BY MONTHLY-SALES-INDEX.
         10  IE-UNIT-SALES           PIC S9(5).
         10  IE-DOLLAR-SALES         PIC S9(5)V99.
*
```

**Figure 6-14** The INVEXT COPY member for the inventory extension record

last month's sales, the average dollar sales for the last three months should be printed for each inventory item listed. This, of course, is a more realistic indication of how many months' stock of an item is on hand, because the data for just one month can be misleading. To derive this data, the program must read the extension record for an item and average the dollar sales for the last three months.

### The structure chart

Figure 6-16 presents the structure chart for the investment-listing program of this chapter. This chart is like the chart in figure 5-10, except that module 320 has been modified so it only calculates the investment amount for an item, and modules 325, 326, 327, and 328 have been added to the program. This illustrates how easy it is to make a modification to a structured program.

### The COBOL listing

Figure 6-17 presents the COBOL listing for the new version of the investment-listing program. Like the other program listings in this book, this one is for an IBM mainframe using the VS COBOL compiler under the DOS/VSE operating system. I've shaded the code that differs from the code in figure 5-11.

**The Environment Division** If you check the SELECT statements for the disk files in the Environment Division, you can see that they follow the formats given in figure 6-10. Both are indexed files with item-number key fields. The master file will be accessed sequentially. The extension file will be accessed randomly. To distinguish one file's key field from the other's, the first key field is named INVMAST-ITEM-NUMBER, while the second one is named INVEXT-ITEM-NUMBER.

**The Data Division** In the File Section, you can see that the key fields are defined in the record descriptions after the FD statements for the files. This is a COBOL requirement.

```
DATE:  99/99/99                                          MIKE MURACH & ASSOCIATES, INC.                                      PAGE: ZZ9
TIME:  99:99 XX                                                                                                              INV3520
                                   INVENTORY INVESTMENT LISTING -- ITEMS WITH RETAIL VALUE OVER $10,000

ITEM                               UNIT   QUANTITY   LAST        AVG. SALES          INVESTMENT      NO. OF MONTHS
 NO.     ITEM DESCRIPTION          PRICE  ON HAND  ORDER DATE    LAST 3 MOS.         IN RETAIL $    INVENTORY ON HAND

ZZZZZ  XXXXXXXXXXXXXXXXXXXX      ZZZ.99   -----9   99/99/99     ---,---.99       --,---,---.99        ----.9

ZZZZZ RECORDS IN THE MASTER FILE                             $$$$,$$$,$$$.99 *  $$$$,$$$,$$$.99 *     ZZZ.9 *
ZZZZZ RECORDS IN THIS SELECTED LISTING
```

**Figure 6-15** The revised print chart for the investment listing

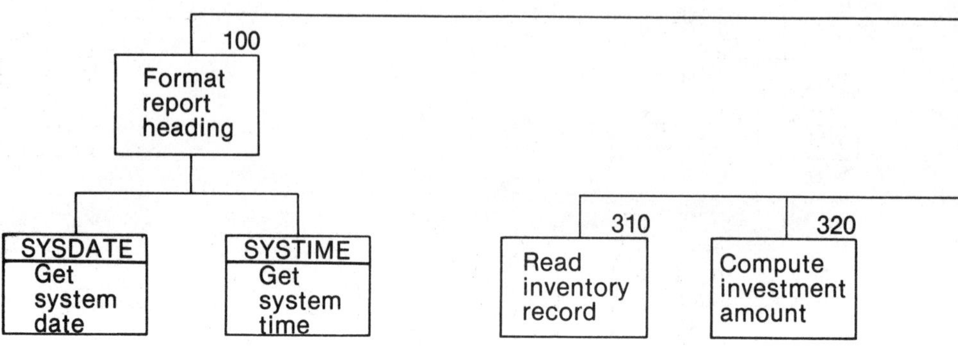


**Figure 6-16** The revised structure chart for the investment-listing program

Then, in the Working-Storage Section, you can see that a RECORD-FOUND-SWITCH has been defined that will be used in the read module for the extension file. You can see a number of minor changes that provide for the change from last month's sales on the investment listing to average sales for the last three months. And you can see that the complete record description for the extension file has been copied into the program with a COPY statement.

**The Procedure Division** In the Procedure Division, it's important that you understand why module 300 is coded the way it is. Here, it first performs module 320 to calculate the investment amount for a record. Then, if the investment amount isn't greater than $10,000, the module doesn't do anything. As a result, the program processes the next master record in sequence.

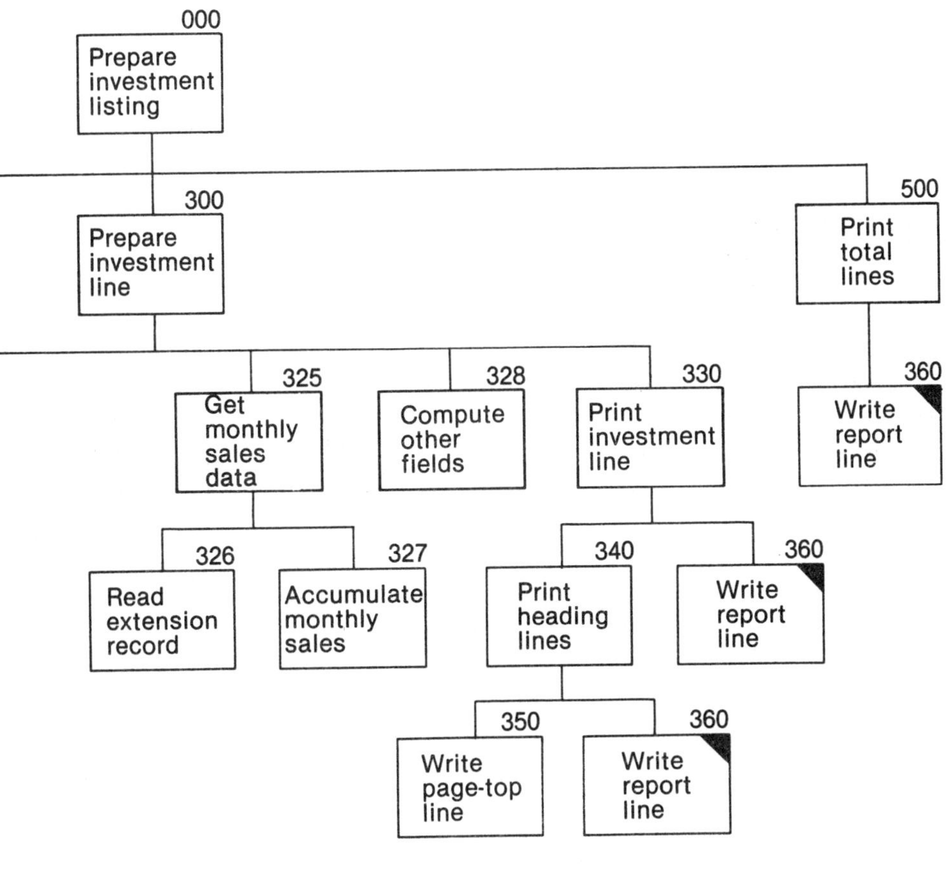


In contrast, the module could be coded like this:

```
PERFORM 310-READ-INVENTORY-RECORD.
IF NOT INVMAST-EOF
     PERFORM 320-COMPUTE-INVESTMENT-AMOUNT
     PERFORM 325-GET-MONTHLY-SALES-DATA
     PERFORM 328-COMPUTE-OTHER-FIELDS
     IF INVESTMENT-AMOUNT > 10000
          PERFORM 330-PRINT-INVESTMENT-LINE.
```

Although this coding would produce the same investment listing, it would read the inventory extension file for each master record. As a result, it wouldn't be nearly as efficient as the coding in figure 6-17.

```
000100 IDENTIFICATION DIVISION.
000200*
000300 PROGRAM-ID.          INV3520.
000400*AUTHOR.              MIKE MURACH.
000500*
000600 ENVIRONMENT DIVISION.
000700*
000800 INPUT-OUTPUT SECTION.
000900*
001000 FILE-CONTROL.
001100     SELECT INVMAST ASSIGN TO SYS020-INVMAST
001200                    ORGANIZATION IS INDEXED
001300                    ACCESS IS SEQUENTIAL
001400                    RECORD KEY IS INVMAST-ITEM-NUMBER.
001500     SELECT INVEXT  ASSIGN TO SYS021-INVEXT
001600                    ORGANIZATION IS INDEXED
001700                    ACCESS IS RANDOM
001800                    RECORD KEY IS INVEXT-ITEM-NUMBER.
001900     SELECT INVLIST ASSIGN TO SYS006-UR-1403-S.
002000*
002100 DATA DIVISION.
002200*
002300 FILE SECTION.
002400*
002500 FD  INVMAST
002600     LABEL RECORDS ARE STANDARD
002700     RECORD CONTAINS 80 CHARACTERS.
002800*
002900 01  INVENTORY-MASTER.
003000*
003100     05  INVMAST-ITEM-NUMBER      PIC 9(5).
003200     05  FILLER                   PIC X(75).
003300*
003400 FD  INVEXT
003500     LABEL RECORDS ARE STANDARD
003600     RECORD CONTAINS 149 CHARACTERS.
003700*
003800 01  INVENTORY-EXTENSION.
003900*
004000     05  INVEXT-ITEM-NUMBER       PIC 9(5).
004100     05  FILLER                   PIC X(144).
004200*
004300 FD  INVLIST
004400     LABEL RECORDS ARE OMITTED
004500     RECORD CONTAINS 132 CHARACTERS.
004600*
004700 01  PRINT-AREA               PIC X(132).
004800*
004900 WORKING-STORAGE SECTION.
005000*
005100 01  SWITCHES.
005200*
005300     05  INVMAST-EOF-SWITCH              PIC X       VALUE 'N'.
005400         88  INVMAST-EOF                             VALUE 'Y'.
005500     05  INVESTMENT-SIZE-ERROR-SWITCH    PIC X.
005600         88  INVESTMENT-SIZE-ERROR                   VALUE 'Y'.
005700     05  RECORD-FOUND-SWITCH             PIC X.
005800         88  RECORD-FOUND                            VALUE 'Y'.
005900*
```

**Figure 6-17** The revised COBOL listing for the investment-listing program (part 1 of 7)

```
006000 01  PRINT-FIELDS                 COMP-3.
006100*
006200     05  SPACE-CONTROL            PIC S9.
006300     05  LINES-ON-PAGE            PIC S999 VALUE +55.
006400     05  LINE-COUNT               PIC S999 VALUE +99.
006500     05  PAGE-COUNT               PIC S999 VALUE ZERO.
006600*
006700 01  DATE-FIELDS.
006800*
006900     05  TODAYS-DATE                  PIC 9(6).
007000     05  TODAYS-DATE-R REDEFINES TODAYS-DATE.
007100         10  TODAYS-MONTH             PIC 99.
007200         10  TODAYS-DAY               PIC 99.
007300         10  TODAYS-YEAR              PIC 99.
007400*
007500 01  COUNT-FIELDS                     COMP-3.
007600*
007700     05  RECORD-COUNT                 PIC S9(5)       VALUE ZERO.
007800     05  SELECTED-RECORD-COUNT        PIC S9(5)       VALUE ZERO.
007900*
008000 01  CALCULATED-FIELDS                      COMP-3.
008100*
008200     05  INVESTMENT-AMOUNT                  PIC S9(7)V99.
008300     05  NO-OF-MONTHS-STOCK                 PIC S9(3)V9.
008400     05  SALES-LAST-3-MONTHS                PIC S9(7)V99.
008500     05  AVG-SALES-LAST-3-MONTHS            PIC S9(5)V99.
008600*
008700 01  TOTAL-FIELDS                           COMP-3.
008800*
008900     05  SELECTED-L3-SALES-TOTAL            PIC S9(9)V99    VALUE ZERO.
009000     05  SELECTED-INVESTMENT-TOTAL          PIC S9(9)V99    VALUE ZERO.
009100*
009200 COPY INVMAST.
C              01  INVENTORY-MASTER-RECORD.
C             *
C                  05  IM-DESCRIPTIVE-DATA.
C                      10  IM-ITEM-NO                 PIC 9(5).
C                      10  IM-ITEM-DESC               PIC X(20).
C                      10  IM-UNIT-COST               PIC 999V99.
C                      10  IM-UNIT-PRICE              PIC 999V99.
C                  05  IM-INVENTORY-DATA.
C                      10  IM-REORDER-POINT           PIC S9(5).
C                      10  IM-ON-HAND                 PIC S9(5).
C                      10  IM-ON-ORDER                PIC S9(5).
C                  05  IM-SALES-DATA.
C                      10  IM-LAST-ORDER-DATE         PIC 9(6).
C                      10  IM-LAST-ORDER-DATE-R REDEFINES IM-LAST-ORDER-DATE.
C                          15  IM-LAST-ORDER-MONTH PIC 99.
C                          15  IM-LAST-ORDER-DAY   PIC 99.
C                          15  IM-LAST-ORDER-YEAR  PIC 99.
C                      10  IM-LAST-MONTH-SALES        PIC S9(5)V99.
C                      10  IM-LAST-YEAR-SALES         PIC S9(7)V99.
C                  05  FILLER                         PIC X(8).
009300*
009400 COPY INVEXT.
C              01  INVENTORY-EXTENSION-RECORD.
C             *
C                  05  IE-ITEM-NO                 PIC 9(5).
C                  05  MONTHLY-SALES-DATA         OCCURS 12 TIMES
C                                                 INDEXED BY MONTHLY-SALES-INDEX.
```

Figure 6-17 The revised COBOL listing for the investment-listing program (part 2 of 7)

```
C                    10  IE-UNIT-SALES          PIC S9(5).
C                    10  IE-DOLLAR-SALES        PIC S9(5)V99.
C          *
    009500*
    009600 COPY RPTHDG14.
C          01  HEADING-LINE-1.
C          *
C              05  FILLER             PIC X(7)     VALUE 'DATE:'.
C              05  HDG1-DATE          PIC 99/99/99.
C              05  FILLER             PIC X(36)    VALUE SPACE.
C              05  FILLER             PIC X(20)    VALUE 'MIKE MURACH & ASSOCI'.
C              05  FILLER             PIC X(20)    VALUE 'ATES, INC.          '.
C              05  FILLER             PIC X(31)    VALUE SPACE.
C              05  FILLER             PIC X(6)     VALUE 'PAGE:'.
C              05  HDG1-PAGE-NO       PIC ZZ9.
C              05  FILLER             PIC X        VALUE SPACE.
C          *
C          01  HEADING-LINE-2.
C          *
C              05  HDG2-TIME-DATA.
C                  10  FILLER               PIC X(7)     VALUE 'TIME:'.
C                  10  HDG2-HOURS           PIC 99.
C                  10  FILLER               PIC X        VALUE ':'.
C                  10  HDG2-MINUTES         PIC 99.
C                  10  FILLER               PIC X        VALUE SPACE.
C                  10  HDG2-TIME-SUFFIX     PIC X(8).
C              05  FILLER                   PIC X(101)   VALUE SPACE.
C              05  HDG2-REPORT-NUMBER       PIC X(10)    VALUE 'XXXX9999'.
    009700*
    009800 01  HEADING-LINE-3.
    009900*
    010000     05  FILLER  PIC X(20)  VALUE '                    '.
    010100     05  FILLER  PIC X(20)  VALUE '           INVENTOR'.
    010200     05  FILLER  PIC X(20)  VALUE 'Y INVESTMENT LISTING'.
    010300     05  FILLER  PIC X(20)  VALUE ' -- ITEMS WITH RETAI'.
    010400     05  FILLER  PIC X(20)  VALUE 'L VALUE OVER $10,000'.
    010500     05  FILLER  PIC X(20)  VALUE '                    '.
    010600     05  FILLER  PIC X(12)  VALUE '            '.
    010700*
    010800 01  HEADING-LINE-4.
    010900*
    011000     05  FILLER  PIC X(20)  VALUE 'ITEM                '.
    011100     05  FILLER  PIC X(20)  VALUE '         UNIT   QUAN'.
    011200     05  FILLER  PIC X(20)  VALUE 'TITY   LAST     AVG.'.
    011300     05  FILLER  PIC X(20)  VALUE ' SALES         INVEST'.
    011400     05  FILLER  PIC X(20)  VALUE 'MENT     NO. OF MONTH'.
    011500     05  FILLER  PIC X(20)  VALUE 'S                   '.
    011600     05  FILLER  PIC X(12)  VALUE '            '.
    011700*
    011800 01  HEADING-LINE-5.
    011900*
    012000     05  FILLER  PIC X(20)  VALUE ' NO.   ITEM DESCRIPT'.
    012100     05  FILLER  PIC X(20)  VALUE 'ION       PRICE  ON H'.
    012200     05  FILLER  PIC X(20)  VALUE 'AND ORDER DATE  LAST'.
    012300     05  FILLER  PIC X(20)  VALUE ' 3 MOS.        IN RET'.
    012400     05  FILLER  PIC X(20)  VALUE 'AIL $  INVENTORY ON '.
    012500     05  FILLER  PIC X(20)  VALUE 'HAND                '.
    012600     05  FILLER  PIC X(12)  VALUE '            '.
    012700*
    012800 01  INVESTMENT-LINE.
```

Figure 6-17 The revised COBOL listing for the investment-listing program (part 3 of 7)

```
012900*
013000         05  IL-ITEM-NO                PIC Z(5).
013100         05  FILLER                    PIC X(2)     VALUE SPACE.
013200         05  IL-ITEM-DESC              PIC X(20).
013300         05  FILLER                    PIC X(2)     VALUE SPACE.
013400         05  IL-UNIT-PRICE             PIC ZZZ.99.
013500         05  FILLER                    PIC X(2)     VALUE SPACE.
013600         05  IL-ON-HAND                PIC -----9.
013700         05  FILLER                    PIC X(2)     VALUE SPACE.
013800         05  IL-LAST-ORDER-DATE        PIC 99/99/99.
013900         05  FILLER                    PIC X(3)     VALUE SPACE.
014000         05  IL-AVG-SALES-LAST-3-MONTHS
014100                                       PIC ---,---.99
014200                                       BLANK WHEN ZERO.
014300         05  IL-AVG-SALES-LAST-3-MESSAGE
014400                 REDEFINES IL-AVG-SALES-LAST-3-MONTHS
014500                                       PIC X(10).
014600         05  FILLER                    PIC X(6)     VALUE SPACE.
014700         05  IL-INVESTMENT-AMOUNT      PIC --,---,---.99.
014800         05  IL-INVESTMENT-AMT-MESSAGE REDEFINES IL-INVESTMENT-AMOUNT
014900                                       PIC X(13).
015000         05  FILLER                    PIC X(6)     VALUE SPACE.
015100         05  IL-NO-OF-MONTHS-STOCK     PIC ----.9.
015200         05  IL-NO-OF-MONTHS-STOCK-MESSAGE
015300                 REDEFINES IL-NO-OF-MONTHS-STOCK
015400                                       PIC X(6).
015500         05  FILLER                    PIC X(35)    VALUE SPACE.
015600*
015700 01  TOTAL-LINE-1.
015800*
015900         05  TL1-RECORD-COUNT          PIC Z(5).
016000         05  FILLER                    PIC X(15)    VALUE ' RECORDS IN THE'.
016100         05  FILLER                    PIC X(12)    VALUE ' MASTER FILE'.
016200         05  FILLER                    PIC X(19)    VALUE SPACE.
016300         05  TL1-SEL-L3-SALES-TOTAL        PIC $$$$,$$$,$$$.99.
016400         05  FILLER                    PIC X(2)     VALUE ' *'.
016500         05  FILLER                    PIC X(2)     VALUE SPACE.
016600         05  TL1-SEL-INVESTMENT-TOTAL      PIC $$$$,$$$,$$$.99.
016700         05  FILLER                    PIC X(2)     VALUE ' *'.
016800         05  FILLER                    PIC X(5)     VALUE SPACE.
016900         05  TL1-SEL-NO-OF-MONTHS-STOCK PIC ZZZ.9.
017000         05  FILLER                    PIC X(2)     VALUE ' *'.
017100         05  FILLER                    PIC X(33)    VALUE SPACE.
017200*
017300 01  TOTAL-LINE-2.
017400*
017500         05  TL2-SEL-RECORD-COUNT  PIC Z(5).
017600         05  FILLER            PIC X(15)  VALUE ' RECORDS IN THI'.
017700         05  FILLER            PIC X(18)  VALUE 'S SELECTED LISTING'.
017800         05  FILLER            PIC X(94)  VALUE SPACE.
017900*
018000 PROCEDURE DIVISION.
018100*
018200 000-PREPARE-INVESTMENT-LISTING.
018300*
018400         OPEN INPUT  INVMAST
018500                     INVEXT
018600              OUTPUT INVLIST.
018700         PERFORM 100-FORMAT-REPORT-HEADING.
018800         PERFORM 300-PREPARE-INVESTMENT-LINE
```

**Figure 6-17** The revised COBOL listing for the investment-listing program (part 4 of 7)

```
           UNTIL INVMAST-EOF.
       PERFORM 500-PRINT-TOTAL-LINES.
       CLOSE INVMAST
             INVEXT
             INVLIST.
       DISPLAY 'INV3520   I   1   NORMAL EOJ'.
       STOP RUN.
*
100-FORMAT-REPORT-HEADING.
*
       CALL 'SYSDATE' USING TODAYS-DATE.
       MOVE TODAYS-DATE TO HDG1-DATE.
       CALL 'SYSTIME' USING HDG2-TIME-DATA.
       MOVE 'INV3520' TO HDG2-REPORT-NUMBER.
*
300-PREPARE-INVESTMENT-LINE.
*
       PERFORM 310-READ-INVENTORY-RECORD.
       IF NOT INVMAST-EOF
           PERFORM 320-COMPUTE-INVESTMENT-AMOUNT
           IF INVESTMENT-AMOUNT > 10000
               PERFORM 325-GET-MONTHLY-SALES-DATA
               PERFORM 328-COMPUTE-OTHER-FIELDS
               PERFORM 330-PRINT-INVESTMENT-LINE.
*
310-READ-INVENTORY-RECORD.
*
       READ INVMAST RECORD INTO INVENTORY-MASTER-RECORD
           AT END
               MOVE 'Y' TO INVMAST-EOF-SWITCH.
       IF NOT INVMAST-EOF
           ADD 1 TO RECORD-COUNT.
*
320-COMPUTE-INVESTMENT-AMOUNT.
*
       MOVE 'N' TO INVESTMENT-SIZE-ERROR-SWITCH.
       COMPUTE INVESTMENT-AMOUNT = IM-ON-HAND * IM-UNIT-PRICE
           ON SIZE ERROR
               MOVE 9999999.99 TO INVESTMENT-AMOUNT
               MOVE 'Y' TO INVESTMENT-SIZE-ERROR-SWITCH.
*
325-GET-MONTHLY-SALES-DATA.
*
       PERFORM 326-READ-EXTENSION-RECORD.
       IF RECORD-FOUND
           MOVE ZERO TO SALES-LAST-3-MONTHS
           PERFORM 327-ACCUMULATE-MONTHLY-SALES
               VARYING MONTHLY-SALES-INDEX FROM 10 BY 1
               UNTIL MONTHLY-SALES-INDEX > 12.
*
326-READ-EXTENSION-RECORD.
*
       MOVE 'Y' TO RECORD-FOUND-SWITCH.
       MOVE IM-ITEM-NO TO INVEXT-ITEM-NUMBER.
       READ INVEXT RECORD INTO INVENTORY-EXTENSION-RECORD
           INVALID KEY
               MOVE 'N' TO RECORD-FOUND-SWITCH.
*
327-ACCUMULATE-MONTHLY-SALES.
*
```

**Figure 6-17** The revised COBOL listing for the investment-listing program (part 5 of 7)

```
        ADD IE-DOLLAR-SALES (MONTHLY-SALES-INDEX)
            TO SALES-LAST-3-MONTHS.
*
 328-COMPUTE-OTHER-FIELDS.
*
        IF RECORD-FOUND
            COMPUTE AVG-SALES-LAST-3-MONTHS
                = SALES-LAST-3-MONTHS / 3
        ELSE
            MOVE ZERO TO AVG-SALES-LAST-3-MONTHS.
        IF          NOT INVESTMENT-SIZE-ERROR
                AND AVG-SALES-LAST-3-MONTHS POSITIVE
            COMPUTE NO-OF-MONTHS-STOCK ROUNDED =
                INVESTMENT-AMOUNT / AVG-SALES-LAST-3-MONTHS
                ON SIZE ERROR
                    MOVE 999.9 TO NO-OF-MONTHS-STOCK
        ELSE
            MOVE 999.9 TO NO-OF-MONTHS-STOCK.
*
 330-PRINT-INVESTMENT-LINE.
*
        IF LINE-COUNT > LINES-ON-PAGE
            PERFORM 340-PRINT-HEADING-LINES.
        MOVE IM-ITEM-NO                  TO IL-ITEM-NO.
        MOVE IM-ITEM-DESC                TO IL-ITEM-DESC.
        MOVE IM-UNIT-PRICE               TO IL-UNIT-PRICE.
        MOVE IM-ON-HAND                  TO IL-ON-HAND.
        MOVE IM-LAST-ORDER-DATE          TO IL-LAST-ORDER-DATE.
        IF RECORD-FOUND
            MOVE AVG-SALES-LAST-3-MONTHS
                TO IL-AVG-SALES-LAST-3-MONTHS
            ADD AVG-SALES-LAST-3-MONTHS
                TO SELECTED-L3-SALES-TOTAL
        ELSE
            MOVE '    NO DATA'
                TO IL-AVG-SALES-LAST-3-MESSAGE.
        IF NOT INVESTMENT-SIZE-ERROR
            MOVE INVESTMENT-AMOUNT   TO IL-INVESTMENT-AMOUNT
            ADD INVESTMENT-AMOUNT    TO SELECTED-INVESTMENT-TOTAL
            MOVE NO-OF-MONTHS-STOCK  TO IL-NO-OF-MONTHS-STOCK
        ELSE
            MOVE '    SIZE ERROR'    TO IL-INVESTMENT-AMT-MESSAGE
            MOVE '    N/A'           TO IL-NO-OF-MONTHS-STOCK-MESSAGE.
        MOVE INVESTMENT-LINE             TO PRINT-AREA.
        PERFORM 360-WRITE-REPORT-LINE.
        MOVE 1 TO SPACE-CONTROL.
        ADD 1 TO SELECTED-RECORD-COUNT.
*
 340-PRINT-HEADING-LINES.
*
        ADD 1 TO PAGE-COUNT.
        MOVE PAGE-COUNT TO HDG1-PAGE-NO.
        PERFORM 350-WRITE-PAGE-TOP-LINE.
        MOVE HEADING-LINE-2 TO PRINT-AREA.
        MOVE 1 TO SPACE-CONTROL.
        PERFORM 360-WRITE-REPORT-LINE.
        MOVE HEADING-LINE-3 TO PRINT-AREA.
        PERFORM 360-WRITE-REPORT-LINE.
        MOVE HEADING-LINE-4 TO PRINT-AREA.
        MOVE 2 TO SPACE-CONTROL.
```

**Figure 6-17** The revised COBOL listing for the investment-listing program (part 6 of 7)

```
030900         PERFORM 360-WRITE-REPORT-LINE.
031000         MOVE HEADING-LINE-5 TO PRINT-AREA.
031100         MOVE 1 TO SPACE-CONTROL.
031200         PERFORM 360-WRITE-REPORT-LINE.
031300         MOVE 2 TO SPACE-CONTROL.
031400*
031500 350-WRITE-PAGE-TOP-LINE.
031600*
031700         WRITE PRINT-AREA FROM HEADING-LINE-1
031800             AFTER ADVANCING PAGE.
031900         MOVE 1 TO LINE-COUNT.
032000*
032100 360-WRITE-REPORT-LINE.
032200*
032300         WRITE PRINT-AREA
032400             AFTER ADVANCING SPACE-CONTROL LINES.
032500         ADD SPACE-CONTROL TO LINE-COUNT.
032600*
032700 500-PRINT-TOTAL-LINES.
032800*
032900         MOVE RECORD-COUNT TO TL1-RECORD-COUNT.
033000         MOVE SELECTED-L3-SALES-TOTAL TO TL1-SEL-L3-SALES-TOTAL.
033100         MOVE SELECTED-INVESTMENT-TOTAL
033200             TO TL1-SEL-INVESTMENT-TOTAL.
033300         COMPUTE TL1-SEL-NO-OF-MONTHS-STOCK ROUNDED =
033400             SELECTED-INVESTMENT-TOTAL / SELECTED-L3-SALES-TOTAL
033500             ON SIZE ERROR
033600                 MOVE 999.9 TO TL1-SEL-NO-OF-MONTHS-STOCK.
033700         MOVE TOTAL-LINE-1 TO PRINT-AREA.
033800         MOVE 3 TO SPACE-CONTROL.
033900         PERFORM 360-WRITE-REPORT-LINE.
034000         MOVE SELECTED-RECORD-COUNT TO TL2-SEL-RECORD-COUNT.
034100         MOVE TOTAL-LINE-2 TO PRINT-AREA.
034200         MOVE 1 TO SPACE-CONTROL.
034300         PERFORM 360-WRITE-REPORT-LINE.
```

**Figure 6-17** The revised COBOL listing for the investment-listing program (part 7 of 7)

Otherwise, you should be able to follow the coding in the Procedure Division without too much trouble. It processes the table in the extension record as described in topic 1 of this chapter. And it reads the indexed master and extension records as described in topic 2. Note in module 325 that the index for the monthly sales data in the extension record is varied from an occurrence number of 10 by 1 until the number is greater than 12. This means that the data for the last three months is processed.

### Other acceptable structures for this program

As your programs require more modules, you'll find there's often more than one structure that leads to an acceptable program. For instance, figure 6-18 presents two other portions of a structure chart that would be acceptable for this revised version of the investment-listing program. Both alternatives use modules with similar names, but they are arranged in slightly different structures.

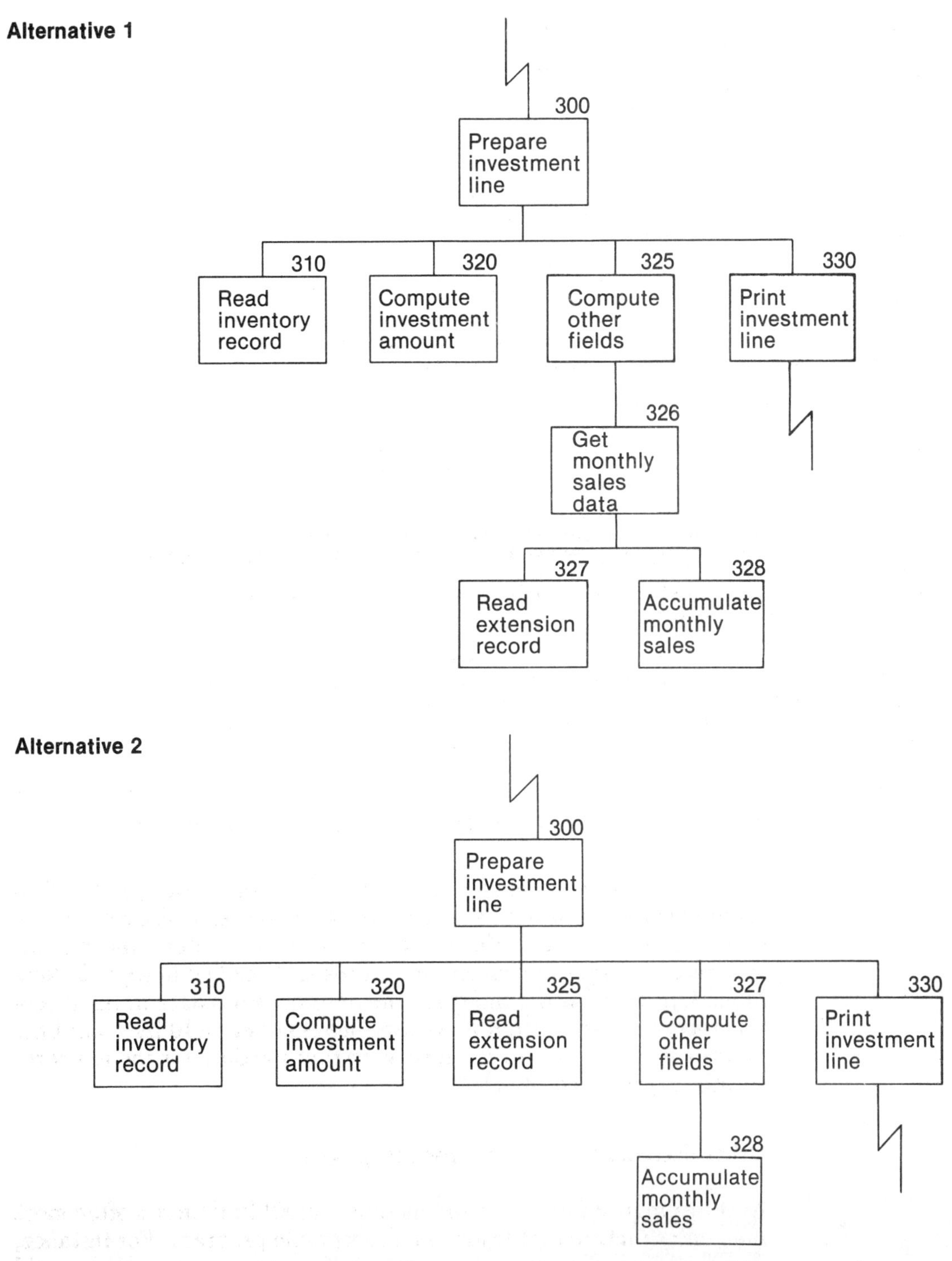


**Figure 6-18** Two other acceptable structures for the main processing modules of the investment-listing program

In alternative 1, module 300 calls module 310 to read an inventory master record. Next, it calls module 320 to compute the investment amount for the record. Then, if the investment amount is greater than $10,000, module 300 calls module 325 to compute the other fields required by the program and module 330 to print the investment line. In this structure, module 325 calls module 326 to get the monthly sales data, and module 326 calls module 327 to read an extension record and module 328 to accumulate the table data within the extension record.

In alternative 2, one less module is used to produce the investment listing. After module 310 reads an inventory master record, module 300 calls module 320 to compute the investment amount. Then, if the investment amount is greater than $10,000, module 300 calls module 325 to read an extension record and module 327 to compute the other fields required by the investment listing. To accumulate the table data within an extension record, module 327 calls module 328.

At this stage of your training, you should be able to write the code for either of the structures in figure 6-18. Of course, the code for either structure is similar to the code in figure 6-17. It's just arranged differently.

My point in showing you these structural alternatives is to make you aware that you can usually design acceptable processing structures in more than one way. This is particularly true at the lower levels of the structure chart. For all three structures (the structure in figure 6-16 and the two structures in figure 6-18, the modules at the first two levels are the same. It's only the modules at the third, fourth and fifth levels that differ. All three structures, however, are logical, and the modules in all three structures have clearly defined functions. As a result, all three are acceptable structures.

### Changes required for reading the extension file on a sequential basis

It's not always best to read a file like the extension file on a random basis. Often, in fact, a program like the investment-listing program will run more efficiently if both input files are read sequentially. This is particularly true if all of the records in both files must be processed. If, for example, the investment-listing program printed a line on the listing for each inventory master record, it would probably be more efficient to read the extension file sequentially, in tandem with the master file.

For most programs, you can read an indexed file sequentially or randomly using the same structure chart. If, for example, you decided it was more efficient to read the extension file sequentially in the investment-listing program, you could modify the COBOL code as shown in figure 6-19. As you can see, only a few lines of code have to be added to the program in figure 6-17 and only a few lines need to be changed.

```
000100 IDENTIFICATION DIVISION.
000200*
000300 PROGRAM-ID.          INV3520.
000400*AUTHOR.              MIKE MURACH.
000500*
000600 ENVIRONMENT DIVISION.
000700*
000800 INPUT-OUTPUT SECTION.
000900*
001000 FILE-CONTROL.
001100     SELECT INVMAST  ASSIGN TO SYS020-INVMAST
001200                     ORGANIZATION IS INDEXED
001300                     ACCESS IS SEQUENTIAL
001400                     RECORD KEY IS INVMAST-ITEM-NUMBER.
001500     SELECT INVEXT   ASSIGN TO SYS021-INVEXT
001600                     ORGANIZATION IS INDEXED
001700                     ACCESS IS SEQUENTIAL
001800                     RECORD KEY IS INVEXT-ITEM-NUMBER.
001900     SELECT INVLIST  ASSIGN TO SYS006-UR-1403-S.
002000*
002100 DATA DIVISION.
002200*
002300 FILE SECTION.
002400*
002500 FD  INVMAST
002600     LABEL RECORDS ARE STANDARD
002700     RECORD CONTAINS 80 CHARACTERS.
002800*
002900 01  INVENTORY-MASTER.
003000*
003100     05  INVMAST-ITEM-NUMBER       PIC 9(5).
003200     05  FILLER                    PIC X(75).
003300*
003400 FD  INVEXT
003500     LABEL RECORDS ARE STANDARD
003600     RECORD CONTAINS 149 CHARACTERS.
003700*
003800 01  INVENTORY-EXTENSION.
003900*
004000     05  INVEXT-ITEM-NUMBER        PIC 9(5).
004100     05  FILLER                    PIC X(144).
004200*
        .
        .
004900 WORKING-STORAGE SECTION.
005000*
005100 01  SWITCHES.
005200*
005300     05  INVMAST-EOF-SWITCH              PIC X        VALUE 'N'.
005400         88  INVMAST-EOF                              VALUE 'Y'.
005500     05  INVEXT-EOF-SWITCH               PIC X        VALUE 'N'.
005600         88  INVEXT-EOF                               VALUE 'Y'.
005700     05  INVESTMENT-SIZE-ERROR-SWITCH    PIC X.
005800         88  INVESTMENT-SIZE-ERROR                    VALUE 'Y'.
005900     05  RECORD-FOUND-SWITCH             PIC X.
006000         88  RECORD-FOUND                             VALUE 'Y'.
006100*
        .
        .
```

Figure 6-19 Coding for the investment-listing program when the extension file is read sequentially (part 1 of 3)

```
  009600 COPY INVEXT.
C         01   INVENTORY-EXTENSION-RECORD.
C        *
C              05  IE-ITEM-NO                     PIC 9(5).
C              05  MONTHLY-SALES-DATA             OCCURS 12 TIMES
C                                                 INDEXED BY MONTHLY-SALES-INDEX.
C                  10  IE-UNIT-SALES              PIC S9(5).
C                  10  IE-DOLLAR-SALES            PIC S9(5)V99.
C        *
         :

  018200 PROCEDURE DIVISION.
  018300*
  018400 000-PREPARE-INVESTMENT-LISTING.
  018500*
  018600     OPEN INPUT  INVMAST
  018700                 INVEXT
  018800          OUTPUT INVLIST.
  018900     PERFORM 100-FORMAT-REPORT-HEADING.
  019000     MOVE ZERO TO IE-ITEM-NO.
  019100     PERFORM 300-PREPARE-INVESTMENT-LINE
  019200         UNTIL INVMAST-EOF.
  019300     PERFORM 500-PRINT-TOTAL-LINES.
  019400     CLOSE INVMAST
  019500           INVEXT
  019600           INVLIST.
  019700     DISPLAY 'INV3520  I  1  NORMAL EOJ'.
  019800     STOP RUN.
  019900*
  020000 100-FORMAT-REPORT-HEADING.
  020100*
  020200     CALL 'SYSDATE' USING TODAYS-DATE.
  020300     MOVE TODAYS-DATE TO HDG1-DATE.
  020400     CALL 'SYSTIME' USING HDG2-TIME-DATA.
  020500     MOVE 'INV3520' TO HDG2-REPORT-NUMBER.
  020600*
  020700 300-PREPARE-INVESTMENT-LINE.
  020800*
  020900     PERFORM 310-READ-INVENTORY-RECORD.
  021000     IF NOT INVMAST-EOF
  021100         PERFORM 320-COMPUTE-INVESTMENT-AMOUNT
  021200         IF INVESTMENT-AMOUNT > 10000
  021300             PERFORM 325-GET-MONTHLY-SALES-DATA
  021400             PERFORM 328-COMPUTE-OTHER-FIELDS
  021500             PERFORM 330-PRINT-INVESTMENT-LINE.
  021600*
         :

  023300  325-GET-MONTHLY-SALES-DATA.
  023400*
  023500     PERFORM 326-READ-EXTENSION-RECORD
  023600         UNTIL IE-ITEM-NO NOT < IM-ITEM-NO.
  023700     IF IE-ITEM-NO = IM-ITEM-NO
  023800         MOVE 'Y' TO RECORD-FOUND-SWITCH
  023900     ELSE
  024000         MOVE 'N' TO RECORD-FOUND-SWITCH.
  024100     IF RECORD-FOUND
  024200         MOVE ZERO TO SALES-LAST-3-MONTHS
  024300         PERFORM 327-ACCUMULATE-MONTHLY-SALES
  024400             VARYING MONTHLY-SALES-INDEX FROM 10 BY 1
  024500             UNTIL MONTHLY-SALES-INDEX > 12.
```

**Figure 6-19** Coding for the investment-listing program when the extension file is read sequentially (part 2 of 3)

```
*
 326-READ-EXTENSION-RECORD.
*
     READ INVEXT RECORD INTO INVENTORY-EXTENSION-RECORD
         AT END
             MOVE 99999 TO IE-ITEM-NO
             MOVE 'Y' TO INVEXT-EOF-SWITCH.
*
 327-ACCUMULATE-MONTHLY-SALES.
*
     ADD IE-DOLLAR-SALES (MONTHLY-SALES-INDEX)
         TO SALES-LAST-3-MONTHS.
*
```

**Figure 6-19** Coding for the investment-listing program when the extension file is read sequentially (part 3 of 3)

Note in module 326 in figure 6-19 that 99999 is moved to IE-ITEM-NO when there are no more records in the file. As a result, the first PERFORM statement in module 325 won't execute module 326 after the last record has been read. In other words, IE-ITEM-NO with its value of 99999 will always be greater than the item number in the inventory master file. If module 325 did perform 326 after the last record in the extension file had been read, the program would be cancelled because a sequential READ statement for a file can't be executed after the end-of-file condition has occurred.

Likewise, the statement in module 000 that sets IE-ITEM-NO to zero at the start of the program is needed to control the logic in module 325. (If we didn't set IE-ITEM-NO to zero, it might contain any data—it would depend on how those bytes of storage were used last.) The first time module 325 is executed, the first PERFORM statement finds that IE-ITEM-NO (with its value of zero) is less than the value of IM-ITEM-NO for the inventory record just read in module 310. So, it performs module 326 to read an extension record. If the item number in that record is less than the inventory master item number, the program continues to read extension records until the condition in the PERFORM statement is true.

At that point, the program compares item numbers more carefully. If they're equal, the extension record is for the correct inventory item, so the RECORD-FOUND-SWITCH is set to Y and the program continues with module 327. If the extension item number is greater than the inventory master item number, it means there's no extension record to match the inventory master, and the RECORD-FOUND-SWITCH is set to N.

After the program finishes processing one master record, it starts again by reading another. Then, when module 325 is executed, if the extension record that was read the *last* time through is equal to or greater than the new inventory master, no new extension records are read. Instead, module 325 continues with the processing for the equal or greater-than condition. If there's a less-than condition, though, then another extension record is read.

I hope you understand this matching logic. It's very common in programs that read interdependent files sequentially. If you're not sure how it works, make up some values for the item numbers in the inventory master and extension files and follow them through the program. I think you'll quickly grasp how this code handles any kind of equal/not-equal condition that can occur. Then, in chapter 12, you'll learn how to design a program like this.

## Discussion

Although the investment-listing program in this topic doesn't do much more than the ones in the preceding chapters, it does illustrate the use of the table handling elements and the indexed file handling elements of COBOL. It also starts to demonstrate how the structural decisions become more complex as your programs become more complex. In fact, as you become more experienced with COBOL, coding itself gets to be the easy part of programming. The difficult tasks are designing the modules of the program and organizing the code so it's both efficient and readable.

## Objective

Apply the COBOL elements presented in this chapter to your application programs.

## Topic 4 Compiler dependent code

The program in figure 6-17 is written for an IBM mainframe using the VS COBOL compiler running under DOS/VSE. However, because the COBOL code in the program is standard, it should run with only a couple of changes on any system that uses 1974 or 1985 ANS COBOL. As I explained in chapter 3, you should code the program name, the Configuration Section, the system names in the SELECT statements, and the FD statements to conform to your compiler and your computer system. As I explained in chapter 4, you should code computational usages so they meet the requirements of your system and you should know how simple DISPLAY statements work on your system. And as I explained in chapter 5, you may have to code the COPY library name in COPY statements on your system.

As for the code presented in this chapter, it should run on all systems. Nevertheless, there are two compiler dependencies that you should be aware of just in case they apply to your system. These involve SEARCH ALL statements and system names in the SELECT statements for indexed files.

### SEARCH ALL statements

The ANS standards for the SEARCH ALL statement say that "a nonserial type of search operation *may* take place" during its execution "in a manner specified by the implementor." That means that the implementor (the developer of the compiler) can decide how the search will take place. It doesn't necessarily have to be a nonserial, or binary, search.

In practice, then, the SEARCH ALL statement as implemented on the compilers for microcomputers or minicomputers often doesn't do a binary search. Instead, it does the same kind of sequential search that a regular SEARCH statement does. As a result, the SEARCH ALL statement won't perform any faster than a SEARCH statement. In this case, there's no point in coding the extra clauses to define the table along with the SEARCH ALL statement, unless you intend to convert your programs to a compiler with a binary search later on.

Also, the compilers for micorocomputers and minicomputers don't always support the extra clauses for table definition, regardless of how they implement the SEARCH ALL statement. For example, the Wang VS COBOL compiler doesn't support the DEPENDING ON clause, even though it implements the SEARCH ALL statement as a binary search. As a result, a binary search on that system won't be adjusted to the actual length of the variable-length table.

In contrast, the compilers for mainframes usually do implement the SEARCH ALL statement with a binary search. For instance, the VS COBOL and VS COBOL II compilers for IBM mainframes provide binary searches, and they use the value you specify in the DEPENDING ON clause to adjust the search to the actual length of the table.

The point of all this is that you should find out how the SEARCH ALL statement is implemented on your system. Then, you can decide whether it's worth using.

### System names for indexed files

For many compilers, the system names used in the SELECT statements for indexed files are coded the same way as for sequential files. This is true for the Microsoft compiler for IBM PC's and the VS compiler for Wang VS systems.

For the compilers on IBM mainframes, though, the system name for an indexed file is slightly different than the system name for a sequential file. On a DOS system, the system name for an indexed file is usually coded as follows:

```
SYSnnn-filename
```

For an OS system, the system name for an indexed file is usually coded just as:

```
filename
```

On either system, indexed files are implemented as VSAM files.

### Objectives

1. Find out what the COBOL manuals for your system say about the use of SEARCH ALL statements.

2. Find out what your shop standards are for coding the system names for indexed files.

Chapter 7

# The 1985 COBOL elements for structured programming

Many of the new elements in the 1985 COBOL standards are designed to make it easier for you to code structured programs. In contrast, most of the other new elements are relatively trivial. In this chapter, you will learn how to use the 1985 COBOL elements for structured programming so you can take advantage of them as soon as a 1985 compiler is available to you.

As I write this, only the COBOL II compiler for IBM mainframes running under OS/MVS has already implemented the code described in this chapter. The compiler's available already because it was developed before the 1985 standards were approved. Other 1985 compilers are promised, however. So you may have one available to you by the time you read this book.

In this chapter, I'll first present the most important new elements for structured coding. I'll show you how they work and give you recommendations for their use. Then, I'll show you how they can be used in the investment-listing program that I presented in the last chapter. As you will see, these new elements won't have much effect on the way you design and code your programs, but they're useful at times.

## Structured delimiters

Figure 7-1 shows the verbs that can have *structured delimiters* under the 1985 standards (some of the verbs aren't covered in this book, but don't worry about that). Simply stated, the purpose of a structured delimiter is to show where a statement ends. So, in the first example in figure 7-1, the READ statement ends with the END-READ delimiter;

**Input/output verbs**

| | | |
|---|---|---|
| READ | REWRITE | RETURN |
| WRITE | DELETE | START |

**Example**

```
IF CONDITION-A
    READ TRANREC
        INVALID KEY
            MOVE 'Y' TO INVALID-KEY-SW
    END-READ
    MOVE TR-RECORD-KEY TO OLD-RECORD-KEY.
```

**Computational verbs**

| | | |
|---|---|---|
| ADD | MULTIPLY | COMPUTE |
| SUBTRACT | DIVIDE | |

**Example**

```
IF CONDITION-A
    ADD B TO C
        ON SIZE ERROR
            MOVE ZERO TO C
    END-ADD
    ADD C TO D.
```

**Miscellaneous verbs**

| | | |
|---|---|---|
| IF | EVALUATE | STRING |
| PERFORM | SEARCH | UNSTRING |
| CALL | | |

**Example**

```
IF CONDITION-A
    IF CONDITION-B
        PERFORM 100-PROCESS-CONDITION-B
    ELSE
        PERFORM 200-PROCESS-OTHER-CONDITION
    END-IF
    PERFORM 300-PROCESS-CONDITION-A.
```

**Figure 7-1** Verb list for structured delimiters

however, the IF condition is still in effect for the MOVE statement that follows.

In general, structured delimiters are only useful when one conditional statement is used within another one. This is illustrated by the

**Coding without END-IF**

```
*
 100-PRODUCE-EMPLOYEE-LINE.
*
     PERFORM 110-READ-EMPLOYEE-RECORD.
     IF NOT EMPLOYEE-EOF
         IF SR-ACTIVE-EMPLOYEE
             PERFORM 120-PRINT-ACTIVE-LINE
         ELSE
             PERFORM 130-PRINT-INACTIVE-LINE.
     IF NOT EMPLOYEE-EOF
         PERFORM 140-ACCUMULATE-GRAND-TOTAL.
*
```

**Coding with END-IF**

```
*
 100-PRODUCE-EMPLOYEE-LINE.
*
     PERFORM 110-READ-EMPLOYEE-RECORD.
     IF NOT EMPLOYEE-EOF
         IF SR-ACTIVE-EMPLOYEE
             PERFORM 120-PRINT-ACTIVE-LINE
         ELSE
             PERFORM 130-PRINT-INACTIVE-LINE
         END-IF
         PERFORM 140-ACCUMULATE-GRAND-TOTAL.
*
```

**Figure 7-2** How END-IF can improve the readability of a module

examples in figure 7-1. If a statement isn't used within another statement, it doesn't need a structured delimiter, because the period at the end of the statement is the delimiter. As a result, structured delimiters should have only a minor effect on your coding and little or no effect on the way you design programs.

Of all the structured delimiters, you'll probably use the END-IF delimiter the most. Because structured programming makes extensive use of nested IF statements, the END-IF can help you improve the readability of your modules as illustrated in figure 7-2. In the top example, the programmer had to code the IF NOT EMPLOYEE-EOF condition twice because the only way he could end the second IF statement was with a period. In the bottom example, the programmer ends the second IF statement with an END-IF so the code for the module is easier to read.

You should notice in figure 7-2 that the structured delimiter in the second example is aligned with the IF statement it ends. This makes it obvious which IF statement it's associated with. Whenever you use structured delimiters, you should align them in this way.

With the exception of END-IF, I don't think you'll use delimiters much. If you isolate I/O statements in their own modules as shown in this book, you won't ever need the delimiters for the I/O verbs. And you should have only an occasional need for delimiters on the computational verbs and the other miscellaneous verbs. As a general rule, then, you should only use structured delimiters when they improve readability...and this should be infrequently.

### The inline PERFORM

The *inline PERFORM* is a structure that many structured programming advocates have wanted for years. When you use an inline PERFORM, you code the performed function right after the PERFORM statement, and you end the function with the END-PERFORM delimiter or a period. In other words, the performed function is not coded in a separate paragraph. This is illustrated by the example in figure 7-3.

When the inline PERFORM is used as shown in figure 7-3, we agree that it is useful. Here, module 000 simply calls module 200 to load the price table. Then, module 200 uses an inline PERFORM VARYING statement to load the table. Without the inline PERFORM, module 000 must call module 200 with a PERFORM VARYING statement. In other words, without the inline PERFORM, module 200 really just loads a single table entry; with the inline PERFORM, the module does what its name implies and loads the entire table. For functions like this, we believe that the coding with the inline PERFORM is preferable to the coding without it.

The problem with the inline PERFORM is that it makes it relatively easy for you to code more than one function in a single COBOL paragraph. And that can lead to complex paragraphs that are difficult to read, test, and maintain. As a result, we don't think you should use inline PERFORMs much. As we see it, you should only use them when 1974 COBOL forces you to divide a function in a way that you wouldn't otherwise divide it. Then, the use of an inline PERFORM can help you consolidate the code in a single module so you improve both the structure and coding of your program.

### The PERFORM UNTIL statement WITH TEST AFTER

As you've already learned, the condition stated in a PERFORM UNTIL statement is tested before the performed module is called. Then, if the condition is true, the module isn't called. Although this is acceptable most of the time, there are times when it would be nice to have the statement test the condition after the module is called. And

**Coding without an inline PERFORM**

```
 000-PREPARE-PRICE-LISTING.
*
      .
      .
      PERFORM 200-LOAD-PRICE-TABLE
          VARYING PRICE-TABLE-INDEX FROM 1 BY 1
          UNTIL PTABLE-EOF.
      .
      .
*
 200-LOAD-PRICE-TABLE.
*
      PERFORM 210-READ-PRICE-TABLE-RECORD.
      IF NOT PTABLE-EOF
          MOVE PT-ITEM-NUMBER
              TO ITEM-NUMBER (PRICE-TABLE-INDEX)
          MOVE PT-ITEM-PRICE
              TO ITEM-PRICE (PRICE-TABLE-INDEX)
      ELSE
          SET PRICE-TABLE-INDEX DOWN BY 1
          SET PT-ENTRY-COUNT TO PRICE-TABLE-INDEX.
```

**Coding with an inline PERFORM**

```
 000-PREPARE-PRICE-LISTING.
*
      .
      .
      PERFORM 200-LOAD-PRICE-TABLE.
      .
      .
*
 200-LOAD-PRICE-TABLE.
*
      PERFORM
          VARYING PRICE-TABLE-INDEX FROM 1 BY 1
          UNTIL PTABLE-EOF
              PERFORM 210-READ-PRICE-TABLE-RECORD
              IF NOT PTABLE-EOF
                  MOVE PT-ITEM-NUMBER
                      TO ITEM-NUMBER (PRICE-TABLE-INDEX)
                  MOVE PT-ITEM-PRICE
                      TO ITEM-PRICE (PRICE-TABLE-INDEX)
               ELSE
                   SET PRICE-TABLE-INDEX DOWN BY 1
                   SET PT-ENTRY-COUNT TO PRICE-TABLE-INDEX
      END-PERFORM.
```

**Figure 7-3** How an inline PERFORM can improve the code of a load-table module

Coding with test before

```
 100-GENERATE-DEPT-STATISTICS.
*
           .
           .
           PERFORM 130-SEARCH-DEPT-TABLE
               VARYING DT-INDEX FROM 1 BY 1
               UNTIL DT-ENTRY-FOUND
                  OR DT-INDEX > DT-TABLE-LIMIT.
           SET DT-INDEX DOWN BY 1.
           .
           .
*
 130-SEARCH-DEPT-TABLE.
*
           IF DEPT-LOOKUP = DT-ENTRY (DT-INDEX)
               MOVE 'Y' TO DT-ENTRY-FOUND-SW.
```

Coding with test after

```
 100-GENERATE-DEPT-STATISTICS.
*
           .
           .
           PERFORM 130-SEARCH-DEPT-TABLE
               WITH TEST AFTER
               VARYING DT-INDEX FROM 1 BY 1
               UNTIL DT-ENTRY-FOUND
                  OR DT-INDEX =  DT-TABLE-LIMIT.
           .
           .
*
 130-SEARCH-DEPT-TABLE.
*
           IF DEPT-LOOKUP = DT-ENTRY (DT-INDEX)
               MOVE 'Y' TO DT-ENTRY-FOUND-SW.
```

**Figure 7-4** How WITH TEST AFTER can improve the code of a search function

that is what the WITH TEST AFTER language of the 1985 standards provides for.

Figure 7-4 illustrates how this statement can be useful. Without this clause, the search module derives an index that is one larger than the index of the desired table entry. As a result, the search module has to set the index down by 1 before passing control back to its calling module. But when the WITH TEST AFTER clause is used, the index has the desired value when the table entry is found.

Figure 7-5 presents flowcharts for the operation of PERFORM statements with tests before and after. As you saw in chapter 6, when

**PERFORM with test before**

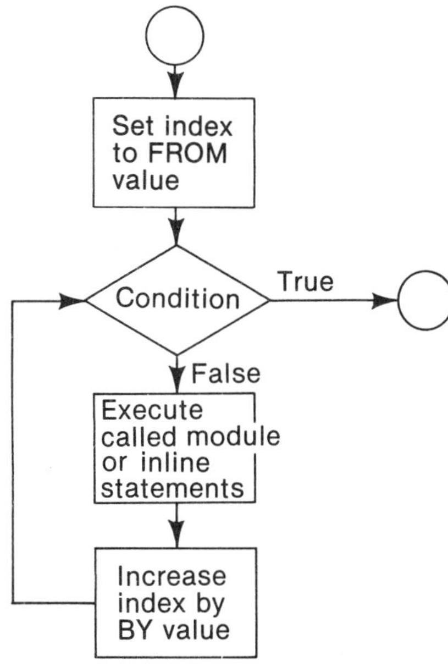


**PERFORM with test after**

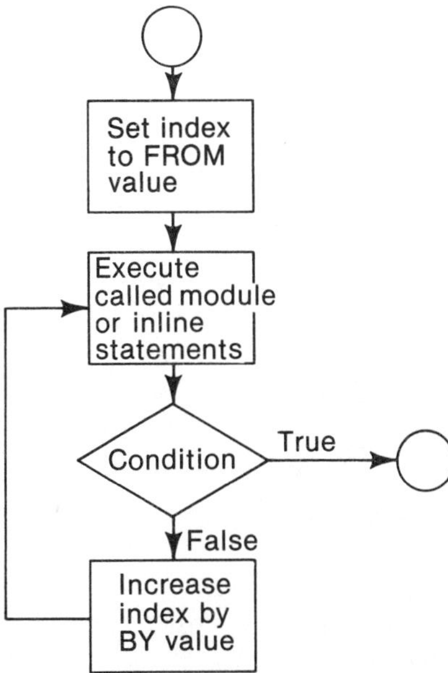


**Figure 7-5** Flowcharts for the logic of PERFORM statements with before and after tests

you use a before test, the index named in the VARYING clause is increased after the called module or inline statements have been executed. But that's not always what you want. In contrast, when you use an after test, the index is *not* increased if the condition is true after the called module or the inline statements have been executed. This explains why you have to reduce the index in the example in figure 7-4 by an occurrence value of one when the before test is used, but you don't have to reduce it at all when the after test is used.

Because the WITH TEST AFTER clause has limited application, you probably won't use it much. In fact, you can do anything with the traditional before test that you can do WITH TEST AFTER. Nevertheless, you should use this clause whenever it improves the clarity of your code.

### The SET TO TRUE statement

The SET TO TRUE statement is designed to be used with condition names. By using this statement, you can set a condition to true without knowing the value required by the condition. This is illustrated in figure 7-6. As you can see, using the SET TO TRUE statement is equivalent to moving the value of a condition to a field.

If you follow the examples in this book for coding and testing switches and flags, your coding will be quite readable. As a result, the SET TO TRUE statement won't do much to improve the clarity of your code. But it may make it easier for you to write the code in your Procedure Divisions.

In particular, you may want to use the SET TO TRUE statement when the value assigned to a condition name is not directly related to the condition name. In figure 7-6, for example, numeric values are assigned to mnemonic condition names. In a case like this, it's easier for you to remember a condition name than the value assigned to it. So it's somewhat easier for you to code the program if you use SET TO TRUE statements for turning conditions on. And this can also make your code somewhat easier to follow.

### The 1985 elements as used in the investment-listing program

To give you a better idea of how you can make use of the 1985 COBOL elements in your report preparation programs, I've rewritten the investment-listing program of chapter 6 using 1985 COBOL elements wherever appropriate. This made it possible for me to simplify the structure chart somewhat as shown by the portion of the structure chart in figure 7-7. This also made it possible for me to improve the readability of the coding somewhat as shown by the portion of the program in figure 7-8.

**Field description with condition names**

```
 DATA DIVISION.
*
        .
        .
        05  COMMISSION-STATUS       PIC X.
            88  TRAINEE             VALUE '1'.
            88  ASSISTANT           VALUE '2'.
            88  ASSOCIATE           VALUE '3'.
            88  MANAGER             VALUE '4'.
*
        .
        .
```

**Turning a condition on with a MOVE statement**

```
 PROCEDURE DIVISION.
*
        .
        .
        MOVE '3' TO COMMISSION-STATUS.
        .
        .
*
```

**Turning a condition on with a SET TO TRUE statement**

```
 PROCEDURE DIVISION.
*
        .
        .
        SET ASSOCIATE TO TRUE.
        .
        .
*
```

**Figure 7-6** The SET TO TRUE statement

If you compare the portion of the structure chart in figure 7-7 with the comparable portion of the chart in figure 6-16, you can see that three fewer modules are used in figure 7-7. Also, the logic of the program is a bit more apparent in the structure of figure 7-7 than it is in the structure of figure 6-16. In figure 7-7, module 300 calls module 310 to read a master record. Then, if the investment amount is greater than $10,000, module 300 calls module 320 to read an extension record, calls module 330 to compute all required output fields, and calls module 340 to print an investment line. As you will see, this structure is made possible by the use of one delimiter and one inline PERFORM. This structure couldn't be coded using only the elements of 1974 COBOL.

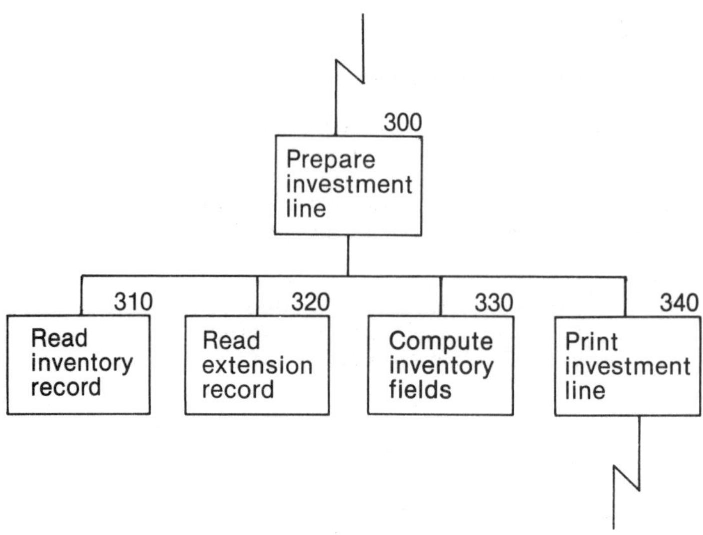


**Figure 7-7** A revised portion of the structure chart for the investment-listing program of chapter 6

In module 300 in figure 7-8, an END-COMPUTE delimiter is used to end the COMPUTE statement. As a result, this statement can be coded within a nested IF statement. Without the delimiter, this COMPUTE statement has to end with a period and the IF NOT INVMAST-EOF condition has to be repeated, or the COMPUTE statement has to be coded in a separate module and performed as shown in figure 6-17. So the END-COMPUTE delimiter saves some coding here. I think it also makes the program somewhat more readable than it would be otherwise.

In module 300, I used the SET TO TRUE statement to turn the INVESTMENT-SIZE-ERROR condition on. I also used it in the other modules to turn conditions on. Frankly, I don't think this improves the readability of the program at all. Also, for simple switches, I think you should be able to set a condition to false as well as to true. But why quibble? If you think this statement improves readability, by all means use it.

In module 330, I used an inline PERFORM to accumulate the monthly sales for the last three months. In this case, the END-PERFORM delimiter is essential because the PERFORM is within an IF statement. Since I used a WITH TEST AFTER clause in this PERFORM statement, it ends with this condition:

```
UNTIL MONTHLY-SALES-INDEX = 12
```

To me, this is a bit more logical than the greater-than condition you would have to code with a test before. However, this is only a minor improvement in readability.

```
 300-PREPARE-INVESTMENT-LINE.
*
     PERFORM 310-READ-INVENTORY-RECORD.
     IF NOT INVMAST-EOF
         MOVE 'N' TO INVESTMENT-SIZE-ERROR-SWITCH
         COMPUTE INVESTMENT-AMOUNT = IM-ON-HAND * IM-UNIT-PRICE
             ON SIZE ERROR
                 MOVE 9999999.99 TO INVESTMENT-AMOUNT
                 SET INVESTMENT-SIZE-ERROR TO TRUE
         END-COMPUTE
         IF INVESTMENT-AMOUNT > 10000
             PERFORM 320-READ-EXTENSION-RECORD
             PERFORM 330-COMPUTE-INVENTORY-FIELDS
             PERFORM 340-PRINT-INVESTMENT-LINE.
*
 310-READ-INVENTORY-RECORD.
*
     READ INVMAST RECORD INTO INVENTORY-MASTER-RECORD
         AT END
             SET INVMAST-EOF TO TRUE.
     IF NOT INVMAST-EOF
         ADD 1 TO RECORD-COUNT.
*
 320-READ-EXTENSION-RECORD.
*
     SET RECORD-FOUND TO TRUE.
     MOVE IM-ITEM-NO TO INVEXT-ITEM-NUMBER.
     READ INVEXT RECORD INTO INVENTORY-EXTENSION-RECORD
         INVALID KEY
             MOVE 'N' TO RECORD-FOUND-SWITCH.
*
 330-COMPUTE-INVENTORY-FIELDS.
*
     IF RECORD-FOUND
         MOVE ZERO TO SALES-LAST-3-MONTHS
         PERFORM
             WITH TEST AFTER
             VARYING MONTHLY-SALES-INDEX FROM 10 BY 1
             UNTIL MONTHLY-SALES-INDEX = 12
                 ADD IE-DOLLAR-SALES (MONTHLY-SALES-INDEX)
                     TO SALES-LAST-3-MONTHS
         END-PERFORM
         COMPUTE AVG-SALES-LAST-3-MONTHS
             = SALES-LAST-3-MONTHS / 3
     ELSE
         MOVE ZERO TO AVG-SALES-LAST-3-MONTHS.
     IF         NOT INVESTMENT-SIZE-ERROR
           AND AVG-SALES-LAST-3-MONTHS POSITIVE
         COMPUTE NO-OF-MONTHS-STOCK ROUNDED =
             INVESTMENT-AMOUNT / AVG-SALES-LAST-3-MONTHS
             ON SIZE ERROR
                 MOVE 999.9 TO NO-OF-MONTHS-STOCK
     ELSE
         MOVE 999.9 TO NO-OF-MONTHS-STOCK.
*
```

**Figure 7-8** Revised code using 1985 COBOL for the investment-listing program of chapter 6

The 1985 elements for structured programming don't apply to any of the other paragraphs in this program. As you can see, then, these elements won't have much effect on most of your programs. Nevertheless, these elements can be useful at times.

## Discussion

In this chapter, I haven't covered all of the new Procedure Division code that is part of the 1985 standards. For instance, a CONTINUE statement, which does nothing, and an INITIALIZE statement, which sets fields to starting values, are part of the new standards. Also, an EVALUATE statement is available for coding some complex structures. Although I will cover these elements in *Part 2* of this series, you will only use them occasionally and you can certainly get by without them.

## Terminology

structured delimiter
inline PERFORM

## Objective

If you have a 1985 compiler available to you, apply the elements presented in this chapter to your application programs.

# Section 3

# Program development techniques

This section contains three chapters. Chapter 8 is an introduction to procedures and job control language (JCL) for compiling and testing COBOL programs. Since the procedures vary from one system to another, topic 1 makes no attempt to give you specific procedures for your system. However, topic 2 presents specific JCL information for users of IBM mainframes running under DOS/VSE, and topic 3 gives specific JCL information for users of IBM mainframes running under OS/MVS. You can read this chapter any time after you complete chapter 3, but we recommend that you read it before you compile and test your first program.

Chapter 9 shows you how to compile a source program and correct any diagnostic errors it contains. You can read this chapter any time after you complete chapter 3, but we recommend that you read it just before you compile your first program or right after you get your first diagnostics.

Chapter 10 shows you how to test and debug a program. Again, you can read this chapter any time after you complete chapter 3, but we recommend that you read it just before you test your first program.

Chapter 8

# Procedures and JCL for compiling and testing a program

After you enter your source program into your system, you can compile and test it. However, the procedure you use to do this varies from one system to another. On some systems, you can start a compilation by pressing one key on the keyboard of your terminal. On other systems, it's a good deal more complicated than that.

In topic 1 of this chapter, I'm going to introduce you to the types of procedures that you may use to compile and test a program on your system. As you will see, before you can use some of these procedures, you need to code job control language, or JCL, that directs the compilations and tests. As a result, in topics 2 and 3, I'll introduce you to the JCL you use for compiling and testing programs on IBM mainframes operating under the DOS/VSE operating system (topic 2) or the OS/MVS operating system (topic 3).

You can read this chapter any time after you complete chapter 3. But the best time to read it is probably right before or right after you enter your first program into your system.

No matter what system you're using, you should read topic 1 of this chapter to get some idea of how to go about compiling and testing on your system. Then, if you're using a DOS/VSE system, read topic 2, and if you're using an OS/MVS system, read topic 3. If your system isn't an IBM mainframe but it requires the use of job control language, you should skip topics 2 and 3 and find out what job control language you need to use on your system.

## Topic 1 Procedures for compiling and testing a program

As I said in chapter 2, this book doesn't show you how to enter a source program into a computer system using an interactive editor. There are just too many systems and too many editors to present them all in one book.

Similarly, this book doesn't show you how to compile and test a program once it has been entered into the system. Again, there are just too many systems and too many different ways that this can be done.

In this topic, then, the best I can do is introduce you to some of the most common procedures for compiling and testing programs on an interactive system. Because I believe a few specific examples are better than dozens of generalities, I'm going to present some typical interactive procedures for compiling and testing programs on an IBM PC, a Wang VS minicomputer, an IBM mainframe running under DOS/VSE, and an IBM mainframe running under OS/MVS. Before I start this presentation, though, let me refresh your memory on what needs to be done in order to compile and test a program.

### The three steps for compiling and testing a program

In general, it takes three computer steps to compile and test a program as flowcharted in figure 8-1. The three steps make up one *job*, and each of the steps can be referred to as a *job step*. In the third job step in figure 8-1, a program is tested that reads one or more disk files and produces printed output. This is the type of program you'll be writing in this course.

In step 1, the source program is compiled into an object program by the COBOL compiler. If the source program uses any COPY members (as presented in chapter 5), they are inserted into the program. During the compilation, the compiler output is printed on the system's printer. (You'll see samples of typical compiler output in the next chapter.)

In step 2, the linkage editor turns the object program into an executable program. If the object program requires any subprograms (as presented in chapter 5), the linkage editor links them with the object program. As the linkage editor links the main program and any subprograms, the linkage editor output is printed on the system's printer. The linkage editor output shows which modules have been linked.

Finally, in step 3, the executable application program can be tested. When a report preparation program is executed, it reads any disk files required by the program and prints the specified output.

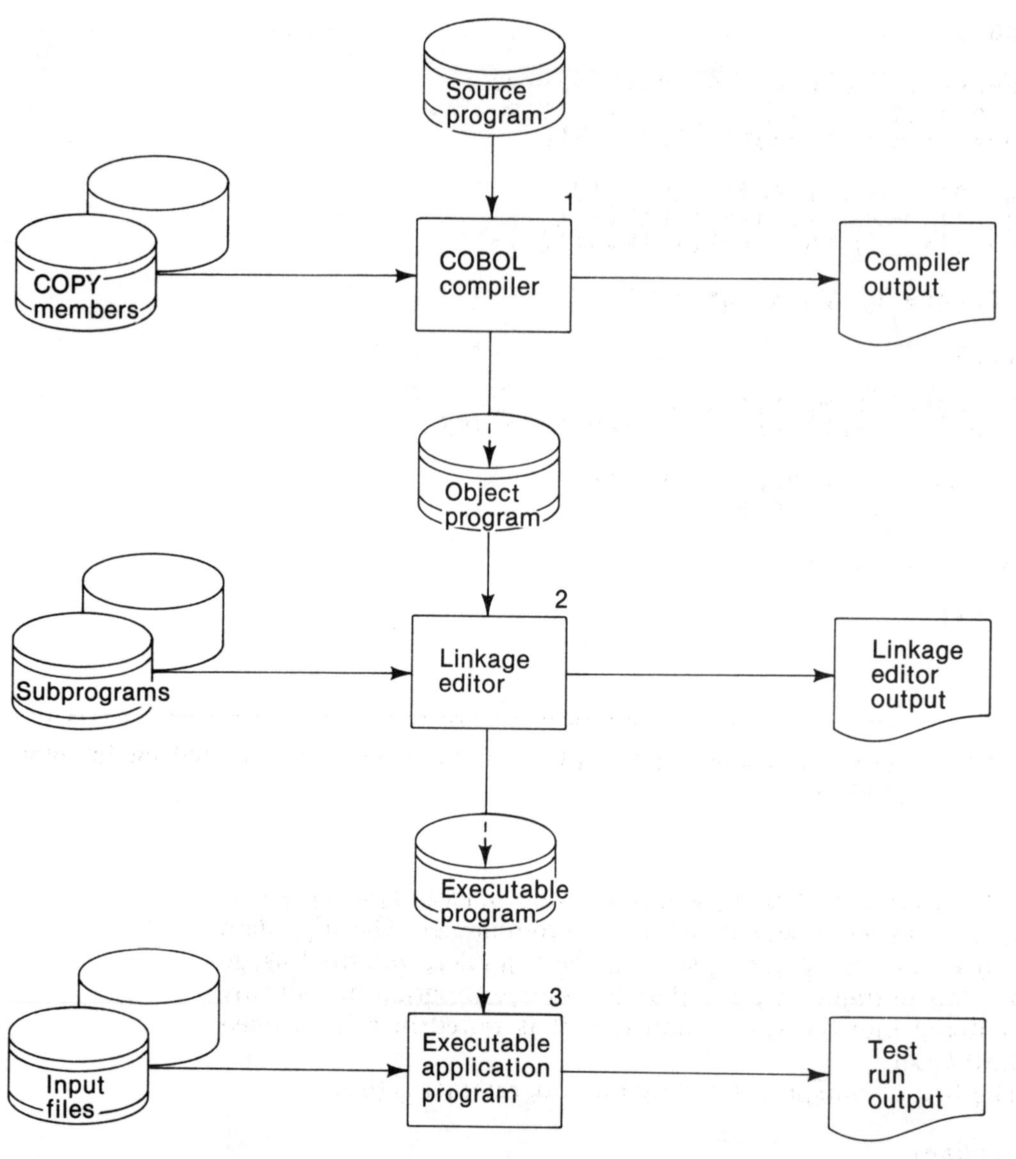


**Figure 8-1** The three steps in a procedure to compile, link, and test a COBOL source program

As you will now see, these three steps are normally done whether the system is a microcomputer, a minicomputer, or a mainframe. Sometimes, the linkage editing step isn't required, but most of the time it is.

## Procedures on an IBM PC

Figure 8-2 shows the commands used to compile and test the inventory-listing program during an interactive session on an IBM PC

```
B>A:COBOL

IBM Personal Computer COBOL Compiler
Version 1.00 (C) Copyright IBM Corp 1982
(C)Copyright Microsoft, Inc. 1982

Source filename [.COB]: INV3510
Object filename [INV3510.OBJ]:
Source listing [NUL.LST]: INV3510.LST

  No Errors or Warnings

B>A:LINK

IBM Personal Computer Linker
Version 1.10 (C) Copyright IBM Corp 1982

Object modules [.OBJ]: INV3510
Run file [INV3510.EXE]:
List file [NUL.MAP]:
Libraries [.LIB]:

B>INV3510

B>
```

Figure 8-2 An interactive session on an IBM PC to compile, link, and test the inventory-listing program

using the Microsoft COBOL compiler. The shaded data represents commands and responses entered by the programmer. The other data is displayed by the operating system, the compiler, and the linkage editor. This example assumes that the source program has already been entered into the system and that it is stored in a file named INV3510.COB.

The first command entered by the programmer is this:

```
A:COBOL
```

This tells the operating system to load the program named COBOL (the COBOL compiler) from diskette drive A and to execute the program.

When the COBOL compiler is executed, it asks the programmer for the file names to be used for the source file, the object file, and the source listing (that is, the compiler listing). In this example, the programmer responds with INV3510 and INV3510.LST. Based on these responses and the default values given in brackets, the compiler assumes that the source program is in INV3510.COB, the object program should be stored in INV3510.OBJ, and the compiler listing should be stored in INV3510.LST.

On this system, the compiler listing is stored in a print file by the compiler. Then, if the programmer decides that she wants to print it, she can do so using another command. At the end of the compilation, the compiler prints a message indicating how many diagnostics the program has generated.

Since the compilation has no diagnostics, the programmer enters this second command:

```
A:LINK
```

This tells the operating system to load the program named LINK (the linkage editor) from diskette drive A and to execute it. The linkage editor then asks for the names of the object program file, the run file (the executable program), the linkage editor listing file, and the library files. In this example, the programmer responds with only INV3510. As a result, the linkage editor assumes that the object program is in INV3510.OBJ, that the run file should be stored in INV3510.EXE, that no linkage editor listing should be prepared (NUL.MAP), and that the default libraries should be used.

When the linkage editor finishes executing, the programmer enters the last command: INV3510. Since a Microsoft COBOL program gives the names of the input files to be used during the test run, the system requires no further information. As a result, it starts the test run of the executable module named INV3510.EXE. When the test run is over, the operating system indicates that it is ready for another command.

Of course, this is only one way that you can compile and test programs on a PC. There are other COBOL compilers for the IBM PC. And there are sophisticated editors that make it much easier for you to compile and test a COBOL program. Nevertheless, this is a typical procedure on a PC, so it should give you some idea of what you might have to do when using one.

### Procedures on a Wang VS minicomputer

The Wang VS minicomputer has a sophisticated interactive editor that you use for entering, compiling, and testing a COBOL program. When you finish entering a program into the system using this editor, the screen displays a menu like the one in figure 8-3. As you can see, it offers up to 16 functions that you can start by pressing one function key. At the time this screen was displayed, functions 11, 12, and 14 weren't reasonable, so they weren't offered. At other times in the development of a program, though, they are offered.

To start the three-step process for compiling, linking, and testing a program, you press function key 9 on the keyboard of your terminal. The compiler then compiles your program. If it compiles without any serious diagnostics, the system automatically continues by link editing

```
   *** WANG VS INTEGRATED PROGRAM DEVELOPMENT EDITOR - VERSION  6.09.15 ***
INPUT FILE IS INV3510   IN LIBRARY SC1SRCE  ON VOLUME SYS1
THERE ARE      125 LINES IN THE EDITED TEXT.


PLEASE SELECT THE DESIRED FUNCTION AND PRESS THE APPROPRIATE PF KEY:

 (1) DISPLAY       - RESUME TEXT EDITING
 (2) SET           - SET WORKSTATION DEFAULTS AND EDITOR/COMPILER OPTIONS
 (3) MENU          - ACTIVATE THE NORMAL MENU
 (4) RESTART       - EDIT ANOTHER FILE
 (5) CREATE        - CREATE A NEW FILE FROM THE EDITED TEXT
 (6) REPLACE       - REPLACE THE INPUT FILE WITH THE EDITED TEXT
 (7) RENUMBER      - GENERATE NEW LINE NUMBERS FOR THE EDITED TEXT
 (8) EXTERNAL COPY - COPY A RANGE OF LINES FROM ANOTHER FILE TO THE WORK FILE
 (9) RUN           - COMPILE AND RUN PROGRAM
(10) COMPILE       - COMPILE THE EDITED TEXT


(13) UTILITIES     - RUN VS UTILITY (OR OTHER) PROGRAMS

(15) PRINT         - PRINT THE EDITED TEXT
(16) EXIT          - END EDITOR PROCESSING
```

**Figure 8-3** The program development screen for compiling and testing a program on a Wang VS minicomputer

the object program. Then, if the link editing is done successfully, the system automatically continues by testing your program.

During compilation, if a program needs any information that it doesn't have, the system asks you for it. If, for example, the compiler can't find a COPY member that the source program requests, it asks you to identfy it by giving its file name, library name, and volume name. And if your program doesn't give the names of the test files it's supposed to read, the system asks you to identity them.

## Procedures on an IBM mainframe under DOS/VSE

To enter a program into an IBM mainframe that runs under the DOS/VSE operating system, you can use any one of several editors. One of the most popular is called ICCF (the Interactive Computing and Control Facility). After you use it to enter a program, you can use it to compile and test a program, but you can do so in more than one way.

Figure 8-4 illustrates one way of compiling and testing a program when using ICCF. After the programmer finishes entering the source program, he adds some job control language to the source file. In the top portion of figure 8-4, the shaded lines in the screen represent the first portion of the JCL that is put into the source file along with the inventory-listing program. Some of the JCL precedes the source program; some of it follows the source program. In this example, the JCL will direct the system to compile, link, and test the source program. Together, the JCL and the source program represent one job that can be run by the operating system.

After the programmer stores the job in a single file named INV3510, he submits the job to the operating system as shown in the second screen in figure 8-4. To do this, he uses the SUBMIT command, which is shaded in the illustration. When the SUBMIT command is executed, the job is sent to the operating system for processing.

In topic 2 of this chapter, you'll be introduced to the JCL you need for compiling and testing a program when you use a procedure like this. As I said, though, there are other ways to compile and test a program on a DOS/VSE system. Some of these alternatives don't require you to know anything about JCL as long as you're working with simple COBOL programs. Eventually, though, as your programs become more complex, you'll have to learn how to use JCL.

### Procedures on an IBM mainframe under OS/MVS

To enter a program into an IBM mainframe that runs under the OS/MVS operating system, you can use any one of several editors. One of the most popular is called ISPF (the Interactive System Productivity Facility). After you use it to enter a program, you can use it to compile and test a program, but you can do so in more than one way.

Figure 8-5 illustrates one way of compiling and testing a program when using ISPF. After the programmer finishes entering the source program, he stores it in a source file. Then, he creates another file that contains job control language. This file represents one job that will direct the system to compile, link, and test the source program. After the programmer finishes editing the JCL for the job, he submits it to the operating system. To do this, he uses the SUBMIT command, which is shaded in the illustration.

In topic 3 of this chapter, you'll be introduced to the JCL you need for compiling and testing a program when you use a procedure like this. As I said, though, there are other ways to compile and test a program on an OS/MVS system. Some of these alternatives don't require you to know anything about JCL as long as you're working with simple COBOL programs. Eventually, though, as your programs become more complex, you'll have to learn how to use JCL.

**Storing a job stream in INV3510 using ICCF's full-screen editor**

```
===> FILE INV3510
<<..+....1....+....2....+....3....+....4....+....5....+.. INP=*INPARA*>>..+..FS
***** TOP OF FILE *****                                              /===/
// JOB        MMC4                                                   *===*
// OPTION     LINK                                                   *===*
// EXEC       FCOBOL                                                 *===*
       IDENTIFICATION DIVISION.                                      *===*
      *                                                              *===*
       PROGRAM-ID.         INV3510.                                  *===*
      *AUTHOR.             MIKE MURACH.                              *===*
      *                                                              *===*
       ENVIRONMENT DIVISION.                                         *===*
      *                                                              *===*
       CONFIGURATION SECTION.                                        *===*
      *                                                              *===*
       SOURCE-COMPUTER.  IBM-370.                                    *===*
       OBJECT-COMPUTER.  IBM-370.                                    *===*
      *                                                              *===*
       INPUT-OUTPUT SECTION.                                         *===*
      *                                                              *===*
       FILE-CONTROL.                                                 *===*
           SELECT INVMAST ASSIGN TO SYS020-AS-INVMAST.               *===*
           SELECT INVLIST ASSIGN TO SYS006-UR-1403-S.                *===*
      *                                                              *===*
```

**Submitting the job stream in INV3510 for processing**

```
SUBMIT INV3510
 ...+....1....+....2....+....3....+....4....+....5....+....6....+....7....+..CM
*FULL-SCREEN EDITOR TERMINATED
*READY
```

**Figure 8-4** Compiling and testing the inventory-listing program using the SUBMIT command of ICCF under DOS/VSE on an IBM mainframe

```
EDIT - MM.TEST.CNTL(COBOL) --------------------------------- COLUMNS 001 072
COMMAND INPUT ===> SUBMIT                                    SCROLL ===> 20
****** ***************************** TOP OF DATA ****************************
000100 //MMC4         JOB  (MMA,MURACH),'MIKE MURACH'
000200 //             EXEC PROC=COBUCLG
000300 //COB.SYSIN    DD   DSNAME=MMA.COBOL.SOURCE(INV3510),DISP=SHR
000400 //GO.INVMAST DD     DSNAME=MMA.TEST.INVMAST,DISP=SHR
000500 //GO.INVLIST DD     SYSOUT=A
000600 //GO.SYSOUT    DD   SYSOUT=A
****** **************************** BOTTOM OF DATA **************************
```

Figure 8-5 Compiling and testing the inventory-listing program using the SUBMIT command of ISPF under OS/MVS on an IBM mainframe

### Discussion

As I said at the start of this topic, there are so many different ways to compile and test a program on an interactive system that the best I can do is introduce you to some typical development procedures. With this as background, you can find out what procedures you are supposed to use on your system.

### Terminology

job
job step

### Objective

Find out what procedures you are supposed to use on your system to compile and test your source programs.

## Topic 2 JCL for compiling and testing a program on an IBM mainframe under DOS/VSE

Most of the time, when you write programs for an IBM mainframe using the DOS/VSE operating system, you'll use JCL to control compilation, link editing, and testing. In figure 8-4 in the last topic, for example, I showed you how you can code JCL statements in the same file with the source program you want to compile and test. When you do this, the entire file represents one job. Then, you can submit the job to the system for processing.

In this topic, I'll introduce you to some typical jobs for compiling and testing COBOL programs. I won't try to explain the JCL in these jobs in detail, but I will highlight the code that will vary from one job to another. Specifically, I'll present jobs for: (1) compiling a source program; (2) compiling and testing a disk-to-printer program that doesn't use COPY members or call subprograms; and (3) compiling and testing a program that uses COPY members, calls subprograms, and reads two input files to prepare one report.

### Job 1: A compile-only job

Figure 8-6 presents a simple DOS job for compiling but not testing a COBOL program. A job like this can be used to compile the programs in chapters 3 and 4 of this book.

As you can see, two JCL statements precede the source program and two follow it. In the first statement, which is a JOB statement, I gave the name MMC3 to the job. When you write your own programs, though, you will want to use job names that are consistent with your shop standards. You may also have to code some accounting information after the job name in your JOB statements.

Otherwise, this job should be pretty much the same from one DOS system to another. Here, the second statement, the EXEC statement, starts the execution of the program named FCOBOL, which is the COBOL compiler. As it executes, it reads the source program that follows the EXEC statement. The /* at the end of the source program indicates that there are no more source statements to be compiled. The /& at the end of the job indicates the end of the job.

In general, you won't run a compile-only job very often. Usually, if your program compiles without any diagnostics, you'll want to link and test it right away. So except for the first compilation of a new program when you're almost certain to have diagnostics...or when you're creating subprograms, which you won't learn to do in this book ...you'll use a compile-link-and-test job instead of a compile-only job.

```
// JOB       MMC3
// EXEC      FCOBOL
     .
   Source program
     .
/*
/&
```

Figure 8-6 A DOS/VSE job stream to compile a program without linking and testing it

**Job 2: A compile-link-and-test job**

Figure 8-7 presents a DOS/VSE job for compiling, linking, and testing a COBOL program. A job like this can be used to compile and test the programs in chapters 3 and 4 of this book. And, depending on how the system is set up, a job like this may also be satisfactory for the program in chapter 5 that uses both COPY members and subprograms.

In this example, three JCL statements precede the source program and six follow it. Once again, you should code the job name and the accounting information in the JOB statement in accordance with your shop standards.

The second statement in this job is the OPTION statement. It can be used to specify a number of different options that control what happens and what output is produced during a COBOL compilation. In this case, it specifies only the LINK option. This option means that the compiler should write the object program on disk so it's ready for link editing.

In this topic, I'm only going to present the LINK option because I'm assuming that the other options will be set the way you want them to be for your case studies. In other words, you shouldn't have to change the other options by using an OPTION statement. Often, though, the LINK option is set to NOLINK, so you have to change it to LINK when you're ready to link and test a program.

After the source program has been compiled, the second EXEC statement causes the linkage editor, which is named LNKEDT, to be executed. Then, the third EXEC statement causes the program that has just been link edited to be executed. The system knows that it should do this because the third EXEC statement doesn't specify a program name like FCOBOL or LNKEDT after EXEC. It does, however, specify a SIZE operand that tells the operating system to automatically allocate the proper amount of main memory for the program.

Before the COBOL program can be tested, the operating system needs to know where it can find the input files that the program's going to read. So that's what the two DLBL statements in figure 8-7 tell the system:

```
//DLBL     IJSYSUC,'MMA.USER.CATALOG',,VSAM,CAT=IJSYSCT
//DLBL     INVMAST,'MMA.TEST.INVMAST',,VSAM
```

```
// JOB       MMC4
// OPTION    LINK
// EXEC      FCOBOL
   .
   Source program
   .
/*
// EXEC      LNKEDT
// DLBL      IJSYSUC,'MMA.USER.CATALOG',,VSAM,CAT=IJSYSCT
// DLBL      INVMAST,'MMA.TEST.INVMAST',,VSAM
// EXEC      ,SIZE=AUTO
/&
```

**Figure 8-7** A DOS/VSE job stream to compile, link, and test a program that reads one input file

The first one says that the files used by this program can be located by looking in a VSAM catalog named MMA.USER.CATALOG. (A VSAM catalog contains information that identifies the files on a system.) In other words, this DLBL statement identifies a catalog that is used during the execution of one job. This type of catalog can be called a *job catalog*.

The second DLBL statement says that the file identified as INVMAST in the system name in the SELECT statement in the source program will actually be the VSAM file named MMA.TEST.INVMAST. In other words, it's the DLBL statement that establishes the relationship between a file defined in a program and a file that is stored on the system. To locate MMA.TEST.INVMAST, the system gets information from the job catalog.

With the exception of the shaded data, this job should be pretty much the same from one DOS/VSE system to another. The first DLBL statement identifies the job catalog. The second one identifies the file that is required by the program. You should realize, though, that these DLBL statements apply only to VSAM files. Also, the SIZE operand on the third EXEC statement is required only for programs that handle VSAM files. When you use non-VSAM files, you code your jobs in a slightly different way.

One other point to be aware of is that the compile step in this job will fail if the compiler finds serious diagnostics in your program. When that happens, the rest of the job is cancelled, so the program isn't link-edited and executed.

### Job 3: A compile-link-and-test job that uses both COPY and subprogram libraries

Figure 8-8 presents a DOS/VSE job for compiling, linking, and testing a COBOL program when the program uses both COPY members and subprograms. In addition, the program to be tested requires two input files. A job like this can be used to compile and test the program in

```
// JOB        MMC6
// OPTION     LINK
// LIBDEF     SL,SEARCH=(MMASL)
// EXEC       FCOBOL
   .
   Source program
   .
/*
// LIBDEF     RL,SEARCH=(MMARL)
// EXEC       LNKEDT
// DLBL       IJSYSUC,'MMA.USER.CATALOG',,VSAM,CAT=IJSYSCT
// DLBL       INVMAST,'MMA.TEST.INVMAST',,VSAM
// DLBL       INVEXT,'MMA.TEST.INVEXT',,VSAM
// EXEC       ,SIZE=AUTO
/&
```

**Figure 8-8** A DOS/VSE job stream that specifies the COPY and subprogram libraries to be used in a compile-link-and-test job for a program that reads two input files

chapter 6. In this example, four JCL statements precede the source program in the job and eight follow it. Once again, you should code the job name and the accounting information in the JOB statement in accordance with your shop standards.

This job is like the one in figure 8-7 except for the two LIBDEF statements and the extra DLBL statement. The first LIBDEF statement gives the name of a source statement library (SL) to be used by the compiler when looking for COPY members. The name in the example is MMASL. Depending on how your system is set up, though, you may not need to use a LIBDEF statement like this. In other words, the compiler will search your library for the COPY members you request, whether or not you code a LIBDEF statement.

The second LIBDEF statement gives the name of the relocatable library (RL) to be used by the linkage editor when looking for the subprograms called by the source program. The name of this library is MMARL. Here again, depending on how your system is set up, you may not need to use a LIBDEF statement to identify your relocatable library.

Because the COBOL program uses two input files, there are three DLBL statements in the job before the last EXEC statement. The first one identifies the job catalog. The next two identify the two files used by the program. In this example, INVMAST and INVEXT are the names used in the system names in the SELECT statements for the files in the source program. That's how the DLBL statements relate the actual files used to the file references in the COBOL program.

Once again, with the exception of the shaded data, this job should be pretty much the same from one DOS/VSE system to another. Remember, though, that you may not need the LIBDEF statements, and keep in mind that the DLBL statements apply only to

VSAM files. To identify non-VSAM files, you code your jobs in a slightly different way.

### Discussion

Obviously, this topic isn't designed to teach you job control language. It's only meant as an introduction to JCL so you'll have some idea of what kind of jobs you'll need to compile and test your programs. As a result, you should find out how to code the jobs you'll need on your system. In most cases, they'll be similar to the ones presented in this topic, and in some cases they'll be identical.

If you want to become proficient at using JCL, I'd like to recommend our book by Steve Eckols called *DOS/VSE JCL*. This book also introduces you to ICCF. Then, if you want to learn how to use ICCF for all of the tasks of program development and system maintenance, we recommend another one of Steve's books called *DOS/VSE ICCF*. It's a complete presentation of the capabilities of ICCF.

### Terminology

job catalog

### Objective

Find out how to code the JCL you'll need to compile and test programs on your DOS/VSE system.

## Topic 3 JCL for compiling and testing a program on an IBM mainframe under OS/MVS

Most of the time, when you write programs for an IBM mainframe using the OS/MVS operating system, you'll use JCL to control compilation, link editing, and testing. In figure 8-5 in topic 1, for example, I showed you how you can code JCL statements in a file that represents one job. Then, you can submit the file to the system for processing.

In this topic, I'll introduce you to some typical jobs for compiling and testing COBOL programs. I won't try to explain the JCL in these jobs in detail, but I will highlight the code that will vary from one job to another. Specifically, I'll present jobs for: (1) compiling a source program; (2) compiling and testing a disk-to-printer program that doesn't use COPY members or call subprograms; and (3) compiling and testing a program that uses COPY members, calls subprograms, and reads two input files to prepare one report.

### Job 1: A compile-only job

Figure 8-9 presents a simple OS job for compiling but not testing a COBOL program. A job like this can be used to compile the programs in chapters 3 and 4 in this book.

In the first statement, the JOB statement, I gave the name MMC3 to the job. This job name is printed in large characters on the first and last pages of your job output. I also coded accounting information for the job (in parentheses), including my company code and my name. After the accounting information, I coded my name between single quotation marks so it will be easy to tell whose job this is. When you write your own programs, of course, you will want to code the job names, accounting information, and other data on the JOB statement so it's consistent with your shop standards.

The second statement in this job is an EXEC statement. It tells the operating system to execute a *procedure* named COBUC. This procedure consists of one job step named COB. When the procedure is executed, it compiles a COBOL program, but doesn't link or test it.

The third statement is a DD (Data Definition) statement that identifies the file that contains the source program that is supposed to be compiled. Right after the // in a DD statement, you code the *ddname*. In this example, the ddname is SYSIN, which is the name for the source file that is used by the compiler (it's assigned to the source file in the COBUC procedure itself). The COB that precedes the ddname says that this ddname applies to the first job step of the procedure. However, since this procedure consists of only one job step,

```
//MMC3       JOB  (MMA,MURACH),'MIKE MURACH'
//           EXEC PROC=COBUC
//COB.SYSIN  DD   DSNAME=MMA.COBOL.SOURCE(INV3510),DISP=SHR
```

**Figure 8-9** An OS/MVS job stream to compile a program without linking and testing it

this prefix isn't really necessary. When you use procedures that consist of more than one job step, though, you do need to prefix your ddnames with job step names. You'll see this illustrated in the next two jobs.

In any event, the DD statement for SYSIN says that the source program can be found in a file named INV3510, which is in a library named MMA.COBOL.SOURCE. In a DD statement, the word DSNAME refers to *data set name*, which is the name given to a *data set*. On an OS system, a file or library is often referred to as a data set, so "data set" and "data set name" are interchangeable with "file" and "file name."

Aside from the shaded values, this job should be pretty much the same from one OS system to another. In general, as you go from one compilation to another, you just have to change the job name in the JOB statement and the data set name that identifies the source program.

In practice, though, you won't run a compile-only job very often. Usually, if your program compiles without any diagnostics, you'll want to link and test it right away. So except for the first compilation of a new program when you're almost certain to have diagnostics...or when you're creating subprograms, which you won't learn to do in this book...you'll use a compile-link-and-test job instead of a compile-only job.

### Job 2: A compile-link-and-test job

Figure 8-10 presents an OS/MVS job for compiling, linking, and testing the investment-listing program of chapter 4. This time the procedure name in the EXEC statement is COBUCLG for compile, link, and go. Within this procedure are three job steps named COB (for the compilation), LKED (for the linkage editing), and GO (for the test run).

After the EXEC statement are four DD statements. As in the COBUC procedure, the first DD statement identifies the source program that is to be compiled. This job step is named COB.

The next three DD statements identify the files that are to be used during the test run, the third job step in the procedure. That's why the ddnames used in these statements have a prefix of GO. Of these, the first two are for the files that are called INVMAST and INVLIST in the system names in the SELECT statements for the files in the source

```
//MMC4          JOB   (MMA,MURACH),'MIKE MURACH'
//              EXEC  PROC=COBUCLG
//COB.SYSIN     DD    DSNAME=MMA.COBOL.SOURCE(INV3520),DISP=SHR
//GO.INVMAST    DD    DSNAME=MMA.TEST.INVMAST,DISP=SHR
//GO.INVLIST    DD    SYSOUT=A
//GO.SYSOUT     DD    SYSOUT=A
```

Figure 8-10 An OS/MVS job stream to compile, link, and test a program that reads one input file

program. Thus, these DD statements relate the ddnames in the programs to actual files on the system. For INVMAST, the program will read a file named MMA.TEST.INVMAST. For INVLIST, which is a print file, the program will direct the data to a standard print file that contains class A output.

The last DD statement is only required if your program uses DISPLAY statements as described in chapter 4. If it does, this DD statement says that DISPLAY statement output will be directed to a standard print file that contains class A output. However, this print file will be different than the one for INVLIST. As a result, the INVLIST output can be printed separately from the DISPLAY statement output.

With the exception of the shaded data, this job should be pretty much the same from one program to another. Only the job name, ddnames, and data set names should change.

One other point to be aware of, though, is that the compile step in this job will fail if the compiler finds serious diagnostics in the program. When that happens, the rest of the job is cancelled, so the program isn't link-edited and executed.

### Job 3: A compile-link-and-test job that uses both COPY and subprogram libraries

Figure 8-11 presents an OS/MVS job for compiling, linking, and testing a COBOL program when the program uses both COPY members and subprograms. In addition, the program to be tested requires two input files. This job can be used to test the investment-listing program presented in chapter 6.

This job is like the one in figure 8-10 with the addition of four new statements. The first new statement is the DD statement for SYSLIB in the COB job step. It simply identifies the COPY library to be used during the compilation. The use of a COPY library is presented in chapter 5.

The next new statements are these:

```
//LKED.SYSLIB DD   DSNAME=SYS1.COBLIB,DISP=SHR
//            DD   DSNAME=MMA.SUBLIB,DISP=SHR
```

```
//MMC6          JOB   (MMA,MURACH),'MIKE MURACH'
//              EXEC  PROC=COBUCLG
//COB.SYSLIB    DD    DSNAME=MMA.COBOL.COPY,DISP=SHR
//COB.SYSIN     DD    DSNAME=MMA.COBOL.SOURCE(INV3520),DISP=SHR
//LKED.SYSLIB   DD    DSNAME=SYS1.COBLIB,DISP=SHR
//              DD    DSNAME=MMA.SUBLIB,DISP=SHR
//GO.INVMAST    DD    DSNAME=MMA.TEST.INVMAST,DISP=SHR
//GO.INVEXT     DD    DSNAME=MMA.TEST.INVEXT,DISP=SHR
//GO.INVLIST    DD    SYSOUT=A
//GO.SYSOUT     DD    SYSOUT=A
```

Figure 8-11 An OS/MVS job stream that specifies the COPY and subprogram libraries to be used in a compile-link-and-test job for a program that reads two input files

They identify the libraries that contain the subprograms that are to be link edited with the main program during the linkage editing (LKED) step. The first statement identifies the subprogram library that is used by all COBOL programs, SYS1.COBLIB. The second one identifies a second subprogram library that can be used during the linkage editing step. Note that this second DD statement doesn't specify a ddname. In case you're not yet familiar with subprograms, their use is presented in chapter 5.

The fourth new statement is the DD statement for the file that is referred to as INVEXT in a SELECT statement in the source program. In this case, the DD statement relates this file to an actual file named MMA.TEST.INVEXT.

Once again, with the exception of the shaded data, this job should be pretty much the same from one program to another. Only the job name, ddnames, and data set names should change. You should realize, though, that you may not need to put extra DD statements in your job to specify the COPY and subprogram libraries that your program requires. In many cases, the COBUCLG procedure, which varies from one shop to another, will be set up so it identifies them for you.

## Discussion

Obviously, this topic isn't designed to teach you job control language. It's only meant as an introduction to JCL so you'll have some idea of what kind of jobs you'll need for compiling and testing your programs. As a result, you should find out how to code the jobs you'll need on your system. In most cases, they'll be similar to the ones presented in this topic, and in some cases they'll be identical.

If you want to become proficient at using JCL, I'd like to recommend our *OS JCL* book. It is currently being revised by Doug Lowe under the new name, *OS/MVS JCL*. Also, if you use ISPF on your system, we recommend another one of Doug's books called *MVS TSO*.

It shows you how to use TSO (IBM's Time-Sharing Option for interactive processing) and ISPF for all of the tasks of program development and system maintenance.

**Terminology**

procedure
ddname
data set name
data set

**Objective**

Find out how to code the JCL you'll need to compile and test programs on your OS/MVS system.

Chapter 9

# How to correct compilation diagnostics

After you code a source program and enter it into the system, you must compile it using a procedure like one of those described in chapter 8. Then, if the compilation produces any diagnostics, you must correct them and recompile the program. When the program finally compiles without any diagnostics, it is referred to as a *clean compilation*. Then, you can test and debug the program as described in the next chapter.

This chapter starts by presenting the compiler output you are likely to get when you compile your source programs. Then, it shows you how to go about correcting diagnostics. You can read this chapter any time after you complete chapter 3 in this book, but the best time is probably just before you compile your first program or right after you compile it.

## Compiler output

When a program is compiled, several different types of output can be printed as part of the *compiler output*. Three of the most commonly-used types of compiler output are illustrated in figures 9-1 through 9-3. This compiler output is for the inventory-listing program presented in chapter 3. However, we've put a few coding errors into the program so the compilation produces some diagnostics.

Each type of compiler output starts on a new page and continues for as many pages as needed. In sequence, the usual compiler output consists of (1) the compiler listing, (2) the cross-reference listing, and (3) the diagnostic listing. The output in this chapter is from a VS COBOL compiler used on an IBM mainframe running under DOS/VSE, but the compiler output for other systems will be similar.

```
 CBL LIB,APOST,SXREF
00001    000100 IDENTIFICATION DIVISION.
00002    000200*
00003    000300 PROGRAM-ID.        INV3510.
00004    000400*AUTHOR.            MIKE MURACH.
00005    000500*
00006    000600 ENVIRONMENT DIVISION.
00007    000700*
00008    000800 CONFIGURATION SECTION.
00009    000900*
00010    001000 SOURCE-COMPUTER.  IBM-370.
00011    001100 OBJECT-COMPUTER.  IBM-370.
00012    001200*
00013    001300 INPUT-OUTPUT SECTION.
00014    001400*
00015    001500 FILE-CONTROL.
00016    001600     SELECT INVMAST ASSIGN TO SYS020-AS-INVMAST.
00017    001700     SELECT INVLIST ASSIGN TO SYS006-UR-1403-S.
00018    001800*
00019    001900 DATA DIVISION.
00020    002000*
00021    002100 FILE SECTION.
00022    002200*
00023    002300 FD  INVMAST
00024    002400     LABEL RECORDS ARE STANDARD
00025    002500     RECORD CONTAINS 80 CHARACTERS.
00026    002600*
00027    002700 01  INVENTORY-MASTER-RECORD.
00028    002800*
00029    002900     05  IM-ITEM-NO          PIC 9(5).
00030    003000     05  IM-ITEM-DESC        PIC X(24)
00031    003100     05  IM-UNIT-COST        PIC 999V99.
00032    003200     05  IM-UNIT-PRICE       PIC 999V99.
00033    003300     05  IM-REORDER-POINT    PIC 9(5).
00034    003400     05  IM-ON-HAND          PIC 9(5).
00035    003500     05  IM-ON-ORDER         PIC 9(5).
00036    003600     05  FILLER              PIC X(30).
00037    003700*
00038    003800 FD  INVLIST
00039    003900     LABEL RECORDS ARE OMITTED
00040    004000     RECORD CONTAINS 132 CHARACTERS.
00041    004100*
00042    004200 01  PRINT-AREA              PIC X(132).
00043    004300*
00044    004400 WORKING-STORAGE SECTION.
00045    004500*
00046    004600 01  SWITCHES.
00047    004700*
00048    004800     05  INVMAST-EOF-SWITCH  PIC X       VALUE 'N'.
00049    004900*
```

**Figure 9-1** The compiler listing for the inventory-listing program with some coding errors (part 1 of 3)

```
2                       16.01.16        07/07/86

00050   005000 01  PRINT-FIELDS.
00051   005100*
00052   005200         05  SPACE-CONTROL        PIC 9.
00053   005300         05  LINES-ON-PAGE        PIC 99       VALUE 55.
00054   005400         05  LINE-COUNTER         PIC 99       VALUE 70.
00055   005500*
00056   005600 01  HEADING-LINE.
00057   005700*
00058   005800         05  FILLER               PIC X(8)     VALUE 'ITEM NO.'.
00059   005900         05  FILLER               PIC X(2)     VALUE SPACE.
00060   006000         05  FILLER               PIC X(16)    VALUE 'ITEM DESCRIPTION'.
00061   006100         05  FILLER               PIC X(8)     VALUE SPACE.
00062   006200         05  FILLER               PIC X(10)    VALUE 'UNIT PRICE'.
00063   006300         05  FILLER               PIC X(5)     VALUE SPACE.
00064   006400         05  FILLER               PIC X(7)     VALUE 'ON HAND'.
00065   006500         05  FILLER               PIC X(5)     VALUE SPACE.
00066   006600         05  FILLER               PIC X(13)    VALUE 'REORDER POINT'.
00067   006700         05  FILLER               PIC 9(58)    VALUE SPACE.
00068   006800 *
00069   006900 01  INVENTORY-LINE.
00070   007000*
00071   007100         05  IL-ITEM-NO           PIC Z(5).
00072   007200         05  FILLER               PIC X(5)     VALUE SPACE.
00073   007300         05  IL-ITEM-DESC         PIC X(20).
00074   007400         05  FILLER               PIC X(7).    VALUE SPACE.
00075   007500         05  IL-UNIT-PRICE        PIC ZZZ.99.
00076   007600         05  FILLER               PIC X(7)     VALUE SPACE.
00077   007700         05  IL-ON-HAND           PIC ZZZZ9.
00078   007800         05  FILLER               PIC X(11)    VALUE SPACE.
00079   007900         05  IL-REORDER-POINT     PIC Z(5).
00080   008000         05  FILLER               PIC (61)     VALUE SPACE.
00081   008100*
00082   008200 PROCEDURE DIVISION.
00083   008300*
00084   008400 000-PREPARE-INVENTORY-LISTING.
00085   008500*
00086   008600         OPEN INPUT  INVMAST
00087   008700              OUTPUT INVLIST.
00088   008800         PERFORM 100-PREPARE-INVENTORY-LINE
00089   008900             UNTIL INVMAST-EOF-SWITCH = 'Y'.
00090   009000         CLOSE INVMAST
00091   009100               INVLIST.
00092   009200         STOP RUN.
00093   009300*
00094   009400 100-PREPARE-INVENTORY-LINE.
00095   009500*
00096   009600       PERFORM 110-READ-INVENTORY-RECORD.
00097   009700         IF INVMAST-EOF-SWITCH NOT = 'Y'
00098   009800             PREFORM 120-PRINT-INVENTORY-LINE.
00099   009900*
```

**Figure 9-1** The compiler listing for the inventory-listing program with some coding errors (part 2 of 3)

```
     3                              16.01.16        07/07/86

00100    010000 110-READ-INVENTORY-RECORD.
00101    010100*
00102    010200         READ INVMAST RECORD
00103    010300             AT END
00104    010400                 MOVE 'Y' TO INVMAST-EOF-SWITCH.
00105    010500*
00106    010600 120-PRINT-INVENTORY-LINE.
00107    010700*
00108    010800         IF LINE-COUNT > LINES-ON-PAGE
00109    010900             PERFORM 130-PRINT-HEADING-LINE.
00110    011000         MOVE IM-ITEM-NO          TO IL-ITEM-NO.
00111    011100         MOVE IM-ITEM-DESC        TO IL-ITEM-DESC.
00112    011200         MOVE IM-UNIT-PRICE       TO IL-UNIT-PRICE.
00113    011300         MOVE IM-ON-HAND          TO IL-ON-HAND.
00114    011400         MOVE IM-REORDER-POINT    TO IL-REORDER-POINT.
00115    011500         MOVE INVENTORY-LINE      TO PRINT-AREA.
00116    011600         PERFORM 140-WRITE-INVENTORY-LINE.
00117    011700*
00118    011800 130-PRINT-HEADING-LINE.
00119    011900*
00120    012000         MOVE HEADING-LINE TO PRINT AREA.
00121    012100         WRITE PRINT-AREA
00122    012200             AFTER ADVANCING PAGE.
00123    012300         MOVE ZERO TO LINE-COUNT.
00124    012400         MOVE 2 TO SPACE-CONTROL.
00125    012500*
00126    012600 140-WRITE-INVENTORY-LINE.
00127    012700*
00128    012800         WRITE PRINT-AREA
00129    012900             AFTER ADVANCING SPACE-CONTROL LINES.
00130    013000         ADD 1 TO LINE-COUNT.
00131    013100         MOVE 1 TO SPACE-CONTROL.

*STATISTICS*           SOURCE RECORDS =      131    DATA ITEMS =     39     PROC DIV SZ =     30
*STATISTICS*           PARTITION SIZE =4687752      LINE COUNT =     53     BUFFER SIZE =     2048
*OPTIONS IN EFFECT*    PMAP RELOC ADR =    NONE     SPACING    =     1      FLOW        =     NONE
*OPTIONS IN EFFECT*     NOLISTX        APOST      NOSYM    NOCATALR      LIST          LINK    NOSTXIT        LIB
*OPTIONS IN EFFECT*     NOCLIST        FLAGW        ZWB    NOSUPMAP    NOXREF          ERRS      SXREF      NOOPT
*OPTIONS IN EFFECT*     NOSTATE        TRUNC        SEQ    NOSYMDMP    NODECK        NOVERB   NOSYNTAX      NOLVL
*OPTIONS IN EFFECT*     LANGLVL(2)   NOCOUNT        ADV             NOVERBSUM     NOVERBREF
*LISTER OPTIONS*           NONE
```

**Figure 9-1** The compiler listing for the inventory-listing program with some coding errors (part 3 of 3)

```
    4          INV3510            13.30.57          07/07/86

                                            CROSS-REFERENCE DICTIONARY

DATA NAMES                             DEFN      REFERENCE

HEADING-LINE                           000056
IL-ITEM-DESC                           000073    000111
IL-ITEM-NO                             000071    000110
IL-ON-HAND                             000077    000113
IL-REORDER-POINT                       000079    000114
IL-UNIT-PRICE                          000075    000112
IM-ITEM-DESC                           000030    000111
IM-ITEM-NO                             000029    000110
IM-ON-HAND                             000034    000113
IM-ON-ORDER                            000035
IM-REORDER-POINT                       000033    000114
IM-UNIT-COST                           000031
IM-UNIT-PRICE                          000032    000112
INVENTORY-LINE                         000069    000115
INVENTORY-MASTER-RECORD                000027
INVLIST                                000017    000086    000090    000121    000128
INVMAST                                000016    000086    000090    000102
INVMAST-EOF-SWITCH                     000048    000088    000097    000104
LINES-ON-PAGE                          000053
PRINT-AREA                             000042    000115    000121    000128
PRINT-FIELDS                           000050
SPACE-CONTROL                          000052    000124    000128    000131
SWITCHES                               000046
TALLY  TGT                             000000    000130
```

**Figure 9-2** The cross-reference listing for the inventory-listing program (part 1 of 2)

```
    5          INV3510            13.30.57          07/07/86

PROCEDURE NAMES                        DEFN      REFERENCE

000-PREPARE-INVENTORY-LISTING          000084
100-PREPARE-INVENTORY-LINE             000094    000088
110-READ-INVENTORY-RECORD              000100    000096
120-PRINT-INVENTORY-LINE               000106
130-PRINT-HEADING-LINE                 000118    000109
140-WRITE-INVENTORY-LINE               000126    000116
```

**Figure 9-2** The cross-reference listing for the inventory-listing program (part 2 of 2)

```
    6          INV3510          13.30.57          07/07/86

CARD    ERROR MESSAGE

00016   ILA2007I-C      RECORD CONTAINS CLAUSE CONFLICTS WITH RECORD DESCRIPTION. CLAUSE IGNORED.
00031   ILA1043I-W      END OF SENTENCE SHOULD PRECEDE 05 . ASSUMED PRESENT.
00054   ILA1001I-E      NUMERIC LITERAL NOT RECOGNIZED AS LEVEL NUMBER BECAUSE ' LINE-COUNTER 'ILLEGAL AS
                        USED. SKIPPING TO NEXT LEVEL, SECTION OR DIVISION.
00068   ILA1004I-E      INVALID WORD ASTERISK . SKIPPING TO NEXT RECOGNIZABLE WORD.
00067   ILA2075I-C      NUMERIC PIC- DIGIT LENGTH GT 18. PICTURE REPLACED BY 9(1).
00067   ILA2129I-C      VALUE CLAUSE LITERAL DOES NOT CONFORM TO PICTURE. CHANGED TO ZERO.
00074   ILA1004I-E      INVALID WORD VALUE . SKIPPING TO NEXT RECOGNIZABLE WORD.
00080   ILA2039I-C      PICTURE CONFIGURATION ILLEGAL. PICTURE CHANGED TO 9 UNLESS USAGE IS 'DISPLAY-ST',
                        THEN L(6)BDZ9BDZ9.
00080   ILA2129I-C      VALUE CLAUSE LITERAL DOES NOT CONFORM TO PICTURE. CHANGED TO ZERO.
00096   ILA1087I-W      ' PERFORM ' SHOULD NOT BEGIN IN AREA A.
00097   ILA3001I-E      ' PREFORM ' NOT DEFINED. DELETING TILL LEGAL ELEMENT FOUND.
00097   ILA4032I-C      NO ACTION INDICATED IF PRECEDING CONDITION IS TRUE. NEXT SENTENCE ASSUMED.
00097   ILA4072I-W      EXIT FROM PERFORMED PROCEDURE ASSUMED BEFORE PROCEDURE-NAME .
00104   ILA4072I-W      EXIT FROM PERFORMED PROCEDURE ASSUMED BEFORE PROCEDURE-NAME .
00108   ILA3001I-E      ' LINE-COUNT ' NOT DEFINED. TEST DISCARDED.
00120   ILA3001I-E      ' PRINT ' NOT DEFINED. DISCARDED.
00120   ILA4052I-E      AREA(S)    MAY NOT BE TARGET FIELD FOR DNM=2-120  (GRF) IN MOVE STATEMENT, AND IS
                        DISCARDED.
00123   ILA3001I-E      ' LINE-COUNT ' NOT DEFINED. DISCARDED.
00130   ILA3001I-E      ' LINE-COUNT ' NOT DEFINED. SUBSTITUTING TALLY .
00130   ILA5011I-W      HIGH ORDER TRUNCATION MIGHT OCCUR.
```

**Figure 9-3** The diagnostic listing for the inventory-listing program (part 1 of 2)

```
    7          INV3510          13.30.57          07/07/86

ILA0004I- OUTPUT OPTIONS SUPPRESSED DUE TO ERROR SEVERITY

END OF COMPILATION
```

**Figure 9-3** The diagnostic listing for the inventory-listing program (part 2 of 2)

**The compiler listing** Figure 9-1 presents the *compiler listing* for the inventory-listing program. Primarily, this is a listing of the source program just as you entered it into the system. In the left column of the listing, though, is a column of statement numbers generated by the compiler. Thus, each source statement of this program can be referred to by a statement number from 1 through 131.

Between the statement number column and the source listing are three spaces. If a statement number (positions 1-6 in each source statement) is out of sequence, an asterisk is printed in this area and a message is printed on the diagnostic listing. In figure 9-1, no statements are out of sequence.

When you enter your source program into the system using a modern interactive editor, it's impossible to have sequence errors in your source program because the editor keeps track of the statement numbers for you. However, when you use the COPY library as described in chapter 5, it is possible to have sequence errors on your compiler listing because the statement numbers in the COPY members aren't likely to be in sequence with the statement numbers of your source program. As a result, you're likely to have one sequence error for each COPY member you use.

When you use COPY members, the lines copied into the program are identified in the area between the generated statement numbers and the statement numbers in the source program. For instance, the IBM compilers put a C in this area as illustrated by the program in chapter 5. In contrast, the Wang compiler puts a plus sign in this area. In either case, though, it's easy to tell which statements have been copied into the program.

At the end of the source code in the compiler listing in figure 9-1 is a list of statistics and options. The statistics present some data about the source program such as the number of source records and the number of data items in the program. The options tell what compiler and listing options were in effect during the compilation. For instance, the LINK option is on for this compilation (meaning the object program should be written on disk so it's ready for link editing) and so are the SXREF option (which produces a sorted cross-reference listing) and the ERRS option (which produces the diagnostic listing). In most cases, you'll use the default options for your system.

**The cross-reference listing** Figure 9-2 presents the *cross-reference listing* for the inventory-listing program. As you can see, it is a listing of all names created by the programmer, both data names and paragraph (procedure) names. The DEFN column gives the compiler-generated number of the statement in which each name is defined. For example, IM-ITEM-NO is defined in statement 29. Then, the REFERENCE column gives the compiler-generated numbers of the statements that refer to each name. For instance, only statement 110 refers to IM-ITEM-NO. If necessary, multiple lines are used to list the numbers of all statements that refer to a name.

On a modern system, the cross-reference listing is likely to be sorted like the one in figure 9-2. As you can see, all of the names are in alphanumeric sequence. On older or smaller systems, though, the names in the cross-reference listing may be in the sequence in which they appear in the source program. On IBM mainframes, you can request the cross-reference listing in either sorted or unsorted form.

In short programs, I think you'll find that the cross-reference listing isn't that useful. This is particularly true if you group your fields in the Working-Storage Section as illustrated by the programs in this book. Then, you'll usually be able to find the fields you're looking for just as easily without the cross-reference listing as with it. Similarly, if you use an editor that makes it easy for you to find the fields and paragraphs within a program, you may not have much use for cross-reference listings. That's why we rarely use cross-reference listings on our Wang VS system.

On some systems, though, cross-reference listings do come in handy. This is particularly true when you are working on long programs that contain dozens of different data names.

**The diagnostic listing** Figure 9-3 presents the *diagnostic listing* for the inventory-listing program. Each line on this listing refers to an error in the source program.

In the lefthand column of the diagnostic listing, the compiler-generated numbers of the statements in error are given. Thus, the first two diagnostics refer to statement numbers 16 and 31. In figure 9-3, this column is labelled CARD. This relates back to the days when source programs were punched into source cards. When you use other compilers, you may see this column referred to as LINE NUMBER, as REFERENCE, or as nothing at all. Regardless of the column title, it should be obvious what the data in the leftmost column contains.

To the right of the statement number column, you'll usually find an error message code, an indication of the error level, and the *diagnostic message* itself. In figure 9-3, for example, the error message code for statement 31 is ILA1043I; the -W at the end of the code indicates that it's a "warning" diagnostic; and the message is:

```
END OF SENTENCE SHOULD PRECEDE 05 . ASSUMED PRESENT.
```

When you use other compilers, you'll find similar information for each diagnostic although it may be in a slightly different form.

In general, you don't need to use the error message code. It just refers you to an explanation of the diagnostic message that you can find in one of the COBOL reference manuals for your compiler. In most cases, though, the diagnostic message is self-explanatory, so you don't need an expanded explanation. In addition, the explanation in the manual is often the same as the diagnostic message, so the manual doesn't tell you anything you don't already know.

On the other hand, the error level is useful information because it tells you how the compiler handled the error. On an IBM mainframe, for example, there are four levels of errors: W for "warning," C for "conditional," E for "error," and D for "disaster." On most other systems, you'll find similar levels of errors.

When a *warning diagnostic* occurs, the program is compiled and can be tested. In most cases, in fact, the statements with warning diagnostics will execute the way you want them to.

When a *conditional diagnostic* occurs, the program is also compiled, but only after the compiler makes an assumption to correct the error. Unfortunately, the assumption usually isn't the one you want, so the statements won't execute the way you want them to.

When an *error diagnostic* occurs, the compiler stops trying to create the object code for the program. For the remainder of the source code, the compiler only tries to check the syntax of the statements and list any errors it finds on the diagnostic listing.

When a *disaster diagnostic* occurs, the compiler can't even complete the compilation. Unlike the other types of diagnostics, this type usually occurs when some limit of the compiler has been reached or when the compiler itself has a bug in it. As a result, you should rarely, if ever, encounter a disaster diagnostic.

### How to correct diagnostics

To correct diagnostics, you normally take them in sequence and correct each statement as needed. If you come to a message you can't figure out, skip over it since one of the later diagnostics may indicate its cause. As you will see, it's relatively easy to correct coding errors, even though the diagnostic messages aren't always clear. To illustrate, let's go through some of the diagnostics in figure 9-3.

The first diagnostic is conditional and refers to statement 16, the SELECT statement for the inventory master file. The error message says the program has tried to describe a record that doesn't have the number of characters given in the RECORD CONTAINS clause for the file. In this case, the pictures of the record description add up to 84 characters because the PIC for IM-ITEM-DESC is X(24) when it should be X(20). However, as this conditional diagnostic message indicates, the compiler will treat the input record as though it had 84 characters. As a result, this error must be corrected before the program is tested.

The second diagnostic is a warning and refers to statement 31. It indicates that a period is missing before statement 31 and that one is assumed by the compiler. This is the problem and the proper correction, so statements 30 and 31 will be compiled properly. Nevertheless, you should correct statement 30 the next time you modify the program so this diagnostic won't be printed in the diagnostic listing.

The third diagnostic is an error diagnostic that refers to statement 54. It says that this statement is skipped because LINE-COUNTER is "illegal as used." The problem is that LINE-COUNTER is a COBOL reserved word. As a result, the programmer can't use it as the name of one of his fields. In this case, the programmer meant to use LINE-COUNT, but he entered it into the system incorrectly. In any event, this error must be corrected before testing.

Note that this error is also the cause of three other errors: statements 108, 123, and 130. These statements refer to LINE-COUNT, which has never been properly defined due to the error in statement 54. As a result, by correcting statement 54, these diagnostics will also be corrected.

Now, look at the diagnostic for statement 96. It says that the word PERFORM starts in the A margin. If you check the source listing, you can see that the diagnostic is correct since PERFORM starts in position 11 of the statement, not position 12. Remember that the A margin is positions 8-11, not just position 8. Although this is only a warning diagnostic, the error should be corrected because it's not clear how the compiler handles the statement: Does it ignore it or does it ignore the margin error and compile the statement correctly?

One diagnostic that you're likely to see quite frequently when using IBM systems is the one given for statements 97 and 104:

```
EXIT FROM PERFORMED PROCEDURE ASSUMED BEFORE
PROCEDURE-NAME .
```

This diagnostic occurs when a performed paragraph ends in a conditional statement. For example, statement 104 is the last statement in the paragraph named 110-READ-INVENTORY-RECORD, but it's part of the AT END clause in the READ statement. Normally, then, if the AT END condition hasn't been met, the program should continue with the next statement of the program (the first statement of the next paragraph). Fortunately, though, the compiler realizes that this is a performed paragraph and assumes a proper paragraph exit; that is, it returns to the statement following the PERFORM statement that called the paragraph.

Incidentally, this diagnostic isn't really needed because that's the way a PERFORM statement should work. Nevertheless, it's still generated by the VS compilers for IBM mainframes, unless the software specialist for the shop has deleted it from the compiler. On other systems, you're less likely to encounter diagnostics like this. And we don't expect them to be used by future compilers.

With this as background, you should be able to figure out the other errors indicated by the diagnostic listing in figure 9-3. They are all relatively simple coding errors.

As you go down the list of diagnostics for one of your programs, you should mark all corrections on the compiler listing, usually in red so they're easy to spot. Then, after you modify the source program to correct the errors, the source program can be recompiled.

Sometimes, after going through all the diagnostics, there are still a few you can't figure out. In this case, it's often worth taking the time to recompile the program with all of the other errors corrected. This may remove the diagnostics that were giving you trouble because they were caused by errors you had already corrected.

One final thought: Should warning diagnostics be corrected? We say, yes, whenever possible. Otherwise, it is too easy to overlook error and conditional diagnostics in a maze of warning diagnostics. In practice, though, it's usually not worth correcting all of the warning diagnostics that your program generates. Some relate to efficiency considerations that you're already aware of but choose to ignore. Some warn you of conditions that you know will never occur in your program. As a result, a typical production program will have some warning diagnostics. In practice, then, a clean compilation is one with only warning diagnostics, not one without any diagnostics at all.

### Discussion

If you're not using the VS compiler on an IBM mainframe, of course, your compiler output will differ in some ways from the output shown in figures 9-1 through 9-3. On some systems, for example, if your program has diagnostics, the errors will be indicated in the compiler listing next to the statements in error as well as in the diagnostic listing. This can save some page flipping when you correct diagnostics. Similarly, cross-reference listings and diagnostic listings may vary in form somewhat from the listings shown in this chapter.

No matter what the variations, though, you shouldn't have much trouble correcting diagnostics. Every diagnostic indicates some violation of a coding rule as defined in the COBOL manuals for your system. As a result, if you run into a diagnostic that's particularly tough to figure out, you can normally solve the problem by reading about the related code in the appropriate reference manual. That's one reason why you must eventually become familiar with the manuals for your system.

### Terminology

clean compilation
compiler output
compiler listing
cross-reference listing
diagnostic listing
diagnostic message
warning diagnostic
conditional diagnostic
error diagnostic
disaster diagnostic

### Objective

Given the compiler output for a program including the diagnostic listing, correct the diagnostics so the program will compile cleanly.

Chapter 10

# How to test and debug a program

When you *test* a program, you try to find all the errors the program contains. When you *debug* a program, you try to correct the errors that you found when you tested it. In topic 1 of this chapter, you'll learn a general procedure for testing a program. Then, in topic 2, you'll learn some techniques for debugging a program. You can read this chapter any time after you complete chapter 3, but the best time is probably right before you test your first COBOL program.

# Topic 1 How to test a program

In general, programs are tested in three phases: unit test, system test, and acceptance test. The *unit test* is the programmer's test of his or her own program. In this phase of testing, you should do your best to make sure that all the modules in your program work properly. Since you know your program better than anyone else, you are the person most qualified to test it.

The *system test* is designed to test the interfaces between the programs within a system. For instance, suppose you're working on an inventory-listing program like the one in chapter 3. Then, the system test will determine whether or not the inventory master file that's produced by a file-creation program is acceptable to your program. But if the test data for the file-creation program is incomplete, the resulting master file won't be an adequate test of your listing program. So you can't rely on the system test to test all aspects of your program.

The *acceptance test* is designed to determine whether the programs in a system perform the way that the user intended them to. Although the data for this test should be developed by a creative person with plenty of testing experience, this isn't always the case. So you can't count on this phase of testing to test all aspects of your program either. To a large extent, then, the burden of proof is on the programmer in the unit test.

Although this book isn't designed to teach you precise procedures for unit testing a production program, I would like to give you a few ideas that will help you test your programs effectively. Most important, we recommend that you take the time to plan your test runs. All too often, it seems, programmers test their programs without any planning. As a result, the programs are *not* tested by all the possible combinations of data, and they're put into production with dozens of bugs.

It's relatively easy, though, to create a test plan for a program. Once you have one, you're more likely to create test data that adequately tests your program. Then, you'll have a solid basis for believing that your program is free of bugs after you test it on the data you have created.

### How to create a test plan

Before you start your *test plan*, you should review your program and list all the conditions that you must test for. To do this, you should review your program specifications, your structure chart, and even your COBOL code, writing down any conditions that come to mind. Then, if you create test data that tests for all of these conditions, you increase the likelihood that your program will be adequately tested.

Figure 10-1 is a *condition list* that I developed for the investment-listing program of chapter 4. If you haven't read chapter 4 yet, this program reads an inventory master file like the one in chapter 3 and prints a listing of all items in inventory with an investment amount of more than $10,000. It also calculates some results that may be larger than the receiving fields for the results, so ON SIZE ERROR conditions may occur. Even if you haven't studied the investment-listing program yet, the testing procedures and documents presented in this topic should make sense to you. However, you may want to review them after you read chapter 4 so you can see more specifically how they apply to the investment-listing program.

If you review the condition list in figure 10-1, you can see that it is a list of the conditions in each module that should be tested. Although making a list like this can be a laborious job if the program is large, you really have no other choice. If your job as a programmer is to prove that your program works for all possible conditions, you must know what those conditions are. As you will see, however, your test data usually won't have to be extensive just because your list of conditions is long.

After you've made your list of conditions, you're ready to create the test plan. Specifically, you want to decide in what sequence the conditions should be tested. The intent here is to discover the major problems first. As a result, you should start by testing the main functions and conditions of your program. Then, once you are satisfied that they are working properly, you can go on to test the less critical conditions.

Figure 10-2 shows my test plan for the investment-listing program of chapter 4. Although this program is extremely limited when compared to a typical production program, I think figure 10-2 will give you an idea of what a test plan should look like. As you can see, I've decided that I will only need to have three test runs. The first run will test the main logic of the program with "clean" data (data that won't lead to ON SIZE ERROR conditions). The second run will test the main logic with both clean data and data that will lead to ON SIZE ERROR conditions. The third run will test any other conditions plus the one volume condition, page overflow.

You should notice in figure 10-2 that I didn't provide for every condition listed in figure 10-1. When I reflected upon them, I decided that I didn't need to test the program using a master file with no records in it since this condition shouldn't occur in the first place and since it shouldn't cause any problem if it does occur no matter how the program handles it. When you create a test plan, you should consider every condition on your condition list even though you may conclude that you don't have to test some of them. If you decide *not* to test a condition, you should of course have a good reason for your decision.

As you create your test plan, you should also decide where the test data will come from. Will you code the data yourself and create the proper input files using utilities? Can you copy some "live" data (that

| Program: INV3520 Prepare investment listing | Page: 1 |
|---|---|
| Designer: Mike Murach | Date: 04/03/86 |

| Module | Conditions |
|---|---|
| 000 | Are all records in the inventory master file processed?<br>Does the DISPLAY statement execute properly? |
| 100 | Are the time and date printed correctly in the heading lines? |
| 300 | Does the program only list the inventory records with an investment of over $10,000? |
| 310 | What happens if there are no records in the master file? |
| 320 | Are all calculated fields on the listing correct? |
| 330 | Are all fields in the investment lines edited properly on the listing?<br>Are the ON SIZE ERROR fields handled correctly on the listing?<br>Do the correct number of lines print on each page?<br>Is the spacing on the listing correct? |
| 340 | Are all heading lines printed correctly? |
| 500 | Are all total lines printed correctly?<br>Is the ON SIZE ERROR field handled correctly? |

**Figure 10-1** A module-by-module listing of test conditions for the investment-listing program of chapter 4

| Program: INV3520 Prepare investment listing | Page: 1 |
| --- | --- |
| Designer: Mike Murach | Date: 04/03/86 |

| Test phase | Data | Data source |
| --- | --- | --- |
| 1. Main branching logic with clean data | Three records: one with investment amount less than $10,000; one with investment amount equal to $10,000; one with investment amount greater than $10,000 | Self |
| 2. Main logic with data that tests the limits of all calculations | Phase 1 data plus records that test the ON SIZE ERROR conditions of the arithmetic statements | Self |
| 3. Page overflow | Phase 2 data plus enough records to cause page overflow | Utility |

**Figure 10-2** A test plan for the investment-listing program of chapter 4

| Item no. | Item description | Unit cost | Unit price | Reorder point | On hand | On order | Last order date | Last month's sales | Last year's sales |
|---|---|---|---|---|---|---|---|---|---|
| 00001 | AAAAAAAAAAAAAAAAAAAA | 00001 | 00002 | 05000 | 10000 | 00000 | 040386 | 1234567 | 123456789 |
| 55555 | BBBBBBBBBBBBBBBBBBBB | 00050 | 00100 | 10000 | 10000 | 10000 | 030386 | 1111111 | 222222222 |
| 99999 | ZZZZZZZZZZZZZZZZZZZZ | 10000 | 20000 | 00050 | 00051 | 00000 | 040386 | 0100000 | 001200000 |

**Figure 10-3** Test data for the first test run of the investment-listing program of chapter 4

is, actual production data) for your test files? Does another program create test data that you can use? Here again, you should make these decisions in a controlled manner.

### How to create test data

As a general rule, the *test data* you use in your first test runs for a program should be low in volume, often just a few records for each input file. That way, it's relatively easy to figure out what output your program should produce. For instance, the three records listed in figure 10-3 are enough for the first phase of testing in the test plan in figure 10-2. For record 1, the investment amount (on hand times unit price) will be less than $10,000; for record 2, it will be equal to $10,000; and for record 3, it will be greater than $10,000.

After a program has been tested on small volumes of data, the program can be tested on a volume of data that is large enough to test all of the conditions that may occur. In the case of the investment-listing program, for example, the input file must be large enough to force page overflow. If a program is large, the test plan may require several low-volume tests and several high-volume tests.

If you don't know what the output of a test run should be, you can't tell if your program worked properly. So, after you create the test data for a test run, you should figure out what the output should be. In some cases, doing this will help you uncover problems in your specifications and program design.

### How to document a test run

After you have created the necessary test data for each test phase, you are ready to perform the test run. Then, after each test run, you compare the actual output of the test run with the expected output. If the program involves tape or disk input or output, appropriate listings of the input and output files must be made before and after the test run. In a disk-update run, for example, the contents of the disk file must be printed before testing and after testing to see what changes were made in the file. In a disk-to-printer program, though, only the printed output usually needs to be checked because you already know what data

**The documentation for a test run**

1. The compiler output for the test run marked with the changes that should be made for the next test run
2. A listing of each input file used for the test run
3. The printed output for the test run
4. A listing of each file that is created or updated by the test run

**Figure 10-4** The documentation for a test run

the disk file contains. Then, if the actual output disagrees with the expected output, you must find the error, change the source code, and test again.

After a test run, you should document the run so you can review it if that becomes necessary. In some shops, in fact, you may be required to document each of your test runs. In general, your documentation for a test run should consist of the items listed in figure 10-4. Because a typical programmer works on more than one program at a time, this documentation can save a considerable amount of backtracking and confusion.

## Discussion

Normally, in a programming course, you don't have to develop your own test data. Instead, it's provided for you. That way, everyone in the class should get the same test results if they write the program correctly. This makes it easier for your instructor to check your work. Nevertheless, you should know how to create test data for a program so you can do production work later on.

The point of this topic, of course, is to get you to test your programs in an orderly fashion. If you take the time to develop condition lists and test plans before you start to test your programs, we're confident that you'll test your programs more effectively.

## Terminology

unit test
system test
acceptance test
test plan
condition list
test data

## Objective

Given a COBOL program's specifications and its structure chart, create a test plan and test data for it.

## Topic 2 How to debug a program

When you test a program, there are two possible outcomes. First, the program can run until it executes its STOP RUN statement. This is referred to as *normal termination* of a program. Second, the program can be cancelled before it reaches its STOP RUN statement. This is referred to as *abnormal termination* of a program. In this topic, I'll show you how to debug programs that end normally or abnormally.

### How to debug a program that ends in a normal termination

If a program runs to a normal termination, you start by comparing the actual output with the expected output. To illustrate, suppose the inventory-listing program of chapter 3 runs to completion using the test data shown in figure 10-5. Suppose also that the expected output differs from the actual output as shown in figure 10-5. Here, I've highlighted some of the differences: (1) there's some data in the heading line that doesn't belong there; and (2) the on-hand and reorder point fields are incorrect in some of the data lines. In addition, the listing is double-spaced when it should be single-spaced.

**Listing of test data**

| Item no. | Item description | Unit cost | Unit price | Reorder point | On hand | On order |
|---|---|---|---|---|---|---|
| 00001 | AAAAAAAAAAAAAAAAAAAA | 00001 | 00001 | 00000 | 00000 | 00000 |
| 11111 | BBBBBBBBBBBBBBBBBBBB | 22222 | 33333 | 44444 | 55555 | 66666 |
| 99999 | ZZZZZZZZZZZZZZZZZZZZ | 99999 | 99999 | 99999 | 99999 | 99999 |

**Expected printer output**

```
ITEM NO.  ITEM DESCRIPTION          UNIT PRICE     ON HAND      REORDER POINT

     1    AAAAAAAAAAAAAAAAAAAA            .01           0
11111     BBBBBBBBBBBBBBBBBBBB         333.33       55555              44444
99999     ZZZZZZZZZZZZZZZZZZZZ         999.99       99999              99999
```

**Actual printer output**

```
ITEM NO.  ITEM DESCRIPTION    #    #UNIT PRICE     ON HAND      REORDER POINT

     1    AAAAAAAAAAAAAAAAAAAA            .01           0

11111     BBBBBBBBBBBBBBBBBBBB         333.33       45555               4444

99999     ZZZZZZZZZZZZZZZZZZZZ         999.99       99999               9999
```

**Figure 10-5** The test data, expected output, and actual output for the first test run of the inventory-listing program of chapter 3

To correct these bugs, you analyze the code that has produced the output, because something must be wrong with it. Since the heading line has unexpected data in it, it must not have been set properly to spaces at the start of the program. Since both on-hand and reorder point are printed incorrectly, something is either wrong with the data in the input file or in the COBOL definitions that define the file. Since the listing is double spaced, the SPACE-CONTROL field must not be set to a value of one at the proper time.

Figure 10-6 gives the COBOL listing for the program that produced the actual output in figure 10-5. I'll tell you now that the data in the input file is just as it's shown in figure 10-5, so all the bugs are due to the coding, not the data. Now, take a few minutes and see if you can correct these bugs.

Since you can encounter so many different kinds of bugs when you test a program, I can't give you a precise procedure for pinpointing the causes. As I see it, this is an analytical part of the programmer's job that can't easily be taught. Although certain types of bugs seem to repeat themselves from one program to the next, some bugs are so rare that they baffle the most experienced programmers. Nevertheless, when a program runs to a normal termination, you should be able to find and correct its bugs most of the time without any further training and without any other assistance.

### How to debug a program that ends in an abnormal termination

When an abnormal termination occurs, you must find the cause of the termination. Often, though, finding the cause of an abnormal termination is far more difficult than finding the bugs when a program terminates normally. As a result, you can usually use all the information you can get when an abnormal termination occurs. If, for example, you can find out what statement the program was trying to execute when the termination occurred, it makes your debugging job easier. And, if you know the common causes of abnormal program terminations, that makes your job simpler too.

**Finding the statement that caused an abnormal termination** In this book, I can't give you a precise procedure for finding the statement that caused an abnormal termination because the procedure varies from one system to another. On some interactive systems, debugging output is displayed on the screen at the time of program termination to tell you what source statement was being executed when the program failed. On the Wang VS system, for example, a screen like the one in the top part of figure 10-7 is displayed. In this case, the screen tells you that statement 127 was being executed at the time of program termination.

```
000100 IDENTIFICATION DIVISION.
000200*
000300 PROGRAM-ID.          INV3510.
000400*AUTHOR.              MIKE MURACH.
000500*
000600 ENVIRONMENT DIVISION.
000700*
000800 CONFIGURATION SECTION.
000900*
001000 SOURCE-COMPUTER.  IBM-370.
001100 OBJECT-COMPUTER.  IBM-370.
001200*
001300 INPUT-OUTPUT SECTION.
001400*
001500 FILE-CONTROL.
001600     SELECT INVMAST ASSIGN TO SYS020-AS-INVMAST.
001700     SELECT INVLIST ASSIGN TO SYS006-UR-1403-S.
001800*
001900 DATA DIVISION.
002000*
002100 FILE SECTION.
002200*
002300 FD  INVMAST
002400     LABEL RECORDS ARE STANDARD
002500     RECORD CONTAINS 80 CHARACTERS.
002600*
002700 01  INVENTORY-MASTER-RECORD.
002800*
002900     05  IM-ITEM-NO            PIC 9(5).
003000     05  IM-ITEM-DESC          PIC X(20).
003100     05  IM-UNIT-COST          PIC 999V99.
003200     05  IM-UNIT-PRICE         PIC 999V99.
003300     05  IM-REORDER-POINT      PIC 9(4).
003400     05  IM-ON-HAND            PIC 9(5).
003500     05  IM-ON-ORDER           PIC 9(6).
003600     05  FILLER                PIC X(30).
003700*
003800 FD  INVLIST
003900     LABEL RECORDS ARE OMITTED
004000     RECORD CONTAINS 132 CHARACTERS.
004100*
004200 01  PRINT-AREA                PIC X(132).
004300*
004400 WORKING-STORAGE SECTION.
004500*
004600 01  SWITCHES.
004700*
004800     05  INVMAST-EOF-SWITCH    PIC X        VALUE 'N'.
004900*
005000 01  PRINT-FIELDS.
005100*
005200     05  SPACE-CONTROL         PIC 9.
005300     05  LINES-ON-PAGE         PIC 99       VALUE 55.
005400     05  LINE-COUNT            PIC 99       VALUE 70.
005500*
005600 01  HEADING-LINE.
005700*
005800     05  FILLER                PIC X(8)     VALUE 'ITEM NO.'.
005900     05  FILLER                PIC X(2)     VALUE SPACE.
```

**Figure 10-6** The compiler listing for the inventory-listing program that produced the output in figure 10-5 (part 1 of 3)

```
006000         05   FILLER                    PIC X(16)   VALUE 'ITEM DESCRIPTION'.
006100         05   FILLER                    PIC X(8).
006200         05   FILLER                    PIC X(10)   VALUE 'UNIT PRICE'.
006300         05   FILLER                    PIC X(5)    VALUE SPACE.
006400         05   FILLER                    PIC X(7)    VALUE 'ON HAND'.
006500         05   FILLER                    PIC X(5)    VALUE SPACE.
006600         05   FILLER                    PIC X(13)   VALUE 'REORDER POINT'.
006700         05   FILLER                    PIC X(58)   VALUE SPACE.
006800*
006900 01   INVENTORY-LINE.
007000*
007100         05   IL-ITEM-NO                PIC Z(5).
007200         05   FILLER                    PIC X(5)    VALUE SPACE.
007300         05   IL-ITEM-DESC              PIC X(20).
007400         05   FILLER                    PIC X(7)    VALUE SPACE.
007500         05   IL-UNIT-PRICE             PIC ZZZ.ZZ.
007600         05   FILLER                    PIC X(7)    VALUE SPACE.
007700         05   IL-ON-HAND                PIC ZZZZ9.
007800         05   FILLER                    PIC X(11)   VALUE SPACE.
007900         05   IL-REORDER-POINT          PIC Z(5).
008000         05   FILLER                    PIC X(61)   VALUE SPACE.
008100*
008200 PROCEDURE DIVISION.
008300*
008400 000-PREPARE-INVENTORY-LISTING.
008500*
008600         OPEN INPUT  INVMAST
008700              OUTPUT INVLIST.
008800         PERFORM 100-PREPARE-INVENTORY-LINE
008900             UNTIL INVMAST-EOF-SWITCH = 'Y'.
009000         CLOSE INVMAST
009100               INVLIST.
009200         STOP RUN.
009300*
009400 100-PREPARE-INVENTORY-LINE.
009500*
009600         PERFORM 110-READ-INVENTORY-RECORD.
009700         IF INVMAST-EOF-SWITCH NOT = 'Y'
009800             PERFORM 120-PRINT-INVENTORY-LINE.
009900*
010000 110-READ-INVENTORY-RECORD.
010100*
010200         READ INVMAST RECORD
010300             AT END
010400                 MOVE 'Y' TO INVMAST-EOF-SWITCH.
010500*
010600 120-PRINT-INVENTORY-LINE.
010700*
010800         IF LINE-COUNT > LINES-ON-PAGE
010900             PERFORM 130-PRINT-HEADING-LINE.
011000         MOVE IM-ITEM-NO             TO IL-ITEM-NO.
011100         MOVE IM-ITEM-DESC           TO IL-ITEM-DESC.
011200         MOVE IM-UNIT-PRICE          TO IL-UNIT-PRICE.
011300         MOVE IM-ON-HAND             TO IL-ON-HAND.
011400         MOVE IM-REORDER-POINT       TO IL-REORDER-POINT.
011500         MOVE INVENTORY-LINE         TO PRINT-AREA.
011600         PERFORM 140-WRITE-INVENTORY-LINE.
011700*
011800 130-PRINT-HEADING-LINE.
011900*
```

**Figure 10-6** The compiler listing for the inventory-listing program that produced the output in figure 10-5 (part 2 of 3)

```
00120   012000          MOVE HEADING-LINE TO PRINT-AREA.
00121   012100          WRITE PRINT-AREA
00122   012200              AFTER ADVANCING PAGE.
00123   012300          MOVE ZERO TO LINE-COUNT.
00124   012400          MOVE 2 TO SPACE-CONTROL.
00125   012500*
00126   012600 140-WRITE-INVENTORY-LINE.
00127   012700*
00128   012800          WRITE PRINT-AREA
00129   012900              AFTER ADVANCING SPACE-CONTROL LINES.
00130   013000          ADD 1 TO LINE-COUNT.
```

**Figure 10-6** The compiler listing for the inventory-listing program that produced the output in figure 10-5 (part 3 of 3)

At the other extreme, a termination message like the one in the middle of figure 10-7 may be printed when your program terminates abnormally. This message was printed by an IBM mainframe using VS COBOL under DOS/VSE. The message was printed after the data that was printed by the program prior to the termination. In this case, the message says that the program terminated due to a "data exception" and that the instruction at address 3AFD0 was the one being executed when the program failed. Unfortunately, 3AFD0 is in hexadecimal code. To find out which COBOL statement this refers to, you have to go through a conversion process using output from the linkage editor and some optional output from the COBOL compiler called a Procedure Division map. Although I'm not going to explain this conversion process in this book, it's relatively straightforward, so your instructor may choose to teach it to you. On the other hand, you shouldn't need to know the process just to do the case studies for this course.

The third type of output shown in figure 10-7 is debugging output that is produced by a DOS/VSE system when the STATE compiler option is on. This output is produced in addition to a termination message. As you can see, it gives the number of the statement that was being executed at the time of the termination. In this case, the program failed while statement 127 was being executed.

If you can't easily find out which source statement was executing at the time of program termination for a report preparation program, you can usually narrow it down by analyzing the output printed by the program before its termination. If, for example, the program terminates before any lines are printed, you can guess that the program terminated while the first record was being processed. If the heading lines are printed but no data lines, you know the program probably terminated while it was executing the print routines for the first record. And if all of the detail lines are printed but no total lines, you can guess that the program failed during the routines for preparing and printing the total lines. By using these clues, you can usually debug report preparation programs without knowing exactly which

**Debugging output as displayed on a Wang VS system**

```
00124 *
00125  140-WRITE-INVENTORY-LINE.
00126 *
00127       WRITE PRINT-AREA
00128           AFTER ADVANCING SPACE-CONTROL LINES.
00129       ADD 1 TO LINE-COUNT.
00130       MOVE 1 TO SPACE-CONTROL.
------------------------------------------------------------------------------

                      ***   WANG VS DEBUG PROCESSOR   ***

ERROR PC07 REPORTED BY DEBUG
        IN ACTIVE PROGRAM SC1C10V3                    CODE SECTION = INV3510
                                                      STATEMENT # =     127
                                                      VERB          = WRITE
                                                      PCW = 071001F4 27004100

DATA EXCEPTION - AN ATTEMPT WAS MADE TO CONVERT OR PERFORM AN ARITHMETIC
                 OPERATION WITH NON-NUMERIC DECIMAL DATA
```

**Termination message as printed by a DOS/VSE system**

```
0S03I   PROGRAM CHECK INTERRUPTION - HEX LOCATION 03AFD0 - CONDITION CODE 0 - DATA EXCEPTION
0S00I   JOB INV3510  CANCELED
0S071   PROBLEM PROGRAM  PSW     031D00000003AFD4
```

**STATE output as printed by a DOS/VSE system**

```
PROGRAM INV3510

LAST CARD NUMBER/VERB NUMBER EXECUTED -- CARD NUMBER 000127/VERB NUMBER 01.
```

**Figure 10-7** Three types of output that may be issued when a program terminates abnormally

COBOL statement caused program termination. This is particularly true if you know the common causes of abnormal terminations.

**Common causes of abnormal program terminations** Figure 10-8 presents some of the common causes of abnormal terminations. On IBM systems, these are referred to as *exceptions*, so I'll use that terminology in this topic. The four most common causes of abnormal terminations are data, overflow, divide, and operation exceptions.

A *data exception*—the type that caused the program termination in figure 10-7—occurs when a statement tries to operate on invalid data. This can happen when an arithmetic statement is executed or when two fields are compared numerically by an IF statement. If, for example, blanks are read into a storage field with a picture of 9(3), a data exception will result when the field is operated upon by an ADD statement or when it's compared numerically with another field in an IF statement. A data exception can also occur if a MOVE statement results in an invalid edit (see figure 4-11 for some examples). These types of errors are caused either by faulty input data or by faulty data descriptions.

**Data exception**

This happens when a statement tries to operate on data that is invalid for it. This is usually caused by invalid input data, incorrect data descriptions, or improperly initialized values. To avoid it, make sure that your data descriptions are coordinated with your input data and that all fields are initialized properly.

This can also happen when you send data to a subprogram in one form, but it expects it in another form. Then, the abnormal termination is likely to occur while the subprogram is being executed. This problem is described in more detail in chapter 5.

**Overflow exception**

This happens when an arithmetic operation develops a result that is too large for the receiving field. This is often caused by invalid input data. To avoid it, you can make sure the fields have valid sizes before the arithmetic operations are performed. Otherwise, use the ON SIZE ERROR clause as described in chapters 4 and 5 whenever it is appropriate.

**Divide exception**

This happens when a divide operation tries to divide by zero. To avoid it, make sure the divisor isn't zero before you execute a DIVIDE statement.

**Operation exception**

This happens when the computer tries to execute an operation with an invalid operation code. In COBOL programs, this often means an I/O problem. To avoid it, make sure your program doesn't:

1. Try to read or write a file before it is opened.
2. Try to read or write a file after it is closed.
3. Refer to fields in the record description for a file in the File Section after the AT END clause for the file has been executed.
4. Refer to fields in the record description for a file in the File Section before the first READ statement for the file has been executed.
5. Issue a STOP RUN statement before all files are closed.

**Figure 10-8** Some common causes of abnormal program terminations

A data exception can also occur when a field in working storage isn't initialized properly. If, for example, a field is supposed to have a starting value of zero but it isn't given a starting value, a data exception will occur when an ADD statement tries to add a number to the field.

An *overflow exception* occurs when the execution of an arithmetic operation leads to a result that is larger than the receiving field can hold. This in turn means that either your size specifications in the Data Division are inaccurate or the data exceeds its expected limits. However, the exception doesn't take place if you use the ON SIZE ERROR clause in your arithmetic statements, as described in chapters 4 and 5. Instead, you handle the overflow condition by the statements in your ON SIZE ERROR clause.

A *divide exception* occurs when a divide operation tries to divide by zero. Here again, the exception doesn't take place if you code the ON SIZE ERROR clause, even if the division is an intermediate calculation within a COMPUTE statement.

An *operation exception* occurs when the computer tries to perform an invalid operation code. In a COBOL program, this often means an I/O problem. If you make sure that your programs don't do any of the illogical operations listed at the bottom of figure 10-8, you should be able to avoid operation exceptions in most of your report preparation programs.

You should realize, though, that the illogical operations listed in figure 10-8 don't always cause abnormal terminations. It depends upon the system you're using. On some systems, for example, one or more of the conditions in figure 10-8 may be ignored so the program will continue until it terminates normally or is cancelled for some other reason.

**Two debugging examples** I can't give you a precise procedure for debugging abnormal terminations. However, I can give you a couple of examples so you can see that debugging is a manageable task if you go about it logically. Both examples were run on an IBM mainframe using DOS/VSE.

Figure 10-9 presents the compiler listing and the termination message for the inventory-listing program with one bug in it. There was no printed output for the program before the program terminated. As you can see, the message indicates a data exception. Can you find the bug and correct it?

One of your clues is that no lines have been printed on the inventory listing, not even the first heading line. This means that only a few statements were executed before the program terminated. Now can you find the bug?

If you're still having trouble finding the bug, it should help you to know that the program terminated as statement 108 was executing. As I said before, many systems will give you this extra item of information. Once you know the statement number, you should quickly be able to figure out that LINE-COUNT wasn't initialized to a value of zero, so a data exception occurred when it was compared numerically with LINES-ON-PAGE.

Figure 10-10 presents another compiler listing, the printed output to the point of the termination, and the termination message for another test run of the inventory-listing program. This time the bug in the first example has been corrected, but the program has a new bug.

```
000100 IDENTIFICATION DIVISION.
000200*
000300 PROGRAM-ID.         INV3510.
000400*AUTHOR.             MIKE MURACH.
000500*
000600 ENVIRONMENT DIVISION.
000700*
000800 CONFIGURATION SECTION.
000900*
001000 SOURCE-COMPUTER.  IBM-370.
001100 OBJECT-COMPUTER.  IBM-370.
001200*
001300 INPUT-OUTPUT SECTION.
001400*
001500 FILE-CONTROL.
001600        SELECT INVMAST ASSIGN TO SYS020-AS-INVMAST.
001700        SELECT INVLIST ASSIGN TO SYS006-UR-1403-S.
001800*
001900 DATA DIVISION.
002000*
002100 FILE SECTION.
002200*
002300 FD  INVMAST
002400        LABEL RECORDS ARE STANDARD
002500        RECORD CONTAINS 80 CHARACTERS.
002600*
002700 01  INVENTORY-MASTER-RECORD.
002800*
002900     05  IM-ITEM-NO            PIC 9(5).
003000     05  IM-ITEM-DESC          PIC X(20).
003100     05  IM-UNIT-COST          PIC 999V99.
003200     05  IM-UNIT-PRICE         PIC 999V99.
003300     05  IM-REORDER-POINT      PIC 9(5).
003400     05  IM-ON-HAND            PIC 9(5).
003500     05  IM-ON-ORDER           PIC 9(5).
003600     05  FILLER                PIC X(30).
003700*
003800 FD  INVLIST
003900        LABEL RECORDS ARE OMITTED
004000        RECORD CONTAINS 132 CHARACTERS.
004100*
004200 01  PRINT-AREA                PIC X(132).
004300*
004400 WORKING-STORAGE SECTION.
004500*
004600 01  SWITCHES.
004700*
004800     05  INVMAST-EOF-SWITCH    PIC X       VALUE 'N'.
004900*
005000 01  PRINT-FIELDS.
005100*
005200     05  SPACE-CONTROL         PIC 9.
005300     05  LINES-ON-PAGE         PIC 99      VALUE 55.
005400     05  LINE-COUNT            PIC 99.
005500*
005600 01  HEADING-LINE.
005700*
005800     05  FILLER                PIC X(8)    VALUE 'ITEM NO.'.
005900     05  FILLER                PIC X(2)    VALUE SPACE.
```

**Figure 10-9** Debugging example 1: The compiler listing (part 1 of 4)

```
006000        05  FILLER                   PIC X(16)  VALUE 'ITEM DESCRIPTION'.
006100        05  FILLER                   PIC X(8)   VALUE SPACE.
006200        05  FILLER                   PIC X(10)  VALUE 'UNIT PRICE'.
006300        05  FILLER                   PIC X(5)   VALUE SPACE.
006400        05  FILLER                   PIC X(7)   VALUE 'ON HAND'.
006500        05  FILLER                   PIC X(5)   VALUE SPACE.
006600        05  FILLER                   PIC X(13)  VALUE 'REORDER POINT'.
006700        05  FILLER                   PIC X(58)  VALUE SPACE.
006800*
006900 01    INVENTORY-LINE.
007000*
007100        05  IL-ITEM-NO               PIC Z(5).
007200        05  FILLER                   PIC X(5)   VALUE SPACE.
007300        05  IL-ITEM-DESC             PIC X(20).
007400        05  FILLER                   PIC X(7)   VALUE SPACE.
007500        05  IL-UNIT-PRICE            PIC ZZZ.99.
007600        05  FILLER                   PIC X(7)   VALUE SPACE.
007700        05  IL-ON-HAND               PIC ZZZZ9.
007800        05  FILLER                   PIC X(11)  VALUE SPACE.
007900        05  IL-REORDER-POINT         PIC Z(5).
008000        05  FILLER                   PIC X(61)  VALUE SPACE.
008100*
008200 PROCEDURE DIVISION.
008300*
008400 000-PREPARE-INVENTORY-LISTING.
008500*
008600        OPEN INPUT  INVMAST
008700             OUTPUT INVLIST.
008800        PERFORM 100-PREPARE-INVENTORY-LINE
008900            UNTIL INVMAST-EOF-SWITCH = 'Y'.
009000        CLOSE INVMAST
009100              INVLIST.
009200        STOP RUN.
009300*
009400 100-PREPARE-INVENTORY-LINE.
009500*
009600        PERFORM 110-READ-INVENTORY-RECORD.
009700        IF INVMAST-EOF-SWITCH NOT = 'Y'
009800            PERFORM 120-PRINT-INVENTORY-LINE.
009900*
010000 110-READ-INVENTORY-RECORD.
010100*
010200        READ INVMAST RECORD
010300            AT END
010400                MOVE 'Y' TO INVMAST-EOF-SWITCH.
010500*
010600 120-PRINT-INVENTORY-LINE.
010700*
010800        IF LINE-COUNT > LINES-ON-PAGE
010900            PERFORM 130-PRINT-HEADING-LINE.
011000        MOVE IM-ITEM-NO          TO IL-ITEM-NO.
011100        MOVE IM-ITEM-DESC        TO IL-ITEM-DESC.
011200        MOVE IM-UNIT-PRICE       TO IL-UNIT-PRICE.
011300        MOVE IM-ON-HAND          TO IL-ON-HAND.
011400        MOVE IM-REORDER-POINT    TO IL-REORDER-POINT.
011500        MOVE INVENTORY-LINE      TO PRINT-AREA.
011600        PERFORM 140-WRITE-INVENTORY-LINE.
011700*
011800 130-PRINT-HEADING-LINE.
011900*
```

Figure 10-9    Debugging example 1: The compiler listing (part 2 of 4)

```
00120    012000        MOVE HEADING-LINE TO PRINT-AREA.
00121    012100        WRITE PRINT-AREA
00122    012200            AFTER ADVANCING PAGE.
00123    012300        MOVE ZERO TO LINE-COUNT.
00124    012400        MOVE 2 TO SPACE-CONTROL.
00125    012500*
00126    012600 140-WRITE-INVENTORY-LINE.
00127    012700*
00128    012800        WRITE PRINT-AREA
00129    012900            AFTER ADVANCING SPACE-CONTROL LINES.
00130    013000        ADD 1 TO LINE-COUNT.
00131    013100        MOVE 1 TO SPACE-CONTROL.
```

**Figure 10-9** Debugging example 1: The compiler listing (part 3 of 4)

```
0S03I PROGRAM CHECK INTERRUPTION - HEX LOCATION 038180 - CONDITION CODE 1 - DATA EXCEPTION
0S00I JOB CLG1      CANCELED
0S07I PROBLEM PROGRAM  PSW     031D100000038186
```

**Figure 10-9** Debugging example 1: The termination message (part 4 of 4)

As the message says, the termination is due to another data exception. Can you find the bug and correct it?

In figure 10-10, one of your clues is that only the heading line of the inventory listing has been printed. This means that the program terminated between the time it printed the first heading line and the time it was supposed to print the first detail line. Now can you find the bug?

If you're still having trouble finding the bug, it may help you to know that the program was executing statement 127 at the time of the termination. Since statement 127 is a WRITE statement, you must then ask how an I/O statement can terminate due to a data exception. In this case, SPACE-CONTROL was never given a valid starting value because module 130 didn't set it to a value of two after it printed the heading line.

In these two examples, we didn't bother to show you the test data because the statements that led to the abnormal terminations weren't working with any input. Remember, though, that data exceptions are often caused by faulty input data. So when you're debugging on your own, your input file may be the first place to look for the cause of the termination.

## Debugging aids

Whether your program runs to normal or abnormal termination, it can be difficult indeed to determine why it doesn't work as expected. Worse, as your programs become longer and more complex, your

```
000100 IDENTIFICATION DIVISION.
000200*
000300 PROGRAM-ID.        INV3510.
000400*AUTHOR.            MIKE MURACH.
000500*
000600 ENVIRONMENT DIVISION.
000700*
000800 CONFIGURATION SECTION.
000900*
001000 SOURCE-COMPUTER.   IBM-370.
001100 OBJECT-COMPUTER.   IBM-370.
001200*
001300 INPUT-OUTPUT SECTION.
001400*
001500 FILE-CONTROL.
001600     SELECT INVMAST ASSIGN TO SYS020-AS-INVMAST.
001700     SELECT INVLIST ASSIGN TO SYS006-UR-1403-S.
001800*
001900 DATA DIVISION.
002000*
002100 FILE SECTION.
002200*
002300 FD  INVMAST
002400     LABEL RECORDS ARE STANDARD
002500     RECORD CONTAINS 80 CHARACTERS.
002600*
002700 01  INVENTORY-MASTER-RECORD.
002800*
002900     05  IM-ITEM-NO            PIC 9(5).
003000     05  IM-ITEM-DESC          PIC X(20).
003100     05  IM-UNIT-COST          PIC 999V99.
003200     05  IM-UNIT-PRICE         PIC 999V99.
003300     05  IM-REORDER-POINT      PIC 9(5).
003400     05  IM-ON-HAND            PIC 9(5).
003500     05  IM-ON-ORDER           PIC 9(5).
003600     05  FILLER                PIC X(30).
003700*
003800 FD  INVLIST
003900     LABEL RECORDS ARE OMITTED
004000     RECORD CONTAINS 132 CHARACTERS.
004100*
004200 01  PRINT-AREA                PIC X(132).
004300*
004400 WORKING-STORAGE SECTION.
004500*
004600 01  SWITCHES.
004700*
004800     05  INVMAST-EOF-SWITCH    PIC X        VALUE 'N'.
004900*
005000 01  PRINT-FIELDS.
005100*
005200     05  SPACE-CONTROL         PIC 9.
005300     05  LINES-ON-PAGE         PIC 99       VALUE 55.
005400     05  LINE-COUNT            PIC 99       VALUE 70.
005500*
005600 01  HEADING-LINE.
005700*
005800     05  FILLER                PIC X(8)     VALUE 'ITEM NO.'.
005900     05  FILLER                PIC X(2)     VALUE SPACE.
```

Figure 10-10 Debugging example 2: The compiler listing (part 1 of 5)

```
006000      05  FILLER               PIC X(16)  VALUE 'ITEM DESCRIPTION'.
006100      05  FILLER               PIC X(8)   VALUE SPACE.
006200      05  FILLER               PIC X(10)  VALUE 'UNIT PRICE'.
006300      05  FILLER               PIC X(5)   VALUE SPACE.
006400      05  FILLER               PIC X(7)   VALUE 'ON HAND'.
006500      05  FILLER               PIC X(5)   VALUE SPACE.
006600      05  FILLER               PIC X(13)  VALUE 'REORDER POINT'.
006700      05  FILLER               PIC X(58)  VALUE SPACE.
006800*
006900 01  INVENTORY-LINE.
007000*
007100      05  IL-ITEM-NO           PIC Z(5).
007200      05  FILLER               PIC X(5)   VALUE SPACE.
007300      05  IL-ITEM-DESC         PIC X(20).
007400      05  FILLER               PIC X(7)   VALUE SPACE.
007500      05  IL-UNIT-PRICE        PIC ZZZ.99.
007600      05  FILLER               PIC X(7)   VALUE SPACE.
007700      05  IL-ON-HAND           PIC ZZZZ9.
007800      05  FILLER               PIC X(11)  VALUE SPACE.
007900      05  IL-REORDER-POINT     PIC Z(5).
008000      05  FILLER               PIC X(61)  VALUE SPACE.
008100*
008200 PROCEDURE DIVISION.
008300*
008400 000-PREPARE-INVENTORY-LISTING.
008500*
008600     OPEN INPUT  INVMAST
008700          OUTPUT INVLIST.
008800     PERFORM 100-PREPARE-INVENTORY-LINE
008900         UNTIL INVMAST-EOF-SWITCH = 'Y'.
009000     CLOSE INVMAST
009100           INVLIST.
009200     STOP RUN.
009300*
009400 100-PREPARE-INVENTORY-LINE.
009500*
009600     PERFORM 110-READ-INVENTORY-RECORD.
009700     IF INVMAST-EOF-SWITCH NOT = 'Y'
009800         PERFORM 120-PRINT-INVENTORY-LINE.
009900*
010000 110-READ-INVENTORY-RECORD.
010100*
010200     READ INVMAST RECORD
010300         AT END
010400             MOVE 'Y' TO INVMAST-EOF-SWITCH.
010500*
010600 120-PRINT-INVENTORY-LINE.
010700*
010800     IF LINE-COUNT > LINES-ON-PAGE
010900         PERFORM 130-PRINT-HEADING-LINE.
011000     MOVE IM-ITEM-NO           TO IL-ITEM-NO.
011100     MOVE IM-ITEM-DESC         TO IL-ITEM-DESC.
011200     MOVE IM-UNIT-PRICE        TO IL-UNIT-PRICE.
011300     MOVE IM-ON-HAND           TO IL-ON-HAND.
011400     MOVE IM-REORDER-POINT     TO IL-REORDER-POINT.
011500     MOVE INVENTORY-LINE       TO PRINT-AREA.
011600     PERFORM 140-WRITE-INVENTORY-LINE.
011700*
011800 130-PRINT-HEADING-LINE.
011900*
```

**Figure 10-10** Debugging example 2: The compiler listing (part 2 of 5)

```
012000           MOVE HEADING-LINE TO PRINT-AREA.
012100           WRITE PRINT-AREA
012200               AFTER ADVANCING PAGE.
012300           MOVE ZERO TO LINE-COUNT.
012400*
012500 140-WRITE-INVENTORY-LINE.
012600*
012700           WRITE PRINT-AREA
012800               AFTER ADVANCING SPACE-CONTROL LINES.
012900           ADD 1 TO LINE-COUNT.
013000           MOVE 1 TO SPACE-CONTROL.
```

**Figure 10-10** Debugging example 2: The compiler listing (part 3 of 5)

```
ITEM NO.  ITEM DESCRIPTION        UNIT PRICE     ON HAND      REORDER POINT
```

**Figure 10-10** Debugging example 2: The test run output (part 4 of 5)

```
0S03I PROGRAM CHECK INTERRUPTION - HEX LOCATION 0398B0 - CONDITION CODE 0 - DATA EXCEPTION
0S00I JOB CLG1      CANCELED
0S07I PROBLEM PROGRAM  PSW    031D0000000398B4
```

**Figure 10-10** Debugging example 2: The termination message (part 5 of 5)

debugging problems become more difficult. That's why modern interactive systems usually provide *debugging aids* that help you locate bugs with relative efficiency.

On the Wang VS system, for example, the debugging aids tell you which statement was being executed at the time of an abnormal termination by displaying a message on the programmer's screen as shown in figure 10-7. Then, using additional debugging aids, the programmer can examine the values in any of the fields at the time of the termination. If a program has some bugs that are extremely difficult to isolate, the programmer can use the debugging aids to step through the program a few statements at a time, examining the data in fields whenever she wants to, until it's obvious where the bugs are. With aids like these, it's relatively easy to debug even the most complex programs.

If your system doesn't have debugging aids like those I've just described, you can use the debugging module provided by both the 1974 and 1985 COBOL standards. However, this module has been marked for deletion in the 1985 standards, which means it won't be continued in the next revision of the COBOL standards. In addition, it's not that useful because it's relatively difficult to use. As a result, we're not going to teach the debugging module of COBOL in this book.

There is one facility of the debugging module, though, that is going to be continued in future versions of the COBOL standards. This facility provides for the use of *debugging statements*. These are regular COBOL statements that are used to print or display data that helps you locate a program's bugs. When you use this facility, you put a D in position 7 of each debugging statement to identify it as a *debugging line*. Then, when you want the debugging lines to be compiled and executed, you add a WITH DEBUGGING MODE clause after the name of the source computer in the Environment Division, as in this example:

```
 ENVIRONMENT DIVISION.
*
 CONFIGURATION SECTION.
*
 SOURCE-COMPUTER.  IBM-370 WITH DEBUGGING MODE.
 OBJECT-COMPUTER.  IBM-370.
```

If you don't want the debugging lines to be compiled, you remove the WITH DEBUGGING MODE clause. Then, the debugging lines are treated as comments, so they're ignored.

Although this debugging facility can be useful, you don't have to use it to put debugging statements into your programs. Instead, you can put whatever debugging statements you want into your program before you compile and test it just as if they were part of the program. If, for example, you want to know the value of one or more fields as a module is being executed, you can put statements in the module that print the contents of the fields in alphanumeric form. Or, you can use the DISPLAY statement, which is described in chapter 4, to print or display fields. Then, after you've debugged your program, you remove these statements.

To illustrate the use of debugging statements, whether or not you use the standard debugging facility, suppose you just can't find the bug in the example in figure 10-10. Suppose that you don't know the number of the last statement executed and that you can't even figure out in which module the program ended. You can then put DISPLAY statements in all of the modules of the program except for module 000 as shown in modules 100 and 110 in figure 10-11. When the program is executed, the DISPLAY statements will either display or print the paragraph names of the modules as they are executed. As a result, you'll get a sequence of paragraph names like the one shown in the second portion of figure 10-11. With this extra information, it's easy to see that the program was cancelled while module 140 was being executed. Incidentally, if you used the debugging facility of COBOL, each DISPLAY statement in figure 10-11 would have a D in position 7.

**Modules of the inventory-listing program including DISPLAY statements for debugging**

```
 100-PREPARE-INVENTORY-LINE.
*
     DISPLAY '100-PREPARE-INVENTORY-LINE'.
     PERFORM 110-READ-INVENTORY-RECORD.
     IF INVMAST-EOF-SWITCH NOT = 'Y'
         PERFORM 120-PRINT-INVENTORY-LINE.
*
 110-READ-INVENTORY-RECORD.
*
     DISPLAY '110-READ-INVENTORY-RECORD'.
     READ INVMAST RECORD
         AT END
             MOVE 'Y' TO INVMAST-EOF-SWITCH.
*
     .
     .
```

**DISPLAY statement output as printed by a DOS/VSE system**

```
100-PREPARE-INVENTORY-LINE
110-READ-INVENTORY-RECORD
120-PRINT-INVENTORY-LINE
130-PRINT-HEADING-LINE
140-WRITE-INVENTORY-LINE
```

**Figure 10-11** Using DISPLAY statements as debugging statements in the program in figure 10-10

In a similar fashion, you can design debugging statements to help you solve other debugging problems. As the years progress, however, we can expect to see more sophisticated, interactive debugging aids that should make the need for debugging statements just about obsolete.

## Discussion

In this course, your case study programs shouldn't require many more than 500 lines of code each. As a result, your debugging problems should be relatively manageable. In general, you should be able to debug your normal or abnormal terminations without using any debugging aids or debugging statements, even if your system doesn't tell you the number of the last statement to be executed in a program that terminates abnormally.

As you progress in your programming career, however, you will want to become proficient in the use of the debugging aids that are available to you. If effective ones are available on your system, they can save you dozens of hours of debugging time each year. If, on the other hand, your system doesn't provide effective debugging aids, you can still do an adequate job of debugging by using debugging statements. It just puts more of a burden on you to be organized and logical during your testing and debugging efforts.

## Terminology

normal termination
abnormal termination
exception
data exception
overflow exception
divide exception
operation exception
debugging aids
debugging statement
debugging line

## Objective

Given test run output for a COBOL report preparation program, debug the program. The test run output will include test data listings, compiler output, the printed output for the test run, and the abnormal termination message (if any).

Section 4

# Structured programming techniques

This section presents the techniques you need to know to develop a COBOL program on a structured basis. Chapter 11 introduces you to the four major techniques of structured programming: top-down design, structured module planning using pseudocode, structured coding, and top-down testing. You can read this chapter any time after you complete chapter 4.

Chapter 12 introduces you to the structure and logic of report preparation programs. By studying the examples in this chapter, you should begin to understand the basic structure of any report preparation program. You can read this chapter any time after you read chapter 11, but we recommend that you read it before you start to design your own report preparation programs.

Chapter 11

# An introduction to structured programming

The term *structured programming* refers to a collection of techniques that are designed to help you improve both your productivity and the quality of your programs. The techniques include structured program design, structured module planning using pseudocode, structured coding, and top-down testing. In this book, all of the programs have been developed using structured design and structured coding.

I'll start this chapter by presenting the theory of structured programming. Next, I'll show you how to design a program using a structure chart and how to plan the modules of a program using pseudocode. Then, I'll show you how to code the structures of structured programming in COBOL and how to code and test a program from the top down.

You can read this chapter any time after you complete chapter 4. In fact, we recommend that you read it right after you complete chapter 4. Then, you can use structured techniques in your work on the case study programs for this course.

## The theory of structured programming

The basic theory of structured programming is that any program, in any language, can be written using three logical structures: sequence, selection, and iteration. These structures, illustrated in figure 11-1, have only one entry point and one exit point. (In contrast, unstructured programs allow for multiple entry and exit points; for an example, look back at MAINLINE-ROUTINE in figure 3-19.)

The first structure, the *sequence structure*, is simply a set of imperative statements executed in sequence, one after another. The

**The sequence structure**

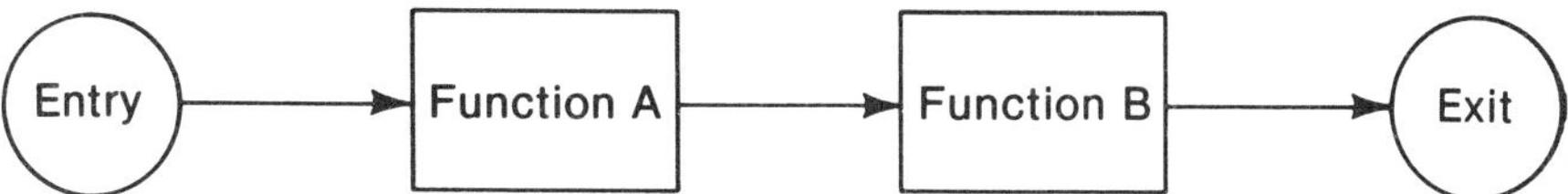


**The selection structure (IF-THEN-ELSE)**

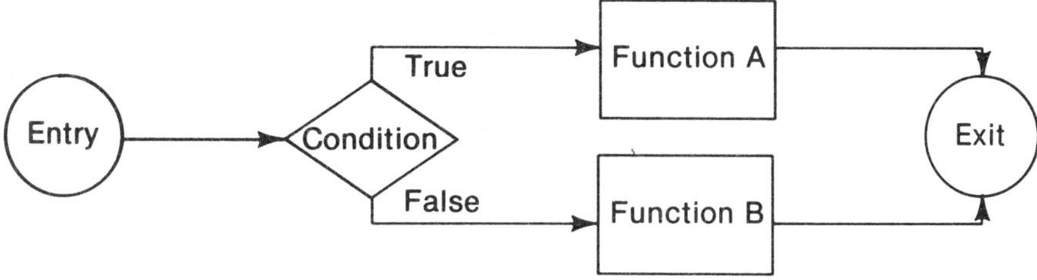


**Variation 1 of the iteration structure (DO-WHILE)**

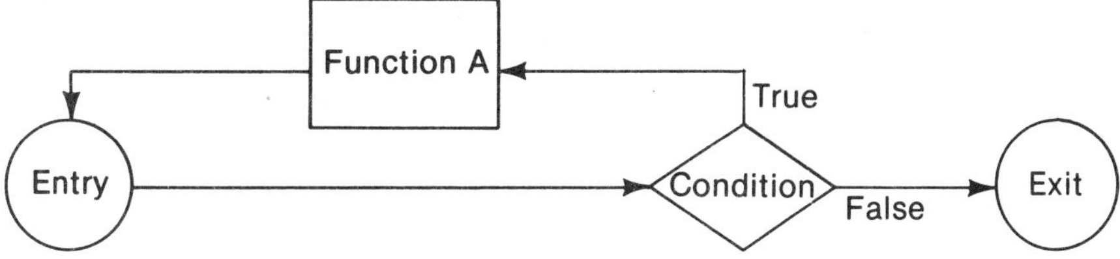


**Variation 2 of the iteration structure (DO-UNTIL)**

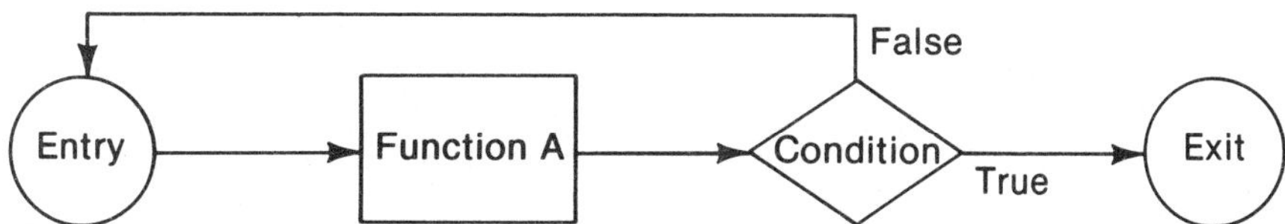


**Variation 3 of the iteration structure (COBOL PERFORM-UNTIL)**

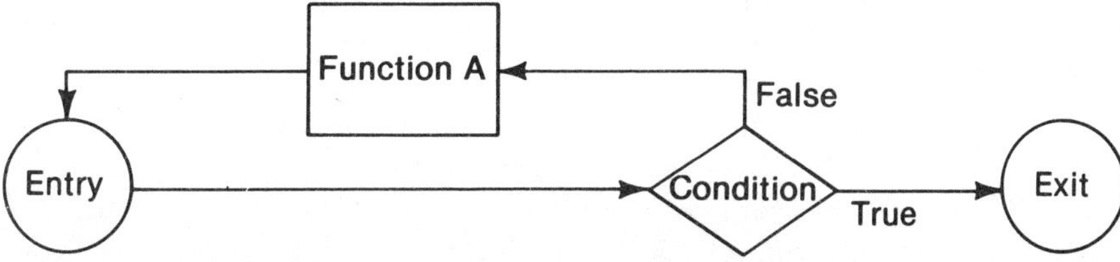


**Figure 11-1** The basic structures of structured programming

entry point is at the start of the sequence; the exit point is after the last statement in the sequence. A sequence structure may consist of a single function or of many functions.

The second structure, the *selection structure*, is a choice between two, and only two, functions based on a condition. You should realize, though, that one of the functions may be null. In other words, if the condition is not met, the flow of control may pass directly to the structure's exit point with no intervening statements or structures. This structure is often referred to as the IF-THEN-ELSE structure, and most programming languages have code that approximates it.

The third structure, the *iteration structure*, is often called the DO-WHILE structure. It provides for doing a function as long as a condition is true. As you can see in variation 1 of the iteration structure, the condition is tested before the function is performed. When the condition is no longer true, the program continues with the next structure.

Related to the DO-WHILE structure are the DO-UNTIL and the COBOL PERFORM-UNTIL structures. As you can see in the DO-UNTIL structure in figure 11-1, the condition is tested *after* the function is performed and the function is performed until a condition is true. In the PERFORM-UNTIL structure, the function is also performed until the condition is true, but the condition is tested *before* the function is performed.

Again, let me stress that all of the structures in figure 11-1 have only one entry point and one exit point. As a result, a program made up of these structures will have only one entry point and one exit point. This means the program will be executed in a controlled manner from the first statement to the last. These characteristics make up a *proper program*.

To create a proper program, any of the three structures can be substituted for a function box in any of the other structures. The result will still be a proper program. Conversely, two or more of the basic structures in sequence can be treated as a single function box. This means that structures of great complexity can be created with the assurance that they will have only one entry point and one exit point.

If you've never written an unstructured program in another language, you may have a hard time understanding the significance of structured programming. But take my word for it: Allowing for multiple entry and exit points makes a program hard to read, understand, and change. It also makes it hard to code and debug in the first place. And the difficulty increases dramatically as the programs get longer (if you've ever written even a simple, unstructured BASIC program, you'll realize that a production program in COBOL could get out of hand in a hurry). So the theory of structured programming is an important contribution to the art of programming because it places necessary restrictions on program structure.

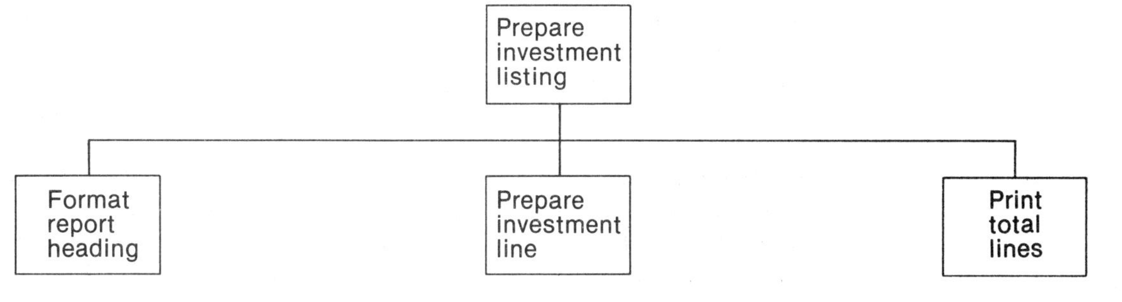


**Figure 11-2** The first two levels of the structure chart for the investment-listing program of chapters 4 and 5

### How to design a program using a structure chart

In this book, each program is presented with the structure chart for its design. However, I haven't yet shown you how to create a structure chart for one of your own programs.

Now, I'm going to present a five-step procedure for designing structure charts. This introductory procedure should help you design any of the programs required by the case studies for this course.

**Step 1: Design the function boxes for the first two levels** To design a structure chart, you start with a top-level module that represents the entire program. Next, you decide on the one functional module that will be performed repeatedly during the execution of the program, and you draw this module at the second level of the chart. Then, you decide whether your program requires any functional modules that need to be performed before or after this primary module at the second level. If so, you draw boxes for these functions to the left or the right of the primary module.

To illustrate, figure 11-2 represents the first two levels of the chart for the investment-listing program of chapters 4 and 5. The top-level box is named "prepare investment listing," and the primary module at the second level is named "prepare investment line." The prepare-investment-line module is the primary module because it will be executed repeatedly during the program—once for each master record until all records in the master file have been read and processed. In other words, a primary module represents the processing for one input record or one set of input records.

Because the investment-listing program must get the date and time into the first heading line of the investment listing, the module to the left of the prepare-investment-line module is named "format report heading." This module will get the date and time and edit them into the appropriate fields in the heading lines. If other functions must be performed before the primary module is executed, they can also be drawn to the left of the primary module. For instance, a program that uses a table might require a module to load the table from a file into storage at the start of the program (table handling is covered in chapter 6).

Because the investment-listing program must print two total lines after all investment lines have been printed, the module to the right of the prepare-investment-line module is named "print total lines." If other functions must be performed after the function of the primary module has been completed, they can also be drawn to the right of the primary module.

To name the functions and subfunctions represented by the boxes of a chart, you use a verb, one or two adjectives, and a noun. Thus, the name of the top-level box in the chart in figure 11-2 is "prepare investment listing." And the names of the modules in the second level of the chart are "format report heading," "prepare investment line," and "print total lines."

As you get more experience with structured program development, you'll realize that all programs can be charted at the first two levels with a structure similar to the one in figure 11-2. Every program has at least one primary function, although it may not be related to a set of input records. And most programs require functions that must be performed before or after the primary function.

**Step 2: Design the subordinate function boxes until each module of the program can be coded in a single COBOL paragraph** Step 2 is to divide the modules at the second level into their subordinate functions and subfunctions until each module of the program can be coded in a single COBOL paragraph. To illustrate, figure 11-3 shows the functions and subfunctions that I designed for the modules in figure 11-2.

To start, I asked what subordinate modules (if any) the format-report-heading module required. Without any subordinates, I knew that I could code the format-report-heading box in a single COBOL paragraph. However, I also knew that two subprograms were available for getting the system date and system time. As a result, I drew boxes for these subprograms on the structure chart.

Subprograms are presented in chapter 5. When you use a subprogram, it should be shown as a separate box on the structure chart for the program. Also, a stripe should be drawn at the top of each subprogram box, and the name of the subprogram should be written in this striped area. Thus, the names of the two subprograms in the chart in figure 11-3 are SYSDATE and SYSTIME.

After I designed the subordinates for the format-report-heading module, I designed the subordinate functions for the prepare-investment-line module. As you can see in figure 11-3, I designed three functions subordinate to this module. Each time the prepare-

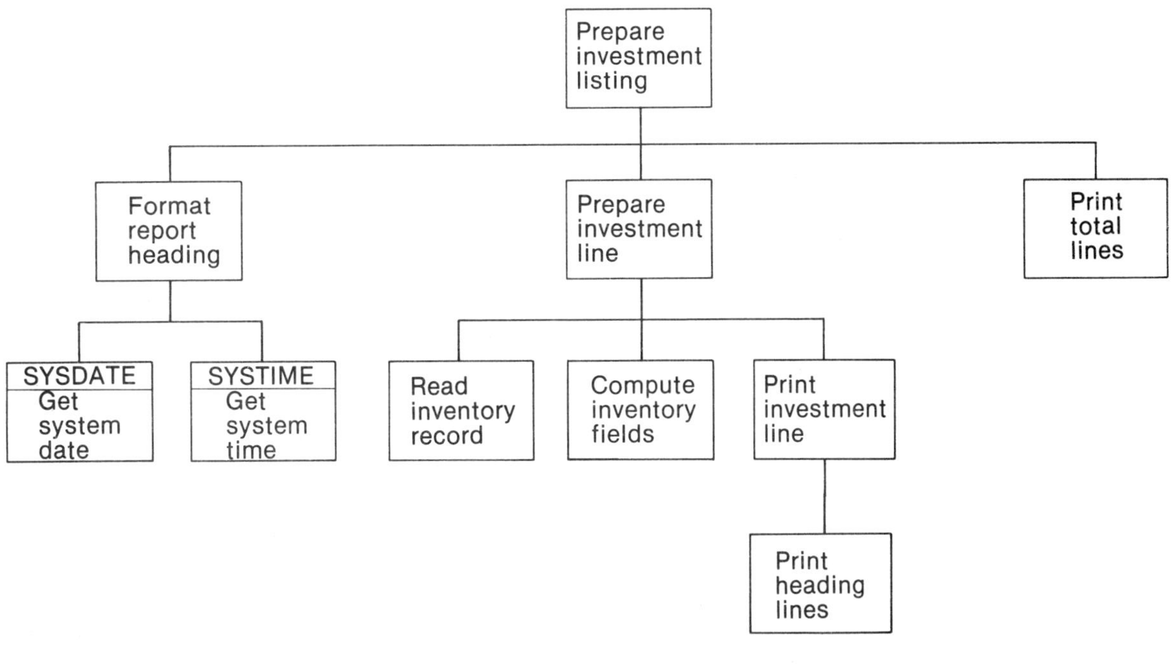


**Figure 11-3** The expanded structure chart for the investment-listing program of chapter 5

investment-line module is executed, it must (1) read an inventory master record, (2) compute the required inventory fields, and (3) print an investment line if the investment amount is greater than $10,000.

I then asked if any of these modules required subordinates, and I decided that only the print-investment-line module needed one. Whenever page overflow occurs, the report headings must be printed on the new page. As a result, the print-heading-lines module is subordinate to the print-investment-line module.

If the read or compute modules required subordinates, of course, I would have drawn them at the next level of the chart. And I would have continued this process until I had designed down to the lowest level. For this simple program, though, figure 11-3 presents all of the functional modules that are required by the prepare-investment-line module.

Last, I asked whether the print-total-lines module required any subordinates. I decided that it didn't. As a result, figure 11-3 represents all the functional modules required by the investment-listing program. In addition, I'm confident that I can code any one of them in a single COBOL paragraph.

When you draw modules on a structure chart, keep in mind that a left-to-right sequence of execution is expected at each level of subordination. At the third level in figure 11-3, for example, you would expect the subordinates for the prepare-investment-line module to be

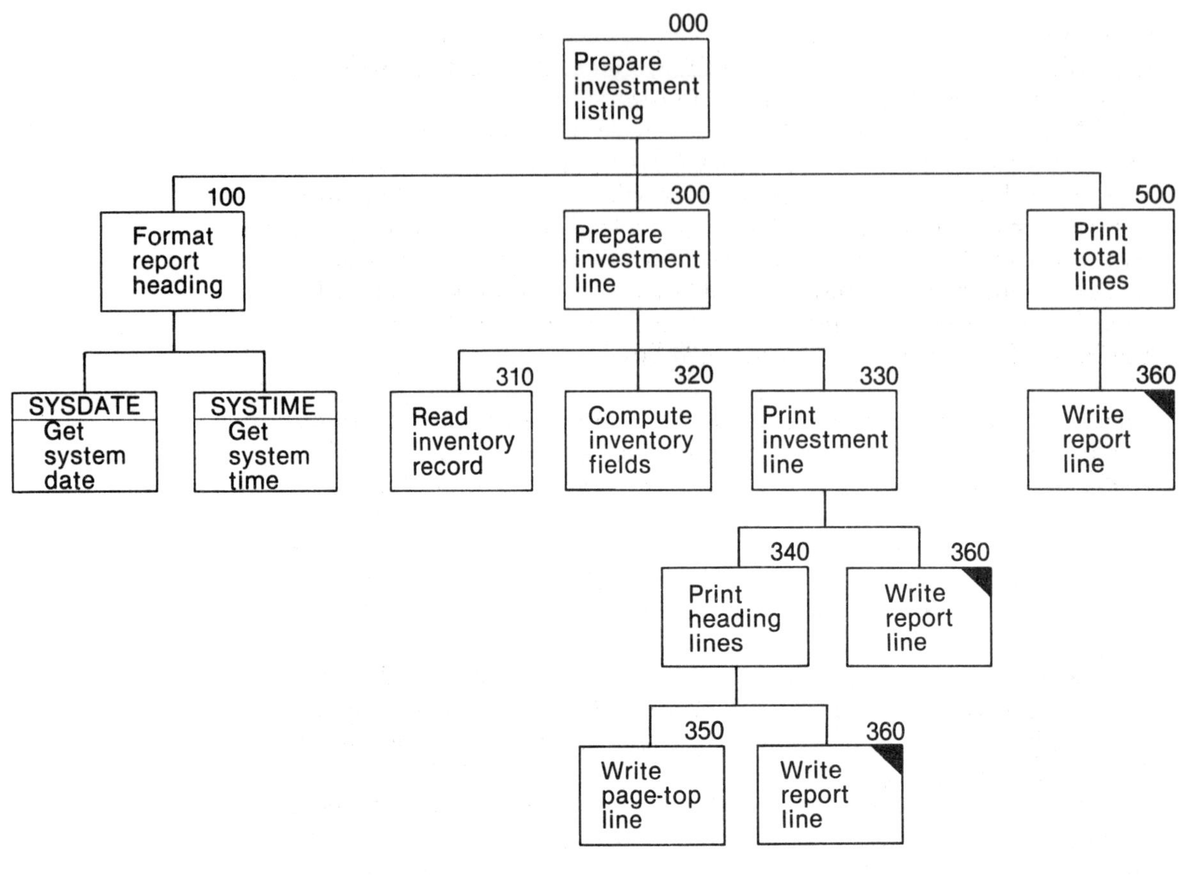


**Figure 11-4** The complete structure chart for the investment-listing program of chapter 5

executed in the sequence of read, compute, and print. However, when you actually code the program, that may not be the case. So the expected sequence can be varied as required by the program specifications. In other words, you can't always tell what the sequence will be at the time that you design a program's modules.

**Step 3: Add one function box for each I/O statement** In step 3, you add one function box for each I/O operation required by a program. If you look at the chart in figure 11-4, for example, you can see that I added four write modules for the printer file, though three of them are the same. I didn't add a read module for the inventory master file, because the chart already had one.

In general, when you add I/O modules to a program, the objective is for you to code only one READ or WRITE statement for each file used by the program. But this isn't always possible. For instance, a print file usually requires one WRITE statement that skips to the top of a page as well as one WRITE statement that spaces one or more lines based on the value in a space-control field. As a result, each print file will usually require two WRITE statements (and two different types of WRITE modules on the structure chart).

When you isolate the I/O statements in their own modules like this, you end up with a more efficient program and one that is easier to modify. This also makes it easier to provide for functions like counting the number of records read or written by a program, because you can code functions like this in the related I/O module. The alternative in a large program is to have several READ or WRITE statements for each file dispersed throughout the program, a practice that can make the logic of the program difficult to follow.

**Step 4: Shade the common modules** In step 4, you shade the upper righthand corners of the modules that are used in more than one place in the program. These modules are called *common modules*. In figure 11-4, for example, the write-report-line modules are common modules, so their corners are shaded. Although this program doesn't illustrate it, modules that aren't I/O modules can also be common modules, in which case they should be shaded too.

**Step 5: Number the modules** In step 5, you number all of the modules except the subprogram modules. For most programs, a simple numbering system like the one used in figure 11-4 is adequate. That means you give the top-level module a number of 000. Next, you number the modules in the second level by hundreds, but you leave enough space between the hundreds to provide for the modules at the lower levels of the chart. That's why the modules in the second level of figure 11-4 are numbered 100, 300, and 500. Finally, you number the modules at the next levels by tens.

Note that the numbers do *not* indicate at what level a module can be found. This means that you can add modules to the chart at any level without changing the numbers of any of the other modules. For instance, you could add a module 200 as a subordinate to module 000. You could add a module 325 as a subordinate to module 300. Or, you could add a module 335 as a subordinate to module 330. As a result, a structure chart like this is easy to enhance or modify.

## How to plan the modules of a program using pseudocode

Once you have completed the structure chart for a program, you can use *pseudocode* to plan the code for the program modules before you actually code them. For instance, figure 11-5 gives the pseudocode for all of the modules charted in figure 11-4. Pseudocode lets you plan the operations and logic of a module using only the legal structures of structured programming. And it lets you plan the modules quickly and easily.

When you use pseudocode, you should remember that it is a personal language. As a result, you don't have to follow rigid coding

```
000-prepare-investment-listing.

    Open files.
    DO 100-format-report-heading.
    DO 300-prepare-investment-line
        UNTIL all master records have been read.
    DO 500-print-total-lines.
    Close files.
    Stop run.

100-format-report-heading.

    Format report heading.

300-prepare-investment-line.

    DO 310-read-inventory-record.
    IF NOT invmast-eof
        DO 320-compute-inventory-fields
        IF investment-amount > 10000
            DO 330-print-investment-line.

310-read-inventory-record.

    Read record
        AT END
            move 'Y' to invmast-eof-switch.
    IF NOT invmast-eof
        add 1 to record-count.

320-compute-inventory-fields.

    Compute inventory fields.

330-print-investment-line.

    IF page-overflow
        DO 340-print-heading-lines.
    Format investment-line.
    DO 360-write-report-line.
    Move 1 to space-control.
```

**Figure 11-5** Pseudocode for the investment-listing program charted in figure 11-4 (part 1 of 2)

rules. In general, you should capitalize all of the structure words like DO, UNTIL, IF, and ELSE. Beyond this, you simply try to state what each module must do in a style that you feel comfortable with.

To illustrate typical variations in the ways that people use pseudocode, figure 11-6 shows three different forms of pseudocode for module 000 of the structure chart in figure 11-4. In the first style, only the structure words DO and UNTIL are capitalized. In the second style, PERFORM is used instead of DO and all COBOL words are capitalized. In the third style, all of the words are capitalized. If you

```
340-print-heading-lines.

    Print the heading lines using modules 350 and 360
    to actually write the lines.

350-write-page-top-line.

    Write a page-top line.
    Move 1 to line-count.
    Move 2 to space-control.

360-write-report-line.

    Write a line after advancing space-control lines.
    Add space-control to line-count.

500-print-total-lines.

    Format total lines and print them using module 360 to
    write them.
```

**Figure 11-5** Pseudocode for the investment-listing program charted in figure 11-4 (part 2 of 2)

compare the differences, you can see they're trivial. But books on pseudocode often stress these kinds of differences, and you may work in a shop someday that stresses them too. So I want you to be aware that differences do exist.

When you use pseudocode, you should use indentation to make the code as readable as possible. This is illustrated by the code in figure 11-5. In the DO-UNTIL statement in module 000, for example, the UNTIL portion is indented four spaces. Similarly, in the nested IF statements in module 300, indentation is used to show the levels of nesting.

When you use pseudocode, you should realize that you don't have to plan every aspect of a module. You'll note in figure 11-5, for example, that I didn't bother to plan the logic of modules 100, 320, 340, and 500 in detail because I know the logic is trivial. Similarly, you may decide that a "format" statement like the one in module 330 is obvious so you don't have to show it in your pseudocode.

Similarly, you don't necessarily have to plan every module in a program when you use pseudocode. For instance, modules 100, 320, 330, 340, 350, 360, and 500 in figure 11-5 are relatively trivial. As a result, you may only want to plan modules 000, 300, and 310 for this program. When you design a structured program, you'll usually find that just a few modules are complicated enough to require planning, because all of the modules will be relatively short. On the other hand, if you're not sure how a module should be coded, it's worth taking the time to plan it with pseudocode.

**Simple pseudocode**

```
Open files.
DO 100-format-report-heading.
DO 300-prepare-investment-line
    UNTIL all master records have been read.
DO 500-print-total-lines.
Close files.
Stop run.
```

**Pseudocode plus COBOL**

```
OPEN files.
PERFORM 100-FORMAT-REPORT-HEADING.
PERFORM 300-PREPARE-INVESTMENT-LINE
    UNTIL INVMAST-EOF.
PERFORM 500-PRINT-TOTAL-LINES.
CLOSE files.
STOP RUN.
```

**Pseudocode plus COBOL using all capital letters**

```
OPEN FILES.
PERFORM 100-FORMAT-REPORT-HEADING.
PERFORM 300-PREPARE-INVESTMENT-LINE
    UNTIL INVMAST-EOF.
PERFORM 500-PRINT-TOTAL-LINES.
CLOSE FILES.
STOP RUN.
```

**Figure 11-6** Different forms of pseudocode for module 000 of the investment-listing program

### How to code a structured program in COBOL

When it comes to coding, structured programming implies three things. First, it implies that you have a structured design for the program. Second, it implies that the program will be coded using only the accepted structures of structured programming. And third, it implies a style of coding that is designed to increase the readability of a program. Since I've just shown you how to design a program using a structure chart, I will now discuss briefly the coding for the accepted structures and give you some guidelines for increasing the readability of your programs.

**How to code the accepted structures in COBOL** To review, the accepted structures of structured programming are the sequence, iteration, and selection structures. To code these structures in COBOL, you use the techniques shown in chapters 3 through 7 in this book.

In COBOL, any statement without conditions is a sequence structure. Similarly, a succession of two or more of these statements is a sequence structure. Thus, a simple PERFORM statement is a sequence structure, a series of MOVE statements is a sequence structure, and a series of arithmetic statements without ON SIZE ERROR clauses is a sequence structure.

To code a selection structure, you code an IF statement. As you have already seen, you use indentation to show how the IF and ELSE parts of a statement are related. You also use indentation to show how the parts of nested IF statements are related.

To code an iteration structure, you code a PERFORM UNTIL statement. This has the logic shown in variation 3 of the iteration structure in figure 11-1. Using 1985 COBOL, you can also code variation 2 of the iteration structure. You do this by coding the WITH TEST AFTER clause in the PERFORM UNTIL statement as described in chapter 7.

**Guidelines for readability** A primary goal of structured programming is to create code that is easy to read because a program that is readable is easier to develop, test, debug, and maintain than one that isn't. As a result, all of the programs in this book have been coded using guidelines that help produce more readable code. In case these guidelines aren't obvious, let me summarize them.

In general, the code in all of the programs is presented in the same sequence. The SELECT statements and FD statements for the files are in sequence with input files first followed by output files. The groups in the working-storage section are in sequence by (1) work fields such as switches and counters, and (2) record descriptions in the same order as the related files listed in the SELECT statements. Within the record descriptions, the print line descriptions are in sequence by heading lines, body lines, and total lines. In the Procedure Division, all paragraphs are in sequence by module number. When you use standard sequences like this, it makes it easier for you to locate code as you test and maintain your programs.

Although there are many ways to achieve vertical spacing in a source listing, we recommend that blank comment lines be used for this purpose. In general, we use these lines to set off division and section headers and to highlight groups of data names in the Data Division and paragraphs in the Procedure Division.

In the Data Division, we group related data items to make it easier to find them. We also try to create data names that are meaningful so it's easy to tell what they represent. We use condition names whenever we think they can improve clarity. And, we use indentation and align clauses to improve readability.

In the Procedure Division, we code each box on the structure chart with a single COBOL paragraph. That way the structure chart is a guide to the COBOL code. We also use indentation and alignment to make all statements as easy to read as possible.

These, then, are the main guidelines for readability that are illustrated by the programs in this book. If you use them in your programs, we're confident that you will develop programs that are relatively easy to read, test, debug, and maintain.

## How to test a program using top-down testing

When you design a program on a top-down basis using structured design, you can develop it using *top-down coding and testing*. In fact, we recommend that you use top-down coding and testing on any program that takes more than a day to develop.

When you use top-down coding and testing, you don't code the entire program and then test it. Instead, you code and test in phases. You normally start by coding the top-level module and one or more of the modules in the second level. Then, after correcting any bugs, you add one or more modules to this coding and test again. When this much of the program runs correctly, you code a few more modules, add them to what you have, and test again. You continue in this way until all the modules have been coded and you are testing the entire program. Because top-down coding and testing always go together, the phrase *top-down testing* implies top-down coding.

The primary benefit of top-down testing is improved testing efficiency (or improved productivity). To illustrate, imagine a typical COBOL program of 2000 lines or more. If you test the entire program at once with all of its bugs, it's likely that your testing will proceed very inefficiently. For example, it may take several hours of testing just to debug a couple of minor clerical errors. But if you test on a top-down basis, testing proceeds in increments of a few modules at a time. Then, it is relatively easy to find any bugs that are discovered during a test phase because they almost have to be in the modules just added or in the interfaces between the old modules and the new.

**How to create a top-down test plan** When you use top-down testing, you start by developing a top-down test plan like the one in figure 11-7. In this plan for the investment-listing program that is charted in figure 11-4, five modules are tested in phase 1, three more are added in phase 2, and the last two are added in phase 3. Then, phase 4 tests data complexities and phase 5 is a volume test. Since the read module (module 310) isn't tested until phase 3, no test data is needed for the first two phases.

When you create a test plan, you have considerable choice as to what modules you test in each phase. As long as you proceed from the top down and add one or more modules in each phase, you are adhering to the principles of top-down testing. Whether you add one, two, or more modules at a time depends on your experience and on the length and complexity of the modules. In a short program like the investment-listing program, it doesn't matter too much what sequence you use, but in a larger, more realistic program, you must carefully plan the development sequence.

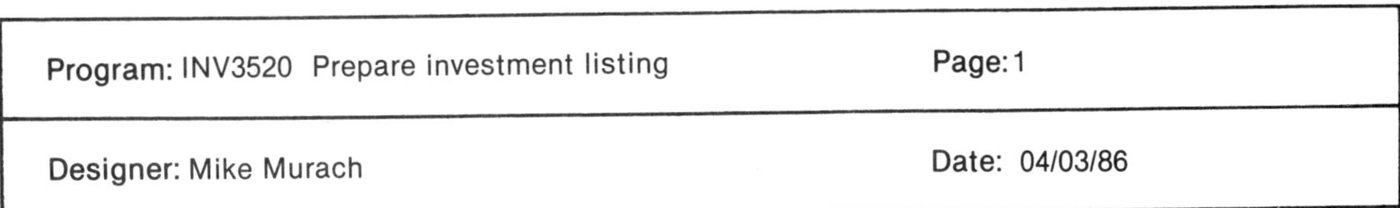

| Program: INV3520 Prepare investment listing | Page: 1 |
|---|---|
| Designer: Mike Murach | Date: 04/03/86 |

| Test phase | Data | Data source |
|---|---|---|
| 1. Modules 000, 100, 300, 500 and 360 | None | Not applicable |
| 2. Add modules 330, 340, and 350 | None | Not applicable |
| 3. Add modules 310 and 320 | Three records: one with investment amount less than $10,000; one with investment amount equal to $10,000; one with investment amount greater than $10,000 | Self |
| 4. All modules | Phase 3 data plus records that test the ON SIZE ERROR conditions of the arithmetic statements | Self |
| 5. Page overflow | Phase 4 data plus enough records to cause page overflow | Utility |

**Figure 11-7** A top-down test plan for the investment-listing program of chapters 4 and 5

In general, your goal should be to use the sequence of testing that will be most efficient in terms of coding and testing. As a result, when you develop your test plan, you should ask questions like: Where are the major module interfaces in the program? Where, if anywhere, in the structure chart do I have doubts about the design? In what modules do I have doubts about how the coding should be done? In most cases, you should try to code and resolve the major problems first.

After you test the first two or three levels of a program, it often becomes a case of mop up. Eventually, you have to code and test all of the modules, so you may as well take them one group at a time, introducing data that applies to each group as you go along.

Incidentally, you don't have to code the file or data definitions required by a module until you add the module to the program. For instance, since the read module in figure 11-4 isn't added to the program until phase 3, you don't have to code the FD statement for the inventory master file until phase 3. On the other hand, since module 330 requires the data descriptions for the fields in the inventory master file, you have to code its record description as part of your coding for phase 2.

**How to code program stubs** To use top-down testing, you must code *program stubs*, or *dummy modules*, for the modules in a phase that are called, but not tested. Using the test plan in figure 11-7, for example, modules 310, 320, and 330 are dummy modules in phase 1 so you must code program stubs for them. Similarly, modules 310 and 320 are dummy modules in phase 2.

In phase 1 of figure 11-7, the program stubs for modules 320 and 330 don't have to do anything because the modules that are being tested don't require any data that is developed by them. As a result, you can code just the paragraph name for each module. Module 310, however, should contain the following statement:

```
MOVE 'Y' TO INVMAST-EOF-SWITCH.
```

This simulates the end of the input file so the program can end properly.

If you want to make sure that the modules are called correctly, you can code program stubs to display messages to that effect. For instance, you can code this statement at the beginning of the stub for module 310:

```
DISPLAY '310-READ-INVENTORY-RECORD'.
```

When executed, this stub will display or print the paragraph name of the module to show that it has been executed. Then, if you code similar statements in the stubs for modules 320 and 330, the printed output will indicate whether or not the dummy modules were called.

**The input stub**

```
 310-READ-INVENTORY-RECORD.
*
     DISPLAY '310-READ-INVENTORY-RECORD'.
     IF FIRST-RECORD
         MOVE '11111AAAAAAAAAAAAAAAAAAAA2222233333'
             TO IM-DESCRIPTIVE-DATA
         MOVE '444445555566666' TO IM-INVENTORY-DATA
         MOVE '77777888888899999999' TO IM-SALES-DATA
         MOVE 'N' TO FIRST-RECORD-SWITCH
     ELSE
         MOVE 'Y' TO INVMAST-EOF-SWITCH.
*
```

**The processing stub**

```
 320-COMPUTE-INVENTORY-FIELDS.
*
     DISPLAY '320-COMPUTE-INVENTORY-FIELDS'.
     MOVE 12000.00 TO INVESTMENT-AMOUNT.
     MOVE 12.0 TO NO-OF-MONTHS-STOCK.
```

**Figure 11-8** The program stubs for phase 2 of the test plan in figure 11-7

In phase 2 of figure 11-7, the program stubs should develop some data in order to test module 330. To do this, the program stubs can be coded as in figure 11-8. Here, module 310 is expanded. It now simulates the reading of one input record the first time it is executed by moving data into the record area for the inventory master file. The second time it's executed, the FIRST-RECORD condition is false, so Y is moved to INVMAST-EOF-SWITCH indicating that all records in the master file have been read. Similarly, module 320 simulates the calculation of the inventory fields by moving values into INVESTMENT-AMOUNT and NO-OF-MONTHS-STOCK. If the stubs are coded like this, module 330 can print the data for one investment line so all of the modules except the stubs will get tested.

When you code program stubs, you must try to be practical. At some point, it becomes more practical to code the actual module than it is to simulate the function of the module. If, for example, you look at the stub for the read module in figure 11-8, you can see that the code for the stub is longer than the code for the actual module will be. So is it worth coding this stub? That, of course, depends on the program, the module, and your experience. In the case of the read stub in figure 11-8, I think it's worth coding it that way, because you simulate a one-record file before you even have to create a test file.

## Discussion

You should now be able to use structured design, pseudocode, structured coding, and top-down testing as you develop the case studies for this course. If you use these techniques, I believe you'll be able to develop high-quality programs in a minimum of time.

You should realize, though, that this chapter is just an introduction to structured programming. Although the techniques presented in this chapter should be adequate for most of the report preparation programs you'll write, they don't present everything you need to know as you start to develop more complex programs. That's why we offer two other books on structured programming for the COBOL programmer. The first, called *How to Design and Develop COBOL Programs*, presents all aspects of structured programming, including other techniques for design, planning, and coding. The second, called *The COBOL Programmer's Handbook*, presents complete guidelines for developing structured programs as well as model programs that you can use as a basis for developing your own programs. These books are used in thousands of COBOL shops throughout the country, and we believe that at least one set belongs in every COBOL shop to answer the development questions that frequently occur.

Up to this point in the text, you have only seen the design for one type of report preparation program, a relatively simple listing program. As a result, you may have difficulty designing structure charts for other types of report preparation programs. That's why the next chapter introduces you to some other types of report preparation programs as well as to the structure charts and pseudocode for some other programs. Although you should be able to do the listing program required by the case study in appendix C without reading the next chapter, we recommend that you read it before you try to develop the structure charts for other types of report preparation programs.

## Terminology

structured programming
sequence structure
selection structure
iteration structure
proper program
common module
pseudocode
top-down coding and testing
top-down testing
program stub
dummy module

## Objectives

1. Explain the theory of structured programming.

2. Given program specifications, design the program using a structure chart, plan the coding of its modules using pseudocode, code it in structured style using the guidelines for readability presented in this chapter, and test it using top-down testing.

Chapter 12

# The structure and logic of report preparation programs

All of the programs in chapters 3 through 7 have the same basic design because all of the programs prepare simple reports called listings. In this chapter, though, you'll be introduced to other types of reports and the basic structure and logic that is used in the programs that prepare these reports. You can read this chapter any time after you've completed chapter 11.

I'll start this chapter by presenting some basic reporting terminology. Then, I'll present the structure charts and pseudocode for four different report preparation programs. I'll conclude by presenting the basic structures of all report preparation programs.

## Reporting terminology

In this chapter, I'm going to introduce you to four types of reports: listings, summary reports, multilevel summary reports, and exception reports. Once you can identify them, you'll be ready to study the structure and logic of the programs that prepare these different types of reports.

**Listings** The inventory listing presented in chapter 3 and the investment listing presented in chapter 4 are both *listings*. Also, the report in figure 12-1 is a listing. In a listing, none of the lines in the body of the report represent summary data. In other words, all of the data can be derived from one record or one set of records. In most listings, one line on the report is prepared from one input record, but some listing programs print more than one line for each input record. And some listing programs print one or more lines from two or more

```
              SALES BY ITEM

ITEM          ITEM              SALES
 NO.       DESCRIPTION          AMOUNT

11202   SQ SHANK SWIVEL        1464.75
11202   SQ SHANK SWIVEL         279.00
11202   SQ SHANK SWIVEL         116.25
11202   SQ SHANK SWIVEL         348.75
11202   SQ SHANK SWIVEL        2325.00
11202   SQ SHANK SWIVEL         232.50
16102   SQ SOCKET RIGID        1230.89
16102   SQ SOCKET RIGID        2076.20
16102   SQ SOCKET RIGID         148.30
16102   SQ SOCKET RIGID         963.95
17203   EXT SHANK WITH BRK      899.25
17203   EXT SHANK WITH BRK       81.75
17203   EXT SHANK WITH BRK       32.70
17203   EXT SHANK WITH BRK      294.30
17203   EXT SHANK WITH BRK     3760.50
21103   SQ SHANK RIGID          253.60
21103   SQ SHANK RIGID        40259.00
23302   EXTENSION SHANK         322.50
23302   EXTENSION SHANK       19350.00

                              74439.19 **
```

**Figure 12-1** A sales-by-item listing

records that represent a record set. You'll see an example of a listing program that produces more than one line of data for each set of records later on in this chapter.

The identifying characteristic of a listing is that no summary data is printed in the body of the report. In other words, all of the body lines are *detail lines*. They present the detailed data that is stored in each input record or set of input records.

**Summary reports** Figure 12-2 presents a *summary report*. The program that prepared it read the same data that is listed in figure 12-1. As you can see, the summary report in figure 12-2 contains detail lines, but it also contains *summary lines*, or *total lines*, in the body of the report. These summary lines are interspersed with the detail lines.

Each summary line in figure 12-2 is identified by one asterisk next to its total. The program that created this summary report accumulated the summary totals by adding the sales amounts in the detail lines for each item group. For instance, the total in the first summary line is $4,766.25, which is the sum of the totals in the six detail lines that precede it.

```
                SALES BY ITEM

 ITEM           ITEM              SALES
  NO.        DESCRIPTION          AMOUNT

11202   SQ SHANK SWIVEL          1464.75
11202   SQ SHANK SWIVEL           279.00
11202   SQ SHANK SWIVEL           116.25
11202   SQ SHANK SWIVEL           348.75
11202   SQ SHANK SWIVEL          2325.00
11202   SQ SHANK SWIVEL           232.50
                                 4766.25 *

16102   SQ SOCKET RIGID          1230.89
16102   SQ SOCKET RIGID          2076.20
16102   SQ SOCKET RIGID           148.30
16102   SQ SOCKET RIGID           963.95
                                 4419.34 *

17203   EXT SHANK WITH BRK        899.25
17203   EXT SHANK WITH BRK         81.75
17203   EXT SHANK WITH BRK         32.70
17203   EXT SHANK WITH BRK        294.30
17203   EXT SHANK WITH BRK       3760.50
                                 5068.50 *

21103   SQ SHANK RIGID            253.60
21103   SQ SHANK RIGID          40259.00
                                40512.60 *

23302   EXTENSION SHANK           322.50
23302   EXTENSION SHANK         19350.00
                                19672.50 *

                                74439.19 **
```

**Figure 12-2** A sales-by-item summary report with detail lines

Sometimes, to improve the readability of a report like the one in figure 12-2, some of the repeated data in the detail lines isn't printed. For instance, the report in figure 12-3 is the same as the one in figure 12-2, but the repeated data isn't printed. When the identifying data for a summary group is only printed in the first line of a group, as in figure 12-3, it is sometimes referred to as *group indication*.

Often, summary reports are printed without any detail lines. For instance, the report in figure 12-4 is the same as the one in figure 12-3, but none of the detail lines are printed. As a result, all of the lines in the body of the report are summary lines.

```
              SALES BY ITEM

ITEM            ITEM               SALES
 NO.         DESCRIPTION          AMOUNT

11202  SQ SHANK SWIVEL           1464.75
                                  279.00
                                  116.25
                                  348.75
                                 2325.00
                                  232.50
                                 4766.25 *

16102  SQ SOCKET RIGID           1230.89
                                 2076.20
                                  148.30
                                  963.95
                                 4419.34 *

17203  EXT SHANK WITH BRK         899.25
                                   81.75
                                   32.70
                                  294.30
                                 3760.50
                                 5068.50 *

21103  SQ SHANK RIGID             253.60
                                40259.00
                                40512.60 *

23302  EXTENSION SHANK            322.50
                                19350.00
                                19672.50 *

                                74439.19 **
```

**Figure 12-3** A sales-by-item summary report with detail lines and group indication

**Multilevel summary reports** The summary reports in figures 12-2, 12-3, and 12-4 are all *one-level reports* because summary lines are printed for only one type of group. In all of these reports, one summary line is printed for each group of records that represents one item number. Often, however, you'll want to prepare reports with more than one level of totals. A report with two or more levels of totals can be called a *multilevel report*.

For instance, the report in figure 12-5 has two levels of totals, although you can't tell that from the report alone. To prepare the line for each customer, the program has to read all of the records for that customer and accumulate the sales total. In other words, there can be

SALES BY ITEM

| ITEM NO. | ITEM DESCRIPTION | SALES AMOUNT |
|---|---|---|
| 11202 | SQ SHANK SWIVEL | 4766.25 |
| 16102 | SQ SOCKET RIGID | 4419.34 |
| 17203 | EXT SHANK WITH BRK | 5068.50 |
| 21103 | SQ SHANK RIGID | 40512.60 |
| 23302 | EXTENSION SHANK | 19672.50 |
| | | 74439.19 ** |

Figure 12-4 A sales-by-item summary report without detail lines

SALES BY SALES REPRESENTATIVE

| SALES REP NO. | CUST. NO. | SALES AMOUNT |
|---|---|---|
| 11 | 12321 | 1,497.45 |
| | | 1,497.45 * |
| 12 | 54356 | 279.00 |
| 12 | 56987 | 2,116.80 |
| 12 | 76334 | 2,192.45 |
| 12 | 84736 | 232.50 |
| | | 4,820.75 * |
| 16 | 25639 | 442.60 |
| | | 442.60 * |
| 17 | 23432 | 671.25 |
| | | 671.25 * |
| 19 | 11111 | 40,259.00 |
| 19 | 23333 | 19,431.75 |
| 19 | 23658 | 7,316.39 |
| | | 67,007.14 * |
| | | 74,439.19 ** |

Figure 12-5 A multilevel report showing sales by customer within sales representative

more than one record for each customer. Then, to prepare the total line for each salesman, the program must accumulate all of the customer totals for that salesman.

When you look at the report in figure 12-5, you can't tell whether it is a one-level or a two-level report. The customer lines could be detail lines or they could be total lines derived from a group of detail records. When you look at the program specifications for a report preparation program, though, you should be able to tell how many levels a report has. Since this has an effect on how you design a program, you should be sure that you understand what a multilevel report is and how you tell how many levels it has.

**Exception reports** An *exception report* is simply a report that includes only the data for those records or sets of records that meet an exceptional condition. For instance, the investment listing in chapters 4 and 5 is an exception report; it doesn't list all of the items in inventory, just the ones with an investment amount over $10,000. Similarly, a summary report showing all customers who owe more than $5,000 to your company is an exception report. An exception report can be a listing or a summary report, but it usually isn't a multilevel report.

Exception reporting is important because it reduces the amount of printed output that a system has to prepare. It can also improve the management of a business, because it highlights the items of data that need attention, rather than all items of data. Nevertheless, most of the reports prepared by a business computer are *not* exception listings.

## The structure and logic of four report preparation programs

To help you understand the structure and logic of report preparation programs, I'm going to present four programs. For each program, I'll present the record layouts, the print chart, the structure chart, and the pseudocode for the critical modules. I won't present program overviews for the programs, because none of the reports are exception reports and each program simply prepares the data shown on the print chart by reading the records in the input files. After you've studied the design and logic for these programs, I think you'll recognize that there's a basic structure for all report preparation programs.

**Program 1: A listing program that uses matching record logic** Figure 12-6 presents the record descriptions for the two files required by the first report preparation program. One file consists of customer master records with one record per customer, while the other file consists of accounts receivable records with one record per customer. Both files are in sequence by customer key.

Figure 12-7 gives a print chart for the report prepared from the data in these two files. As you can see, three different lines are supposed to be printed for each customer. The customer key and name and address fields are printed from the customer master record for each customer. The other fields are printed from the accounts receivable record for the customer. All three lines for each customer

**The record description for the customer master record**

```
 01   CUSTOMER-MASTER-RECORD.
*
      05   CM-CUST-KEY                PIC 9(5).
      05   CM-CUST-NAME               PIC X(22).
      05   CM-CUST-ADDRESS            PIC X(22).
      05   CM-CUST-CITY-STATE-ZIP     PIC X(22).
*
```

**The record description for the accounts receivable record**

```
 01   ACCOUNTS-RECEIVABLE-RECORD.
*
      05   AR-CUST-KEY                PIC 9(5).
      05   AR-CURRENT                 PIC 9(5)V99.
      05   AR-OVER-30                 PIC 9(5)V99.
      05   AR-OVER-60                 PIC 9(5)V99.
      05   AR-OVER-90                 PIC 9(5)V99.
*
```

Note: The records in both of these files are in sequence by customer key.

Figure 12-6 The record descriptions for the accounts receivable listing program

| Record Name | Line | Print positions |
|---|---|---|
| Heading-Line-1 | 1 | DATE: 99/99/99 PAGE: ZZ9 |
| Heading-Line-2 | 2 | TIME: 99:99 XX ACCOUNTS RECEIVABLE LISTING AR3110 |
| | 3 | |
| Heading-Line-3 | 4 | CUST. TOTAL |
| Heading-Line-4 | 5 | NO. NAME AND ADDRESS CURRENT OVER 30 OVER 60 OVER 90 OWED |
| | 6 | |
| Customer-Line-1 | 7 | 99999 XXXXXXXXXXXXXXXXXXXXXX ZZ,ZZZ.99 ZZ,ZZZ.99 ZZ,ZZZ.99 ZZ,ZZZ.99 ZZ,ZZZ.99 |
| Customer-Line-2 | 8 | XXXXXXXXXXXXXXXXXXXXXX |
| Customer-Line-3 | 9 | XXXXXXXXXXXXXXXXXXXXXX |
| | 10 | |
| Customer-Line-1 | 11 | 99999 XXXXXXXXXXXXXXXXXXXXXX ZZ,ZZZ.99 ZZ,ZZZ.99 ZZ,ZZZ.99 ZZ,ZZZ.99 ZZ,ZZZ.99 |
| Customer-Line-2 | 12 | XXXXXXXXXXXXXXXXXXXXXX |
| Customer-Line-3 | 13 | XXXXXXXXXXXXXXXXXXXXXX |
| | 14 | |
| Total-Line | 15 | Z,ZZZ,ZZZ.99 Z,ZZZ,ZZZ.99 Z,ZZZ,ZZZ.99 Z,ZZZ,ZZZ.99 Z,ZZZ,ZZZ.99 |
| | 16 | |
| | 17 | |
| | 18 | |

Figure 12-7 The print chart for the accounts receivable listing

are detail, rather than total lines, because they simply contain data taken from the input records.

Figure 12-8 presents an acceptable structure chart for this program, and figure 12-9 presents pseudocode for the critical modules of the chart. To prepare the accounts receivable listing, the program must *match* the records in the accounts receivable file with the records

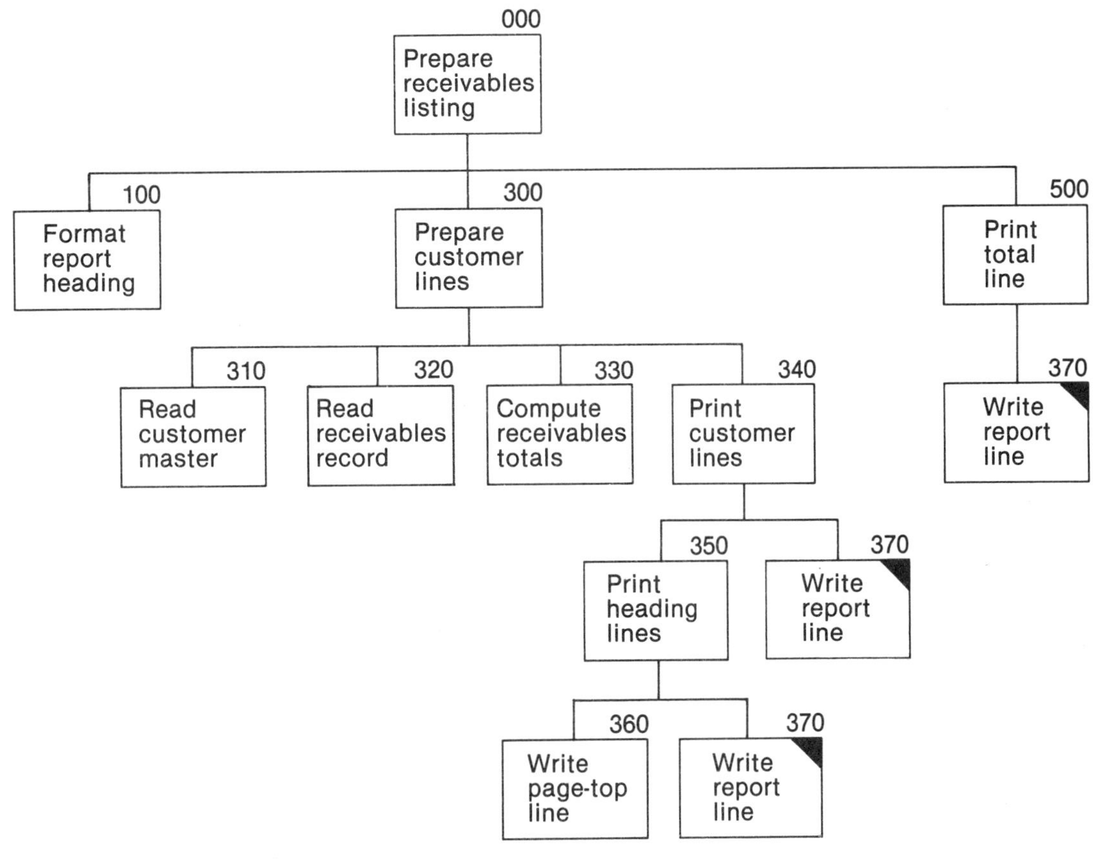


**Figure 12-8** The structure chart for the program that prepares an accounts receivable listing using matching record logic

in the customer master file. This matching is done based on the contents of a *control field*. Usually, the control field is the key field for each of the files. For this program, the control field is the customer key, which is CM-CUST-KEY in the customer master record and AR-CUST-KEY in the accounts receivable record. The logic in a program like this can be referred to as *matching record logic*, and you should become familiar with it.

The matching record logic in the pseudocode in figure 12-9 is shaded. In module 300, after a customer master record has been read, the shaded pseudocode moves N to a switch that indicates whether the accounts receivable record that matches the key of the master record has been found. Then, the code performs module 320 until an accounts receivable record has been read that matches the customer master record or until the key in the accounts receivable record is greater than the key in the customer master record.

```
000-prepare-receivables-listing.

    Open files.
    DO 100-format-report-heading.
    Move zero to ar-cust-key.
    DO 300-prepare-customer-lines
        UNTIL custmast-eof.
    DO 500-print-total-line.
    Close files.
    Stop run.

300-prepare-customer-lines.

    DO 310-read-customer-master.
    IF NOT custmast-eof
        move 'N' to record-found-switch
        DO 320-read-receivables-record
            UNTIL record-found
               OR ar-cust-key not less than cm-cust-key
        IF record-found
            DO 330-compute-receivables-totals
            DO 340-print-customer-lines
        ELSE
            DO 340-print-customer-lines.

310-read-customer-master.

    Read custmast record
        AT END
            move 'Y' to custmast-eof-switch.

320-read-receivables-record.

    Read receive record
        AT END
            move 99999 to ar-cust-key.
    IF ar-cust-key = cm-cust-key
        move 'Y' to record-found-switch.

330-compute-receivables-totals.

    Compute receivables totals.

340-print-customer-lines.

    IF page-overflow
        DO 350-print-heading-lines.
    Format customer-line-1.
    DO 370-write-report-line.
    Move 1 to space-control.
    Format customer-line-2.
    DO 370-write-report-line.
    Format customer-line-3.
    DO 370-write-report-line.
    Move 2 to space-control.
    Add 4 to line-count.
```

**Figure 12-9** Pseudocode for the critical modules of the program charted in figure 12-8

If you check the code in module 320, you can see that the record-found switch is turned on when the key in the accounts receivable record matches the key in the customer master record. For this program, the record-found switch should be turned on each time module 300 executes module 320 since there should be one accounts receivable record for each master record. On the other hand, if a customer record isn't matched by an accounts receivable record, the record-found switch won't be turned on. Similarly, if an accounts receivable record isn't matched by a customer record, the accounts receivable record will be skipped by this logic.

So that this logic will work for the first and last records in the customer master record, module 000 moves zero to the key in the accounts receivable record before it starts executing module 300. Also, 99999 is moved to this key when the AT END clause for the accounts receivable file is excecuted.

This coding assumes, of course, that there can't be an actual customer key with a value of all zeroes or all 9's. To allow for those possibilities, you can move LOW-VALUE (instead of zero) and HIGH-VALUE (instead of 99999) to the accounts receivable key field, as long as the field is defined as alphanumeric. Then, the accounts receivable key will always be less than or greater than any field it's compared to. Be aware, though, that this method won't work if the accounts receivable key field—or any field it's compared to—is defined as numeric.

Otherwise, the pseudocode for this program should be relatively easy to understand. After both records are read for a file, module 340 prints three lines for each set of records by formatting each print line and executing module 370. If a matching accounts receivable record can't be found for a customer record, module 340 should move an appropriate message into print positions 35-95 of the first line for the customer.

**Program 2: A summary report preparation program that uses control break logic** Figure 12-10 presents the record descriptions for the two files required by the second report preparation program. One file consists of customer master records with one record per customer, while the other file consists of open item records with zero, one, or more records per customer. Here again, both files are in sequence by customer key.

An open item record represents one invoice that was billed to a customer, but not paid by the customer. That's why it's "open." As a result, if you add up the amounts in the open items for a customer, you derive the total amount owed by the customer. When an open item is paid, it is removed from the open item file, so the open item file always reflects the total amount of money owed by all the customers of a company.

Figure 12-11 gives a print chart for the summary accounts receivable report prepared from the data in these two files. It is

**The record description for the customer master record**

```
 01   CUSTOMER-MASTER-RECORD.
*
      05   CM-CUST-KEY              PIC 9(5).
      05   CM-CUST-NAME             PIC X(22).
      05   CM-CUST-ADDRESS          PIC X(22).
      05   CM-CUST-CITY-STATE-ZIP   PIC X(22).
*
```

**The record description for the open item record**

```
 01   OPEN-ITEM-RECORD.
*
      05   OI-CUST-KEY              PIC 9(5).
      05   OI-REFERENCE-NO          PIC 9(5).
      05   OI-REFERENCE-DATE.
           10   OI-REFERENCE-MONTH  PIC 99.
           10   OI-REFERENCE-DAY    PIC 99.
           10   OI-REFERENCE-YEAR   PIC 99.
      05   OI-AMOUNT                PIC S9(5)V99.
*
```

Note: The records in both of these files are in sequence by customer key.

**Figure 12-10** The record descriptions for the summary report preparation program

| Record Name | Line | | | | | | | | |
|---|---|---|---|---|---|---|---|---|---|
| Heading-Line-1 | 1 | DATE: | 99/99/99 | | | | | | PAGE: ZZ9 |
| Heading-Line-2 | 2 | TIME: | 99:99 XX | ACCOUNTS RECEIVABLE REPORT | | | | | AR3110 |
| | 3 | | | | | | | | |
| Heading-Line-3 | 4 | CUST. | | | | | | | TOTAL |
| Heading-Line-4 | 5 | NO. | CUSTOMER NAME | CURRENT | OVER 30 | OVER 60 | OVER 90 | | OWED |
| | 6 | | | | | | | | |
| Customer-Total-Line | 7 | 99999 | XXXXXXXXXXXXXXXXXXXXXX | ZZ,ZZZ.99 | ZZ,ZZZ.99 | ZZ,ZZZ.99 | ZZ,ZZZ.99 | | ZZ,ZZZ.99 |
| Customer-Total-Line | 8 | 99999 | XXXXXXXXXXXXXXXXXXXXXX | ZZ,ZZZ.99 | ZZ,ZZZ.99 | ZZ,ZZZ.99 | ZZ,ZZZ.99 | | ZZ,ZZZ.99 |
| Customer-Total-Line | 9 | 99999 | XXXXXXXXXXXXXXXXXXXXXX | ZZ,ZZZ.99 | ZZ,ZZZ.99 | ZZ,ZZZ.99 | ZZ,ZZZ.99 | | ZZ,ZZZ.99 |
| | 10 | | | | | | | | |
| Final-Total-Line | 11 | | | Z,ZZZ,ZZZ.99 | Z,ZZZ,ZZZ.99 | Z,ZZZ,ZZZ.99 | Z,ZZZ,ZZZ.99 | | Z,ZZZ,ZZZ.99 |
| | 12 | | | | | | | | |
| | 13 | | | | | | | | |
| | 14 | | | | | | | | |

**Figure 12-11** The print chart for the summary accounts receivable report

similar to the one in figure 12-7, but only one line is printed for each customer. The customer key and name are printed from the customer master record for each customer. The other fields are calculated by accumulating the receivable amounts in the open items for each customer. As a result, each line in the body of the report is a total line, and the entire report is a summary report, not a listing.

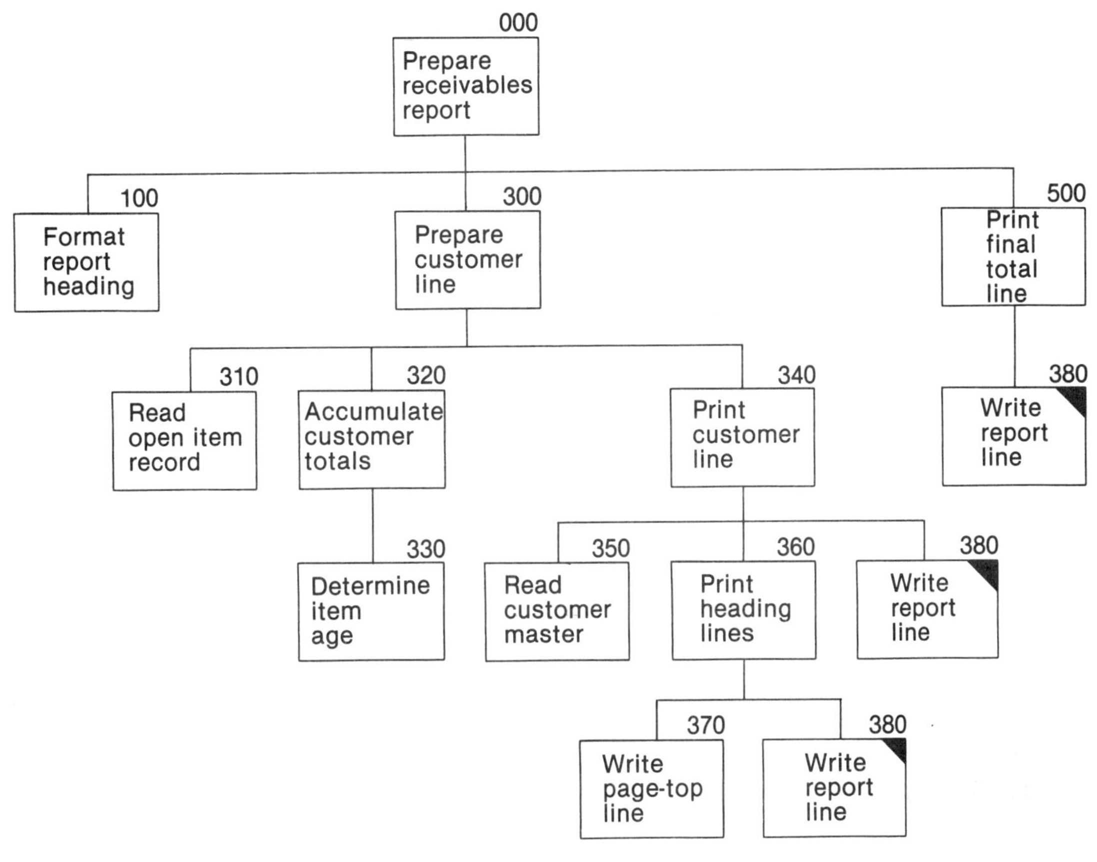


**Figure 12-12** The structure chart for the program that prepares a summary accounts receivable report using control break logic

Figure 12-12 presents an acceptable structure chart for this program, and figure 12-13 presents pseudocode for the critical modules of the chart. To prepare the accounts receivable report, the program must read all of the open item records for a customer before it prints a customer total line. It does this by determining when a *control break* occurs in the open item file based on the values in a control field. Usually, the control field is the key field for the primary file that is read by a program. For this program, the control field is the customer key in the open item file (OI-CUST-KEY). The logic in a program like this can be referred to as *control break logic*, and you should become familiar with it.

The control break logic in the pseudocode in figure 12-13 is shaded. In module 300, after the first open item record has been read, the program moves the customer key to a working-storage field named OLD-CUST-KEY. Then, it moves N into the first-record switch so

```
000-prepare-receivables-report.

    Open files.
    DO 100-format-report-heading.
    Move zero to cm-cust-key.
    DO 300-prepare-customer-line
        UNTIL openitem-eof.
    DO 500-print-final-total-line.
    Close files.
    Stop run.

300-prepare-customer-line.

    DO 310-read-open-item-record.
    IF first-record
        move oi-cust-key to old-cust-key
        move 'N' to first-record-switch
    ELSE
        IF oi-cust-key is greater than old-cust-key
            DO 340-print-customer-line
            move oi-cust-key to old-cust-key.
    IF NOT openitem-eof
        DO 320-accumulate-customer-totals.

310-read-open-item-record.

    Read openitem record
        AT END
            move 99999 to oi-cust-key
            move 'Y' to openitem-eof-switch.

320-accumulate-customer-totals.

    DO 330-determine-item-age.
    Add oi-amount to cust-total-owed.
    IF item-age is less than 31
        add oi-amount to cust-current
    ELSE
        IF item-age is less than 61
            add oi-amount to cust-over-30
        ELSE
            IF item-age is less than 91
                add oi-amount to cust-over-60
            ELSE
                add oi-amount to cust-over-90.

330-determine-item-age.

    Calculate number of days between item date
        and current date.
```

**Figure 12-13** Pseudocode for the critical modules of the program charted in figure 12-12 (part 1 of 2)

this portion of the nested IF statement won't be executed for any of the other records in the open item file. In contrast, if the open item record that has just been read isn't the first record in the file and the

```
340-print-customer-line.

    IF page-overflow
        DO 360-print-heading-lines.
    Move 'N' to record-found-switch.
    DO 350-read-customer-master
        UNTIL record-found
            OR cm-cust-key greater than old-cust-key.
    IF record-found
        move cm-cust-name to cl-cust-name
    ELSE
        move 'NO RECORD FOUND' to cl-cust-name.
    Move old-cust-key to cl-cust-key.
    Move customer totals to fields in customer-total-line.
    Move customer-total-line to print-area.
    DO 380-write-report-line.
    Move 1 to space-control.
    Add 1 to line-count.
    Add customer totals to corresponding final totals.
    Move zero to customer total fields.

350-read-customer-master.

    Read custmast record
        AT END
            move 99999 to cm-cust-key.
    IF cm-cust-key = old-cust-key
        move 'Y' to record-found-switch.
```

**Figure 12-13** Pseudocode for the critical modules of the program charted in figure 12-12 (part 2 of 2)

key in the open item record is greater than the old customer key, a control break has occurred. This means that the value of the control field has changed. Then, module 300 calls module 340 to print a customer total line on the accounts receivable report. The last IF statement in module 300 calls module 320 to accumulate the receivables totals for a customer whether or not the open item that has just been read is the first record in the file or a subsequent record.

So this logic will work for the last group of records in the open item file, module 310 moves 99999 to the control field when the AT END clause for the open item file is excecuted. That way the open item key will be greater than the old customer key so module 300 will call module 340 to print the last customer total line on the report. As in the first report program, you can move HIGH-VALUE instead of 99999 to the open item key as long as the key field and any fields it's compared to are defined as alphanumeric.

Module 320 is relatively straightforward, but it's worth mentioning nonetheless. After it calls module 330 to determine the age in days of the open item, it adds the open item amount to the appropriate customer fields. It also adds the amount to the total amount owed by a customer no matter what the age of the item is.

In modules 340 and 350, you should note that matching record logic is used to read the customer master record that matches each group of open item records. So that this logic will work for the first and last records in the customer master file, zero is moved to its key field in module 000 and 99999 is moved to its key field in module 350 when the AT END clause of its READ statement is executed. Again, this assumes that the actual key value can never be all zeroes or all 9's. If the key field and all the fields it's compared to are defined as alphanumeric, you may want to use LOW-VALUE and HIGH-VALUE instead.

The last two lines in the pseudocode for module 340 are important because they represent functions that must be done in the print modules of all summary or multilevel report preparation programs. The next to last line adds the totals for one customer to the totals for the entire file. In other words, the current customer total is added to the current final total, the over 30 customer total is added to the over 30 final total, and so on. This is sometimes referred to as "rolling a total over" from one level to the next. After the customer totals have been rolled over, the last line in this module moves zeros to the customer totals. As a result, these fields can be used to accumulate the totals for the next customer.

This shows that a print module can be used to do quite a bit more than just print one or more lines. In this program, module 340 calls a module to read a related master record. It rolls over totals from the customer level to the final total level. And it zeros out total fields at the customer level so they can be used for the next customer. You'll see these same functions in the print modules of the next two programs, both of which prepare multilevel reports.

**Program 3: A multilevel report preparation program that uses control break logic** Figure 12-14 presents the record description for the one file required by the third report preparation program. It contains one record for each sales transaction such as an invoice. It gives the reference number, date, and amount of each transaction along with the keys of the customer, sales representative, and branch associated with the transaction. This file has been sorted into sequence by customer key within sales rep key.

If you accumulate transactions like these for a time period like a week, month, or year, you can prepare a variety of sales reports from them. For this program, assume that the transactions have been saved for one month. As a result, the report prepared from the file will be a monthly report.

Figure 12-15 gives a print chart for the sales report prepared from the data in the sales transaction file. It gives totals by customer and by sales rep, so it can be called a sales by customer within sales rep report. To prepare a customer total line, the program must accumulate all of the transaction records for one customer. Then, when a control break on the customer key occurs, the program must

**The record description for the sales transaction record**

```
 01   SALES-TRANSACTION-RECORD.
*
      05   ST-TRANSACTION-CODE        PIC X.
      05   ST-REFERENCE-NO            PIC 9(5).
      05   ST-REFERENCE-DATE.
           10   ST-REFERENCE-MONTH    PIC 99.
           10   ST-REFERENCE-DAY      PIC 99.
           10   ST-REFERENCE-YEAR     PIC 99.
      05   ST-BRANCH-KEY              PIC 99.
      05   ST-SALES-REP-KEY           PIC 99.
      05   ST-CUST-KEY                PIC 9(5).
      05   ST-SALES-AMOUNT            PIC S9(5)V99.
*
```

Note: The records in this file are in sequence by customer key within sales rep key.

Figure 12-14 The record description for the sales transaction record required by the program that prepares a two-level sales report

```
Record Name
Heading-Line-1         1  DATE:   99/99/99         TWO-LEVEL          PAGE: ZZ9
Heading-Line-2         2  TIME:   99:99 XX        SALES REPORT        MKTG5100
                       3
Heading-Line-3         4  SALES REP     CUST.          SALES
Heading-Line-4         5     NO.         NO.           AMOUNT
                       6
Customer-Total-Line    7     99         99999        ZZ,ZZZ.99
Customer-Total-Line    8     99         99999        ZZ,ZZZ.99
Customer-Total-Line    9     99         99999        ZZ,ZZZ.99
Sales-Rep-Total-Line  10                          Z,ZZZ,ZZZ.99 *
                      11
Customer-Total-Line   12     99         99999        ZZ,ZZZ.99
Customer-Total-Line   13     99         99999        ZZ,ZZZ.99
Sales-Rep-Total-Line  14                          Z,ZZZ,ZZZ.99 *
                      15
Grand-Total-Line      16        GRAND TOTAL   $$$$,$$$,$$$.99 **
                      17
                      18
                      19
```

Figure 12-15 The print chart for the two-level sales report

print a customer total line. Similarly, to prepare a sales rep total line, the program must accumulate all of the sales for one sales representative. Then, when a control break occurs on the sales rep key, the program should print a sales rep total line as well as a customer total line. In other words, this program requires control break logic at two different levels, so this is a multilevel report.

Figure 12-16 presents an acceptable structure chart for this program, and figure 12-17 presents pseudocode for the critical modules of

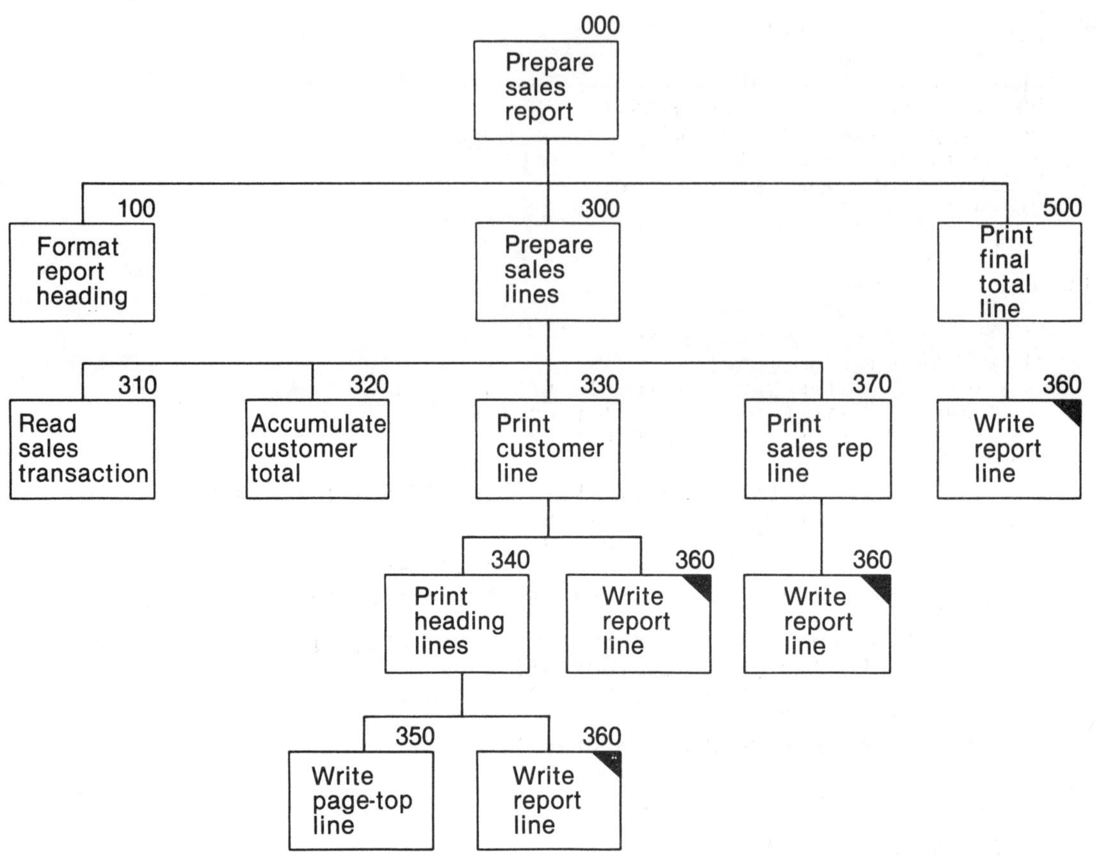


**Figure 12-16** The structure chart for the program that prepares a two-level sales report using control break logic

the chart. Module 300 in this program contains the critical control break logic of the program, and it's similar to module 300 in the previous program. After the first transaction record has been read, the program moves the customer key and sales rep key to working-storage fields named OLD-CUST-KEY and OLD-SALES-REP-KEY. Then, it moves N into the first-record switch so this portion of the nested IF statement won't be executed for any of the other records in the transaction file.

If the transaction record that has just been read isn't the first record in the file, the nested IF statement continues. If the sales rep key has changed, the program calls modules 330 and 370 to print both customer and sales rep total lines. Then, it moves the new sales rep and customer keys to the old key fields in working storage. If the sales rep key hasn't changed but the customer key has, the program calls module 330 to print a customer line and moves the new customer key

```
000-prepare-sales-report.

    Open files.
    DO 100-format-report-heading.
    DO 300-prepare-sales-lines
        UNTIL slstran-eof.
    DO 500-print-final-total-line.
    Close files.
    Stop run.

300-prepare-sales-lines.

    DO 310-read-sales-transaction.
    IF first-record
        move st-sales-rep-key to old-sales-rep-key
        move st-cust-key      to old-cust-key
        move 'N' to first-record-switch
    ELSE
        IF st-sales-rep-key is greater than old-sales-rep-key
            DO 330-print-customer-line
            DO 370-print-sales-rep-line
            move st-cust-key      to old-cust-key
            move st-sales-rep-key to old-sales-rep-key
        ELSE
            IF st-cust-key is greater than old-cust-key
                DO 330-print-customer-line
                move st-cust-key to old-cust-key.
    IF NOT slstran-eof
        DO 320-accumulate-customer-total.

310-read-sales-transaction.

    Read slstran record
        AT END
            move 99999 to st-sales-rep-key
            move 'Y'   to slstran-eof-switch.

320-accumulate-customer-total.

    Add st-sales-amount to customer-total.
```

Figure 12-17 Pseudocode for critical modules of the program charted in figure 12-16 (part 1 of 2)

to the old key field in working storage. The last IF statement in module 300 performs module 320 to accumulate the customer sales total for each transaction record whether or not a control break has occurred and whether or not the record is the first record in the file.

In print modules 330 and 370, you should note that totals at one level are rolled over to the next level and that the totals are then reset to zero so they can be used for the next group of records. In module 330, the customer total is set to zero after it is added to the sales rep total. In module 370, the sales rep total is reset to zero after it is added to the final sales total.

```
330-print-customer-line.

    IF page-overflow
        DO 340-print-heading-lines.
    Move old-sales-rep-key   to cl-sales-rep-key.
    Move old-cust-key        to cl-cust-key.
    Move customer-total      to cl-customer-total.
    Move customer-total-line to print-area.
    DO 360-write-report-line.
    Add space-control to line-count.
    Move 1 to space-control.
    Add customer-total to sales-rep-total.
    Move zero to customer-total.

370-print-sales-rep-line.

    Move sales-rep-total      to sl-sales-rep-total.
    Move sales-rep-total-line to print-area.
    DO 360-write-report-line.
    Add space-control to line-count.
    Move 2 to space-control.
    Add sales-rep-total to final-total.
    Move zero to sales-rep-total.
```

**Figure 12-17** Pseudocode for critical modules of the program charted in figure 12-16 (part 2 of 2)

**Program 4: A more realistic multilevel report preparation program** Figures 12-18 through 12-21 present the specifications, design, and pseudocode for a more realistic report preparation program. This program reads a sequential customer file, but it also reads an indexed salesman file whenever it needs to get additional salesman data. Since this program is a good deal more complicated than the other programs presented in this chapter, the entire program including its COBOL code is presented in appendix B of this text. As a result, you can study it in detail if you want to.

Figure 12-18 presents the record descriptions for the two files required by this program. One file contains one record for each of the company's customers. The other file contains one record for each of the company's sales representatives. The customer master file is in sequence by customer number within salesman number within branch number. The salesman master file is in sequence by salesman number within branch number.

If you study the record descriptions, you can see that the key fields for these files are more than just customer number and salesman number. The customer key actually consists of branch, salesman, and customer number. The salesman key actually consists of branch and salesman number. This means that more than one salesman can have the same salesman number, but only one salesman in a branch will have the same salesman number. Similarly, more than one customer can have the same customer number, but only one customer for each salesman within a branch will have the same customer number.

```
 01   CUSTOMER-MASTER-RECORD.
*
      05   CM-CUSTOMER-KEY.
           10   CM-SALESMAN-KEY.
                15   CM-BRANCH-NUMBER       PIC XX.
                15   CM-SALESMAN-NUMBER     PIC XX.
           10   CM-CUSTOMER-NUMBER          PIC X(5).
      05   CM-CUSTOMER-NAME                 PIC X(25).
      05   CM-SALES-THIS-YTD                PIC S9(5)V99   COMP-3.
      05   CM-SALES-LAST-YTD                PIC S9(5)V99   COMP-3.
```

Note: The records in this file are in sequence by customer key.

```
 01   SALESMAN-MASTER-RECORD.
*
      05   SM-SALESMAN-KEY.
           10   SM-BRANCH-NUMBER           PIC XX.
           10   SM-SALESMAN-NUMBER         PIC XX.
      05   SM-SALESMAN-NAME                PIC X(25).
```

Note: The records in this file are in sequence by salesman key.

**Figure 12-18** The record descriptions required by a more realistic program that prepares a two-level sales report

Figure 12-19 gives a print chart for the sales report prepared from the data in the customer and salesman files. It prints lines for customers, salesmen, and branches, but only the salesman and branch lines are total lines. If you check the record description for a customer master record, you can see that all the data required by a customer line can be derived from the data in one master record. Note that this report requires group indication in the customer lines. In other words, the branch number, salesman number, and salesman name should only print in the first line for each salesman.

Figure 12-20 presents an acceptable structure chart for this program, and figure 12-21 presents pseudocode for the critical modules of the chart. Module 200 in this program contains the control break logic. As you study it, keep in mind that the salesman key consists of both branch number and salesman number. As a result, when a control break occurs on salesman key, it can mean either a change in branch number or a change in salesman number. That's why this module requires one more level of nesting than module 300 in the previous program, even though both prepare two-level reports. In addition, the calls to print customer lines (detail lines) and to accumulate sales totals are included within the one nested IF statement in this module. If you prefer, of course, you could code this module so it was more similar to module 300 in figure 12-17.

```
Record Name              Line
Heading-Line-1            1  DATE:    99/99/99                    MIKE MURACH & ASSOCIATES, INC.                                       PAGE: ZZ9
Heading-Line-2            2  TIME:    99:99 XX                                                                                     MKT3/1200
Heading-Line-3            3                                            YEAR-TO-DATE SALES REPORT
                          4
Heading-Line-4            5  BRANCH   SALESMAN  SALESMAN                      CUSTOMER  CUSTOMER                       SALES          SALES        CHANGE    CHANGE
Heading-Line-5            6    NO        NO     NAME                             NO     NAME                        THIS YTD       LAST YTD        AMOUNT       %
                          7
Customer-Line             8    XX        XX     X----------------------X      ZZZZ9     X-----------------------X   ZZ,ZZ9.99-     ZZ,ZZ9.99-    ZZ,ZZ9.99-  ZZZ9-
                          9                                                   ZZZZ9     X-----------------------X   ZZ,ZZ9.99-     ZZ,ZZ9.99-    ZZ,ZZ9.99-  ZZZ9-
                         10                                                   ZZZZ9     X-----------------------X   ZZ,ZZ9.99-     ZZ,ZZ9.99-    ZZ,ZZ9.99-  ZZZ9-
                         11                                                   ZZZZ9     X-----------------------X   ZZ,ZZ9.99-     ZZ,ZZ9.99-    ZZ,ZZ9.99-  ZZZ9-
                         12                                                   ZZZZ9     X-----------------------X   ZZ,ZZ9.99-     ZZ,ZZ9.99-    ZZ,ZZ9.99-  ZZZ9-
                         13
Salesman-Total-Line      14                                                      SALESMAN TOTALS:  Z,ZZZ,ZZ9.99-  Z,ZZZ,ZZ9.99-  Z,ZZZ,ZZ9.99-  ZZZ9-
                         15
                         16              XX     X----------------------X      ZZZZ9     X-----------------------X   ZZ,ZZ9.99-     ZZ,ZZ9.99-    ZZ,ZZ9.99-  ZZZ9-
                         17                                                   ZZZZ9     X-----------------------X   ZZ,ZZ9.99-     ZZ,ZZ9.99-    ZZ,ZZ9.99-  ZZZ9-
                         18                                                   ZZZZ9     X-----------------------X   ZZ,ZZ9.99-     ZZ,ZZ9.99-    ZZ,ZZ9.99-  ZZZ9-
                         19                                                   ZZZZ9     X-----------------------X   ZZ,ZZ9.99-     ZZ,ZZ9.99-    ZZ,ZZ9.99-  ZZZ9-
                         20
                         21                                                      SALESMAN TOTALS:  Z,ZZZ,ZZ9.99-  Z,ZZZ,ZZ9.99-  Z,ZZZ,ZZ9.99-  ZZZ9-
                         22
                         23
Branch-Total-Line        24                                                        BRANCH TOTALS:  Z,ZZZ,ZZ9.99-  Z,ZZZ,ZZ9.99-  Z,ZZZ,ZZ9.99-  ZZZ9-
                         25
                         26
                         27    XX        XX     X----------------------X      ZZZZ9     X-----------------------X   ZZ,ZZ9.99-     ZZ,ZZ9.99-    ZZ,ZZ9.99-  ZZZ9-
                         28                                                   ZZZZ9     X-----------------------X   ZZ,ZZ9.99-     ZZ,ZZ9.99-    ZZ,ZZ9.99-  ZZZ9-
                         29                                                   ZZZZ9     X-----------------------X   ZZ,ZZ9.99-     ZZ,ZZ9.99-    ZZ,ZZ9.99-  ZZZ9-
                         30                                                   ZZZZ9     X-----------------------X   ZZ,ZZ9.99-     ZZ,ZZ9.99-    ZZ,ZZ9.99-  ZZZ9-
                         31
                         32                                                      SALESMAN TOTALS:  Z,ZZZ,ZZ9.99   Z,ZZZ,ZZ9.99-  Z,ZZZ,ZZ9.99-  ZZZ9-
                         33
                         34              XX     X----------------------X      ZZZZ9     X-----------------------X   ZZ,ZZ9.99-     ZZ,ZZ9.99-    ZZ,ZZ9.99-  ZZZ9-
                         35                                                   ZZZZ9     X-----------------------X   ZZ,ZZ9.99-     ZZ,ZZ9.99-    ZZ,ZZ9.99-  ZZZ9-
                         36                                                   ZZZZ9     X-----------------------X   ZZ,ZZ9.99-     ZZ,ZZ9.99-    ZZ,ZZ9.99-  ZZZ9-
                         37                                                   ZZZZ9     X-----------------------X   ZZ,ZZ9.99-     ZZ,ZZ9.99-    ZZ,ZZ9.99-  ZZZ9-
                         38                                                   ZZZZ9     X-----------------------X   ZZ,ZZ9.99-     ZZ,ZZ9.99-    ZZ,ZZ9.99-  ZZZ9-
                         39
                         40                                                      SALESMAN TOTALS:  Z,ZZZ,ZZ9.99-  Z,ZZZ,ZZ9.99-  Z,ZZZ,ZZ9.99-  ZZZ9-
                         41
                         42
                         43                                                        BRANCH TOTALS:  Z,ZZZ,ZZ9.99-  Z,ZZZ,ZZ9.99-  Z,ZZZ,ZZ9.99-  ZZZ9-
                         44
                         45
                         46
Grand-Total-Line         47                                                    GRAND TOTALS: ZZZ,ZZZ,ZZ9.99-ZZZ,ZZZ,ZZ9.99-ZZZ,ZZZ,ZZ9.99-  ZZZ9-
                         48
                         49
                         50
```

**Figure 12-19** The print chart for a more realistic two-level sales report

To show you how much trouble a requirement like group indication can cause, figure 12-22 shows the COBOL code used for module 220 of this program. The first sentence in this module, which is one long nested IF statement, provides for group indication by moving spaces or values to the branch number, salesman number, and salesman name fields in each customer line. If group indication weren't required, this IF statement could be replaced by three MOVE statements.

The code in figure 12-22 also shows how the print module calls module 230 to read a salesman record. In this program, the salesman file is indexed so this module reads each record on a random basis. This type of file handling is presented in chapter 6 of this book. Although this file could also be read on a sequential basis, it would make the coding for this program even more complicated.

If you compare the chart in figure 12-20 with the one in figure 12-16, you should notice a difference in the structure for printing report lines. In figure 12-16, the program will skip to a new page before printing a customer line, but it can't skip to a new page before printing a salesman or final total line. If it were to skip to a new page before printing any type of line, module 340 would have to be common to modules 370 and 500 as well as to module 330. In contrast, the program in figure 12-20 uses common module 240, named "print report line," to print all of the lines of the program. This module tests to see whether page overflow should occur. Then, if it's necessary, it skips to a new page and prints heading lines. If it isn't, it just prints the next line of the report. Depending on how and when you want page overflow to take place, a common printing routine like the one made up of modules 240 through 270 in figure 12-20 can come in handy.

When you use a common print routine like the one in figure 12-20, the print modules must format the next record to be printed in an intermediate area, not the print area. This is illustrated by the third line from the end of the print module in figure 12-22:

```
MOVE CUSTOMER-LINE TO NEXT-REPORT-LINE.
```

Then, when module 240 is executed, it will move NEXT-REPORT-LINE to the print area when it's ready to print the next line. If module 220 moved the next customer line directly into the print area, it would be destroyed whenever module 240 had to print headings before the next report line.

### The basic structure of a report preparation program

Now that you've seen some typical structures for report preparation programs, you should begin to see the basic structure in all report preparation programs. This structure is illustrated in figure 12-23. As

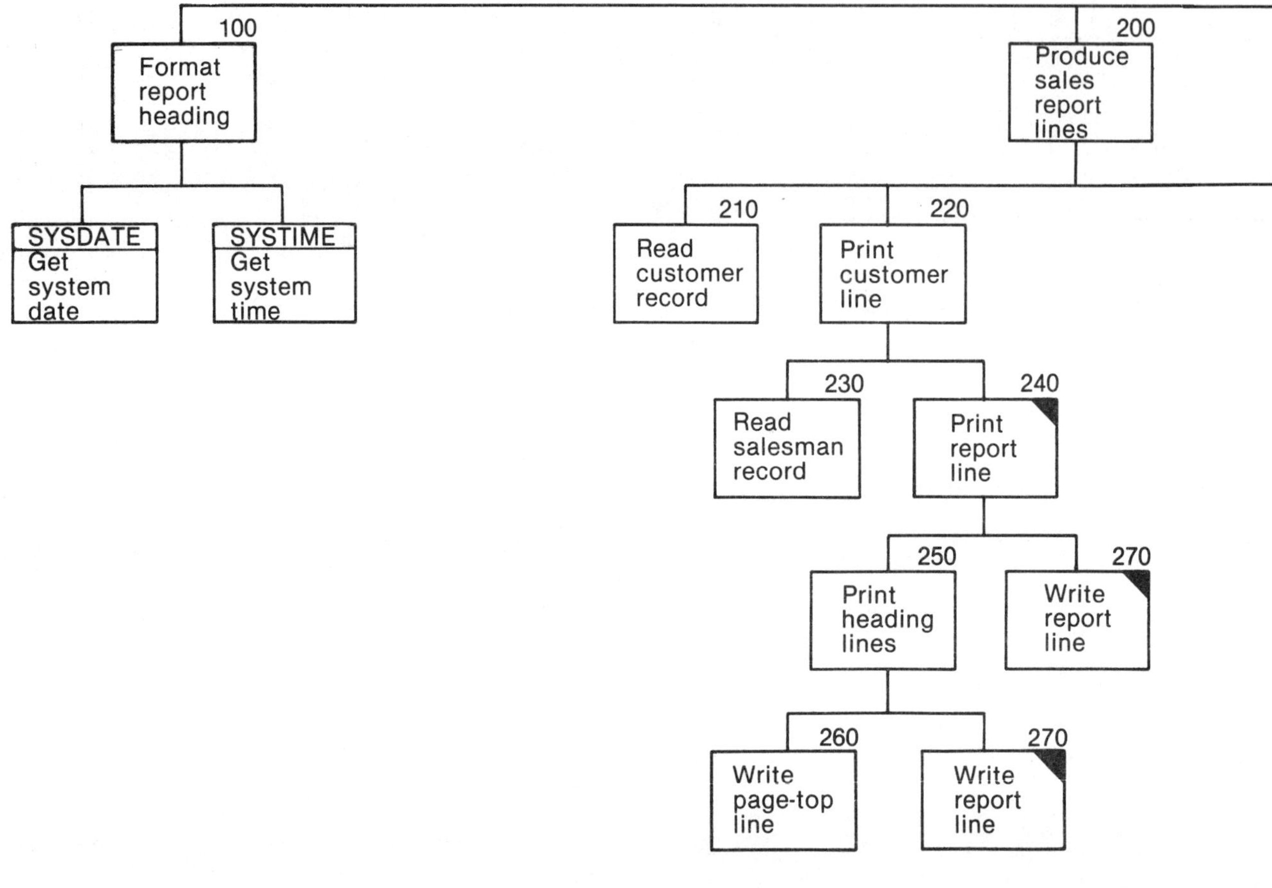


**Figure 12-20** The structure chart for the program that prepares a more realistic two-level sales report

you can see, the modules at the third level of the chart read the next record sequentially and print one or more lines based on the contents of that record. If intermediate or final totals are accumulated by a program, an accumulate module is also needed in the third level of the chart.

Because report preparation programs vary greatly in size and complexity, I'm not saying that the structure in figure 12-23 applies to every report preparation program. In fact, some programs may require a structure that is unique. For most report preparation pro-

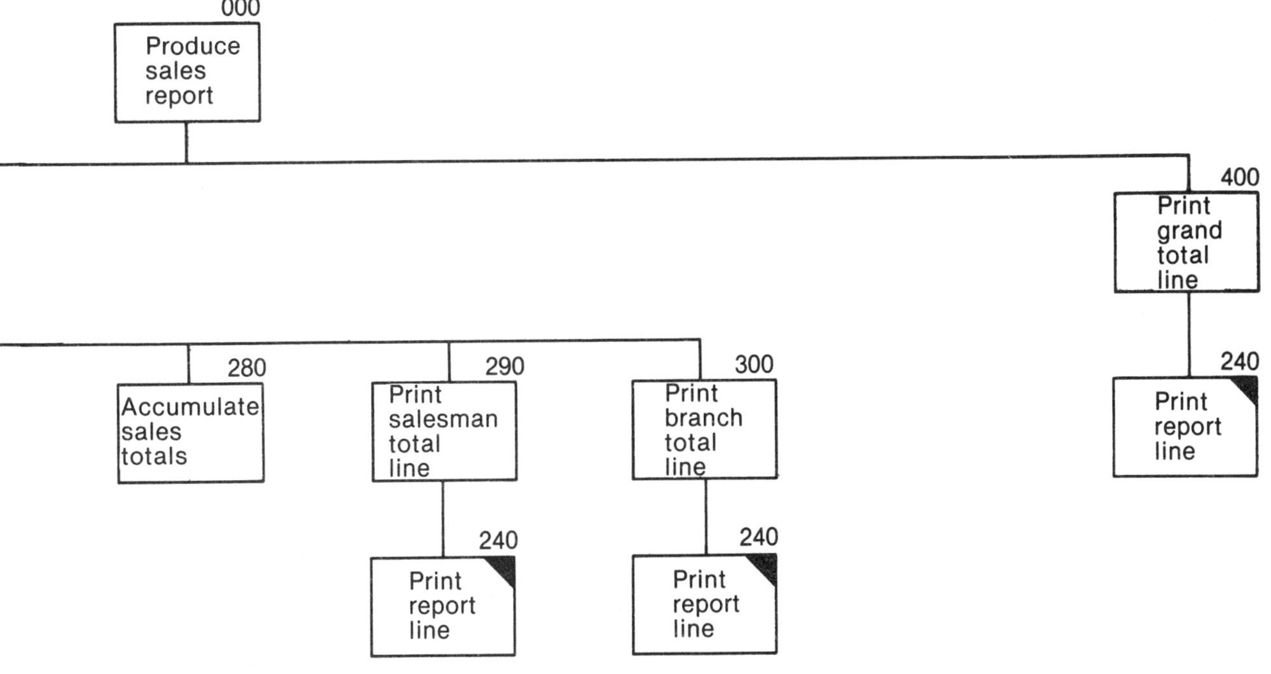


grams, though, the structure in figure 12-23 should be a good starting point for you.

Figure 12-24 shows some modules that can be called by a typical print module. First, if the program must read other records in order to get all the data required for a print line, the print module may call a read module. If the program must get data from more than one secondary file, it may call more than one read module. Second, if the operations or calculations for developing the required output data are complicated, the print module may call a module to develop the data.

```
000-produce-sales-report.

    Open files.
    DO 100-format-report-heading.
    DO 200-produce-sales-report-lines
        UNTIL custmast-eof.
    DO 400-print-grand-total-line.
    Close files.
    Stop run.


200-produce-sales-report-lines.

    DO 210-read-customer-record.
    IF NOT custmast-eof
        IF first-record
            move cm-salesman-key to old-salesman-key
            DO 220-print-customer-line
            DO 280-accumulate-sales-totals
            move 'N' to first-record-switch
        ELSE
            IF cm-salesman-key NOT > old-salesman-key
                DO 220-print-customer-line
                DO 280-accumulate-sales-totals
            ELSE
                IF cm-branch-no > old-branch-no
                    DO 290-print-salesman-total-line
                    DO 300-print-branch-total-line
                    DO 220-print-customer-line
                    DO 280-accumulate-sales-totals
                    move cm-salesman-key to old-salesman-key
                ELSE
                    DO 290-print-salesman-total-line
                    DO 220-print-customer-line
                    DO 280-accumulate-sales-totals
                    move cm-salesman-no to old-salesman-no
    ELSE
        DO 290-print-salesman-total-line
        DO 300-print-branch-total-line.


210-read-customer-record.

    Read custmast
        AT END
            move 'Y' to custmast-eof-switch.
```

Note: To understand this pseudocode, you must realize that the salesman key consists of both salesman number and branch number. Also, the input file of customer records is in sequence by customer number within salesman number within branch number; in other words, it's in sequence by customer number within salesman key.

**Figure 12-21** Pseudocode for some of the critical modules of the program charted in figure 12-20

```
 220-PRINT-CUSTOMER-LINE.
*
     IF FIRST-RECORD
         MOVE CM-BRANCH-NUMBER    TO CL-BRANCH-NO
         MOVE CM-SALESMAN-NUMBER TO CL-SALESMAN-NO
         MOVE CM-SALESMAN-KEY     TO SM-SALESMAN-KEY
         MOVE 'Y'                 TO RECORD-FOUND-SW
         PERFORM 230-READ-SALESMAN-RECORD
         IF RECORD-FOUND
             MOVE SM-SALESMAN-NAME TO CL-SALESMAN-NAME
         ELSE
             MOVE 'SALESMAN RECORD NOT FOUND'
                 TO CL-SALESMAN-NAME
     ELSE
         IF CM-SALESMAN-KEY GREATER OLD-SALESMAN-KEY
             IF CM-BRANCH-NUMBER GREATER OLD-BRANCH-NUMBER
                 MOVE CM-BRANCH-NUMBER    TO CL-BRANCH-NO
                 MOVE CM-SALESMAN-NUMBER TO CL-SALESMAN-NO
                 MOVE CM-SALESMAN-KEY     TO SM-SALESMAN-KEY
                 MOVE 'Y'                 TO RECORD-FOUND-SW
                 PERFORM 230-READ-SALESMAN-RECORD
                 IF RECORD-FOUND
                     MOVE SM-SALESMAN-NAME TO CL-SALESMAN-NAME
                 ELSE
                     MOVE 'SALESMAN RECORD NOT FOUND'
                         TO CL-SALESMAN-NAME
             ELSE
                 MOVE SPACE               TO CL-BRANCH-NO
                 MOVE CM-SALESMAN-NUMBER TO CL-SALESMAN-NO
                 MOVE CM-SALESMAN-KEY     TO SM-SALESMAN-KEY
                 MOVE 'Y'                 TO RECORD-FOUND-SW
                 PERFORM 230-READ-SALESMAN-RECORD
                 IF RECORD-FOUND
                     MOVE SM-SALESMAN-NAME TO CL-SALESMAN-NAME
                 ELSE
                     MOVE 'SALESMAN RECORD NOT FOUND'
                         TO CL-SALESMAN-NAME
         ELSE
             MOVE SPACE TO CL-SALESMAN-NAME
                           CL-SALESMAN-NO
                           CL-BRANCH-NO.
     MOVE CM-CUSTOMER-NUMBER TO CL-CUSTOMER-NO.
     MOVE CM-CUSTOMER-NAME   TO CL-CUSTOMER-NAME.
     MOVE CM-SALES-THIS-YTD  TO CL-SALES-THIS-YTD.
     MOVE CM-SALES-LAST-YTD  TO CL-SALES-LAST-YTD.
     COMPUTE CHANGE-AMOUNT = CM-SALES-THIS-YTD
                           - CM-SALES-LAST-YTD.
     MOVE CHANGE-AMOUNT TO CL-CHANGE-AMOUNT.
     IF CM-SALES-LAST-YTD NOT EQUAL ZERO
         COMPUTE CHANGE-PERCENT ROUNDED = CHANGE AMOUNT
                                        / CM-SALES-LAST-YTD
                                        * 100
         MOVE CHANGE-PERCENT TO CL-CHANGE-PERCENT
     ELSE
         MOVE 'N/A' TO CL-CHANGE-PERCENT-R.
     MOVE CUSTOMER-LINE TO NEXT-REPORT-LINE.
     PERFORM 240-PRINT-REPORT-LINE.
     MOVE 1 TO SPACE-CONTROL.
*
```

**Figure 12-22** The COBOL code for module 220 of the program charted in figure 12-20 when module 200 is coded as shown in figure 12-21

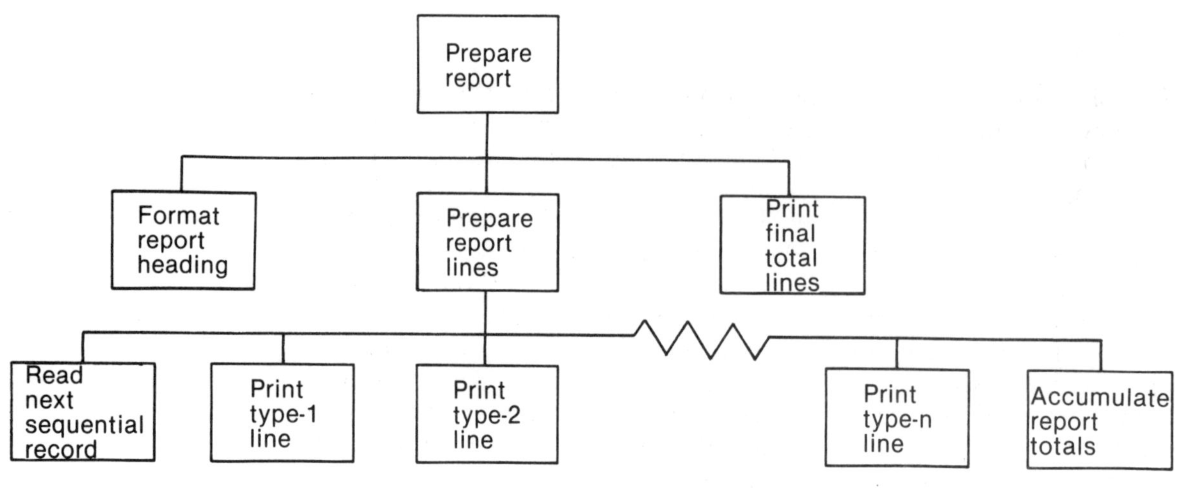


**Figure 12-23** The basic structure of a report preparation program

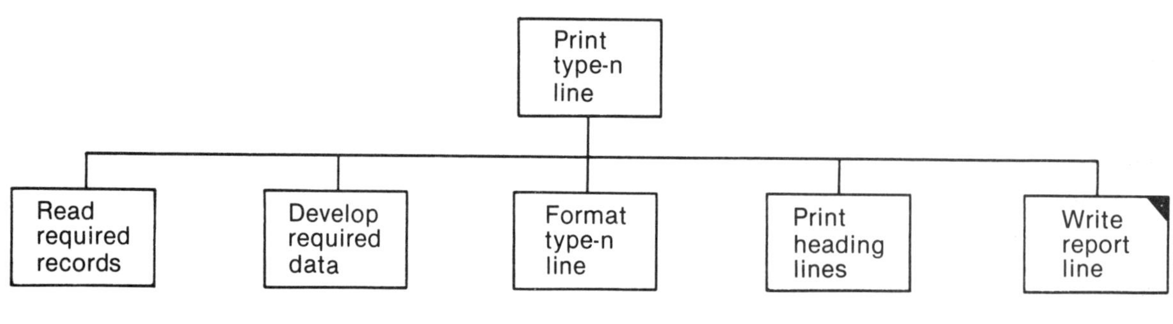


**Figure 12-24** Possible subordinate modules for a print module

Third, if the statements required for formatting the print line are extensive, the print module can call a format module. Fourth, if the print module must provide for page overflow, it must call a print-heading-lines module when overflow is required. And fifth, the print module must always call a module that actually writes the line on the printer (or to a print file).

In many programs, however, the print modules are relatively simple. Then, a print module may not require subordinates to read other records, develop data, and so on. In fact, it may only require the module to write a report line, and, if the module must provide for page overflow, the module to print the report heading. You should keep in mind, though, that you can use subordinates like those in figure 12-24 whenever a print module becomes cumbersome.

## Discussion

By using the structure and pseudocode presented in this chapter as models, you should be able to design any report preparation program that you're assigned. You should realize, though, that designing effective programs doesn't always come easily. In most cases, you will have to study the examples in this chapter until you understand the matching record and control break logic that is used in most report preparation programs. Once you understand this logic, though, report preparation programs shouldn't give you much trouble.

As I mentioned earlier, appendix B presents the complete specifications, structure chart, and COBOL code for the fourth program presented in this chapter. Because this program is more realistic than the other three, we recommend that you study the program in appendix B until you're confident that you understand this program's structure and logic. Then, when you develop multilevel programs of your own, we recommend that you use the program in appendix B as a model for your design and coding. Incidentally, this program is one of the seven model programs presented in our book, *The COBOL Programmer's Handbook*.

## Terminology

listing
detail line
summary report
summary line
total line
group indication
one-level report
multilevel report
exception report
control field
matching record logic
control break
control break logic

## Objective

Given the specifications for a report preparation program, design an acceptable structure chart for it and code the pseudocode for its critical modules.

## Section 5

# Related subjects

This section consists of but one short chapter. It explains what you must know to be an effective COBOL programmer. That includes the COBOL language itself, the facilities of your operating system, and effective programming techniques. You should read this chapter after you have completed the other 12 chapters in this book, or at least a major portion of them.

Chapter 13

# What else an effective COBOL programmer must know

You should read this chapter after you've read the other 12 chapters in this book. Its purpose is to show you what else a COBOL programmer must know in order to be effective. When you complete this book, you should be able to use a professional subset of COBOL for developing report preparation programs. But there's much more to COBOL programming than that.

I present this material in case you're interested in becoming a COBOL programmer. If you've done the case studies for this course without too much trouble, you probably have the aptitude for further study in COBOL and its related subjects. On the other hand, if you've had difficulty in writing and testing the case study programs, this probably isn't the right field for you. So read this chapter only if you want to continue your COBOL training.

In brief, effective COBOL programmers must know how to use all of the standard COBOL language that is available to them on their systems. They must know how to use the non-standard COBOL features that make it possible for them to write interactive programs. If their system uses data base software, they must know how to access data bases in their COBOL programs. They must know how to make use of the features that their operating system provides. And they must know the programming techniques that let them develop reliable programs that are easy to code, test, debug, and maintain.

## Standard COBOL and its features

Figure 13-1 summarizes the COBOL modules that are defined in the 1974 and 1985 ANS standards. In general, both sets of standards consist of the same modules. However, the table handling module of 1974

| Module name | 1974 levels | 1985 levels | Remarks |
|---|---|---|---|
| Nucleus | 2 | 2 | The 1985 nucleus includes table handling code. |
| Table handling | 2 | 0 | Included in the nucleus in 1985 COBOL. |
| Sequential I-O | 2 | 2 | |
| Relative I-O | 2 | 2 | |
| Indexed I-O | 2 | 2 | |
| Library | 2 | 2 | Called "source text manipulation" in 1985 COBOL. Provides for the use of the COPY library. |
| Inter-program communication | 2 | 2 | Provides for the use of subprograms. |
| Sort-merge | 2 | 2 | In common use on large systems. |
| Report Writer | 1 | 1 | Not required in a 1985 compiler. |
| Communication | 2 | 2 | Not required in a 1985 compiler. |
| Segmentation | 2 | 2 | Not required in a 1985 compiler, and it will be deleted from the next set of standards. |
| Debug | 2 | 2 | Not required in a 1985 compiler, and it will be deleted from the next set of standards. |

Note: All of the modules listed are required in a "full standard" 1974 compiler. However, only the modules above the line are required in a "high subset" 1985 compiler; the modules below the line are optional.

**Figure 13-1** The modules of 1974 and 1985 ANS COBOL

COBOL is part of the nucleus module in 1985 COBOL. Similarly, the "library" module of 1974 COBOL is called the "source text manipulation" module in 1985 COBOL.

Each set of standards provides for several levels of language in each module, as shown by the "levels" columns in figure 13-1. For instance, there are three levels to the nucleus in both the 1974 and 1985 standards. In contrast, there are two levels for the inter-program communication module in the 1974 standards, but three levels in the 1985 standards.

Each level consists of different COBOL elements. For example, the simple DIVIDE statement (shown in Format 1 of figure 4-13) is part of level 1 of the nucleus module, while the DIVIDE statement with the REMAINDER clause is part of level 2. To be classified as "standard," a minimum 1974 compiler only has to provide for the lowest level in each of the first three modules listed in figure 13-1, and a 1985 compiler only has to provide for the lowest level in the nucleus, sequential I-O, and inter-program communication modules.

To be classified as a "full standard" compiler, a 1974 compiler has to provide for the highest level in all of the modules. Similarly, to be classified as a "high subset" compiler, a 1985 compiler has to provide for the highest level in the eight modules above the line in figure 13-1; the modules below the line are optional.

Many compilers, though, are neither minimum nor full standard or high subset compilers. Instead, they provide for a subset of COBOL elements that are above the minimum standard but below the full, or high, standard. That's why you must study the COBOL manuals for your system to find out exactly what language it provides.

In this book, chapters 3 through 7 present a subset of the elements in the first seven modules in figure 13-1. Nucleus elements are presented in chapters 3 through 5; table handling elements in chapter 6; sequential I-O elements in chapter 3; indexed I-O elements in chapter 6; relative I-O elements aren't presented at all in this book but they are similar to those for indexed files; library elements are presented in chapter 5; and inter-program communication elements in chapter 5. To learn the rest of the elements for each of these modules is a relatively easy task, one that you can do by reading *Structured ANS COBOL, Part 2.*

If you look at the four modules below the line in figure 13-1, you can see that two will not be included in subsequent sets of standards: the segmentation module and the debug module. Neither of these modules is used much today, and we expect them to be used even less frequently in the future. As a result, we don't present them in our COBOL series. For the same reasons, we don't present the communication module in our series. On the other hand, we believe that effective COBOL programmers should know how to use the sort-merge module and the Report Writer module if they are available on their systems.

**The sort-merge module** The sort-merge module of COBOL is one that is frequently used on large systems. It allows you to code a sort or merge function within a COBOL program. In general, however, this module isn't available on the compilers for small systems.

To illustrate the purpose of the sort-merge module of COBOL, figure 13-2 presents a typical system flowchart for preparing a report.

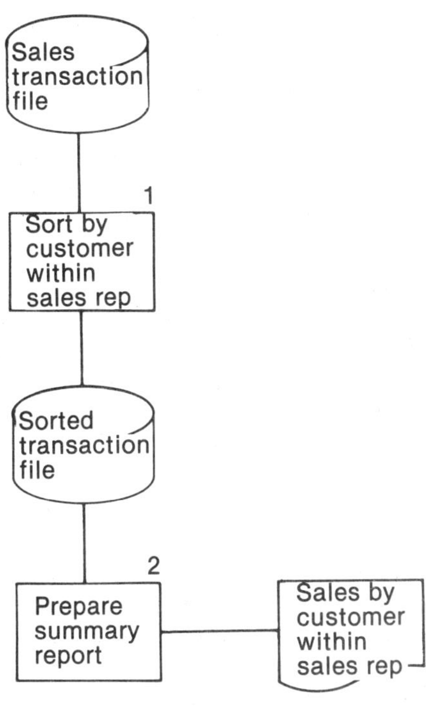


**Figure 13-2** Two system functions that can be done in a single COBOL program by using the sort-merge feature

First, a transaction file is sorted into the sequence that is required for report preparation. Then, a COBOL program is used to prepare the report from the sorted transaction file. By using the sort-merge module of COBOL, though, both functions can be coded in one COBOL program. The sort-merge module is relatively easy to learn and use, and it is covered in *Part 2* of this series.

**The Report Writer module** The Report Writer module of COBOL lets you define a report in detail in the Data Division. Then, you can prepare the report by using just a few statements in the Procedure Division.

For instance, figure 13-3 presents the structure chart for the same multilevel report preparation program that is charted in figure 12-16. If you refer back to that chart, though, you'll find it requires eleven different modules in contrast to the four modules in figure 13-3. Similarly, the number of lines in the Procedure Division of the program when using Report Writer is reduced to less than one-third the number of lines required when the Report Writer module isn't used. Furthermore, the number of lines in the Data Division for this program is actually decreased when using Report Writer, so the complete

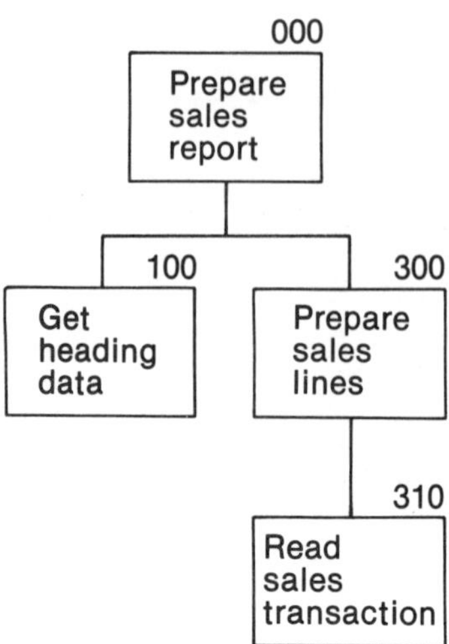


**Figure 13-3** The structure chart for a multilevel report preparation program when using the Report Writer feature of COBOL

program with Report Writer is only 65 percent as long as the complete program without Report Writer.

Because it lets you reduce the number of modules in your structure charts and the number of lines of code in your programs, we believe the Report Writer module will help you increase your productivity. Nevertheless, many compilers don't provide this module and many COBOL shops don't use it even when the compiler does provide it. That's why Report Writer isn't one of the required modules in the 1985 standards. If you do need to learn this module, our *Report Writer* text in this series will help you learn it quickly and use it effectively.

## COBOL for interactive programs

If you refer again to figure 13-1, you can see that neither the 1974 nor the 1985 COBOL standards provide for interactive programs. Today, however, most systems are interactive, so almost all COBOL compilers provide non-standard language that lets a program send data to a terminal screen and receive data from a terminal keyboard.

To illustrate one way that this is done, figure 13-4 shows some interactive COBOL code for a Wang VS compiler. This code sends a customer entry screen to a user's terminal. Then, after the user enters data on the terminal using the keyboard, the program receives this data. In module 420, the shaded statement is the one that sends and receives the screen data. It is the DISPLAY AND READ statement. Otherwise, the Procedure Division code is standard COBOL. Similarly, the Data Division uses only a few non-standard clauses to define

```
 01   CUSTOMER-ENTRY-SCREEN  DISPLAY-WS.
*
     05   FILLER            LINE 1
                            COLUMN 1
                            PIC X(80)
                            SOURCE DSP-HEADING-LINE.
     05   FILLER            LINE 6
                            COLUMN 2
                            PIC X(14)
                            VALUE "CUSTOMER CODE:".
     05   CES-CUST-CODE     LINE 6
                            COLUMN 19
                            PIC X(5)
                            SOURCE CM-CUSTOMER-CODE.
     05   FILLER            LINE 8
                            COLUMN 2
                            PIC X(5)
                            VALUE "NAME:".
     05   CES-NAME          LINE 8
                            COLUMN 19
                            PIC X(30)
                            SOURCE CM-NAME
                            OBJECT CM-NAME.
     05   FILLER            LINE 9
                            COLUMN 2
                            PIC X(8)
                            VALUE "ADDRESS:".
     05   CES-ADDRESS       LINE 9
                            COLUMN 19
                            PIC X(30)
                            SOURCE CM-ADDRESS
                            OBJECT CM-ADDRESS.
     .
     .
     05   FILLER            LINE 24
                            COLUMN 1
                            PIC X(80)
                            SOURCE DSP-MESSAGE-LINE.
*
     .
     .
 420-ACCEPT-CUSTOMER-DATA.
*
     MOVE "PF16 = CANCEL ENTRY" TO DSP-MESSAGE-AREA.
     MOVE SCREEN-ORDER-AREA
         TO ORDER-AREA OF CUSTOMER-ENTRY-SCREEN.
     DISPLAY AND READ CUSTOMER-ENTRY-SCREEN ON SCREEN
         PFKEY 16
         ON PFKEY 16
             MOVE "Y" TO CANCEL-ENTRY-SW.
     SET WCC-BEEP IN SOA-WCC OFF.
*
```

**Figure 13-4** Getting data from a terminal using Wang VS COBOL

```
 1300-SEND-CUSTOMER-SCREEN SECTION.
*
     PERFORM 1310-SET-ENTRY-FACS.
     MOVE CWA-DATE TO CDM-D-DATE.
     EXEC CICS
         SEND MAP('MT21MP2')
              MAPSET('MT21SET')
              FROM(CUSTOMER-DATA-MAP)
              CURSOR
         END-EXEC.
*
     .
     .
*
 2100-RECEIVE-CUSTOMER-SCREEN SECTION.
*
     EXEC CICS
         HANDLE AID CLEAR(2100-CLEAR-KEY)
                    ANYKEY(2100-ANYKEY)
     END-EXEC.
     EXEC CICS
         RECEIVE MAP('MT21MP2')
                 MAPSET('MT21SET')
                 INTO(CUSTOMER-DATA-MAP)
     END-EXEC.
     GO TO 2100-EXIT.
*
```

**Figure 13-5** Getting data from a terminal using CICS on an IBM mainframe

the fields in the terminal screen that is being sent and received. Otherwise, it looks a lot like standard Data Division code.

Figure 13-5 shows another way that data can be sent to and received from terminals. It shows some Procedure Division code when using CICS for handling terminal screens on an IBM mainframe. Here, one COBOL module is used to send the screen to the terminal; another module is used to receive the data from the terminal. The statements that send and receive the data are shaded in this figure. They are EXEC statements that call subprograms to send and receive the data.

In general, each type of system supports interactive processing in COBOL in a different way. Most microcomputers and minicomputers provide language for interactive processing that is similar to standard COBOL, but most mainframes provide for it by using language that is similar to CALL statements. If you're going to develop interactive programs, you have to learn how to use the interactive provisions of your system.

```
 LINKAGE SECTION.
*
 01  INVENTORY-PCB-MASK.
*
     05  IPCB-DBD-NAME                 PIC X(8).
     05  IPCB-SEGMENT-LEVEL            PIC XX.
     05  IPCB-STATUS-CODE              PIC XX.
     05  IPCB-PROC-OPTIONS             PIC X(4).
     05  FILLER                        PIC S9(5)        COMP.
     05  IPCP-SEGMENT-NAME             PIC X(8).
     05  IPCB-KEY-LENGTH               PIC S9(5)        COMP.
     05  IPCB-NUMB-SENS-SEGS           PIC S9(5)        COMP.
     05  IPCB-KEY                      PIC X(11).
*
     .
     .
*
 110-GET-INVENTORY-SEGMENT.
*
     CALL 'CBLTDLI' USING DLI-GN
                          INVENTORY-PCB-MASK
                          SEGMENT-I-O-AREA.
     IF IPCB-STATUS-CODE = 'GB'
         MOVE 'Y' TO END-OF-DATA-BASE-SW
     ELSE
         IF         IPCB-STATUS-CODE NOT = 'GA'
                AND IPCB-STATUS-CODE NOT = SPACE
             MOVE 'Y' TO END-OF-DATA-BASE-SW
             DISPLAY 'INV2100   I  1   DATA BASE ERROR - STATUS CODE '
                     IPCB-STATUS-CODE.
*
```

**Figure 13-6** Accessing a data base using DL/I on an IBM mainframe

## COBOL for processing data bases

Data base software lets you organize the data that your system requires in a way that is both logical and efficient. The resulting collection of data is called a *data base*. I'm not going to describe data bases at all here. Just be aware that they're organized differently than the records and files you've learned to handle in this book.

Data base software is used on most large systems today. In the future, we expect data base software to be used on medium and even small systems. Nevertheless, neither the 1974 nor the 1985 COBOL standards provide language for processing data bases. As a result, the COBOL compiler for a system that uses data base software must have some other way to access its data bases.

Figure 13-6 illustrates one way that a COBOL program can access the data in a data base. This is part of a COBOL program for an IBM mainframe that accesses a data base using DL/I (Data Language I). If you study this code, you can see that it is all standard COBOL since the access to the data base is made by calling a subprogram with a standard CALL statement (shaded). To access the data base using DL/I, you must learn what subprograms to call, what fields must be passed to each subprogram, and so on.

Although many systems use CALLs to access data bases, some provide a special language for it. If you're going to develop programs that access your system's data bases, you must learn how to use whatever facility your system provides.

### The operating system and its features

To be an effective COBOL programmer, it's not enough to master the COBOL for your system. You must also learn how to use the operating system and its features. This includes its interactive editor, its job control language, its debugging aids, and its utilities.

In chapter 2 and chapter 8, I introduced you to interactive editors and job control language. An interactive editor lets you enter your COBOL programs into the system and to modify them later on. It may also let you compile and test your COBOL programs. In addition, you usually need to know the job control language for your system so you can test and run your programs.

The debug module of COBOL isn't presented in this series because most operating systems provide debugging aids that are more efficient than it is. The debugging aids may be part of the interactive editor, or they may be separate programs within the operating system. In any event, you should find out what debugging aids are available on your system and master them. If you do, they can save you many hours of debugging time each month.

In chapter 1, I briefly mentioned the utilities that come with an operating system. These are general-purpose programs that let you list the data in files, generate test data, and so on. Because they can help you during testing, you should learn how to use the utilities that are available on your system.

### Programming techniques

Some programmers do a poor job even though they master the COBOL language and the features of their operating systems. In other words, mastering COBOL and an operating system isn't enough to make you an effective COBOL programmer. In addition, you must learn how to get complete program specifications, how to design programs, how to plan the modules of a program, how to test a program, and so on. I introduced you to some of these techniques in chapters 10, 11, and 12, but there's much more to them than that.

By the mid-1970's, many people realized that most programmers were working at a dismally low level of performance. As a result, many techniques were developed that were designed to improve program quality and programmer productivity. Unfortunately, most COBOL shops didn't make dramatic improvements in programmer performance by changing to these techniques, and there's little doubt that most programmers today still use techniques that are inefficient and ineffective. But programming doesn't have to be that way.

If you're interested in learning techniques that have proven to be effective in thousands of COBOL shops throughout the country, let me recommend two books. The first is a text called *How to Design and Develop COBOL Programs.* This 528-page book is a complete presentation of the techniques that apply to all phases of program development. It assumes that you are an experienced COBOL programmer, but you can use it after mastering the subset of COBOL presented in this book. It will teach you the programming techniques that aren't usually presented in a course that teaches the COBOL language.

The second book is a reference book called *The COBOL Programmer's Handbook.* It presents complete standards for the development of COBOL programs. It also presents seven model programs—four batch and three interactive—that will show you how to apply the COBOL language to common types of business programs. If you use this handbook for reference as you continue your study in COBOL, we're confident that you'll learn COBOL more quickly and more completely.

## Discussion

I hope you can see by now that there's a lot to learn if you want to become an effective COBOL programmer. After you've taken courses like this one for your basic training in COBOL, operating system functions, and programming techniques, you should go through the technical manuals for your system to find out specific details that may be of use to you. You should also go through your shop standards to make sure you use COBOL and all development software in a way that is consistent with the goals of your company.

For instance, our COBOL books present standard COBOL that should work on any full or high subset standard compiler. However, your compiler may not be a full standard compiler. In addition, it may offer extensions to the standards that are useful on your system. That's why you should study the COBOL manuals for your system to learn all of the language that is available to you that wasn't presented in the COBOL courses you've taken. You should also find out whether all of the language that was presented in your COBOL courses is available on your compiler. After you study the manuals, you should study your shop standards to find out what restrictions your shop places on the use of the COBOL language.

I hope this chapter hasn't sounded too much like an advertisement for our books. In case you enjoyed this book, I just wanted you to know that we offer a complete selection of books for COBOL training. In addition, we offer books on operating system features, JCL, and interactive editors. Please check our catalog for books that may apply to your system.

### Terminology

None

### Objective

This chapter is only intended to show you what you must know if you want to become an effective COBOL programmer. As a result, there are no behavioral objectives for it.

Section 6

# Appendixes

Appendix A

# COBOL reference summary

This appendix presents a summary of the COBOL language presented in this text. In sequence, you will find the following:

General Information
Identification Division
Environment Division
Data Division
Procedure Division

Using only the language in this summary, you should be able to develop most report preparation programs.

The notation used in this appendix conforms to the notation used in the ANS COBOL standards. This notation is also used in COBOL reference manuals. The rules for this notation follow:

1. Words printed entirely in capital letters are COBOL reserved words.

2. Words printed in lowercase letters represent names, literals, or statements that must be supplied by the programmer.

3. Braces { } enclosing a group of items indicate that the programmer must choose one of them.

4. When a single item is enclosed in braces, it means the ellipsis that follows applies only to that item—not to the entire statement or clause (see rule 6 below).

5. Brackets [ ] indicate that the enclosed item may be used or omitted, depending on the requirements of the program.

6. The ellipsis ... indicates that an element may be repeated as many times as necessary.

7. Underlined reserved words are required unless the element itself is optional. Words that aren't underlined are optional.

8. In general, the clauses and phrases in a statement should be coded in the sequence shown. This is particularly true for statements in the Procedure Division.

The formats in this summary use the word *identifier* to indicate that the programmer must identify a data item. In contrast, the formats in the text chapters use *data-name*. Most of the time an identifier is coded as a data name, but it can also be a data name followed by an index enclosed in parentheses as described in chapter 6.

This summary presents elements from both the 1974 and the 1985 COBOL standards. If an element is included in the 1985 standards but not in the 1974 standards, it's shaded. That means that you shouldn't use it unless you are using a 1985 compiler. In contrast, all of the unshaded elements are acceptable to both 1974 and 1985 compilers.

## GENERAL INFORMATION

### Character set

#### Characters used for words and names

| | |
|---|---|
| A-Z | Letters |
| 0-9 | Digits |
| - | Hyphen |

#### Characters used for punctuation

| | |
|---|---|
| " | Quotation mark |
| ' | Single quote (apostrophe) |
| ( | Left parenthesis |
| ) | Right parenthesis |
| . | Period |
| | Space |
| , | Comma |

#### Characters used in arithmetic expressions

| | |
|---|---|
| + | Addition |
| - | Subtraction |
| * | Multiplication |
| / | Division |
| ** | Exponentiation |

#### Characters used to show relationships

| | |
|---|---|
| = | Equals |
| < | Less than |
| > | Greater than |

## Characters used in editing

| | |
|---|---|
| Z | Zero suppression |
| , | Comma |
| . | Period |
| - | Minus |
| + | Plus |
| CR | Credit |
| DB | Debit |
| * | Asterisk |
| $ | Dollar sign |
| / | Stroke |
| B | Blank |
| 0 | Zero |

## Logical operators

NOT

OR

AND

## Name formation

### Program name

1. Maximum of 30 characters.
2. Letters, numbers, and hyphens only.
3. Cannot start or end with a hyphen.
4. Should conform to the requirements of your system.

### Data name

1. Maximum of 30 characters.
2. Letters, numbers, and hyphens only.
3. Cannot start or end with a hyphen.
4. Must contain at least one letter.

### Paragraph (procedure) name

1. Maximum of 30 characters.
2. Letters, numbers, and hyphens only.
3. Cannot start or end with a hyphen.

### File name, record name, or condition name

Same as for data name.

## Figurative constants

```
ZERO, ZEROS, ZEROES
SPACE, SPACES
HIGH-VALUE, HIGH-VALUES
LOW-VALUE, LOW-VALUES
QUOTE, QUOTES
ALL literal
```

## Rules for forming literals

### Numeric literals

1. Maximum of 18 digits.
2. Consisting of 0-9, + or −, and the decimal point.
3. Only one sign character (if unsigned, assumed positive).
4. Only one decimal point.

### Non-numeric literals

1. Maximum of 120 characters in the 1974 standards, 160 characters in the 1985 standards.
2. Enclosed in quotation marks.

## Comment lines

1. An asterisk (*) in position 7.
2. Any other characters in positions 8-72.

## Debugging lines

1. The letter D in position 7.
2. Any valid COBOL code in positions 8-72.
3. When the WITH DEBUGGING MODE clause is coded in the SOURCE-COMPUTER paragraph in the Environment Division, the debugging lines are compiled and executed. When the WITH DEBUGGING MODE clause isn't coded, the debugging lines are treated as comments.

## Indexing format

```
data-name ( { index-name } )
            { integer    }
```

## Condition formats

### Relation conditions

```
{ identifier-1            }  { IS [NOT] GREATER THAN }  { identifier-2            }
{ literal-1               }  { IS [NOT] LESS THAN    }  { literal-2               }
{ arithmetic-expression-1 }  { IS [NOT] EQUAL TO     }  { arithmetic-expression-2 }

{ identifier-1            }  { IS [NOT] > }  { identifier-2            }
{ literal-1               }  { IS [NOT] < }  { literal-2               }
{ arithmetic-expression-1 }  { IS [NOT] = }  { arithmetic-expression-2 }
```

### Class condition

```
identifier IS [NOT] { NUMERIC    }
                    { ALPHABETIC }
```

### Sign condition

```
                                    { POSITIVE }
arithmetic-expression IS [NOT]      { NEGATIVE }
                                    { ZERO     }
```

### Condition-name condition

```
condition-name
```

## IDENTIFICATION DIVISION

```
IDENTIFICATION DIVISION.
PROGRAM-ID.  program-name.
```

Notes:

1. Your program name should conform to the requirements of your system.
2. To provide other identifying information in this division, you should use comment lines.

## ENVIRONMENT DIVISION

### General format

```
ENVIRONMENT DIVISION.
CONFIGURATION SECTION.
SOURCE-COMPUTER.  computer-name [WITH DEBUGGING MODE].
OBJECT-COMPUTER.  computer-name.
INPUT-OUTPUT SECTION.
FILE-CONTROL.
    SELECT-statement ...
```

Notes:

1. Computer names are defined by the computer manufacturer.
2. The entire Configuration Section is optional on some compilers.

### SELECT statement formats

#### Format 1: Sequential file

```
SELECT file-name

    ASSIGN TO system-name

    [[ORGANIZATION] IS SEQUENTIAL]

    [ACCESS MODE IS SEQUENTIAL].
```

### Format 2: Indexed file

```
SELECT file-name

    ASSIGN TO system-name

    ORGANIZATION IS INDEXED

    [ACCESS MODE IS {SEQUENTIAL}  ]
                    {RANDOM    }

    RECORD KEY IS data-name.
```

Note: System names are defined by the computer manufacturer.

## DATA DIVISION

### General format

```
DATA DIVISION.
FILE SECTION.
file-control-entry ...

WORKING-STORAGE SECTION.
data-description-entry ...
```

### File control entry format

```
FD  file-name

    [LABEL  {RECORD IS  }  {STANDARD}  ]
            {RECORDS ARE}  {OMITTED }

    [BLOCK CONTAINS integer-1 RECORDS]

    [RECORD CONTAINS integer-2 CHARACTERS].

data-description-entry ...
```

Note: The LABEL RECORDS clause is optional in the 1985 standards, though it is required by most 1974 compilers. It is marked for deletion in future versions of the COBOL standards, so you should stop using it as soon as it becomes optional on your compiler.

### Data description entry format

**Format 1: 01 through 49 levels**

```
level-number [data-name-1]
             [FILLER     ]

      [REDEFINES data-name-2]

      [{PICTURE}  IS character-string]
      [{PIC    }                     ]

      [           {COMPUTATIONAL}]
      [[USAGE IS] {COMP         }]
      [           {DISPLAY      }]

   [{OCCURS integer-2 TIMES                                                }]
   [{                                                                      }]
   [{       [{ASCENDING }  KEY IS {data-name-3} ...] ...                   }]
   [{       [{DESCENDING}                          ]                       }]
   [{        INDEXED BY {index-name-1} ...                                 }]
   [{OCCURS integer-1 TO integer-2 TIMES DEPENDING ON data-name-4          }]
   [{                                                                      }]
   [{       [{ASCENDING }  KEY IS {data-name-3} ...] ...                   }]
   [{       [{DESCENDING}                          ]                       }]
   [{        INDEXED BY {index-name-1} ...                                 }]

     [BLANK WHEN ZERO]

     [VALUE IS literal-1].
```

Note: Although COMP-3 usage is non-standard, it is accepted by many compilers and it is the preferred usage on some systems.

**Format 2: 88 levels**

```
88  condition-name  {VALUE IS  } {literal-1  [{THROUGH}  literal-2]} ... .
                    {VALUES ARE} {            [{THRU   }           ]}
```

## PROCEDURE DIVISION

```
                                {DATE       }
ACCEPT identifier-1 FROM        {DAY        }
                                {DAY-OF-WEEK}
                                {TIME       }
```

```
ADD {identifier-1} ... TO {identifier-2 [ROUNDED]} ...
    {literal-1   }

    [ON SIZE ERROR imperative-statement-1]

    [END-ADD]

ADD {identifier-1} ... TO {identifier-2}
    {literal-1   }        {literal-2   }

    GIVING {identifier-3 [ROUNDED]} ...

    [ON SIZE ERROR imperative-statement-1]

    [END-ADD]

CALL subprogram-name [USING identifier-1 ...]

    [END-CALL]

CLOSE {file-name-1} ...

COMPUTE {identifier-1 [ROUNDED]} ... = arithmetic-expression-1

    [ON SIZE ERROR imperative-statement-1]

    [END-COMPUTE]

COPY text-name [{OF} library-name]
                {IN}

DISPLAY {identifier-1} ...
        {literal-1   }

DIVIDE {identifier-1} INTO {identifier-2 [ROUNDED]} ...
       {literal-1   }

    [ON SIZE ERROR imperative-statement-1]

    [END-DIVIDE]

DIVIDE {identifier-1} INTO {identifier-2} GIVING identifier-3 [ROUNDED]
       {literal-1   }      {literal-2   }

    [REMAINDER identifier-4]

    [ON SIZE ERROR imperative-statement-1]

    [END-DIVIDE]
```

```
DIVIDE {identifier-1} BY {identifier-2} GIVING identifier-3 [ROUNDED]
       {literal-1   }    {literal-2   }

   [REMAINDER identifier-4]

   [ON SIZE ERROR imperative-statement-1]

   [END-DIVIDE]

IF condition-1 {{statement-1} ...} [{ELSE {statement-2} ... [END-IF]}]
               {NEXT SENTENCE    }  {ELSE NEXT SENTENCE              }
                                    {END-IF                          }

MOVE {identifier-1} TO {identifier-2} ...
     {literal-1   }

MULTIPLY {identifier-1} BY {identifier-2 [ROUNDED]} ...
         {literal-1   }

   [ON SIZE ERROR imperative-statement-1]

   [END-MULTIPLY]

MULTIPLY {identifier-1} BY {identifier-2}
         {literal-1   }    {literal-2   }

   GIVING {identifier-3 [ROUNDED]} ...

   [ON SIZE ERROR imperative-statement-1]

   [END-MULTIPLY]

OPEN {INPUT {file-name-1} ... } ...
     {OUTPUT {file-name-2} ...}

PERFORM [procedure-name-1]

   [WITH TEST {BEFORE}] [UNTIL condition-1]
              {AFTER }

   [imperative-statement-1 END-PERFORM]
```

```
PERFORM [procedure-name-1]

    [WITH TEST {BEFORE}]
               {AFTER }

    VARYING {identifier-1}  FROM {identifier-2}
            {index-name-1}       {index-name-2}
                                 {literal-1   }

            BY {identifier-3}  UNTIL condition-1
               {literal-2   }

    [imperative-statement-1 END-PERFORM]

READ file-name-1  RECORD  [INTO identifier-1]

    [AT END imperative-statement-1]

    [END-READ]

READ file-name-1  RECORD  [INTO identifier-1]

    [INVALID KEY imperative-statement-1]

    [END-READ]

SEARCH identifier-1 [VARYING {identifier-2}]
                             {index-name-1}

    [AT END imperative-statement-1]

    {WHEN condition-1  {imperative-statement-2}} ...
                       {NEXT SENTENCE         }

    [END-SEARCH]

SEARCH ALL identifier-1  [AT END imperative-statement-1]

  WHEN  {data-name-1 {IS EQUAL TO} {identifier-2             }}
        {            {IS =       } {literal-1                }}
        {                          {arithmetic-expression-1  }}
        {condition-name-1                                     }

     [AND {data-name-2  {IS EQUAL TO}  {identifier-3           }}] ...
     [    {             {IS =       }  {literal-2              }}]
     [    {                            {arithmetic-expression-2}}]
     [    {condition-name-2                                     }]

      {imperative-statement-2}
      {NEXT SENTENCE         }

     [END-SEARCH]
```

```
SET {index-name-1 | identifier-1} ... TO {index-name-2 | identifier-2 | integer-1}

SET {index-name-1} ... {UP BY | DOWN BY} {identifier-1 | integer-1}

SET {condition-name-1} ... TO TRUE

STOP RUN

SUBTRACT {identifier-1 | literal-1} ... FROM {identifier-2 [ROUNDED]} ...

    [ON SIZE ERROR imperative-statement-1]

    [END-SUBTRACT]

SUBTRACT {identifier-1 | literal-1} ... FROM {identifier-2 | literal-2}

    GIVING {identifier-3 [ROUNDED]} ...

    [ON SIZE ERROR imperative-statement-1]

    [END-SUBTRACT]

WRITE record-name-1 [FROM identifier-1]

    [{BEFORE | AFTER} ADVANCING {{identifier-2 | integer-1} {LINE | LINES} | PAGE}]

    [END-WRITE]
```

Appendix B

# A model report preparation program

This appendix presents the specifications, structure chart, DOS/VSE COBOL listing, and test run output for a fairly realistic report preparation program. Using the reporting terminology presented in chapter 12, this program prepares a two-level summary report with group indication. After you read chapter 12, you should study this program until you feel that you understand its structure and logic. Then, you can use this program as a model for the structure and code that you use in your own report preparation programs. Incidentally, this is just one of seven model programs presented in *The COBOL Programmer's Handbook*.

| Program: | MKTG1200 Produce Sales Report | Page: | 1 |
|---|---|---|---|
| Designer: | Anne Prince | Date: | 08-24-84 |

Input/output specifications

| File | Description | Use |
|---|---|---|
| CUSTMST | Customer master file | Input |
| SALESMN | Salesman master file | Input |
| SALESRPT | Print file: Sales report | Output |

Process specifications

The customer master file is in sequence by customer number within salesman number within branch number. This file should be read sequentially, and one line should be printed for each record in the file.

The year-to-date sales for the current and previous year are contained in each customer record, and the change amount and change percent are calculated from these values.

The salesman master file is indexed by salesman number within branch number. This file should be read randomly by the program, and the salesman records should be used to get the salesmen's names for the sales report.

Totals should be printed for each salesman and branch. At the end of the report, a grand total of all sales should be printed.

| Program: | MKTG1200 Produce Sales Report | Page: | 2 |
|---|---|---|---|
| Designer: | Anne Prince | Date: | 08-24-84 |

Process specifications

The basic processing requirements follow.

Do until the end of the customer master file:

1. Read a customer record.

2. If the salesman key in a customer record is different than the one in the previous customer record, calculate the salesman change amount and change percent and print a salesman total line. Then, reset the salesman totals to zero and read the salesman master file.

3. If the branch number in the customer record is different than the one in the previous customer record, calculate the branch change amount and change percent and print a branch total line. Then, reset the branch totals to zero.

4. Calculate the customer change amount and change percent and print a customer sales line.

5. Add the customer sales totals to the salesman, branch, and grand totals.

After all customers have been processed, calculate the total change amount and change percent and print a grand total line.

The COPY member for the customer master record

```
 01   CUSTOMER-MASTER-RECORD.
*
      05   CM-CUSTOMER-KEY.
           10   CM-SALESMAN-KEY.
                15   CM-BRANCH-NUMBER      PIC XX.
                15   CM-SALESMAN-NUMBER    PIC XX.
           10   CM-CUSTOMER-NUMBER         PIC X(5).
      05   CM-CUSTOMER-NAME                PIC X(25).
      05   CM-SALES-THIS-YTD               PIC S9(5)V99   COMP-3.
      05   CM-SALES-LAST-YTD               PIC S9(5)V99   COMP-3.
```

The COPY member for the salesman master record

```
 01   SALESMAN-MASTER-RECORD.
*
      05   SM-SALESMAN-KEY.
           10   SM-BRANCH-NUMBER      PIC XX.
           10   SM-SALESMAN-NUMBER    PIC XX.
      05   SM-SALESMAN-NAME           PIC X(25).
```

Document name Year-To-Date Sales Report  Date 8-23-84

Program name MKTG1200  Designer Anne Prince

| Record Name | Line | Branch No | Salesman No | Salesman Name | Customer No | Customer Name | Sales This YTD | Sales Last YTD | Change Amount | Change % |
|---|---|---|---|---|---|---|---|---|---|---|
| Heading-Line-1 | 1 | DATE: 99/99/99 | | | MIKE MURACH & ASSOCIATES, INC. | | | | PAGE: ZZ9 | |
| Heading-Line-2 | 2 | TIME: 99:99 XX | | | | | | | MKTG1200 | |
| Heading-Line-3 | 3 | | | | YEAR-TO-DATE SALES REPORT | | | | | |
| | 4 | | | | | | | | | |
| Heading-Line-4 | 5 | BRANCH | SALESMAN | SALESMAN | CUSTOMER | CUSTOMER | SALES | SALES | CHANGE | CHANGE |
| Heading-Line-5 | 6 | NO | NO | NAME | NO | NAME | THIS YTD | LAST YTD | AMOUNT | % |
| | 7 | | | | | | | | | |
| Customer-Line | 8 | XX | XX | X———X | ZZZZ9 | X———X | ZZ,ZZ9.99- | ZZ,ZZ9.99- | ZZ,ZZ9.99- | ZZZ9- |
| | 9 | | | | ZZZZ9 | X———X | ZZ,ZZ9.99- | ZZ,ZZ9.99- | ZZ,ZZ9.99- | ZZZ9- |
| | 10 | | | | ZZZZ9 | X———X | ZZ,ZZ9.99- | ZZ,ZZ9.99- | ZZ,ZZ9.99- | ZZZ9- |
| | 11 | | | | ZZZZ9 | X———X | ZZ,ZZ9.99- | ZZ,ZZ9.99- | ZZ,ZZ9.99- | ZZZ9- |
| | 12 | | | | ZZZZ9 | X———X | ZZ,ZZ9.99- | ZZ,ZZ9.99- | ZZ,ZZ9.99- | ZZZ9- |
| | 13 | | | | | | | | | |
| Salesman-Total-Line | 14 | | | | | SALESMAN TOTALS: | Z,ZZZ,ZZ9.99- | Z,ZZZ,ZZ9.99- | Z,ZZZ,ZZ9.99- | ZZZ9- |
| | 15 | | | | | | | | | |
| | 16 | | XX | X———X | ZZZZ9 | X———X | ZZ,ZZ9.99- | ZZ,ZZ9.99- | ZZ,ZZ9.99- | ZZZ9- |
| | 17 | | | | ZZZZ9 | X———X | ZZ,ZZ9.99- | ZZ,ZZ9.99- | ZZ,ZZ9.99- | ZZZ9- |
| | 18 | | | | ZZZZ9 | X———X | ZZ,ZZ9.99- | ZZ,ZZ9.99- | ZZ,ZZ9.99- | ZZZ9- |
| | 19 | | | | ZZZZ9 | X———X | ZZ,ZZ9.99- | ZZ,ZZ9.99- | ZZ,ZZ9.99- | ZZZ9- |
| | 20 | | | | | | | | | |
| | 21 | | | | | SALESMAN TOTALS: | Z,ZZZ,ZZ9.99- | Z,ZZZ,ZZ9.99- | Z,ZZZ,ZZ9.99- | ZZZ9- |
| | 22 | | | | | | | | | |
| | 23 | | | | | | | | | |
| Branch-Total-Line | 24 | | | | | BRANCH TOTALS: | Z,ZZZ,ZZ9.99- | Z,ZZZ,ZZ9.99- | Z,ZZZ,ZZ9.99- | ZZZ9- |
| | 25 | | | | | | | | | |
| | 26 | | | | | | | | | |
| | 27 | XX | XX | X———X | ZZZZ9 | X———X | ZZ,ZZ9.99- | ZZ,ZZ9.99- | ZZ,ZZ9.99- | ZZZ9- |
| | 28 | | | | ZZZZ9 | X———X | ZZ,ZZ9.99- | ZZ,ZZ9.99- | ZZ,ZZ9.99- | ZZZ9- |
| | 29 | | | | ZZZZ9 | X———X | ZZ,ZZ9.99- | ZZ,ZZ9.99- | ZZ,ZZ9.99- | ZZZ9- |
| | 30 | | | | ZZZZ9 | X———X | ZZ,ZZ9.99- | ZZ,ZZ9.99- | ZZ,ZZ9.99- | ZZZ9- |
| | 31 | | | | | | | | | |
| | 32 | | | | | SALESMAN TOTALS: | Z,ZZZ,ZZ9.99 | Z,ZZZ,ZZ9.99- | Z,ZZZ,ZZ9.99- | ZZZ9- |
| | 33 | | | | | | | | | |
| | 34 | | XX | X———X | ZZZZ9 | X———X | ZZ,ZZ9.99- | ZZ,ZZ9.99- | ZZ,ZZ9.99- | ZZZ9- |
| | 35 | | | | ZZZZ9 | X———X | ZZ,ZZ9.99- | ZZ,ZZ9.99- | ZZ,ZZ9.99- | ZZZ9- |
| | 36 | | | | ZZZZ9 | X———X | ZZ,ZZ9.99- | ZZ,ZZ9.99- | ZZ,ZZ9.99- | ZZZ9- |
| | 37 | | | | ZZZZ9 | X———X | ZZ,ZZ9.99- | ZZ,ZZ9.99- | ZZ,ZZ9.99- | ZZZ9- |
| | 38 | | | | ZZZZ9 | X———X | ZZ,ZZ9.99- | ZZ,ZZ9.99- | ZZ,ZZ9.99- | ZZZ9- |
| | 39 | | | | | | | | | |
| | 40 | | | | | SALESMAN TOTALS: | Z,ZZZ,ZZ9.99- | Z,ZZZ,ZZ9.99- | Z,ZZZ,ZZ9.99- | ZZZ9- |
| | 41 | | | | | | | | | |
| | 42 | | | | | | | | | |
| | 43 | | | | | BRANCH TOTALS: | Z,ZZZ,ZZ9.99- | Z,ZZZ,ZZ9.99- | Z,ZZZ,ZZ9.99- | ZZZ9- |
| | 44 | | | | | | | | | |
| | 45 | | | | | | | | | |
| | 46 | | | | | | | | | |
| Grand-Total-Line | 47 | | | | | GRAND TOTALS: | ZZZ,ZZZ,ZZ9.99- | ZZZ,ZZZ,ZZ9.99- | ZZZ,ZZZ,ZZ9.99- | ZZZ9- |
| | 48 | | | | | | | | | |
| | 49 | | | | | | | | | |
| | 50 | | | | | | | | | |

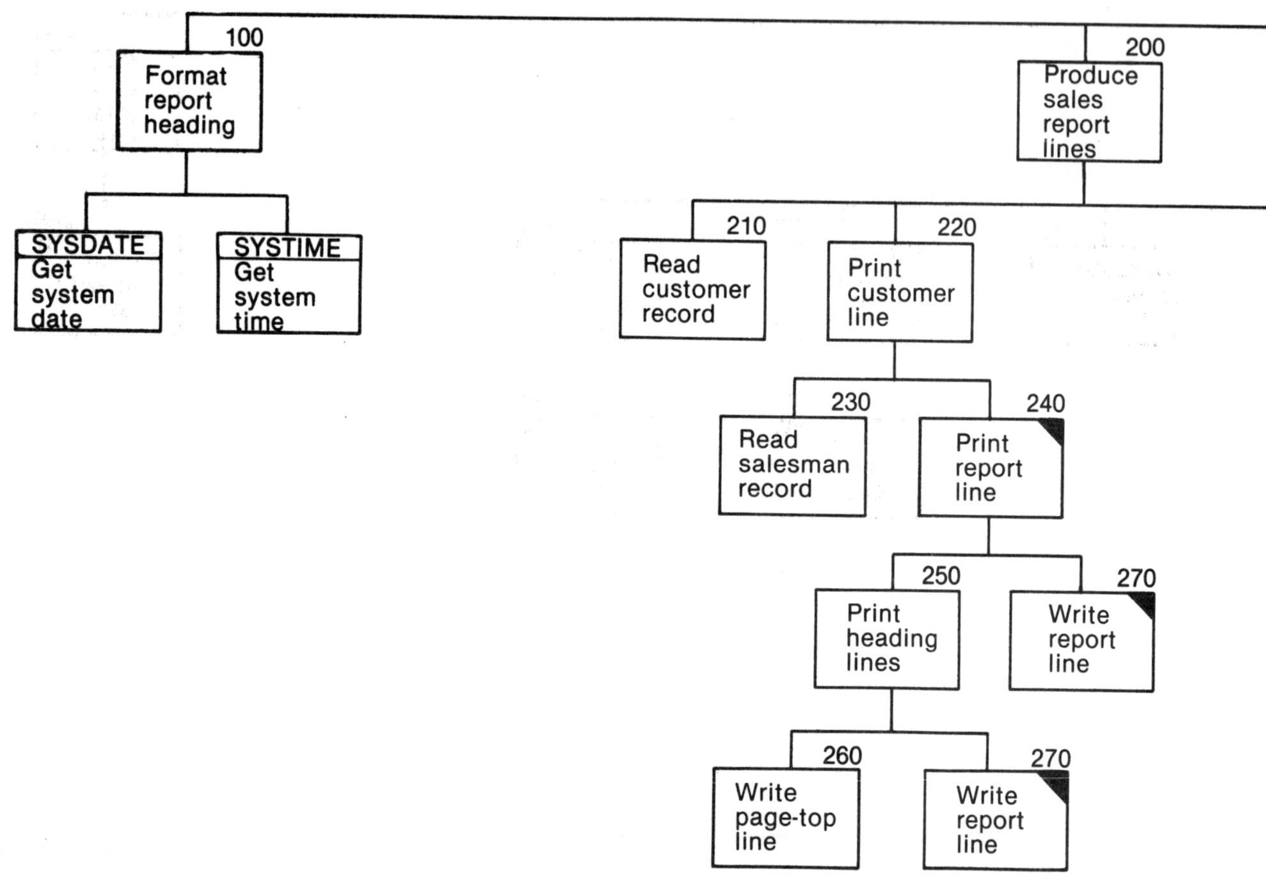
100
Format report heading
SYSDATE
Get system date
SYSTIME
Get system time
200
Produce sales report lines
210
Read customer record
220
Print customer line
230
Read salesman record
240
Print report line
250
Print heading lines
270
Write report line
260
Write page-top line
270
Write report line

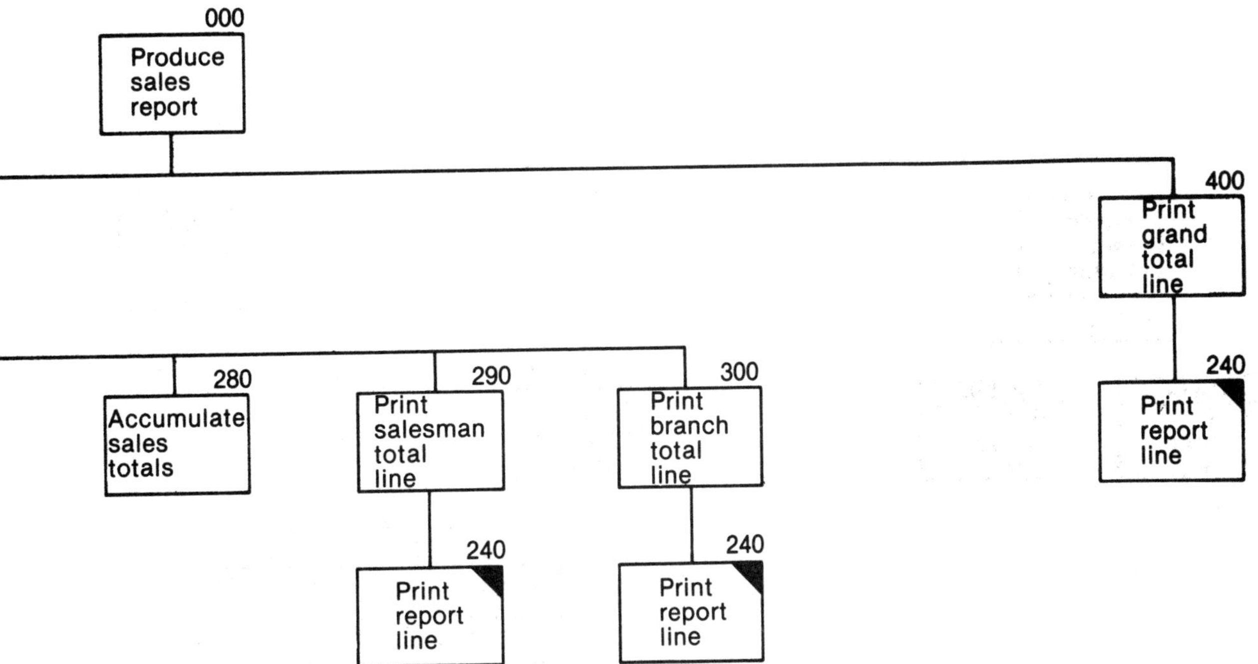
000
Produce sales report
280
Accumulate sales totals
290
Print salesman total line
240
Print report line
300
Print branch total line
240
Print report line
400
Print grand total line
240
Print report line

```
    1   IBM DOS/VS COBOL                                        REL 3.0

 CBL LIB,APOST,SXREF
       000100 IDENTIFICATION DIVISION.
       000200*
       000300 PROGRAM-ID.        MKTG1200.
       000400*AUTHOR.            ANNE PRINCE.
       000500*INSTALLATION.      MMA.
       000600*DATE.              SEPTEMBER 10, 1984.
       000700*
       000800 ENVIRONMENT DIVISION.
       000900*
       001000 INPUT-OUTPUT SECTION.
       001100*
       001200 FILE-CONTROL.
       001300        SELECT CUSTMST  ASSIGN TO SYS005-AS-CUSTMST.
       001400        SELECT SALESMN  ASSIGN TO SYS008-SALESMN
       001500                        ORGANIZATION IS INDEXED
       001600                        ACCESS IS RANDOM
       001700                        RECORD KEY IS SM-SALESMAN-KEY.
       001800        SELECT SALESRPT ASSIGN TO SYS006-UR-1403-S.
       001900*
       002000 DATA DIVISION.
       002100*
       002200 FILE SECTION.
       002300*
       002400 FD    CUSTMST
       002500       LABEL RECORDS ARE STANDARD
       002600       RECORD CONTAINS 42 CHARACTERS.
       002700*
       002800 COPY CUSTMAST.
 C             01   CUSTOMER-MASTER-RECORD.
 C            *
 C                  05  CM-CUSTOMER-KEY.
 C                      10  CM-SALESMAN-KEY.
 C                          15  CM-BRANCH-NUMBER       PIC XX.
 C                          15  CM-SALESMAN-NUMBER     PIC XX.
 C                      10  CM-CUSTOMER-NUMBER         PIC X(5).
 C                  05  CM-CUSTOMER-NAME               PIC X(25).
 C                  05  CM-SALES-THIS-YTD              PIC S9(5)V99 COMP-3.
 C                  05  CM-SALES-LAST-YTD              PIC S9(5)V99 COMP-3.
       002900*
       003000 FD    SALESMN
       003100       LABEL RECORDS ARE STANDARD
       003200       RECORD CONTAINS 29 CHARACTERS.
       003300*
       003400 COPY SALESMAN.
 C             01   SALESMAN-MASTER-RECORD.
 C            *
 C                  05  SM-SALESMAN-KEY.
 C                      10  SM-BRANCH-NUMBER           PIC XX.
 C                      10  SM-SALESMAN-NUMBER         PIC XX.
 C                  05  SM-SALESMAN-NAME               PIC X(25).
       003500*
       003600 FD    SALESRPT
       003700       LABEL RECORDS ARE OMITTED
       003800       RECORD CONTAINS 132 CHARACTERS.
       003900*
       004000 01    PRINT-AREA.
```

```
  2                         10.24.37        07/21/86

004100*
004200        05  PRINT-LINE   PIC X(132).
004300*
004400 WORKING-STORAGE SECTION.
004500*
004600 01  SWITCHES.
004700*
004800        05  FIRST-RECORD-SW PIC X    VALUE 'Y'.
004900            88  FIRST-RECORD         VALUE 'Y'.
005000        05  CUSTOMER-EOF-SW PIC X    VALUE 'N'.
005100            88  CUSTOMER-EOF         VALUE 'Y'.
005200        05  RECORD-FOUND-SW PIC X    VALUE 'Y'.
005300            88  RECORD-FOUND         VALUE 'Y'.
005400*
005500 01  CONTROL-FIELDS.
005600*
005700        05  OLD-SALESMAN-KEY.
005800            10  OLD-BRANCH-NUMBER    PIC 99.
005900            10  OLD-SALESMAN-NUMBER PIC 99.
006000*
006100 01  WORK-FIELDS            COMP-3.
006200*
006300        05  CHANGE-AMOUNT    PIC S9(7)V99     VALUE ZERO.
006400        05  CHANGE-PERCENT   PIC S9(3)V99     VALUE ZERO.
006500*
006600 01  PRINT-FIELDS.
006700*
006800        05  SPACE-CONTROL    PIC S9                      COMP   SYNC.
006900        05  LINE-COUNT       PIC S999     VALUE +999    COMP   SYNC.
007000        05  LINES-ON-PAGE    PIC S999     VALUE +53     COMP   SYNC.
007100        05  PAGE-COUNT       PIC S999     VALUE ZERO    COMP-3.
007200*
007300 01  TOTAL-FIELDS                      COMP-3.
007400*
007500        05  SALESMAN-TOTAL-THIS-YTD PIC S9(7)V99     VALUE ZERO.
007600        05  SALESMAN-TOTAL-LAST-YTD PIC S9(7)V99     VALUE ZERO.
007700        05  BRANCH-TOTAL-THIS-YTD   PIC S9(7)V99     VALUE ZERO.
007800        05  BRANCH-TOTAL-LAST-YTD   PIC S9(7)V99     VALUE ZERO.
007900        05  TOTAL-SALES-THIS-YTD    PIC S9(9)V99     VALUE ZERO.
008000        05  TOTAL-SALES-LAST-YTD    PIC S9(9)V99     VALUE ZERO.
008100*
008200 01  DATE-FIELDS.
008300*
008400        05  TODAYS-DATE       PIC 9(6).
008500*
008600 01  NEXT-REPORT-LINE     PIC X(132).
008700*
008800 01  COMPANY-NAME.
008900*
009000        05  FILLER        PIC X(10)   VALUE SPACE.
009100        05  FILLER        PIC X(20)   VALUE 'MIKE MURACH & ASSOCI'.
009200        05  FILLER        PIC X(20)   VALUE 'ATES, INC.          '.
009300*
009400 01  REPORT-TITLE.
009500*
009600        05  FILLER        PIC X(17)   VALUE SPACE.
009700        05  FILLER        PIC X(20)   VALUE 'YEAR-TO-DATE SALES R'.
```

```
3                       10.24.37        07/21/86

009800          05  FILLER         PIC X(23)    VALUE 'EPORT'.
009900*
010000 COPY RPTHDG14.
C           01   HEADING-LINE-1.
C          *
C                05  FILLER                         PIC X(7)     VALUE 'DATE:'.
C                05  HDG1-DATE                      PIC 99/99/99.
C                05  FILLER                         PIC X(26)    VALUE SPACE.
C                05  HDG1-COMPANY-NAME              PIC X(50).
C                05  FILLER                         PIC X(31)    VALUE SPACE.
C                05  FILLER                         PIC X(6)     VALUE 'PAGE:'.
C                05  HDG1-PAGE-NUMBER               PIC ZZ9.
C          *
C           01   HEADING-LINE-2.
C          *
C                05  HDG2-TIME-DATA.
C                    10  FILLER                 PIC X(7)     VALUE 'TIME:'.
C                    10  HDG2-HOURS             PIC XX.
C                    10  FILLER                 PIC X        VALUE ':'.
C                    10  HDG2-MINUTES           PIC XX.
C                    10  FILLER                 PIC X        VALUE SPACE.
C                    10  HDG2-TIME-SUFFIX       PIC X(8).
C                05  FILLER                     PIC X(101)   VALUE SPACE.
C                05  HDG2-REPORT-NUMBER         PIC X(10).
C          *
C           01   HEADING-LINE-3.
C          *
C                05  FILLER                     PIC X(36)     VALUE SPACE.
C                05  HDG3-REPORT-TITLE          PIC X(60).
010100*
010200 01   HEADING-LINE-4.
010300*
010400          05  FILLER         PIC X(20)    VALUE 'BRANCH  SALESMAN  SA'.
010500          05  FILLER         PIC X(20)    VALUE 'LESMAN              '.
010600          05  FILLER         PIC X(20)    VALUE '    CUSTOMER   CUSTO'.
010700          05  FILLER         PIC X(20)    VALUE 'MER                 '.
010800          05  FILLER         PIC X(20)    VALUE '             SALES  '.
010900          05  FILLER         PIC X(20)    VALUE '      SALES       CH'.
011000          05  FILLER         PIC X(12)    VALUE 'ANGE  CHANGE'.
011100*
011200 01   HEADING-LINE-5.
011300*
011400          05  FILLER         PIC X(20)    VALUE '  NO        NO    NA'.
011500          05  FILLER         PIC X(20)    VALUE 'ME                  '.
011600          05  FILLER         PIC X(20)    VALUE '          NO    NAME '.
011700          05  FILLER         PIC X(20)    VALUE '                    '.
011800          05  FILLER         PIC X(20)    VALUE '          THIS YTD  '.
011900          05  FILLER         PIC X(20)    VALUE ' LAST  YTD        AM'.
012000          05  FILLER         PIC X(20)    VALUE 'OUNT    %'.
012100*
012200 01   CUSTOMER-LINE.
012300*
012400          05  FILLER                   PIC XX      VALUE SPACE.
012500          05  CL-BRANCH-NO             PIC XX.
012600          05  FILLER                   PIC X(7)    VALUE SPACE.
012700          05  CL-SALESMAN-NO           PIC XX.
012800          05  FILLER                   PIC X(5)    VALUE SPACE.
```

```
4                         10.24.37          07/21/86

012900       05  CL-SALESMAN-NAME       PIC X(25).
013000       05  FILLER                 PIC X(4)     VALUE SPACE.
013100       05  CL-CUSTOMER-NO         PIC ZZZZ9.
013200       05  FILLER                 PIC XXX      VALUE SPACE.
013300       05  CL-CUSTOMER-NAME       PIC X(25).
013400       05  FILLER                 PIC X(5)     VALUE SPACE.
013500       05  CL-SALES-THIS-YTD      PIC ZZ,ZZ9.99-.
013600       05  FILLER                 PIC X(5)     VALUE SPACE.
013700       05  CL-SALES-LAST-YTD      PIC ZZ,ZZ9.99-.
013800       05  FILLER                 PIC X(5)     VALUE SPACE.
013900       05  CL-CHANGE-AMOUNT       PIC ZZ,ZZ9.99-.
014000       05  FILLER                 PIC X        VALUE SPACE.
014100       05  CL-CHANGE-PERCENT      PIC ZZZ9-.
014200       05  CL-CHANGE-PERCENT-R REDEFINES CL-CHANGE-PERCENT
014300                                  PIC X(5).
014400*
014500 01  SALESMAN-TOTAL-LINE.
014600*
014700       05  FILLER                 PIC X(63)    VALUE SPACE.
014800       05  FILLER                 PIC X(19)    VALUE 'SALESMAN TOTALS:'.
014900       05  SL-SALES-THIS-YTD      PIC Z,ZZZ,ZZ9.99-.
015000       05  FILLER                 PIC XX       VALUE SPACE.
015100       05  SL-SALES-LAST-YTD      PIC Z,ZZZ,ZZ9.99-.
015200       05  FILLER                 PIC XX       VALUE SPACE.
015300       05  SL-CHANGE-AMOUNT       PIC Z,ZZZ,ZZ9.99-.
015400       05  FILLER                 PIC X        VALUE SPACE.
015500       05  SL-CHANGE-PERCENT      PIC ZZZ9-.
015600       05  SL-CHANGE-PERCENT-R REDEFINES SL-CHANGE-PERCENT
015700                                  PIC X(5).
015800*
015900 01  BRANCH-TOTAL-LINE.
016000*
016100       05  FILLER                 PIC X(65)    VALUE SPACE.
016200       05  FILLER                 PIC X(17)    VALUE 'BRANCH TOTALS:'.
016300       05  BL-SALES-THIS-YTD      PIC Z,ZZZ,ZZ9.99-.
016400       05  FILLER                 PIC XX       VALUE SPACE.
016500       05  BL-SALES-LAST-YTD      PIC Z,ZZZ,ZZ9.99-.
016600       05  FILLER                 PIC XX       VALUE SPACE.
016700       05  BL-CHANGE-AMOUNT       PIC Z,ZZZ,ZZ9.99-.
016800       05  FILLER                 PIC X        VALUE SPACE.
016900       05  BL-CHANGE-PERCENT      PIC ZZZ9-.
017000       05  BL-CHANGE-PERCENT-R REDEFINES BL-CHANGE-PERCENT
017100                                  PIC X(5).
017200*
017300 01  GRAND-TOTAL-LINE.
017400*
017500       05  FILLER                     PIC X(66)    VALUE SPACE.
017600       05  FILLER                     PIC X(14)    VALUE 'GRAND TOTALS:'.
017700       05  GTL-SALES-THIS-YTD         PIC ZZZ,ZZZ,ZZ9.99-.
017800       05  GTL-SALES-LAST-YTD         PIC ZZZ,ZZZ,ZZ9.99-.
017900       05  GTL-CHANGE-AMOUNT          PIC ZZZ,ZZZ,ZZ9.99-.
018000       05  FILLER                     PIC X        VALUE SPACE.
018100       05  GTL-CHANGE-PERCENT         PIC ZZZ9-.
018200       05  GTL-CHANGE-PERCENT-R REDEFINES GTL-CHANGE-PERCENT
018300                                      PIC X(5).
018400*
018500 PROCEDURE DIVISION.
```

```
     5                              10.24.37         07/21/86

018600*
018700 000-PRODUCE-SALES-REPORT.
018800*
018900     OPEN INPUT  CUSTMST
019000                 SALESMN
019100          OUTPUT SALESRPT.
019200     PERFORM 100-FORMAT-REPORT-HEADING.
019300     PERFORM 200-PRODUCE-SALES-REPORT-LINES
019400         UNTIL CUSTOMER-EOF.
019500     PERFORM 400-PRINT-GRAND-TOTAL-LINE.
019600     CLOSE CUSTMST
019700           SALESMN
019800           SALESRPT.
019900     STOP RUN.
020000*
020100 100-FORMAT-REPORT-HEADING.
020200*
020300     CALL 'SYSDATE' USING TODAYS-DATE.
020400     MOVE TODAYS-DATE  TO HDG1-DATE.
020500     MOVE COMPANY-NAME TO HDG1-COMPANY-NAME.
020600     CALL 'SYSTIME' USING HDG2-TIME-DATA.
020700     MOVE 'MKTG1200'   TO HDG2-REPORT-NUMBER.
020800     MOVE REPORT-TITLE TO HDG3-REPORT-TITLE.
020900*
021000 200-PRODUCE-SALES-REPORT-LINES.
021100*
021200     PERFORM 210-READ-CUSTOMER-RECORD.
021300     IF NOT CUSTOMER-EOF
021400         IF FIRST-RECORD
021500             PERFORM 220-PRINT-CUSTOMER-LINE
021600             PERFORM 280-ACCUMULATE-SALES-TOTALS
021700             MOVE CM-SALESMAN-KEY TO OLD-SALESMAN-KEY
021800             MOVE 'N'             TO FIRST-RECORD-SW
021900         ELSE
022000             IF CM-SALESMAN-KEY NOT GREATER OLD-SALESMAN-KEY
022100                 PERFORM 220-PRINT-CUSTOMER-LINE
022200                 PERFORM 280-ACCUMULATE-SALES-TOTALS
022300             ELSE
022400                 IF CM-BRANCH-NUMBER GREATER OLD-BRANCH-NUMBER
022500                     PERFORM 290-PRINT-SALESMAN-TOTAL-LINE
022600                     PERFORM 300-PRINT-BRANCH-TOTAL-LINE
022700                     PERFORM 220-PRINT-CUSTOMER-LINE
022800                     PERFORM 280-ACCUMULATE-SALES-TOTALS
022900                     MOVE CM-SALESMAN-KEY TO OLD-SALESMAN-KEY
023000                 ELSE
023100                     PERFORM 290-PRINT-SALESMAN-TOTAL-LINE
023200                     PERFORM 220-PRINT-CUSTOMER-LINE
023300                     PERFORM 280-ACCUMULATE-SALES-TOTALS
023400                     MOVE CM-SALESMAN-NUMBER
023500                         TO OLD-SALESMAN-NUMBER
023600     ELSE
023700         PERFORM 290-PRINT-SALESMAN-TOTAL-LINE
023800         PERFORM 300-PRINT-BRANCH-TOTAL-LINE.
023900*
024000 210-READ-CUSTOMER-RECORD.
024100*
024200     READ CUSTMST
```

```
6                         10.24.37        07/21/86

024300          AT END
024400              MOVE 'Y' TO CUSTOMER-EOF-SW.
024500*
024600 220-PRINT-CUSTOMER-LINE.
024700*
024800     IF FIRST-RECORD
024900         MOVE CM-BRANCH-NUMBER    TO CL-BRANCH-NO
025000         MOVE CM-SALESMAN-NUMBER  TO CL-SALESMAN-NO
025100         MOVE CM-SALESMAN-KEY     TO SM-SALESMAN-KEY
025200         MOVE 'Y'                 TO RECORD-FOUND-SW
025300         PERFORM 230-READ-SALESMAN-RECORD
025400         IF RECORD-FOUND
025500             MOVE SM-SALESMAN-NAME TO CL-SALESMAN-NAME
025600         ELSE
025700             MOVE 'SALESMAN RECORD NOT FOUND'
025800                 TO CL-SALESMAN-NAME
025900     ELSE
026000         IF CM-SALESMAN-KEY GREATER OLD-SALESMAN-KEY
026100             IF CM-BRANCH-NUMBER GREATER OLD-BRANCH-NUMBER
026200                 MOVE CM-BRANCH-NUMBER    TO CL-BRANCH-NO
026300                 MOVE CM-SALESMAN-NUMBER  TO CL-SALESMAN-NO
026400                 MOVE CM-SALESMAN-KEY     TO SM-SALESMAN-KEY
026500                 MOVE 'Y'                 TO RECORD-FOUND-SW
026600                 PERFORM 230-READ-SALESMAN-RECORD
026700                 IF RECORD-FOUND
026800                     MOVE SM-SALESMAN-NAME TO CL-SALESMAN-NAME
026900                 ELSE
027000                     MOVE 'SALESMAN RECORD NOT FOUND'
027100                         TO CL-SALESMAN-NAME
027200             ELSE
027300                 MOVE SPACE               TO CL-BRANCH-NO
027400                 MOVE CM-SALESMAN-NUMBER  TO CL-SALESMAN-NO
027500                 MOVE CM-SALESMAN-KEY     TO SM-SALESMAN-KEY
027600                 MOVE 'Y'                 TO RECORD-FOUND-SW
027700                 PERFORM 230-READ-SALESMAN-RECORD
027800                 IF RECORD-FOUND
027900                     MOVE SM-SALESMAN-NAME TO CL-SALESMAN-NAME
028000                 ELSE
028100                     MOVE 'SALESMAN RECORD NOT FOUND'
028200                         TO CL-SALESMAN-NAME
028300         ELSE
028400             MOVE SPACE TO CL-SALESMAN-NAME
028500                           CL-SALESMAN-NO
028600                           CL-BRANCH-NO.
028700     MOVE CM-CUSTOMER-NUMBER TO CL-CUSTOMER-NO.
028800     MOVE CM-CUSTOMER-NAME   TO CL-CUSTOMER-NAME.
028900     MOVE CM-SALES-THIS-YTD  TO CL-SALES-THIS-YTD.
029000     MOVE CM-SALES-LAST-YTD  TO CL-SALES-LAST-YTD.
029100     COMPUTE CHANGE-AMOUNT = CM-SALES-THIS-YTD
029200                           - CM-SALES-LAST-YTD.
029300     MOVE CHANGE-AMOUNT TO CL-CHANGE-AMOUNT.
029400     IF CM-SALES-LAST-YTD POSITIVE
029500         COMPUTE CHANGE-PERCENT ROUNDED = CHANGE-AMOUNT
029600                                        / CM-SALES-LAST-YTD
029700                                        * 100
029800         MOVE CHANGE-PERCENT TO CL-CHANGE-PERCENT
029900     ELSE
```

7 10.24.37 07/21/86

```
030000              MOVE 'N/A' TO CL-CHANGE-PERCENT-R.
030100          MOVE CUSTOMER-LINE TO NEXT-REPORT-LINE.
030200          PERFORM 240-PRINT-REPORT-LINE.
030300          MOVE 1 TO SPACE-CONTROL.
030400*
030500 230-READ-SALESMAN-RECORD.
030600*
030700          READ SALESMN
030800              INVALID KEY
030900                  MOVE 'N' TO RECORD-FOUND-SW.
031000*
031100 240-PRINT-REPORT-LINE.
031200*
031300          IF LINE-COUNT GREATER LINES-ON-PAGE
031400              PERFORM 250-PRINT-HEADING-LINES.
031500          MOVE NEXT-REPORT-LINE TO PRINT-AREA.
031600          PERFORM 270-WRITE-REPORT-LINE.
031700*
031800 250-PRINT-HEADING-LINES.
031900*
032000          ADD 1                    TO PAGE-COUNT.
032100          MOVE PAGE-COUNT          TO HDG1-PAGE-NUMBER.
032200          MOVE HEADING-LINE-1 TO PRINT-AREA.
032300          PERFORM 260-WRITE-PAGE-TOP-LINE.
032400          MOVE HEADING-LINE-2 TO PRINT-AREA.
032500          MOVE 1                   TO SPACE-CONTROL.
032600          PERFORM 270-WRITE-REPORT-LINE.
032700          MOVE HEADING-LINE-3 TO PRINT-AREA.
032800          PERFORM 270-WRITE-REPORT-LINE.
032900          MOVE HEADING-LINE-4 TO PRINT-AREA.
033000          MOVE 2                   TO SPACE-CONTROL.
033100          PERFORM 270-WRITE-REPORT-LINE.
033200          MOVE HEADING-LINE-5 TO PRINT-AREA.
033300          MOVE 1                   TO SPACE-CONTROL.
033400          PERFORM 270-WRITE-REPORT-LINE.
033500          MOVE 2                   TO SPACE-CONTROL.
033600*
033700 260-WRITE-PAGE-TOP-LINE.
033800*
033900          WRITE PRINT-AREA
034000              AFTER ADVANCING PAGE.
034100          MOVE 1 TO LINE-COUNT.
034200*
034300 270-WRITE-REPORT-LINE.
034400*
034500          WRITE PRINT-AREA
034600              AFTER ADVANCING SPACE-CONTROL LINES.
034700          ADD SPACE-CONTROL TO LINE-COUNT.
034800*
034900 280-ACCUMULATE-SALES-TOTALS.
035000*
035100          ADD CM-SALES-THIS-YTD TO SALESMAN-TOTAL-THIS-YTD.
035200          ADD CM-SALES-LAST-YTD TO SALESMAN-TOTAL-LAST-YTD.
035300          ADD CM-SALES-THIS-YTD TO BRANCH-TOTAL-THIS-YTD.
035400          ADD CM-SALES-LAST-YTD TO BRANCH-TOTAL-LAST-YTD.
035500          ADD CM-SALES-THIS-YTD TO TOTAL-SALES-THIS-YTD.
035600          ADD CM-SALES-LAST-YTD TO TOTAL-SALES-LAST-YTD.
```

```
8                    10.24.37         07/21/86

035700*
035800 290-PRINT-SALESMAN-TOTAL-LINE.
035900*
036000     MOVE SALESMAN-TOTAL-THIS-YTD TO SL-SALES-THIS-YTD.
036100     MOVE SALESMAN-TOTAL-LAST-YTD TO SL-SALES-LAST-YTD.
036200     COMPUTE CHANGE-AMOUNT = SALESMAN-TOTAL-THIS-YTD
036300                           - SALESMAN-TOTAL-LAST-YTD.
036400     MOVE CHANGE-AMOUNT TO SL-CHANGE-AMOUNT.
036500     IF SALESMAN-TOTAL-LAST-YTD POSITIVE
036600         COMPUTE CHANGE-PERCENT ROUNDED = CHANGE-AMOUNT
036700                                        / SALESMAN-TOTAL-LAST-YTD
036800                                        * 100
036900         MOVE CHANGE-PERCENT TO SL-CHANGE-PERCENT
037000     ELSE
037100         MOVE 'N/A' TO SL-CHANGE-PERCENT-R.
037200     MOVE SALESMAN-TOTAL-LINE TO NEXT-REPORT-LINE.
037300     MOVE 2                   TO SPACE-CONTROL.
037400     PERFORM 240-PRINT-REPORT-LINE.
037500     MOVE ZERO TO SALESMAN-TOTAL-THIS-YTD
037600                  SALESMAN-TOTAL-LAST-YTD.
037700*
037800 300-PRINT-BRANCH-TOTAL-LINE.
037900*
038000     MOVE BRANCH-TOTAL-THIS-YTD TO BL-SALES-THIS-YTD.
038100     MOVE BRANCH-TOTAL-LAST-YTD TO BL-SALES-LAST-YTD.
038200     COMPUTE CHANGE-AMOUNT = BRANCH-TOTAL-THIS-YTD
038300                           - BRANCH-TOTAL-LAST-YTD.
038400     MOVE CHANGE-AMOUNT TO BL-CHANGE-AMOUNT.
038500     IF BRANCH-TOTAL-LAST-YTD POSITIVE
038600         COMPUTE CHANGE-PERCENT ROUNDED = CHANGE-AMOUNT
038700                                        / BRANCH-TOTAL-LAST-YTD
038800                                        * 100
038900         MOVE CHANGE-PERCENT TO BL-CHANGE-PERCENT
039000     ELSE
039100         MOVE 'N/A' TO BL-CHANGE-PERCENT-R.
039200     MOVE BRANCH-TOTAL-LINE TO NEXT-REPORT-LINE.
039300     MOVE 3                 TO SPACE-CONTROL.
039400     PERFORM 240-PRINT-REPORT-LINE.
039500     MOVE ZERO TO BRANCH-TOTAL-THIS-YTD
039600                  BRANCH-TOTAL-LAST-YTD.
039700*
039800 400-PRINT-GRAND-TOTAL-LINE.
039900*
040000     MOVE TOTAL-SALES-THIS-YTD TO GTL-SALES-THIS-YTD.
040100     MOVE TOTAL-SALES-LAST-YTD TO GTL-SALES-LAST-YTD.
040200     COMPUTE CHANGE-AMOUNT = TOTAL-SALES-THIS-YTD
040300                           - TOTAL-SALES-LAST-YTD.
040400     MOVE CHANGE-AMOUNT TO GTL-CHANGE-AMOUNT.
040500     IF TOTAL-SALES-LAST-YTD POSITIVE
040600         COMPUTE CHANGE-PERCENT ROUNDED = CHANGE-AMOUNT
040700                                        / TOTAL-SALES-LAST-YTD
040800                                        * 100
040900         MOVE CHANGE-PERCENT TO GTL-CHANGE-PERCENT
041000     ELSE
041100         MOVE 'N/A' TO GTL-CHANGE-PERCENT-R.
041200     MOVE GRAND-TOTAL-LINE TO NEXT-REPORT-LINE.
041300     PERFORM 240-PRINT-REPORT-LINE.
```

DATE: 07/29/86
TIME: 10:51 AM

MIKE MURACH & ASSOCIATES, INC.

YEAR-TO-DATE SALES REPORT

PAGE: 1
MKTG1200

| BRANCH NO | SALESMAN NO | SALESMAN NAME | CUSTOMER NO | CUSTOMER NAME | SALES THIS YTD | SALES LAST YTD | CHANGE AMOUNT | CHANGE % |
|---|---|---|---|---|---|---|---|---|
| 01 | 01 | LINDA HUGHES | 1 | GEORGE DONALDSON | 456.38 | 235.49 | 220.89 | 93 |
| | | | 2 | BONNIE BRENDT | 52.39 | 425.39 | 373.00- | 87- |
| | | | 5 | YOLANDA PEREZ | 129.38 | 0.00 | 129.38 | 9999 |
| | | | 7 | CELIA PRICE | 0.00 | 253.49 | 253.49- | 100- |
| | | | 12 | GEORGE THOMAS | 1,253.39 | 538.49 | 714.90 | 132 |
| | | | | SALESMAN TOTALS: | 1,891.54 | 1,452.86 | 438.68 | 30 |
| | 02 | WILLIAM YOUNG | 3 | KENNY WRIGHT | 389.38 | 629.39 | 240.01- | 38- |
| | | | 8 | ALEX JONAS | 0.00 | 0.00 | 0.00 | 9999 |
| | | | 13 | JOHN JOHNSON | 35.38 | 74.39 | 39.01- | 52- |
| | | | | SALESMAN TOTALS: | 424.76 | 703.78 | 279.02- | 39- |
| | 03 | ANTHONY LUND | 1 | PATTI LANGE | 545.39 | 235.49 | 309.90 | 131 |
| | | | 4 | INEZ WHITE | 45.29 | 125.39 | 80.10- | 63- |
| | | | 9 | FARRIN LONG | 0.00 | 35.28 | 35.28- | 100- |
| | | | 17 | TINA RANDALL | 37.49 | 58,54 | 21.05- | 35- |
| | | | 19 | THOMAS RICE | 254.39 | 386.39 | 132.00- | 34- |
| | | | | SALESMAN TOTALS: | 882.56 | 841.09 | 41.47 | 4 |
| | 04 | PETER PIPPIN | 4 | LARRY UPTON | 59.38 | 0.00 | 59.38 | 9999 |
| | | | | SALESMAN TOTALS: | 59.38 | 0.00 | 59.38 | 9999 |
| | 05 | TRICIA REED | 7 | LINDA WENDT | 39.49 | 564.39 | 524.90- | 93- |
| | | | 9 | JOHN KELLY | 465.39 | 253.39 | 212.00 | 83 |
| | | | 21 | PATRICIA HARRISON | 49.30 | 69.38 | 20.08- | 28- |
| | | | | SALESMAN TOTALS: | 554.16 | 887.16 | 332.98- | 37- |
| | | | | BRANCH TOTALS: | 3,812.42 | 3,884.89 | 72.47- | 1- |
| 02 | 01 | PAUL JOHNSON | 11 | KELLY FLOYD | 90.39 | 154.29 | 63.90- | 41- |
| | | | 13 | SONYA SIMPSON | 75.39 | 153.29 | 77.90- | 50- |
| | | | 17 | HENRY HART | 89.30 | 523.39 | 434.09- | 82- |
| | | | | SALESMAN TOTALS: | 255.08 | 830.97 | 575.89- | 69- |
| | 02 | GEORGE HARVEY | 2 | FRED RICE | 253.39 | 453.39 | 200.00- | 44- |
| | | | 6 | TOMMY HYDE | 85.39 | 25.39 | 60.00 | 236 |
| | | | 7 | RALPH HARPER | 93.48 | 142.39 | 48.91- | 34- |
| | | | | SALESMAN TOTALS: | 432.26 | 621.17 | 188.91- | 30- |

DATE: 07/29/86 MIKE MURACH & ASSOCIATES, INC. PAGE: 2
TIME: 10:51 AM MKTG1200

YEAR-TO-DATE SALES REPORT

| BRANCH NO | SALESMAN NO | SALESMAN NAME | CUSTOMER NO | CUSTOMER NAME | SALES THIS YTD | SALES LAST YTD | CHANGE AMOUNT | CHANGE % |
|---|---|---|---|---|---|---|---|---|
| | 03 | DONNA TRENT | 12 | SHEILA BARBER | 79.39 | 0.00 | 79.39 | 9999 |
| | | | 24 | HARVEY HILL | 0.00 | 79.49 | 79.49- | 100- |
| | | | 22 | JOHN FRENCH | 94.38 | 143.29 | 48.91- | 34- |
| | | | 23 | SIDNEY TINSLEY | 834.48 | 453.49 | 380.99 | 84 |
| | | | 25 | PATRICK LANGE | 732.38 | 938.29 | 205.91- | 21- |
| | | | | SALESMAN TOTALS: | 1,740.63 | 1,614.56 | 126.07 | 7 |
| | 04 | BETTY KENT | 1 | DOUG ALLEN | 593.49 | 432.53 | 160.96 | 37 |
| | | | 2 | STEVE QUEEN | 634.39 | 243.49 | 390.90 | 160 |
| | | | 5 | PENNY UPTON | 48.39 | 153.29 | 104.90- | 68- |
| | | | 9 | LAURA HARVEY | 49.39 | 253.49 | 204.10- | 80- |
| | | | | SALESMAN TOTALS: | 1,325.66 | 1,082.80 | 242.86 | 22 |
| | | | | BRANCH TOTALS: | 3,753.63 | 4,149.50 | 395.87- | 9- |
| 03 | 01 | CLARK PARKER | 4 | SANDY LOWE | 93.28 | 24.39 | 68.89 | 282 |
| | | | 6 | PAT KEMMER | 78.39 | 293.48 | 215.09- | 73- |
| | | | 9 | CORY WISE | 0.00 | 0.00 | 0.00 | 9999 |
| | | | 11 | RONALD FAYE | 48.39 | 24.39 | 24.00 | 98 |
| | | | 15 | CINDY VANCE | 143.29 | 13.29 | 130.00 | 978 |
| | | | | SALESMAN TOTALS: | 363.35 | 355.55 | 7.80 | 2 |
| | 03 | EDWARD RAND | 7 | RANDALL TREET | 58.39 | 53.39 | 5.00 | 9 |
| | | | 9 | JUDY TRUDEAU | 94.39 | 423.49 | 329.10- | 77- |
| | | | 10 | BARBARA BRICE | 94.38 | 35.49 | 58.89 | 165 |
| | | | 14 | PETER NASH | 745.29 | 253.49 | 491.80 | 194 |
| | | | 17 | ALAN WHITE | 953.39 | 534.39 | 419.00 | 78 |
| | | | 25 | SIDNEY POTTER | 84.39 | 35.49 | 48.90 | 137 |
| | | | | SALESMAN TOTALS: | 2,030.23 | 1,335.74 | 694.49 | 51 |
| | 04 | THOMAS TINKER | 11 | HAROLD SMITH | 49.39 | 243.49 | 194.10- | 79- |
| | | | 15 | CAROL BAKER | 475.39 | 243.49 | 231.90 | 95 |
| | | | 21 | LINDSEY GREEN | 74.39 | 243.54 | 169.15- | 69- |
| | | | | SALESMAN TOTALS: | 599.17 | 730.52 | 131.35- | 17- |
| | 05 | LARRY DARREN | 3 | DONALD NANCE | 0.00 | 253.49 | 253.49- | 100- |
| | | | 8 | PAULA JOHNSON | 74.39 | 253.48 | 179.09- | 70- |
| | | | 9 | TIMOTHY SMITH | 245.39 | 0.00 | 245.39 | 9999 |
| | | | 12 | STEVE SANDERS | 83.29 | 43.29 | 40.00 | 92 |
| | | | 17 | SALLY FRY | 89.39 | 35.49 | 53.90 | 151 |

DATE: 07/29/86 MIKE MURACH & ASSOCIATES, INC. PAGE: 3
TIME: 10:51 AM MKTG1200

YEAR-TO-DATE SALES REPORT

| BRANCH NO | SALESMAN NO | SALESMAN NAME | CUSTOMER NO | CUSTOMER NAME | SALES THIS YTD | SALES LAST YTD | CHANGE AMOUNT | CHANGE % |
|---|---|---|---|---|---|---|---|---|
| | | | 19 | MANNY MANFRED | 384.39 | 243.49 | 140.90 | 57 |
| | | | | SALESMAN TOTALS: | 876.85 | 829.24 | 47.61 | 5 |
| | | | | BRANCH TOTALS: | 3,869.60 | 3,251.05 | 618.55 | 19 |
| 04 | 05 | SALESMAN RECORD NOT FOUND | 12 | TYRONE WHITE | 253.39 | 429.38 | 175.99- | 40- |
| | | | | SALESMAN TOTALS: | 253.39 | 429.38 | 175.99- | 40- |
| | | | | BRANCH TOTALS: | 253.39 | 429.38 | 175.99- | 40- |
| | | | | GRAND TOTALS: | 11,689.04 | 11,714.82 | 25.78- | 0 |

Appendix C

# One chapter-by-chapter case study

The case study that follows asks you to develop one program after you finish chapter 3 in the text. Then, for chapters 4 through 7, you are asked to enhance this program in several different ways. By the time you code and test all the enhancements, you will have coded about 480 lines of code. And you will have used most of the COBOL elements described in this book.

You should be able to do all the tasks required by this case study, because the required programs closely parallel the programs described in chapters 3 through 7. Also, you are given the structure chart for the version of the program required for chapter 3.

After you complete this case study, your instructor should assign one or more of the case studies in appendix D. The programs required by these case studies will be more difficult because they won't be like the programs in the text. Also, you will have to design them yourself. If you are able to do these case studies without too much difficulty, you most likely have enough programming aptitude to become a programmer in industry.

| Program: CUST5230 Produce sales report | Page: 1 |
|---|---|
| Designer: MM | Date: 4-16-86 |

Input/output specifications

| File | Description | Use |
|---|---|---|
| CUSTMST | Customer master file | Input |
| SLSRPT | Print file: Sales report | Output |
| CUSTEXT | Customer extension file (used only for the tasks in chapters 6 and 7) | Input |

Process specifications

This program prepares a year-to-date (YTD) sales report from a sequential file of customer records. The records are in sequence by customer key and the report should be printed in the same sequence. The program should print headings at the top of each page of the report and skip to a new page after 55 detail lines have been printed on a page.

This program is designed so you can add code to it as you proceed through the book. When you complete chapter 3, for example, you aren't expected to be able to write a program that produces the shaded portions of the print chart. As a result, your program should only produce the unshaded data. Then, when you complete chapter 4, you'll be able to enhance your program so it produces the first two heading lines and the first two total lines. When you complete chapter 5, you'll be able to enhance your program so it produces the data in the column headed YTD NET SALES and in the third total line. And so on.

**Compiler dependent code**

Before you can write this program, you need to find out how to code the following on your system:

The program name in the Identification Division
The Configuration Section
The system names in the SELECT statements for the disk file(s)
The system name in the SELECT statement for the printer file
The FD statement for the disk file(s)
The FD statement for the printer file
Quotation marks (single or double)

**File identification**

On all systems, you will have to identify the files used by your programs in order to test them. Unless you're told otherwise, you can assume that the names for the two disk files used in this case study are CUSTMST and CUSTEXT. However, you may also have to get other identifying information, such as what volume they're on, what library they're in, or what catalog is used to locate them.

**Record layout for the customer master record (CUSTMST)**

| Data name | Picture |
|---|---|
| CM-CUST-KEY | X(6) |
| CM-CUST-TYPE-CODE | X |
| CM-CUST-NAME | X(31) |
| CM-CUST-ADDRESS | X(31) |
| CM-CUST-CITY | X(18) |
| CM-CUST-STATE | X(2) |
| CM-CUST-ZIP-5 | 9(5) |
| CM-CUST-ZIP-EXT | 9(4) |
| CM-YTD-GROSS-SALES | 9(7)V99 |
| CM-YTD-GROSS-SALES-UNITS | 9(5) |
| CM-YTD-RETURNS | 9(5)V99 |
| CM-YTD-RETURNS-UNITS | 9(5) |

**COBOL COPY member for the customer extension record (CUSTEXT)**

```
 01  CUSTOMER-EXTENSION-RECORD.
*
     05  CE-CUST-KEY                 PIC X(6).
     05  CE-MONTHLY-SALES-DOLLARS OCCURS 12 TIMES
                                  INDEXED BY CE-MONTH-INDEX.
         10  CE-GROSS-SALES          PIC S9(7)V99.
         10  CE-RETURNS              PIC S9(5)V99.
         10  CE-NET-SALES            PIC S9(7)V99.
*
```

Document name *Sales by customer* Date *4/16/86*

Program name *CUST523Ø* Designer *MM*

| Record Name | Line | Print layout |
|---|---|---|
| Heading line 1 (C4) | 1 | DATE: MM/DD/YY PAGE: ZZ9 |
| Heading line 2 (C4) | 2 | TIME: HH:MM XX YEAR-TO-DATE SALES BY CUSTOMER ($99,999 OR MORE) CUST523Ø |
| | 3 | |
| Heading line 3 | 4 | KEY CUSTOMER NAME TYPE YTD SALES YTD RETURNS YTD NET SALES LAST YTD SALES % CHG FILE MAINTENANCE |
| | 5 | |
| Detail lines | 6 | XXXXXX XXXXXXXXXXXXXXXXXXXXXXXXXXXXXX X Z,ZZZ,ZZZ.99 ZZ,ZZZ.99 Z,ZZZ,ZZZ.99 Z,ZZZ,ZZZ.99CR +999 INVALID STATE CODE |
| | 7 | XXXXXX X——X X Z,ZZZ,ZZZ.99 ZZ,ZZZ.99 Z,ZZZ,ZZZ.99 Z,ZZZ,ZZZ.99CR -999 INVALID ZIP CODE |
| | 8 | XXXXXX X——X X Z,ZZZ,ZZZ.99 ZZ,ZZZ.99 Z,ZZZ,ZZZ.99 Z,ZZZ,ZZZ.99CR +999 NO EXTENSION RECORD |
| | 9 | XXXXXX X——X X Z,ZZZ,ZZZ.99 ZZ,ZZZ.99 Z,ZZZ,ZZZ.99 Z,ZZZ,ZZZ.99CR -999 |
| | 10 | |
| Total line 1 (C4) | 11 | RECORDS IN CUSTOMER FILE = ZZ,ZZZ ZZZ,ZZZ,ZZZ.99 Z,ZZZ,ZZZ.99 ZZZ,ZZZ,ZZZ.99 ZZZ,ZZZ,ZZZ.99 +999 ZZZZZ MAINT RECORDS |
| Total line 2 (C4) | 12 | RECORDS IN LISTING = ZZ,ZZZ |
| Total line 3 (C5) | 13 | AVG. NET SALES/CUSTOMER = $Z,ZZZ,ZZZ |

Chapter 5 (YTD NET SALES)

Chapter 6 (LAST YTD SALES through FILE MAINTENANCE)

## DEVELOPMENT TASKS BY CHAPTER

### Chapter 3 An introduction to COBOL: The basic elements

When you finish chapter 3 in the text, develop a program that produces the report represented by the unshaded portion of the print chart. You'll find a structure chart for this program below. The module numbers used in this chart will make it easy for you to add modules to it as you do the tasks required for the other chapters.

Your instructor will show you how to enter your program into your system. Then, you'll need to learn the procedures for compiling and testing a program on your system as introduced in chapter 8. Next, when you get your first compiler output, you'll want to read chapter 9 to learn how to read the output and correct the diagnostics. Finally, when you test your program, you'll want to read chapter 10 to learn how to solve your debugging problems.

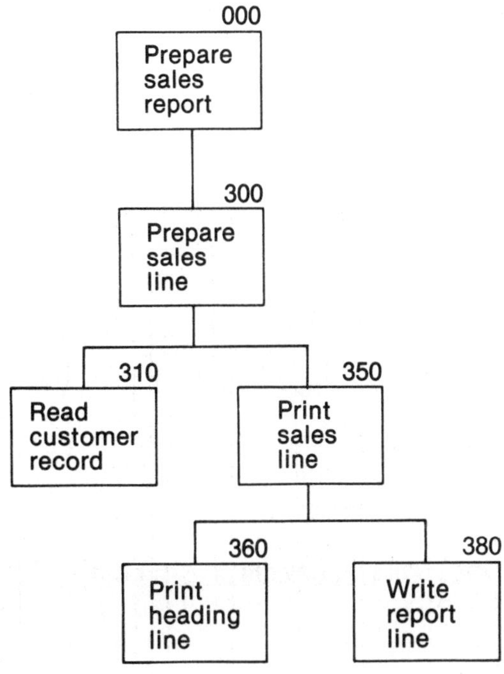

## Chapter 4 Building on the COBOL basics

The tasks for this chapter ask you to enhance the program you developed for chapter 3. Before you make any coding modifications, though, be sure to modify the structure chart you used for the program of chapter 3. When you modify it, try to make the structure and the names of the modules consistent with those used in the program in chapter 4 of the text.

When you complete the program enhancements for this chapter, your program should:

1. Only print a customer line in the body of the report when the customer's type code is R. Valid type codes are R (for retail), W (for wholesale), and S (for special).

2. Print the first two heading lines shown on the print chart. However, nothing should be printed in print positions 74-90 of heading line 2.

3. Print the first two total lines shown on the print chart. The first total line should be blank from position 69 on. The second total line should indicate the number of customers listed on the listing (that is, the number of retail customers).

4. Display this message when the program ends normally:

   ```
   CUST5230   I   1   NORMAL EOJ
   ```

   If you don't already know, find out how to use the DISPLAY statement on your system and find out how it operates. Does it display a message on your screen or does it print a line on the printer?

5. Use condition names and figurative constants whenever appropriate.

6. If you don't already know, find out what the proper usages are for numeric fields on your system. Then, code efficient usages for all of the fields in the program that are operated upon arithmetically or compared numerically. Whenever appropriate, code the usages at the group level.

7. Use ON SIZE ERROR whenever it is appropriate.

## Chapter 5 COBOL elements the professionals use

The tasks for this chapter ask you to enhance the program you developed for chapter 4. Before you make any coding modifications, though, be sure to modify the structure chart you used for the program of chapter 4. When you modify it, try to make your structural changes in a way that is consistent with the techniques used in the text.

When you complete the program enhancements for this chapter, your program should:

1. Only print a customer line in the body of the report when the customer type code is R and the customer's net year-to-date sales are over a certain dollar volume. The minimum dollar volume is the current month minus one times $2000. For example, the minimum dollar volume is $14,000 when the current month is 8 ((8 – 1) × $2000). When the current month is 1, the minimum should be $24,000.

2. Print the data in print positions 74-90 of heading line 2. The number in print positions 75-81 is the minimum dollar volume described in requirement 1. It should be printed with a floating dollar sign.

3. Print the year-to-date net sales column of the report. YTD net sales is calculated by subtracting YTD returns from YTD sales.

4. Print the third total line of the report. Average net sales per customer is YTD net sales divided by the number of records printed in the listing. The result should be rounded to the nearest whole number and printed with a floating dollar sign.

5. Use the COPY member that is available for the customer master record. Assume that it is named CUSTMST, unless your instructor specifies another name. Depending on the defaults for your system, you may have to find out what COPY library this COPY member is in.

6. Use the two subprograms that are available to get the system date and the system time. They are named SYSDATE and SYSTIME. SYSDATE returns the date as a six-byte field in the form MMDDYY. SYSTIME returns the time as formatted in heading line 2. Depending on the defaults for your system, you may have to find out what subprogram library these subprograms are in.

7. Use the following whenever appropriate: READ INTO, WRITE FROM, COMPUTE, compound conditions, and ON SIZE ERROR.

## Chapter 6 Completing the professional subset

In some classes, your instructor may not assign the tasks for both topics 1 and 2 in this chapter. As a result, the tasks in this chapter are divided by topic. You can do the tasks for either topic or both topics, but if you do the tasks for both, you should do them in sequence. For both topics, you enhance the program you developed for chapter 5.

### Topic 1 How to handle one-level tables using indexes

A COPY member is available in one of the COPY libraries. You can assume it is named STTABLE, unless your instructor gives you some other name for it. It contains 51 field descriptions, one for each of the 50 states plus the District of Columbia. This COPY member starts like this:

```
 01   STATE-TABLE-VALUES.
*
      05   FILLER   PIC X(12)   VALUE 'AL3500036999'.
      05   FILLER   PIC X(12)   VALUE 'AK9950099999'.
      05   FILLER   PIC X(12)   VALUE 'AZ8500086599'.
```

It continues with one field description for each of the other 47 states and the District of Columbia.

The first two characters in each value are the state code for the state. The next five characters are the lowest valid zip code for the state. The last five characters are the highest valid zip code for the state. As a result, these values can be used to check the validity of the state codes and the validity of the five-digit zip codes used in an address.

For a state code to be valid, it must match one of the 51 state code entries. For a zip code to be valid, it must be equal to or greater than the first zip code value given for a state, and it must be equal to or less than the second zip code given.

Using this table, enhance your program to produce the data in print positions 112-130 of the print chart. To produce this data, the program should first check each record's state code for validity. If it's invalid, the program should print INVALID STATE CODE in the file maintenance area; in this case, the program shouldn't do the validity checking for the zip code. But if the state code is valid, the program should check the zip code. If it's invalid, the program should print INVALID ZIP CODE in the file maintenance area of the report; if it's valid, the program shouldn't print anything in this area.

If a state or zip code for a record is invalid, the program should add one to a count of records that need file maintenance. Then, at the end of the program, this count should be printed in positions 112-130 of total line 1. However, if none of the records need maintenance, nothing should print in these print positions.

Be sure to modify the structure chart you used for the program of chapter 5 before you make any coding modifications. Also, try to make your structural changes in a way that is consistent with the techniques used in the text.

## Topic 2 How to read records in indexed files

For the tasks in this topic, a customer extension file (CUSTEXT) is available. This file has indexed organization. For each record in the customer master file, there should be a record with a matching key in the extension file.

The format for the records in the extension file is given by the COBOL record description in the program specifications. This record description is available as a COPY member that you can assume is named CUSTEXT, unless your instructor specifies some other name for it.

If you review the record description, you can see that the customer extension file contains the monthly sales data for a customer from the previous year with one group of sales fields for each of the twelve months in the year. The first group contains the sales data for January of the previous year; the second group contains the data for February; and so on. This data is in a separate file because it is only needed for occasional reports.

The extension file is used to produce the data in print positions 87-109 of the print chart. To produce this data, your program must read the extension record that matches a customer master record. Then, your program should accumulate the YTD net sales value by adding the monthly net sales values from January through the current month minus 1. If, for example, the current month is 09, the program should accumulate the net sales values for groups 1 through 8 in the extension record. However, if the current month is 1, the program should accumulate the sales for groups 1 through 12. This assumes that a report is based on data that is accurate to the end of the previous month.

To figure the value for the % CHG field, use the following formula:

$$\text{\% of change} = \left(\frac{\text{YTD net sales} - \text{Last YTD sales}}{\text{Last YTD sales}}\right) \times 100$$

You should realize that if last YTD sales is negative, you'll end up with a negative percent of change, which is misleading. So the program should move all nines into the percent field whenever this happens.

If your program can't find a matching extension record for a customer master record, it should print NO EXTENSION RECORD in print positions 112-130 of the detail line. In this case, print positions 89-109 in the detail line should be blank.

When an extension record can't be found, the program should add one to a count of records that need maintenance. Then, at the end of the program, this count should be printed in print positions 112-130 of the first total line. If no records require maintenance, these print positions should be blank.

If you've done the tasks for topic 1 of this chapter, it's possible that a record may have invalid state or zip codes as well as no extension record. In this case, only the first maintenance message should be printed in positions 112-130 for a record. Also, the maintenance count should only be increased by one for each record, not one for each type of error condition.

If you want to make this program more complicated, assume that two maintenance messages should be printed for a record if it has both an invalid code and no extension record. In this case, the second message should be printed in a second line for the customer. The second line should have blanks in positions 1-111 with the second maintenance message in positions 112-130. Although this aspect of the program is optional, your instructor may require it.

The extension file can be read by this program using either sequential or random access. If your instructor doesn't specify one method or the other, code the program so it accesses the extension file on a random basis. Then, if you have the time, code it so it accesses the file sequentially.

Before you start to code, be sure to modify the structure chart for your last version of the program so it provides for the new requirements. The structure should be the same whether you access the extension file sequentially or randomly.

## Chapter 7 The 1985 COBOL elements for structured programming

If a 1985 COBOL compiler is available to you, revise your program so it uses the 1985 COBOL elements whenever appropriate. Start by modifying the structure chart, because the code can have an effect on the structure. Then, modify the code, but only use the 1985 COBOL elements when you think they improve the clarity of your code.

Appendix D

# Four more case studies

Appendix C presents a case study that asks you to develop one program after you finish chapter 3 in the text. Then, you are asked to enhance this program after you complete chapters 4 through 7 of the text. By the time you complete that case study, you will have used most of the COBOL elements described in this book. However, you will have completed only one type of report preparation program with only one type of structure and logic.

This appendix presents four more case studies. Each of these requires you to develop a report preparation program with a different type of structure and logic. All but the first of these case study programs are considerably more difficult than the program required by the case study in appendix C. Furthermore, you have to design all of these case study programs by yourself. If you are able to do these case studies without too much difficulty, you should be able to develop most report preparation programs and you probably have the programming aptitude required of a professional programmer in industry.

You can do case studies 1 and 2 in this appendix any time after you complete chapter 4 in the text. You can do case studies 3 and 4 after you complete chapter 6. Although the program required by case study 1 has a simple structure and logic, the structure and logic for the programs required by the next three case studies is much more complicated. As a result, we recommend that you read chapters 11 and 12 before you start to design and develop the programs for case studies 2, 3, and 4.

In general, the four case studies are in sequence by degree of difficulty, from the easiest to the hardest. As a result, if your time is limited and you're confident that you can develop the programs for case studies 1 and 2, you can skip them. Then, if you can develop the programs for case studies 3 and 4, you will have proven that you have mastered the material presented in this text. If you are working under the direction of an instructor or advisor, of course, you should get permission to skip the first two case studies.

Within each case study, there are two levels of difficulty. If you start by developing each case study at the lower level, you can modify it later on to provide for the requirements of the higher level. On the other hand, if you're confident that you can develop the program at the higher level from the start, there's no reason to develop it at the lower level.

Test files should be available for each of the case studies, but you will have to get the identifying information for each of the files from your instructor. Similarly, COPY members should be available for the record descriptions provided with the program specifications for each case study, but you will have to get the identifying information for each of the COPY members from your instructor. Once you complete chapter 5, you should use the available COPY members in your programs.

## Case study D-1

| Program: | CASED1 Prepare honors listing | Page: | 1 |
|---|---|---|---|
| Designer: | MM | Date: | 5-14-86 |

### Input/output specifications

| File | Description | Use |
|---|---|---|
| STUDMST | Student master file | Input |
| HONORS | Print file: Honors listing | Output |

### Process specifications

This program prepares an honors listing from a sequential file of student master records. The records are in sequence by student id within class standing. The honors listing includes those students with a grade point average (GPA) of 3.5 or higher. The program should print headings at the top of each page of the report and skip to a new page after 55 detail lines have been printed on a page.

To calculate the grade point average for each student, divide the total grade points by the number of units completed and round to two decimal places.

If a student has a 3.8 average or higher, he or she achieves the special honor of "ranking scholar." As a result, the words RANKING SCHOLAR should be printed in positions 48-62 on the student's line. Otherwise, these print positions should be blank.

#### Difficulty level 1

Write your program so it only prints an honors listing for the senior class. In this case, your report will appear as it's shown on the print chart including the shaded word SENIORS.

#### Difficulty level 2

Write your program so it prints an honors listing for each class: freshman, sophomore, junior, and senior. For the lower classes, the shaded word SENIORS in the print chart should be replaced with the words FRESHMEN, SOPHOMORES, and JUNIORS. For the senior class, it should print as SENIORS. The honors listing for each class should start on a new page that is numbered 1. To prepare all four listings, your program should read the student master file only once.

**COPY member for CASED1**

```
 01  STUDENT-MASTER-RECORD.
*
     05  SM-STUDENT-ID                        PIC 9(9).
     05  SM-STUDENT-STATUS                    PIC X.
         88  ENROLLED                         VALUE 'E'.
         88  INACTIVE                         VALUE 'I'.
     05  SM-STUDENT-NAME-AND-ADDRESS.
         10  SM-STUDENT-NAME                  PIC X(25).
         10  SM-STUDENT-ADDRESS               PIC X(25).
         10  SM-STUDENT-CITY                  PIC X(11).
         10  SM-STUDENT-STATE                 PIC XX.
         10  SM-STUDENT-ZIP-CODE              PIC 9(5).
         10  SM-STUDENT-ZIP-CODE-EXT          PIC 9(4).
     05  SM-STUDENT-PROGRESS-SUMMARY.
         10  SM-CLASS-STANDING                PIC 9.
             88  FRESHMAN                     VALUE 1.
             88  SOPHOMORE                    VALUE 2.
             88  JUNIOR                       VALUE 3.
             88  SENIOR                       VALUE 4.
         10  SM-UNITS-COMPLETED               PIC 9(3).
         10  SM-TOTAL-GRADE-POINTS            PIC 9(3).
         10  SM-UNITS-IN-PROGRESS             PIC 9(3).
```

Document name *Honors listing* Date *5/14/86*

Program name *CASED1* Designer *MM*

Record Name

```
 1 DATE:    99/99/99                                   PAGE: ZZ9
 2 TIME:    99:99 XX                                   CASED1
 3
 4 HONORS LISTING:  SENIORS
 5
 6 STUDENT ID   STUDENT NAME                GPA    SPECIAL HONORS
 7
 8 999-99-9999  XXXXXXXXXXXXXXXXXXXXXXXXX   9.99   XXXXXXXXXXXXXXX
 9 999-99-9999  XXXXXXXXXXXXXXXXXXXXXXXXX   9.99   XXXXXXXXXXXXXXX
10
11 ZZZZ9 STUDENTS IN CLASS     100.0 %
12 ZZZZ9 STUDENTS WITH HONORS   ZZ.9 %
13 ZZZZ9 RANKING SCHOLARS       ZZ.9 %
14
15
16
17
```

## Case study D-2

| Program: | CASED2 Prepare registration summary | Page: | 1 |
|---|---|---|---|
| Designer: | MM | Date: | 5-14-86 |

### Input/output specifications

| File | Description | Use |
|---|---|---|
| STUDMST | Student master file | Input |
| CRSEREG | Course registration file | Input |
| REGSUM | Print file: Registration summary | Output |

### Process specifications

This program prepares a registration summary from two sequential files. The student master file is in sequence by student ID. The course registration file is in sequence by course key within student ID. After printing the data from each student's master record and course registration records, the program should print a total line for the student that shows the total number of credits that the student is taking.

If a course registration record isn't matched by a student master record with the same student ID, the program should still print the course registration data. But it should print NO MASTER RECORD in the area for the student's name. On the other hand, it's okay for a student master record to be unmatched by course registration records, so unmatched master records should be ignored.

#### Difficulty level 1

Write your program so it prints only the unshaded data in the print chart. In other words, only the student's ID and name are taken from the student master record.

#### Difficulty level 2

Write your program so it prints both the shaded and unshaded data in the print chart. This makes the program more complicated because sometimes a student will take less than three courses. Then, the program prints less than three lines related to the course registration records for the student, but it must still print three lines related to the student's master record data (name and address). In a case like this, the total line for a student can be printed after the last address line for the student.

**COPY members for CASED2**

```
 01   STUDENT-MASTER-RECORD.
*
      05   SM-STUDENT-ID                          PIC 9(9).
      05   SM-STUDENT-STATUS                      PIC X.
           88   ENROLLED                          VALUE 'E'.
           88   INACTIVE                          VALUE 'I'.
      05   SM-STUDENT-NAME-AND-ADDRESS.
           10   SM-STUDENT-NAME                   PIC X(25).
           10   SM-STUDENT-ADDRESS                PIC X(25).
           10   SM-STUDENT-CITY                   PIC X(11).
           10   SM-STUDENT-STATE                  PIC XX.
           10   SM-STUDENT-ZIP-CODE               PIC 9(5).
           10   SM-STUDENT-ZIP-CODE-EXT           PIC 9(4).
      05   SM-STUDENT-PROGRESS-SUMMARY.
           10   SM-CLASS-STANDING                 PIC 9.
                88   FRESHMAN                     VALUE 1.
                88   SOPHOMORE                    VALUE 2.
                88   JUNIOR                       VALUE 3.
                88   SENIOR                       VALUE 4.
           10   SM-UNITS-COMPLETED                PIC 9(3).
           10   SM-TOTAL-GRADE-POINTS             PIC 9(3).
           10   SM-UNITS-IN-PROGRESS              PIC 9(3).
```

```
 01   COURSE-REGISTRATION-RECORD.
*
      05   CR-COURSE-KEY.
           10   CR-DEPARTMENT-CODE                PIC X(4).
           10   CR-COURSE-NUMBER                  PIC 9(3).
           10   CR-SECTION-NUMBER                 PIC 9(2).
      05   CR-COURSE-IDENTIFICATION.
           10   CR-COURSE-TITLE                   PIC X(20).
           10   CR-COURSE-START-DATE.
                15   CR-COURSE-START-MONTH        PIC 99.
                15   CR-COURSE-START-YEAR         PIC 99.
           10   CR-COURSE-UNITS                   PIC 9.
           10   CR-COURSE-DAYS                    PIC 9(3).
      05   CR-REGISTRATION-DATA.
           10   CR-TEACHER-NUMBER                 PIC 9(3).
           10   CR-STUDENT-ID                     PIC 9(9).
      05   CR-GRADING-DATA.
           10   CR-6-WEEKS-GRADE                  PIC X.
           10   CR-12-WEEKS-GRADE                 PIC X.
           10   CR-FINAL-EXAM-GRADE               PIC X.
           10   CR-SEMESTER-GRADE                 PIC X.
```

Document name *Registration summary* Date *5/14/86*

Program name *CASE02* Designer *MM*

Record Name

```
1  DATE:    99/99/99                                                                                   PAGE: ZZ9
2  TIME:    99:99 XX                                                                                   CASE02
3                                                REGISTRATION SUMMARY
4
5                                                ---COURSE ID---
6  STUDENT ID       STUDENT NAME & ADDRESS       DEPT COURSE SEC       COURSE TITLE                    UNITS
7
8  999-99-9999      XXXXXXXXXXXXXXXXXXXXXXXXX    XXXX   999    99      XXXXXXXXXXXXXXXXXXXXXXXXX        9
9                   XXXXXXXXXXXXXXXXXXXXXXXXX    XXXX   999    99      XXXXXXXXXXXXXXXXXXXXXXXXX        9
10                  XXXXXXXXXXXXX XX 99999-9999  XXXX   999    99      XXXXXXXXXXXXXXXXXXXXXXXXX        9
11                                               XXXX   999    99      XXXXXXXXXXXXXXXXXXXXXXXXX        9
12                                               XXXX   999    99      XXXXXXXXXXXXXXXXXXXXXXXXX        9
13                                                                                                     Z9 *
14
15 999-99-9999      XXXXXXXXXXXXXXXXXXXXXXXXX    XXXX   999    99      XXXXXXXXXXXXXXXXXXXXXXXXX        9
16                  XXXXXXXXXXXXXXXXXXXXXXXXX    XXXX   999    99      XXXXXXXXXXXXXXXXXXXXXXXXX        9
17                  XXXXXXXXXXXXX XX 99999-9999                                                        Z9 *
18
19
20 ZZZZ9 STUDENTS REGISTERED                                           TOTAL UNITS  ZZZ,ZZ9
21
22
23
```

## Case study D-3

| **Program:** | CASED3 Prepare grading summary | **Page:** | 1 |
|---|---|---|---|
| **Designer:** | MM | **Date:** | 5-14-86 |

### Input/output specifications

| File | Description | Use |
|---|---|---|
| TEACHER | Teacher master file | Input |
| CRSEREG | Course registration file | Input |
| GRADSUM | Print file: Grading summary | Output |

### Process specifications

This program prepares a grading summary from one sequential file and one indexed file. The course registration file is a sequential file in sequence by course number within teacher number within department code. The teacher file is an indexed file that can be read in sequence by teacher key, but it can also be accessed randomly by teacher key.

The grading summary is a report with three levels of summary lines plus a final summary line. The first level is by course; the lines at this level show the average grade for each course taught by a teacher. In other words, each course line printed for a teacher is actually a summary line representing one or more section records for that course. The second level is by teacher; the lines at this level show the average grade given by each teacher for all courses. The third level is by department; the lines at this level show the average grade given in the department. To get the numeric values needed for the average grade fields, the program must convert the letter grades to grade points, using the following scale:

A = 4 grade points
B = 3 grade points
C = 2 grade points
D = 1 grade point
F = 0 grade points

The program should print headings at the top of each page of the report, and it should skip to a new page after 55 lines have been printed on a page. However, it shouldn't skip to a new page until all of the lines for any one teacher have been printed.

To print the department name for a department, the program must look up the department in a table. This table is available in a COPY member named DEPTTAB so you can copy it into your program. As you can see in the specifications, this table isn't in sequence by department code.

To print the teacher name in the report, the program must access the teacher's master record. This access should be done on a random basis.

| Program: CASED3 Prepare grading summary | Page: 2 |
| --- | --- |
| Designer: MM | Date: 5-14-86 |

**Process specifications**

**Difficulty level 1**

Write your program so it prints both the shaded and unshaded data in the print chart. In other words, the report won't be printed with group indication.

**Difficulty level 2**

Write your program so it prints only the unshaded data in the print chart. This means the program will print the report with group indication at both the department and teacher levels.

**COPY members for CASED3**

```
 01   TEACHER-MASTER-RECORD.
*
      05   TM-TEACHER-KEY.
           10   TM-DEPARTMENT-CODE                PIC X(4).
           10   TM-TEACHER-NUMBER                 PIC 9(3).
      05   TM-TEACHER-NAME-AND-ADDRESS.
           10   TM-TEACHER-NAME                   PIC X(24).
           10   TM-TEACHER-ADDRESS                PIC X(24).
           10   TM-TEACHER-CITY                   PIC X(11).
           10   TM-TEACHER-STATE                  PIC XX.
           10   TM-TEACHER-ZIP-CODE               PIC 9(5).
           10   TM-TEACHER-ZIP-CODE-EXT           PIC 9(4).
      05   TM-TEACHER-DATA.
           10   TM-STARTING-DATE                  PIC 9(6).
           10   TM-BIRTH-DATE                     PIC 9(6).
           10   TM-SEX                            PIC X.
                88   MALE                         VALUE 'M'.
                88   FEMALE                       VALUE 'F'.
           10   TM-MARITAL-STATUS                 PIC X.
                88   SINGLE                       VALUE 'S'.
                88   MARRIED                      VALUE 'M'.


 01   COURSE-REGISTRATION-RECORD.
*
      05   CR-COURSE-KEY.
           10   CR-DEPARTMENT-CODE                PIC X(4).
           10   CR-COURSE-NUMBER                  PIC 9(3).
           10   CR-SECTION-NUMBER                 PIC 9(2).
      05   CR-COURSE-IDENTIFICATION.
           10   CR-COURSE-TITLE                   PIC X(20).
           10   CR-COURSE-START-DATE.
                15   CR-COURSE-START-MONTH        PIC 99.
                15   CR-COURSE-START-YEAR         PIC 99.
           10   CR-COURSE-UNITS                   PIC 9.
           10   CR-COURSE-DAYS                    PIC 9(3).
      05   CR-REGISTRATION-DATA.
           10   CR-TEACHER-NUMBER                 PIC 9(3).
           10   CR-STUDENT-ID                     PIC 9(9).
      05   CR-GRADING-DATA.
           10   CR-6-WEEKS-GRADE                  PIC X.
           10   CR-12-WEEKS-GRADE                 PIC X.
           10   CR-FINAL-EXAM-GRADE               PIC X.
           10   CR-SEMESTER-GRADE                 PIC X.
```

**COPY members for CASED3 (continued)**

```
 01   DEPARTMENT-NAMES.
*
      05   FILLER   PIC  X(24)   VALUE 'ENG ENGLISH              '.
      05   FILLER   PIC  X(24)   VALUE 'MATHMATHEMATICS          '.
      05   FILLER   PIC  X(24)   VALUE 'BIOLBIOLOGY              '.
      05   FILLER   PIC  X(24)   VALUE 'CENGCIVIL ENGINEERING    '.
      05   FILLER   PIC  X(24)   VALUE 'MENGMECHANICAL ENGR.     '.
      05   FILLER   PIC  X(24)   VALUE 'NENGNUCLEAR ENGINEERING  '.
      05   FILLER   PIC  X(24)   VALUE 'EENGELECTRICAL ENGR.     '.
      05   FILLER   PIC  X(24)   VALUE 'ZOO ZOOLOGY              '.
      05   FILLER   PIC  X(24)   VALUE 'BOT BOTANY               '.
      05   FILLER   PIC  X(24)   VALUE 'CLITCOMPARATIVE LIT.     '.
      05   FILLER   PIC  X(24)   VALUE 'PSCIPOLITICAL SCIENCE    '.
      05   FILLER   PIC  X(24)   VALUE 'PSYCPSYCHOLOGY           '.
      05   FILLER   PIC  X(24)   VALUE 'SOC SOCIOLOGY            '.
      05   FILLER   PIC  X(24)   VALUE 'CS  COMPUTER SCIENCE     '.
      05   FILLER   PIC  X(24)   VALUE 'BUS BUSINESS             '.
      05   FILLER   PIC  X(24)   VALUE 'ACCTACCOUNTING           '.
      05   FILLER   PIC  X(24)   VALUE 'JOURJOURNALISM           '.
      05   FILLER   PIC  X(24)   VALUE 'CHEMCHEMISTRY            '.
      05   FILLER   PIC  X(24)   VALUE 'LINGLINGUISTICS          '.
      05   FILLER   PIC  X(24)   VALUE 'ECONECONOMICS            '.
      05   FILLER   PIC  X(24)   VALUE 'SPANSPANISH              '.
      05   FILLER   PIC  X(24)   VALUE 'GEOGGEOGRAPHY            '.
      05   FILLER   PIC  X(24)   VALUE 'HLTHHEALTH EDUCATION     '.
      05   FILLER   PIC  X(24)   VALUE 'HISTHISTORY              '.
      05   FILLER   PIC  X(24)   VALUE 'MKTGMARKETING            '.
*
 01   DEPARTMENT-NAME-TABLE REDEFINES DEPARTMENT-NAMES.
*
      05   DEPARTMENT-GROUP          OCCURS 25 TIMES
                                     INDEXED BY DEPT-INDEX.
           10   DEPARTMENT-CODE      PIC  X(4).
           10   DEPARTMENT-NAME      PIC  X(20).
```

Document name Grading summary Date 5/14/86

Program name CASED3 Designer MM

Record Name

```
DATE:     99/99/99                                                                       PAGE: ZZ9
TIME:     99:99 XX                                                                       CASED3
                          GRADING SUMMARY BY TEACHER WITHIN DEPARTMENT

DEPT                     TEACHER                          COURSE                         AVG
CODE  DEPARTMENT NAME      NO.   TEACHER NAME               NO.   COURSE TITLE           GRADE

XXXX  XXXXXXXXXXXXXXXXXXXX  999  XXXXXXXXXXXXXXXXXXXXXXXXX  999   XXXXXXXXXXXXXXXXXXXXX  9.99
XXXX  X------------------X  999  X-----------------------X  999   XXXXXXXXXXXXXXXXXXXXX  9.99
XXXX  X------------------X  999  X-----------------------X  999   XXXXXXXXXXXXXXXXXXXXX  9.99
                                                                                         9.99
                                                                                         9.99 *
XXXX  X------------------X  999  XXXXXXXXXXXXXXXXXXXXXXXXX  999   XXXXXXXXXXXXXXXXXXXXX  9.99
XXXX  X------------------X  999  X-----------------------X  999   XXXXXXXXXXXXXXXXXXXXX  9.99
                                                                                         9.99 *

                                                            DEPARTMENT AVERAGE           9.99 *

XXXX  X------------------X  999  X-----------------------X  999   X-------------------X  9.99
XXXX  X------------------X  999  X-----------------------X  999   X-------------------X  9.99
                                                                                         9.99 *
XXXX  X------------------X  999  X-----------------------X  999   X-------------------X  9.99
XXXX  X------------------X  999  X-----------------------X  999   X-------------------X  9.99
XXXX  X------------------X  999  X-----------------------X  999   X-------------------X  9.99
                                                                                         9.99 *

                                                            DEPARTMENT AVERAGE           9.99 *

                                                            SCHOOL AVERAGE               9.99 *
```

## Case study D-4

| Program: CASED4 Score student tests | Page: 1 |
|---|---|
| Designer: MM | Date: 5-14-86 |

### Input/output specifications

| File | Description | Use |
|---|---|---|
| TESTANS | Test answers file | Input |
| STUDANS | Student answers file | Input |
| STUDMST | Student master file | Input |
| SCORES | Print file: Student test scores | Output |

### Process specifications

This program scores multiple-choice tests that consist of up to 100 questions with only one right answer for each question. The students' answers are read from the student answers file, which is a sequential file in sequence by student ID. The correct answers are read from one record in the test answers file, which is an indexed file that can be accessed by the test key (test number within course number within department).

Within the test answers record, the field named TA-NUMBER-OF-QUESTIONS gives the number of questions on the test; the field named TA-TEST-ANSWERS provides the one-character answers for up to 100 questions. If, for example, a test consists of 50 questions, only the first 50 characters in this area are used. Then, if the answer for the third question is C, the third character in this area will contain the value C.

The student answers file contains two types of records. The first record in the file is a header record that gives the test key so you can find the corresponding record in the test answers file. The remaining records are individual student records that contain identifying information and the student's test answers. The test-answers field is just like the one in the test answers file--it provides for up to 100 one-character answers.

To score a test, you compare one answer in the student answer record with one answer in the test answer record. If they are equal, the student has answered the question correctly. Otherwise, he has answered it incorrectly. To score all of the questions efficiently, you should treat both the correct answers and each student's answers as tables so you can process them by varying the index values. When all of one student's answers have been evaluated, the program should divide the number of questions into the number of correct answers, multiply by 100, and round up to the nearest whole number.

The output of this program is a listing of the students' test scores. After a score has been calculated, the program must read the student's master record to get the student's name (the master file is indexed by student ID). Then, the line for the student can be printed. As always, the program should provide for page overflow in case there are more than 55 students in the class.

| Program: | CASED4 Score student tests | Page: | 2 |
|---|---|---|---|
| Designer: | MM | Date: | 5-14-86 |

## Process specifications

### Difficulty level 1

Write your program so it prints only the unshaded data in the print chart.

### Difficulty level 2

Write your program so it prints both the shaded and unshaded data in the print chart. This means that the program must calculate the median score for the test. The median score is the one that the most students have. To calculate the median, you have to set up a table to accumulate the number of students with each test score. Then, when all the tests have been scored, the program must figure out which score has the highest count. If two or more scores have the highest count, the test has more than one median, so the program should print as many medians as there are on successive lines of the grade report.

### COPY members for CASED4

```
 01 TEST-ANSWERS.
*
      05  TA-TEST-KEY.
          10  TA-DEPARTMENT-CODE             PIC X(4).
          10  TA-COURSE-NUMBER               PIC 9(3).
          10  TA-TEST-NUMBER                 PIC 9(3).
      05  TA-TEST-ANSWER-DATA.
          10  TA-NUMBER-OF-QUESTIONS         PIC 9(3).
          10  TA-TEST-ANSWERS                PIC X(100).
```

```
 01   STUDENT-ANSWERS.
*
      05  SA-RECORD-TYPE                     PIC X.
          88  HEADER-RECORD                  VALUE 'H'.
          88  STUDENT-RECORD                 VALUE 'S'.
      05  SA-TEST-DATA.
          10  SA-TEST-KEY.
              15  SA-DEPARTMENT-CODE         PIC X(4).
              15  SA-COURSE-NUMBER           PIC 9(3).
              15  SA-TEST-NUMBER             PIC 9(3).
          10  SA-SECTION-NUMBER              PIC 9(2).
          10  FILLER                         PIC X(97).
      05  SA-STUDENT-DATA REDEFINES SA-TEST-DATA.
          10  SA-STUDENT-ID                  PIC 9(9).
          10  SA-STUDENT-ANSWERS             PIC X(100).
```

```
 01   STUDENT-MASTER-RECORD.
*
      05  SM-STUDENT-ID                      PIC 9(9).
      05  SM-STUDENT-STATUS                  PIC X.
          88  ENROLLED                       VALUE 'E'.
          88  INACTIVE                       VALUE 'I'.
      05  SM-STUDENT-NAME-AND-ADDRESS.
          10  SM-STUDENT-NAME                PIC X(25).
          10  SM-STUDENT-ADDRESS             PIC X(25).
          10  SM-STUDENT-CITY                PIC X(11).
          10  SM-STUDENT-STATE               PIC XX.
          10  SM-STUDENT-ZIP-CODE            PIC 9(5).
          10  SM-STUDENT-ZIP-CODE-EXT        PIC 9(4).
      05  SM-STUDENT-PROGRESS-SUMMARY.
          10  SM-CLASS-STANDING              PIC 9.
              88  FRESHMAN                   VALUE 1.
              88  SOPHOMORE                  VALUE 2.
              88  JUNIOR                     VALUE 3.
              88  SENIOR                     VALUE 4.
          10  SM-UNITS-COMPLETED             PIC 9(3).
          10  SM-TOTAL-GRADE-POINTS          PIC 9(3).
          10  SM-UNITS-IN-PROGRESS           PIC 9(3).
```

Document name *Student test scores* Date *5-15-86*

Program name *CASED4* Designer *MM*

Record Name

```
 1 DATE:     99/99/99                           PAGE: ZZ9
 2 TIME:     99:99 XX                           CASED4
 3                              STUDENT TEST SCORES
 4
 5 DEPT: XXXX      COURSE: 999   SECTION: 99     TEST: 999
 6
 7 STUDENT ID      STUDENT NAME                 SCORE
 8
 9 999-99-9999     XXXXXXXXXXXXXXXXXXXXXXXXX     ZZ9
10 999-99-9999     XXXXXXXXXXXXXXXXXXXXXXXXX     ZZ9
11 999-99-9999     XXXXXXXXXXXXXXXXXXXXXXXXX     ZZ9
12
13                           AVERAGE SCORE        ZZ9
14                           MEDIAN SCORE         ZZ9
15
16
17
```

# Index

## Comment Form

### Your opinions count

If you have any comments, criticisms, or suggestions for us, I'm eager to hear from you. Your opinions today will affect our products of tomorrow. And if you find any errors in this book, typographical or otherwise, please point them out so we can correct them in the next printing.

Thanks for your help.

Mike Murach

**Book title:** Structured ANS COBOL: Part 1 (Second Edition)

**Dear Mike:**

Name ______________________

Company (if company address) ______________________

Address ______________________

City, State, Zip ______________________

Fold where indicated and tape closed.

No postage needed if mailed in the U.S.

NO POSTAGE
NECESSARY
IF MAILED
IN THE
UNITED STATES

**BUSINESS REPLY MAIL**

FIRST-CLASS MAIL PERMIT NO. 3063 FRESNO, CA

POSTAGE WILL BE PAID BY ADDRESSEE

**Mike Murach & Associates, Inc.**
2560 W SHAW LN STE 101
FRESNO, CA 93711-9866

# Order Form

## Our Unlimited Guarantee

**To our customers who order directly from us:** You must be satisfied. Our books must work for you, or you can send them back for a full refund...no questions asked.

Name & Title ____________________

Company (if company address) ____________________

Street Address ____________________

City, State, Zip ____________________

Phone number (including area code) ____________________

Fax number (if you fax your order to us) ____________________

| Qty | Product code and title | | *Price |
|---|---|---|---|
| **COBOL Language Elements** | | | |
| ___ | SC1R | Structured ANS COBOL, Part 1 | $32.50 |
| ___ | SC2R | Structured ANS COBOL, Part 2 | 32.50 |
| ___ | VC2R | VS COBOL II (Second Edition) | 27.50 |
| **CICS** | | | |
| ___ | CC1R | CICS for the COBOL Programmer Part 1 (Second Edition) | $36.50 |
| ___ | CC2R | CICS for the COBOL Programmer Part 2 (Second Edition) | 36.50 |
| ___ | CRFR | The CICS Programmer's Desk Reference (Second Edition) | 42.50 |
| **MVS Subjects** | | | |
| ___ | MJLR | MVS JCL (Second Edition) | $42.50 |
| ___ | TSO1 | MVS TSO, Part 1: Concepts and ISPF | 36.50 |
| ___ | TSO2 | MVS TSO, Part 2: Commands and Procedures (CLIST and REXX) | 36.50 |
| ___ | MBAL | MVS Assembler Language | 36.50 |
| ___ | OSUT | OS Utilities | 17.50 |

| Qty | Product code and title | | *Price |
|---|---|---|---|
| **Data Base Processing** | | | |
| ___ | DB21 | DB2 for the COBOL Programmer Part 1: An Introductory Course | $36.50 |
| ___ | DB22 | DB2 for the COBOL Programmer Part 2: An Advanced Course | 36.50 |
| ___ | IMS1 | IMS for the COBOL Programmer Part 1: DL/I Data Base Processing | 36.50 |
| ___ | IMS2 | IMS for the COBOL Programmer Part 2: Data Communications and MFS | 36.50 |
| **VSAM** | | | |
| ___ | VSMX | VSAM: Access Method Services and Application Programming | $27.50 |
| ___ | VSMR | VSAM for the COBOL Programmer (Second Edition) | 22.50 |
| **DOS/VSE Subjects** | | | |
| ___ | VJLR | DOS/VSE JCL (Second Edition) | $34.50 |
| ___ | ICCF | DOS/VSE ICCF | 31.00 |
| ___ | VBAL | VSE Assembler Language | 36.50 |

❑ Bill me for the books plus UPS shipping and handling (and sales tax within California).

❑ Bill my company. P.O.# ____________________

❑ I want to **SAVE 10%** by paying in advance. Charge to my ___Visa ___MasterCard ___American Express:

Card number ____________________

Valid thru (mo/yr) ____________________

Cardowner's signature ____________________

❑ I want to **SAVE 10% plus shipping and handling.** Here's my check or money order for the books minus 10% ($__________). California residents, please add sales tax to your total. (Offer valid in U.S.)

***Prices are subject to change. Please call for current prices.**

## To order more quickly,

Call **toll-free** 1-800-221-5528

(Weekdays, 8 to 5 Pacific Time)

**Fax:** 1-209-275-9035

**Mike Murach & Associates, Inc.**

2560 West Shaw Lane, Suite 101
Fresno, California 93711-2765
(209) 275-3335

NO POSTAGE
NECESSARY
IF MAILED
IN THE
UNITED STATES

**BUSINESS REPLY MAIL**

FIRST-CLASS MAIL PERMIT NO. 3063 FRESNO, CA

POSTAGE WILL BE PAID BY ADDRESSEE

**Mike Murach & Associates, Inc.**
2560 W SHAW LN STE 101
FRESNO, CA 93711-9866